THE FICTION OF NARRATIVE

D1082335

The Fiction of Narrative

Essays on History, Literature, and Theory
1957–2007

HAYDEN WHITE
Edited and with an introduction by Robert Doran

The Johns Hopkins University Press
Baltimore

© 2010 The Johns Hopkins University Press
All rights reserved. Published 2010
Printed in the United States of America on acid-free paper
2 4 6 8 9 7 5 3 1

The Johns Hopkins University Press
2715 North Charles Street
Baltimore, Maryland 21218-4363
www.press.jhu.edu

Library of Congress Cataloging-in-Publication Data

White, Hayden V., 1928–
The fiction of narrative : essays on history, literature, and theory, 1957–2007 /
Hayden White ; edited and with an introduction by Robert Doran.
p. cm.
Includes bibliographical references and index.
ISBN-13: 978-0-8018-9479-4 (acid-free paper)
ISBN-10: 0-8018-9479-4 (acid-free paper)
ISBN-13: 978-0-8018-9480-0 (pbk. : acid-free paper)
ISBN-10: 0-8018-9480-8 (pbk. : acid-free paper)
1. Literature, Modern—History and criticism—Theory, etc.   2. Literature
and history.   3. Narration (Rhetoric)   I. Doran, Robert, 1968–   II. Title.
PN511.W58   2010
809.93358—dc22   2009033014

A catalog record for this book is available from the British Library.

*Special discounts are available for bulk purchases of this book. For more information,
please contact Special Sales at 410-516-6936 or specialsales@press.jhu.edu.*

The Johns Hopkins University Press uses environmentally friendly book materials,
including recycled text paper that is composed of at least 30 percent post-consumer
waste, whenever possible. All of our book papers are acid-free, and our jackets and
covers are printed on paper with recycled content.

CONTENTS

This volume brings together twenty-three of Hayden White's previously uncollected essays. To aid the reader in contextualizing the material, the essays have been arranged chronologically, with the original date of publication appearing after each essay's title. Though I consulted with Professor White, the responsibility for the final selection of essays rests with me. Other equally defendable choices could have been made.

I would like to express my gratitude to Professor White for his warm encouragement, advice, and support at every stage of this project. I would also like to thank Hans Kellner for his insightful comments on the original proposal for this volume, which led to important improvements, and Thomas Beebee for his helpful suggestions on my editor's introduction.

Early preparation for the project was aided by several research assistants, who were supported by the Dean of Faculty Research at Middlebury College. These assistants, Melissa Cassis, Sara Jameson, and Gokce Uzumcu, did a terrific job in support of the volume, and I thank them wholeheartedly. I would also like to thank the University of Rochester, where I currently teach, for its generous sponsorship of the conference, "Between History and Narrative: Colloquium in Honor of Hayden White," April 24–25, 2009, which provided a wonderful context for the completion of this project.

A note to the reader about the present volume: All articles appear as they were originally published, with some minor editing for consistency within the book and to conform to current styles and conventions. Brackets in the notes indicate material that I have added to assist the reader.

To the memory of William J. Bossenbrook

I thank Robert Doran for his generous husbandry of my work. In collecting my earliest essays, he has, I fear, made public a certain youthful idealism, both philosophical and political, of which time and experience have long since cured me. I should add that Robert Doran chose these pieces for collection in consultation with but with little advice from me. He no doubt had his own objectives, which he lays out in his introduction. I appreciate the subtlety and precision of Doran's introduction to the volume, which, I think, does a great job of synthesis. I could not have done it. I believe he has caught all of the major issues that have interested me over the course of my career.

I am glad that the essay on Christopher Dawson, the Irish Catholic historian of early medieval Europe, has been republished. Dawson was introduced to me by Professor William J. Bossenbrook, my undergraduate teacher and later colleague at Wayne State University who made history, not only for me but also for legions of students in Detroit during the Depression and World War II, an adventure more compelling than any novel or romance. For Bossenbrook, history was and could only be an art, by which he meant a challenge to the imagination as much as to the rational faculties alone.

Jacques Barzun once said that although one could introduce the young to history, one could not really *teach* it, because history, real history, had to be written. I do not think that Barzun went on to draw the obvious implication of this statement. Which is: history exists only in writing. Barzun was right in one sense. The genre of professional historiography has to be written—oral *history* is a contradiction in terms. If it is not written, it is not history. Information about the past can be conveyed orally. You can carry around in your head all manner of facts and other kinds of information, but you do not have a history until you have brought all of this stuff together and written it up either in a narrative or in an argument of some kind. Then and only then can you submit your history to other historians for assessment and criticism. Those are the rules of the game in professional historiography. And until the rules are changed, oral accounts of historical reality will remain at best a kind of raw material for proper historiography.

Another piece that I am pleased to see reprinted here is "What Is a Historical System?" This was written for presentation at a conference of biologists, historians, and philosophers, the aim of which was to try to bring general systems theory into the discussion of the relation between nature (biology, genetics, evolution) and culture (history, society, language). In this essay, I tried to flesh out Nietzsche's thought about historical change as the substitution of a (historical) past from which one would wish to have descended for that (genetic) past from which one really had descended. The piece was not a great success at its original presentation in Denver in 1967. Scientists, it turns out, do not want history as they know it to change. Their attitude was rather like that of Karl Popper who felt that historical studies could never be a real science—and a good thing too! This is especially the case with these scientists who see it as history's obligation to write the story of their own field's triumphant progress from its origination down to . . . themselves.

In a recent essay in *Daedalus* (the journal of the American Academy of Arts and Sciences, of which, I am proud to say, I am a member—though not in the "History" but in the "Philology" Division), Carolyn Bynum holds forth on the current state of the discipline of History. It appears that, according to Ms. Bynum, all is well in History. The effects of the culture wars of the late twentieth century with its various "turns" appear to have been assimilated; the number of professional historians in the West is growing; and the world is awash in publications by the professional establishment of History—some 48,000 items were published in the last year alone. Ms. Bynum thinks that all of the discussion about the state of History and the condition of historical studies is carried on largely by people who are not "practicing historians." As if only those who are doing history in a professionally accredited way were competent to speak about it. She also, like many other historians, seems to think that people who criticize historical studies on epistemological or ethical or other grounds are too general and fail to analyze specific historical works.

Well, it is worthwhile to point out that an interest in the way historical studies are carried out is or should be a matter of concern to any educated citizen. The professionals may own "history," insofar as by the term "history" they mean that aspect of the past which is studied in the way they study it and write about it. But professional historians do not own the past, and they have no exclusive claim over the study of the way in which the past and the present may be brought together in a comprehensive vision of historical reality. As a matter of fact, that claim can as legitimately be made for literary writers and especially novelists writing in the "modern" mode.

Prior to historiography's scientization, history was regarded as a kind of disciplined memory—memory subjected to authentication by documentation and argument. Moreover, for most of its own history, historiography was regarded as a branch of rhetoric and (like rhetoric itself) a division of moral philosophy. Very few of the great classics of historiography were undertaken out of disinterested motives, and most of them have been undertaken as a search, not so much for the truth of the past as, rather, a search for what the truth *means* for living people. Although the mode of history's presentation of the past is dramatistic—laying out a spectacle of the great events and conflicts of times past—it has always sought to contribute to the question that Kant defined as the soul of ethics: What should I (we) do?

As is well known, science cannot address that question and still remain scientific. And this is where art comes in as both a supplement to science (which can only tell us what is the case) and an organon of the ethical. For the ethical needs the imagination, more specifically what Kant called the *productive* imagination (as against memory or the reproductive imagination) in order to get from contemplation of what is the case to a decision about what I should do. Modern scientific historiography has diminished the role of the imagination in the construction of a past that might be useful for helping living people to make that move.

I entered the field of historical studies because I thought that historical knowledge, being knowledge about what is (or was) the case, was an antidote to ideology. Originally, I thought that this was because history was, if not more scientific, then at least more "realistic" than ideology. I have since come to believe that scientific historiography—in its empiricist as well as in its "grand theoretical" modes—is itself an ideology that, in excluding ethical concerns from its operations, produces apathy, or what my friend Sande Cohen calls "passive nihilism," rather than a will to action. Fortunately, the modern novel, ever since it broke with the romance genre, has kept alive an interest in "history" understood not so much as "the past" as, rather, the spectacle of human self-making (*autopoiesis*, in Niklas Luhmann's terminology). It is precisely because the modern novel takes "history" thus understood as its ultimate referent that it has produced a kind of art that contributes to art's own de-aestheticization. Which is to say, I guess, that in the end I come back to Aristotle's insight that history without poetry is inert, just as poetry without history is vapid.

Humanism, Formalism, and the Discourse of History

All stories are fictions.

—HAYDEN WHITE

Since the publication of *Metahistory: The Historical Imagination in Nineteenth-Century Europe* in 1973,[1] Hayden White's name has been synonymous with the introduction of "theory" into modern historical studies. Indeed, one would have to return to the nineteenth century to find a thinker who has had a greater impact on the way we think about historical representation, the discipline of history, and on how historiography intersects with other domains of inquiry, particularly literary studies. Though White certainly had precursors in his endeavor to probe the discursive foundations of historical writing and of historical consciousness, no one before or since has been able to combine a deep sensitivity to the aims and preoccupations of the professional historian with a philosophical outlook that relentlessly challenges the presuppositions and conventions of his field. In addition, no other historian has had the interdisciplinary influence of White, whose critical works have been a wellspring for literary scholars, philosophers, anthropologists, art historians, and film and media critics, as the large body of secondary literature on his thought attests.[2]

This volume brings together twenty-three of White's uncollected essays, which represent some of his best and most important work. Read in sequence, they form a sort of intellectual autobiography, revealing the trajectory of White's thought as well as its relationship to the theoretical currents of the time of each essay's writing. Though White has published three previous volumes of essays, the texts contained in these collections were selected, and in many cases revised or rewritten, to cleave to a specific theme—theory of tropes (*Tropics of Discourse: Essays in Cultural Criticism*, 1978), theory of narrative (*The Content of the Form: Narrative Discourse and Historical Representation*, 1987), and figuralism (*Figural Realism: Studies in the Mimesis Effect*, 1999)—which meant that many important essays were inevitably left out over the course of his long career.[3] This is particularly true with regard to his first collection, *Tropics of Discourse*, which includes only a fraction of White's output during his first twenty years as an academic. These early essays, many of which are still influential, offer a unique window into the genesis of White's groundbreaking theory of historical writing, and I have been able to include the vast majority of them in this volume.[4]

With the notable exception of *Metahistory*, White has throughout his career preferred the essay as vehicle for his critical insights. Richard Vann, the longtime editor of the journal *History and Theory*, has called White "perhaps the premier academic essayist of our times,"[5] and Dominick LaCapra proclaims him a "master" of the form.[6] Indeed, White's essays reveal a rare degree of craftsmanship, pith, and purpose, elevating a form that has often been neglected by humanists in favor of the monograph—the sine qua non of promotion and prestige in the humanities.

In this introduction, I offer a general overview of White's thought, aiming to show how the essays contained herein might serve to amplify, contextualize, and dramatize White's theses in ways that are perhaps not immediately apparent in his previously published collections and monographs.

From History to Theory

Though generally known as "theorist," Hayden White was trained as a historian. White's interest in intellectual history and the philosophy of history was inspired by his undergraduate mentor, William J. Bossenbrook, a charismatic history professor at Wayne State University, who also taught fellow historian Harry Harootunian and philosopher Arthur Danto.[7] White later expressed his gratitude by editing a collection dedicated to his undergraduate professor: *The Uses of History: Essays in Intellectual and Social History Presented to William J. Bossenbrook*.[8] After completing his B.A. in history in 1951, White pursued graduate study in history at the University of Michigan, earning an M.A. in 1952 and a Ph.D. in 1955, with a 626–page dissertation entitled "The Conflict of Papal Leadership Ideals from Gregory VII to St. Bernard de Clairvaux with Special Reference to the Papal Schism of 1130."[9] At Michigan, White studied under Maurice Mandelbaum who, White recounts, "was the only person in the United States at that time who worked in the philosophy of history."[10] Among the early influences on White were British philosopher and historian R. G. Collingwood and Italian philosopher Benedetto Croce (see "Collingwood and Toynbee: Transitions in English Historical Thought" and "The Abiding Relevance of Croce's Idea of History," chapters 1 and 3 of this volume).

After a brief stint as an instructor at Wayne State, White taught in the history departments of the University of Rochester (1958–68) and the University of California, Los Angeles (1968–73), and held appointments as Director of the Center for the Humanities (1973–77) and as Kenan Professor of History and Letters (1976–78) at Wesleyan University.[11] In 1978, he accepted an appointment as Professor of the History of Consciousness at the University of California, Santa Cruz, where he led an innovative and eclectic department that became one of the nation's premier interdisciplinary programs.[12] Upon White's retirement from UC Santa Cruz in 1995, he accepted part-time appointments at the University of California, Berkeley, in the Department of Rhetoric (1996–97), and at Stanford University in the Department of Comparative Literature (1995–), where he still teaches.

The arc of White's professional career reveals a progressive shift from historian to academic intellectual: from his initial appointments in traditional departments of history; to interdisciplinary studies at the midpoint of his career; and finally, to departments of comparative literature and rhetoric, which have long promoted more general theoretical reflection on the humanities, typically from the perspective of Continental thought. White's peregrinations are also a reflection of his often neuralgic relationship with the field of historical studies, where his ideas have been met with a great deal of resistance, even scorn.[13] While some historians hailed *Metahistory* as a seminal work, others saw White as a gadfly, an unwelcome critic of a hallowed discipline with ancient roots. To them, White's rapprochement between literary or fictional storytelling and the historical or biographical account amounted to an indictment of history as a factual discipline, scientific in spirit, if not in method.

Nevertheless, White's books and articles are standard reading in courses on historiography and the philosophy of history, though for the most part these focus on his pioneering work from the 1970s: *Metahistory* and the essays contained in *Tropics of Discourse*. With a few notable exceptions, historians were generally unmoved by White's later forays into "critical theory," that is, structuralism, poststructuralism, and postmodernism.[14] The essays White published in the early 1980s in the journal *Critical Inquiry*, the main organ for "theory," especially of the poststructuralist variety, brought him a new audience composed largely of literary scholars.[15] Indeed, White's work was well received in literary studies, particularly the essays collected in *The Content of the Form*, which contributed to the field of narratology.

As heterodox as his ideas appeared to historians, White's views were perceived by literary critics as being part of the prevailing orthodoxy. His emphasis on the formal qualities of the verbal artifact appeared to confirm the anti-historicism of literary theorists keen on carving out a specific domain for literary studies as against the contextualist approaches of literary history (which, the former felt, reduced literary criticism to either authorial biography, on the one side, or historical sociology, on the other). White's insistence on the structural identity between factual and fictional representation, as well as his use of the tools of literary analysis to uncover the latent content of historical writing (the content of the form), seemed to lend support to the imperialistic impulse then emerging in literary studies, an impulse that, though the metaphorical power of the term *text,* sought to encompass the study of all aspects of culture.[16]

However, both perspectives on White's work—those of the traditionalist historian and the avant-garde literary critic—betray fundamental misunderstandings. White believes in history, that is, in the inherent value of fostering a historical consciousness—and this is no more in evidence than in the two books of intellectual history White co-authored in the late 1960s: *The Emergence of Liberal Humanism: An Intellectual History of Western Europe,* vol. 1 (McGraw-Hill, 1966), with Wilson H. Coates and J. Salwyn Shapiro; and *The Ordeal of Liberal Humanism: An Intellectual History of Western Europe,* vol. 2 (McGraw-Hill, 1970), again with Coates. And from 1966 to 1973, White served as the general editor of *Major Traditions of World Civilizations,* a seven-volume series published by Harper & Row, to which he contributed the last installment, *The Greco-Roman Tradition* (1973).[17] These projects equipped White with the vast erudition for which he is well known and that is everywhere on display in his work. But these volumes also reveal a special concern for *humanism,* a concern that informs much of White's critical work, though this aspect of his thought is rarely acknowledged.[18]

This is no doubt due to the fact that the thinkers with whom White often professes a certain kinship or fascination—Claude Lévi-Strauss, Michel Foucault, and Roland Barthes—are staunch anti-humanists (or "post-humanists," to use a somewhat anachronistic term) whose critical projects are generally hostile to discourses centered around received concepts of "man" or "the human subject." In addition, this anti-humanism often went hand in hand with an anti-historicism that questioned the very possibility of historical knowledge: whether because historicism anchors a delusive belief in the cultural superiority of the "rational" West as against the "mythological" cast of mind of non-Western, nonhistorical peoples (Lévi-Strauss);[19] or because "history" is best understood as a distinctive discursive practice (Foucault); or because "texts," whether purporting to be history or fiction, should cease to be taken as tokens of subjectivity (Barthes). While White finds these critical attitudes productive and provocative, often putting them at the service of broader arguments, it would be a mistake to confuse White's "linguistic humanism," as Hans Kellner aptly terms it, with linguistic nihilism.[20] For White is as critical of the "theoretical torpor" afflicting academic historians, on the one hand, as he is of "the numerous rebellions against historical consciousness in general," on the other.[21]

What attracted White to the critical avant-garde and to poststructuralist criticism in particular was its linguistic self-awareness, an awareness he found lacking among his fellow historians. He admired Foucault's "counter-history"; and Barthes' textualism was always a source of inspiration. Jacques Derrida was somewhat less of an influence; for, though he commends Derrida for his immanent challenge to the philosophical tradition, appreciating in particular his essay on metaphor, "White Mythology," White could never embrace the idea of interpretative short-circuiting as antidote to the metaphysical proclivities of Western thought. White found in Paul Ricoeur's humanistic hermeneutics—and especially in his massive three-volume *Time and Narrative* (*Temps et récit*, 1983–85), which was written in response to White's *Metahistory*—a more useful model for historical consciousness, to which White's *hommage* in his essay "Guilty of History? The *longue durée* of Paul Ricoeur" (the last chapter of the present volume) is a fitting testament.[22]

Tropology and Rhetoric

Though White sometimes calls himself a "structuralist," this nomenclature is somewhat misleading when applied to White's work. White's point of departure is not Saussurean semiology but Vichian rhetoric.[23] Early eighteenth-century philosopher and rhetorician Giambattista Vico had an important if somewhat subterranean influence on twentieth-century thought, particularly on such figures as Benedetto Croce, Erich Auerbach, and Northrop Frye, whose works were formative for White.[24] (See chapter 3 in the present volume, "The Abiding Relevance of Croce's Idea of History," and chapter 6, "The Culture of Criticism: Gombrich, Auerbach, Popper," as well as the two essays on Frye, chapters 17 and 19.) The basis of Vico's thought is the *verum-factum* principle, which states that the human mind can truly know only what it itself has made. Through this principle, Vico posits the constructed nature of social reality and culture—and by extension, history. As White observes in "Northrop Frye's Place in Contemporary Cultural Studies" (chapter 19):

> [Vico's] theory [of *verum-factum*] is called "maker's knowledge," and it holds that, since nature was made by God, human beings can never hope to have the kind of knowledge of it that only God could possess. However, the theory also says, since culture is a distinctively human creation, human beings can aspire to a knowledge of culture of a kind and degree utterly different from that which they can have of the rest of nature. And since history is the record of this process of cultural creation, human beings can legitimately aspire to a knowledge both

of history and of themselves as the agents of a specifically historical mode of existence that is both truer and more certain than any knowledge they can ever hope to have of nature. Historical knowledge, in short, is human self-knowledge and specifically knowledge of how human beings make themselves through knowing themselves and come to know themselves in the process of making themselves.

The idea of human creativity as self-interpretation that White insists on here is the key to Vico's thought as well as to his own. Vico conceives the poetic mind, the creative mind par excellence, as a mind that thinks in figures (preeminently in terms of metaphor), a prelogical mind, anthropologically primary in that it precedes and conditions rational-logical speech. Vico thus replaces the opposition between literal and figurative speech—a bedrock of Enlightenment rationalism and nineteenth-century scienticism—with a *continuity* wherein stages of consciousness or mind, reflected in shifts in social developments, are defined tropologically, that is, as successions of figural types: from metaphor (age of gods), to metonymy (age of heroes), to synecdoche (age of men), and finally, to irony (age of decadence and dissolution).[25]

From this unification of tropes and stages or states of consciousness, White derives a powerful tool for understanding the relationship between discourse, mind, and world. White sees tropology as a way of transcending the interminable clash between the polar views of philosophical realism (ontologically independent reality that the mind seeks to approximate) and philosophical idealism (identity of mind and world). To hold a figural view of the relation between mind and world is to hold that the world is pre-figured by our linguistic apprehension, which means that "reality" will always be in some sense a fulfillment of a figure. As White remarks in "The Problem of Change in Literary History" (chapter 10 of this volume): "language is . . . what both Vico and Hegel (as well as Marx and Nietzsche) saw it to be, an *instrument of mediation* between human consciousness and the world it occupies" (White's emphasis). Because discourse has a tropological underpinning from which one cannot escape, there is no literal apprehension of the world that is not at the same time a figural interpretation. Literalism is either a latent figuralism, or conversely, is itself a figure (of commonsense speech, truthfulness, etc.). Though White's tropology represents a general conception of language or discourse that is not specific to history, it is of course the particular modalities of representing historical reality that most interests White.

The idea that all language is figurative was a commonplace of ancient rhetoric, and thus there is nothing particularly modern or avant-garde about such a view.

But the use to which this idea has been put—the destabilization of all truth claims and the reduction of subjectivity to language—does indeed point to current concerns in the humanities and social sciences. At first blush, White's Vico-inspired position may seem indistinguishable from the poststructuralist view of language. Indeed, in his essay "Vico and Structuralist/Poststructuralist Thought" (chapter 13 of this volume), White observes: "the structuralist/poststructuralist insistence on the figurative nature of all language and a fortiori all systems of thought might accord nicely with Vico's notions of the 'poetic' origins of all cultural formations." But he then goes on to assert an "unbridgeable divide" between Vico and anti-humanist or nihilistic thought, the same divide that also separates White's work from much of the critical avant-garde. For, as we will see, White's tropology represents an attempt to reinvigorate a concept of human volition—the inherent freedom of every human community to choose its own past and thereby its present.[26]

Metahistory

The theory resulting from the above considerations, as White expounds it in *Metahistory: The Historical Imagination in Nineteenth-Century Europe*, is not easy to describe. For *Metahistory* is at once a theory of historical writing (of the actual *practice* of historians),[27] of historical consciousness (what it means to think historically, and to be aware of ourselves as *historical beings*), of historiography (the *discipline* of history, its particular methodologies, development, and role in the panoply of disciplines), and of history itself as a concept (what is *history*? what does it mean for something to be *historical* as opposed to something else?). A full-scale exegesis of White's 434-page magnum opus is, of course, beyond the scope of this introduction, and the secondary material on this work is rich.[28] Thus my exposition here will be brief.

White presents his theory as "formalist," which already invites a dose of skepticism; for it appears prima facie to smack of the speculative philosophies of history that flourished in the nineteenth century and that became anathema to twentieth-century historians. But White's formalism is not an effort to promulgate putative laws of history, nor to provide an a priori explanatory framework (e.g., a metanarrative along the lines of Marx's "history is the history of class struggle"). It is not White's aim to justify any particular approach to history—not even a "metahistorical" one—but rather to discover what any approach to history necessarily presupposes. White's theory is thus metahistorical in that it seeks to articulate the non-historical ground from which to comprehend the genre of discourse we call history.[29] In effect, White's procedure is analogous to that of Kant in the *Critique of Pure Reason*: just as Kant aims to "find for the conditioned knowledge given through the understanding the unconditioned whereby its unity is brought to completion,"[30] White proposes to sketch out the conditions of possibility of historical writing, which he contends are tropological in nature, in order to assess the unity of what we call "historical knowledge."

White begins his discussion by making a distinction between the manifest and latent levels of historical writing: the manifest level consisting of epistemological, aesthetic, and ethical concerns, and the latent or "deep structural" level consisting of four basic or master tropes: metaphor, metonymy, synecdoche, and irony (the same list as found in Aristotle and Vico). These in turn are characterized by their discursive functions: representational (metaphor), reductionist (metonymy), integrative (synecdoche), and negational (irony).[31] This fourfold structure defines White's theory in general: he distinguishes four modes of *emplotment* (Romantic, Tragic, Comic, Satirical), four modes of *argument* (Formist, Mechanistic, Organicist, Contextualist), and four modes of *ideological implication* (Anarchist, Radical, Conservative, Liberal). The combination of these modes constitutes what he calls a "historiographical style." Different combinations yield the diversity of styles we encounter in historical writing, though there is a limit to the combinatory possibilities (due to inherent incompatibilities). The tropes relate to the modes in that they determine the affinities or compatibilities between different modes; their role is thus prefigurative and precritical.[32] For example, if a historian's or philosopher's apprehension of historical reality can be described as ironic, this will manifest itself in the possibilities of modal combination, that is, in those consistent with an ironic or negational discursive strategy. While there is some confusion with regard to whether the tropes represent a fourth set of variables,[33] I believe that a fair reading shows the tropes to be wedded to corresponding modes of emplotment, forming a dyad: metaphor-romance, metonymy-tragedy, synecdoche-comedy, irony-satire.[34] White also uses the tropes to describe the evolution of nineteenth-century historical consciousness, in the manner of Vico: that is, as beginning with metaphor, continuing through metonymy and synecdoche, and culminating in irony. In the subsequent chapters of *Metahistory*, White demonstrates his thesis through intricate and multilayered readings of four historians (Michelet, Tocqueville, Ranke, Burckhardt) and four philosophers (Hegel, Marx, Nietzsche, Croce).

One wonders what *Metahistory* might have looked like had White, in addition to philosophers and historians, thought to include the four masters of nineteenth-century literary realism: Stendhal, Balzac, Flaubert, and Zola. One of White's little-known essays offers a template: "Romanticism, Historicism, and Realism: Toward a Period Concept for Early Nineteenth-Century Intellectual History" (1968, chapter 4 of this volume), which compares the literary intuitions of Balzac and Stendhal with the historical imaginations of Tocqueville, Ranke, and Hegel. And there is also White's 1979 essay, "The Problem of Style in Realistic Representation: Marx and Flaubert" (chapter 11 of this volume), which does the same for the mid-nineteenth century.

Now the reader may ask: What is White's tropological reduction designed to accomplish? Does it propose itself as a manual for historical writing itself? Decidedly not. It is not prescriptive, but analytical. Is it meant to expose historical writing as being fanciful and thus inherently untruthful, false, illusory? Some conservative critics have read White this way, but this can only be a caricature; for, though White does wish to debunk the idea of a science of history, he nevertheless believes in a concept of historical knowledge as self-knowledge or self-making. In my view, *Metahistory* is a virtuoso *performance* that is not intended to be in any way programmatic but rather to show that a tropological account of historical practice is *possible* and in this manner to reveal the essential contingency of historical writing and of historical consciousness. This revelation of contingency is not a capitulation to nihilism but rather an affirmation of freedom, a freedom born of the necessity of tropes. That is to say, once the fundamentally rhetorical nature of historical writing is made manifest, it can have the effect of liberating the historian, not necessarily to satisfy a will to power (though this cannot be excluded), but to realize his or her *creative* role in the self-understanding of his or her community.[35]

White also seeks through his tropological reduction to address the longstanding animosity evinced by twentieth-century historians toward the philosophy of history. By uncovering their common discursive structure, White deconstructs the opposition between history proper and the speculative philosophies of history, concluding that, despite their manifest differences, "every philosophy of history contains within it the elements of a proper history, just as every proper history contains within it the elements of a full-blown philosophy of history."[36] In his later writings, White will have occasion to extend this argument to the dichotomy between narrative and non-narrative history.

Now it would be a mistake to view *Metahistory* as merely formalist; for it is also a formidable work of intellectual history, continuing White's previous work in that area. Indeed, with its seamless blend of synchronic and diachronic perspectives, *Metahistory* is intellectual history at the highest level of self-consciousness, aware of its performative aspect even as it is performs it. Hence White's disclaimer that his book is cast in the ironic mode, though he intends—ironically—to transcend irony by showing that it is "only one of a *number* of possible perspectives on history."[37] As I said above, *Metahistory* is many things and can be (and has been) read in many different ways.[38] Most important, however, it contains the elements that will define White's subsequent thought, which represents for the most part a fine-tuning, expansion, clarification, and recontextualization of his original theory of historical writing.[39]

Following *Metahistory*, White largely jettisons the more "structuralist" dimension of his theory—that is, the typologies, taxonomies, and multilayered combinations that render *Metahistory* somewhat unwieldy—in favor of a more streamlined approach. Significantly, it is on the *aesthetic* aspect of his theory that White will choose to focus in his later work, and in particular on the consequences of the notion of "emplotment"—a term he coined—which will play an important role in White's writings on narrative.

Emplotment and the Role of Poetic Form

The "natural" or "commonsensical" attitude toward historical representation is that history "exists," that it happened in a certain way and that it is the historian's job to uncover the literal truth of what happened and put it into words as best he or she can. As new sources or artifacts come to light, these will need to be incorporated into the historian's account, but they will not alter the historical reality, only our perception of it. One could conceive of this idea of history as a giant jigsaw puzzle: as each piece falls into place, a clearer picture emerges; historical reality comes into ever sharper focus. Some historical epochs, due to a scant historical record, remain obscure; relatively few pieces are available providing a very incomplete picture. For other periods, the historical record is rich, and it is a matter of putting the pieces together in the right way. Disputes between historians might take the form of emphasizing this or that aspect of the overall picture or of debating the authenticity or importance of a particular source. But even these disagreements have the effect of moving us ever closer to the apprehension of a past reality.

Though seemingly "natural," this view has a history. It is epitomized in the work of influential German historian Leopold von Ranke (1795–1886), who, more than any other figure in modern historical studies, has articulated a vision of history that accords with the scientific (i.e., objectivist) spirit. According to Ranke, the historian should base his insights on original documentary evidence, which alone should guide him. Thus the historian's role is not "to judge the past, nor to instruct one's contemporaries with an eye to the future, but merely to show *how it actually was* (*wie es eigentlich gewesen*)."[40] In *Metahistory*, White endeavors to demonstrate how

Ranke's notion of a transparent, value neutral, "tell it like it was" realism is no more resistant to the influence of tropes and to the attendant modes of aesthetic emplotment and ideological implication than the romantic-historiographical or idealist-philosophical approaches Ranke spurns. For White, *any* approach to history is always an *approach* to history: that is, a perspective that presupposes an interpretative or critical framework that can be theorized as such. (And this goes as well for the literary scholar who adamantly rejects the notion that what he or she does is in any way "theoretical," simply because there is no conscious articulation of critical protocols that are seen as self-evident.)[41]

Narrative appeared to Ranke to be the most "neutral" or "objective" way of representing past events; and indeed the preference for narrative in modern historiography, as well as the emphasis on politics, which is particularly suited to dramatic, narrative presentation, is due in large part to Ranke's influence. Prima facie, narration seems to avoid the twin pitfalls of excessive abstraction (philosophy of history à la Hegel, logical empiricism à la Hempel)[42] and ideological imposition; however, some later historians, such as those of the Annales group in France, challenged this assumption, inveighing against "event history" (*histoire événementielle*)—that is to say, narrative—though in the name of a scientism and an objectivism more extreme than the one espoused by Ranke. Though White sympathizes with many aspects of the Annalistes' critique of narrative, he argues that "one cannot historicize without narrativizing, because it is only by narrativization that a series of events can be transformed into a sequence, divided into periods, and represented as a process in which the substances of things can be said to change while their identities remain the same."[43] In other words, it is not by getting rid of narrative (the unscientific "dramatization" decried by the Annales group) that one has ipso facto solved the problem of *narrativization*, for, in so doing, one has merely substituted an implicit narrativization for an explicit one.

Though Ranke is known for his lively narrative style, he refused to see the specifically aesthetic or literary dimension of his narrative practice—what White calls the "content of the form"—as having any consequences for his objectivist credo. Like Marshall McLuhan's watchword, "the medium is the message," White argues that aesthetic form conveys a content or meaning that cannot be disentangled from the message it is designed to deliver.[44] That story-making requires a certain amount of *art* (in the sense of *technê*—craft or skill) a historian like Ranke could well accept, but with the caveat that the story told is the one dictated by the facts—as if the story were in some sense "waiting to be told," existing in the past events themselves as a kind of narrative-in-itself. White exposes this view as untenable. The "facts" do not "dictate" at all but are subject to the specific choices, inclinations, and prejudices of the historian, which are inevitably moral and aesthetic rather than simply epistemic. The metaphysical view of history as a story existing independently from our apprehension of it is a misunderstanding of what a story most manifestly is, that is, a specifically human way of creating and conferring meaning through verbal figuration. Thus, as White famously says, stories are *made* (*factum*, *poiesis*), not found. The idea of history as art (*techné*) in the service of science is replaced by a *poetic* notion of history, understood in the twofold sense of *poiesis* as making (artistic creation, emplotment) and the revelation of its own constructed-ness in formal or generic analysis (poetics, metahistory).

White thus contends that when a historian transforms a *chronicle* (a simple list of past events arranged chronologically by year of occurrence) into a *story* (a narration that organizes events into a comprehensible whole with beginning, middle, and end), the material is inevitably reconfigured in an aesthetic process White calls *emplotment*. Emplotment means not only that there is no primordial story but also that there is no such thing as a story-in-general (i.e., stories as infinitely diverse as the particularities of the events they recount); there are only stories of particular kinds—those *story-types* that form the cultural patrimony of every civilization and community. Thus, to emplot events, means to organize and arrange them according to a recognizable story-type, which entails a reduction to the number of *possible* story-types available in a given culture. In *Metahistory*, White posits a reduction to four story archetypes (*mythoi*), derived from Northrop Frye's *Anatomy of Criticism*: Romance, Tragedy, Comedy, Satire.[45] Frye's influence on White cannot be understated; for he provides White with the aesthetic justification for his concept of emplotment.

The great controversy surrounding White's notion of emplotment stems, of course, from the idea that fictional story-types should or could describe real events. To use fictional modes to represent real events would appear to fictionalize those events. Any rapprochement, even a structural one, between fictional forms that recall myth and legend, and historical accounts of real events would seem to deprive the category of "historical" of any real significance, marking a regression back to the pre-nineteenth-century notion of history as a branch of rhetoric. Is it White's aim, then, to dismiss the accomplishments of modern historiography, to return to a time when "history" and "literature" were not opposed but considered part of a continuum of "literary" genres?[46]

Let us state, first of all, that White does not at all seek to erase the distinction between real and imaginary (invented) events.[47] And, unlike many critics of objectivist historicism, he does not even wish to dispense with the category of "truth." He does want to suggest, as he observes in his essay "Storytelling: Historical and

Ideological" (chapter 20 of this volume), that "any narrative account of historical events remains contaminated by representational practices of a distinctively fictionalizing and mythicalizing kind." Or, putting the matter more forcefully: "narration itself has been shown to be *inherently* fictive, whatever its subject matter" ("The Discourse of History," chapter 12 of this volume, White's emphasis). What, then, is the relation between the fictional form and its nonfictional subject matter? It is the same relation that inheres between fictional form and fictional content, namely, a *figural* one. The question of reference is thus separated from the question of truth. As White observes:

> Stories are not lived; there is no such thing as a real story. Stories are told or written, not found. And as for the notion of a true story, this is virtually a contradiction in terms. All stories are fictions. Which means, of course, that they can be true only in a metaphorical sense and in the sense in which a figure of speech can be true. Is this true enough?[48]

The answer to this question—which involves the idea of *figural truth* or *figural realism*—has been the subject of White's later work, and I propose to treat it in some detail, for it goes to the most obvious objection to White's theory, that it promotes an irresponsible relativism that endangers the entire historical enterprise.

Historical Relativism and Figural Truth

The charge of relativism has dogged the reception of White's work since the publication of *Metahistory*. If there is no one true way to represent a particular historical epoch, if historical "reality" is nothing but imaginative construction with no ontological substrate, then is it not legitimate to represent past events in any way the historian chooses? And if so, what is to separate "history" from blatant revisionism, state propaganda, Holocaust denial, and so on?

There are two separate issues here: (1) the case of the bad-faith historian who willfully distorts the facts to push a specific ideological agenda and (2) the question of the propriety of certain story-types for the representation of a given set of events (and in particular of the Holocaust for which, in the view of some thinkers, no representation can be deemed adequate or appropriate).

With respect to the first issue, propagandists and Holocaust deniers do not cite White's relativist theory to support their position; for they are not presenting their ideas as an *alternate* account but as the one *true* account that should cancel out the generally accepted account or the one promoted by their rivals. White's relativism is thus as unwelcome to propagandists as it is to the objectivist historian. Furthermore, the Holocaust denier says: "there were no gas chambers." This is a point of fact, not of interpretation, and White is not a relativist when it comes to the facts, which he defines as "singular existential statements." White writes:

> This is not to say that a historical discourse is not properly assessed in terms of the truth value of its factual (singular existential) statements taken individually and the logical conjunction of the whole set taken distributively. For unless a historical discourse acceded to assessment in these terms, it would lose all justification for its claim to represent and provide explanations of specifically real events.[49]

Though White sometimes attacks the fact-fiction opposition, what he means is that there is a structural identity on the level of form between factual and fictional representation, not that there are no such things as facts (understood in the manner defined above). On the most fundamental level, then, to interpret facts is to "fictionalize" them. Facts cease to be *mere* facts once they are interpreted or emplotted—that is, once they are transformed into a historical *discourse*. Thus, the literal fact can always be seen as being a figure *in potentia*, without thereby negating its literal truth content; for, as we shall see in a moment, this is precisely what White means by *figuralism*.

Now the denial of certain facts (or the acceptance of invented "facts") could, of course, lead to an interpretation that would minimize the suffering of the Jews during the Second World War. However, the fault here does not lie in the mode of emplotment or interpretative acuity but in a defective factual record, of which White would be as critical as anyone else. This is not to say, however, that interpretations cannot be morally objectionable *as interpretations*—witness the *Historikerstreit* (Historian's Debate) in Germany.[50] But, White would contend, as morally repugnant and reprehensible as some interpretations may be, they cannot be condemned on epistemological grounds (as if interpretations were subject to the same standards as facts).[51]

In regards to the second issue, White indeed argues that the same set of events can give rise to a multiplicity of possible emplotments, none of which can be held to be "truer" or "more faithful to the facts" than any other, since the story does not inhere *in* the facts but emerges via an interpretative attitude *toward* the facts.[52] As White observes in "Historical Pluralism and Pantextualism" (chapter 15 of this volume), "the demonstration that a given set of events *can be* represented as a comedy implicitly argues for the possibility of representing it with equal plausibility as a tragedy, romance, farce, epic, and so on." All stories are *fictional* in the sense that they are imaginative templates—conventional structures of meaning—whether the events to which they refer are thought to have existed or not. The question of propriety (in the sense of correspondence) only comes into play if one believes that stories are found in the historical record rather than imposed upon it.

For example, the death of a small child would appear to naturally call for emplotment as a tragedy. To emplot such an event as farce would seem incongruous and risk offending against sensibility and taste. But one could nevertheless imagine a successful farcical treatment that ridicules the conduct of the police who investigated the death or the attitudes of a society in which such deaths are only too common. The farcical treatment of a child's death that offends us does so because it fails to accomplish its *aesthetic* goal (of presenting the death in a way that conforms to current and culturally specific standards of taste and decorum) and thus would be judged in exactly the same manner as a purely fictional treatment of the same subject matter (one with no referent). In other words, the question of "appropriateness" here is a matter of aesthetics, not of historical knowledge, and the only aesthetic limitation is that imposed by taste.

This notion lies at the heart of White's contention that modernist or postmodernist techniques of representation, particularly when applied to recent history, may appear to be more convincing or pertinent than traditional techniques of mimesis derived from nineteenth-century authors. Aesthetic standards and conventions evolve over time, and thus what was once held to be an appropriate style of representation of an event may now seem quaint or dated. Thus, as White argues, writing in the "middle voice" (the displacement of the narrating subject, enhanced self-consciousness, and performativity), or other modernist modes that reject historicist conventions, might be looked to as a superior (or at least more relevant) way of capturing an event such as the Holocaust, to the extent that they effectively figure—and thus perform—the "crisis" in historical representation that such an event brings to the fore. (See White's essay "Writing in the Middle Voice," chapter 18 of this volume.)[53]

Only facts (conceived as singular existential statements) can be judged as true or false, that is, as conforming to current standards of scientific inquiry.[54] There are no such standards for historical interpretations (or, for that matter, for any other kind of interpretation). Establishing facts (how many people died, on what date, in what manner, etc.) is not tantamount to conferring meaning in the strong sense of the term; though any articulation of the facts—their elaboration in a discourse— would necessarily entail interpretation. By separating fact from interpretation, White thereby steers a middle course between objectivist historicism (there are no interpretations, only facts) and Nietzschean perspectivism (there are no facts, only interpretations). As White observes:

The distinction between facts and meanings is usually taken to be the basis of historical relativism. This is because in conventional historical inquiry, the facts established about a specific event are taken to be the meaning of that event. Facts are supposed to provide the basis for arbitrating among the variety of different meanings that different social groups can assign to an event for different ideological or political reasons. But the facts are a function of the meaning assigned to events, not some primitive data that determine what meanings an event can have.[55]

But does White's scheme make it impossible to speak of a "bad interpretation" of the facts, in the sense that an interpretation would not merely offend against taste or morality but against our cognitive need for plausibility? Good or bad interpretation cannot be a matter of matching story-type to facts, for the reasons mentioned above; it can only be a matter of the *coherence* of an interpretation, which means using the facts in a way that suggests a well-constructedness: "stories are not true or false, but rather more or less intelligible, coherent, consistent, persuasive, and so on" ("Historical Pluralism and Pantextualism").[56] To be convincing or plausible, interpretations require a host of logical-formal qualities such as those White mentions, but the choice of a particular story-type is not one of them.

Does this suggest that White is simply advocating for a coherence theory over a correspondence theory of truth? Though at times he may give this impression, his thought transcends this dualist choice, for as mentioned above, White argues for a notion of *figural truth*, which involves an *indirect* form of reference or correspondence (that between a prefiguration and a fulfillment).

Consider, for example, Primo Levi's *Se questo è un uomo* (published in English as *Survival in Auschwitz*), of which White offers a figural analysis in a recent article.[57] White shows that Levi's discourse, considered a model of objective portrayal of the death camps, is permeated with figurative language; but far detracting from the realism of his account, his literary style actually constitutes and fulfills it:

> The [conventional view of Levi's text] is that whereas many other Holocaust writers depend upon rhetoric and aestheticization to render the horror of their experiences in the camps, Levi has purged his language of rhetoric, developed an anti-rhetorical, "plain" style, and is all the more effective for eschewing any openly artistic tricks or techniques. In my view, however, it can be easily demonstrated that Levi's text is full of rhetorical figures and tropes, and is never more rhetorical than when he purports to be simply "describing" a place, situation, or individual he knows.[58]

The rhetoric of antirhetoric is the irony of the realistic style. Levi adopts the clinical, understated style to convey an experience the weight of which precludes any "direct" expression of "appropriate" sentiments.

White sees Levi as a prime example of what he calls *figural realism*, or mimesis as figuration. The notion of *figuralism* (as distinguished from tropology, of which it can be considered an aspect) becomes central for White's later work, though it was part of his thinking as early as the essay "What Is a Historical System?" (originally written in 1967, chapter 8 of this volume). White derives this concept from Erich Auerbach's 1939 essay, "Figura," and from his *Mimesis: The Representation of Reality in Western Literature*.[59] As Auerbach notes, figuralism was originally developed as a form of biblical exegesis the goal of which was to show how the Hebrew Tanakh (Old Testament) anticipated or announced Christianity as expressed in the New Testament. According to this notion, persons and events in the Old Testament are said to *prefigure* persons and events in the New Testament, the latter being the *fulfillment* of the former. This relationship was also described as that between "type" and "antitype" (*typos* in Greek, meaning figure, model, archetype).[60] Thus in figural interpretation, or typology, the meaning of the present and the past are shown to be mutually determined: the full meaning of the type is retroactively revealed in the antitype, just as the full meaning of the antitype is revealed only when linked to the type (and every antitype can in turn become a type for a later antitype). Most important, however, figuralism is distinguished from allegory and other figurative modes by an irreducible facticity or historicity; for in figural interpretation, events and persons are considered fully concrete and historical, thereby resisting the abstraction and spiritualization of symbolic interpretation and preserving—albeit paradoxically—the Bible's "literal" truth.

The model for figural interpretation is contained in the New Testament itself: in, for example, Saint Paul's famous phrase "a shadow of things to come" (Col. 2:17), which refers to the relation between Jewish and Christian rites; and in Christ's statement "for had ye believed Moses, ye would have believed me; for he wrote of me" (John 5:45). Moses was indeed interpreted as a prefiguration of Christ by early Christian thinkers such as Saint Augustine, who proclaimed in a sermon: "The Old Testament is the veiling of the New Testament and the New Testament is the unveiling of the Old Testament."[61] The notion of figural correspondences was also extended to the idea that later historical events (such as the advent of the Church) could be seen as fulfillments of biblical persons and events.

This theological understanding of figuralism held the relation between type and antitype to be intrinsic and causal; that is, willed by God, providential. While White sees theological figuralism, in its relational conception of discrete events, as a precursor to a specifically historical consciousness, it is the *aesthetic* notion of figuralism—which animates Auerbach's literary history—that reveals its significance for modern historiography. The literary self-understanding of figuralism, the paradigm of which for Auerbach is Dante, uses the prefiguration-fulfillment model to simultaneously refer to the historical world while *creating*, in a specifically poetic way, connections between literary and biblical figures and ideas, connections that have no causal or intrinsic justification. Though Auerbach uses the notion of figural realism to refer to the type of realism that characterized the Middle Ages, White extends this notion to describe Auerbach's critical practice in *Mimesis* more generally.[62]

For, as White points out, Auerbach's literary history is, on a formal or structural level, constituted by figural relationships, the principle one being the mixture of styles in the Gospels that prefigures and is fulfilled in nineteenth-century literary realism—a relation that is not merely literary-historical but also sociohistorical to the extent that social reality is prefigured in the "aesthetic" performance of stylistic dehierarchization. As White observes in an essay on Auerbach, "the various periods in the history of Western literary realism can be defined in terms of their characteristic mixtures of styles and of the extent to which they succeed in grasping the content of history as a social reality delivered from class division."[63] This historical "content" is a fulfillment of the aesthetic "form" of realism, which does not mean that realistic literature caused, in any direct way, the progressive democratization of Western culture, but that democratization *can be seen or understood as* the completion or concretization of the West's aspiration to realistic representation, inaugurated by the Gospels.

With a slight shift in terminology, White adapts this aesthetic notion of figuralism modeled on literary history to history proper. For example, in "What Is a Historical System?" which was delivered before a group of biologists and historians, White argues that historical systems necessarily differ from biological systems in their conceptions of genetic causation, for historical agents "act *as if they could choose their own ancestors*":

What happened between the third and eighth centuries [in Christian civilization] was that men *ceased to regard themselves as descendents of their Roman forebears and began to treat themselves as descendents of their Judeo-Christian predecessors.* And it was the constitution of this *fictional* cultural ancestry that signaled the abandonment of the Roman sociocultural system. When Western European men began to act *as if* they were descended from the Christian segment of the ancient world; when they began to structure their comportment *as if* they were *genetically* descended from their Christian predecessors; when, in short, they began to honor the Christian past as the most desirable model for creation of a future uniquely their own, and ceased to honor the Roman past as *their* past, the Roman sociocultural system ceased to exist. (White's emphasis)[64]

Though literally chronological, history is figurally anachronistic: for a later event alters the meaning of an earlier event whose fulfillment (as White observes in a later essay on Northrop Frye) "is to be understood as the product or effect of a kind of *reverse causation*."[65] Hence figural interpretation becomes in this example the will to see a later event *as if* it were intrinsically related to an earlier event, in the absence of any efficient-causal connection: to *choose* a past is to choose a *corresponding* present. The idea of history as a linear series of fixed points of reference is thus replaced by the idea of a dynamic system of retrospective correspondences or "repetitions"— to invoke Søren Kierkegaard's enigmatic notion, which White, following Frye, interprets as a secularized version of biblical typology.[66]

Figuralism structures historical consciousness because it structures narrative itself. Hence White's contention that emplotment is essentially a form of verbal *figuration*: the significance of earlier parts of a story are revealed (fulfilled) only in the later moments—as in the literary technique of "foreshadowing" (recalling Saint Paul's "shadow of things to come"). And so with history: to confer meaning retrospectively, to see one event in light of another as narrativistically connected (if not constructed), is precisely what history does.[67] Obviously the French Revolution would have a very different significance if the Axis powers had prevailed during World War II. It would not have been the event that heralded a democratic future, and modern Europe would not have been its fulfillment. And how could the election of the first black president of a nation founded by slave owners not be regarded as the figural and ultimately ironic fulfillment of the national ideals as set forth in this nation's constitution and Declaration of Independence?

In fact, history as an academic discipline emerged from the effort to forge the identity of the nation-state as the fulfillment of its origins. As White observes in "Postmodernism and Textual Anxieties" (chapter 22 of this volume):

> By providing for the nation an equivalent of what the genealogist provided for the family, professional historians of the nineteenth century not only established the purity of the group's bloodlines but also confirmed the claim of the dominant ethnic group within the nation to the land it ruled.

Figural relationships define history as a quintessentially creative enterprise, inherently political and ideological to the extent it affirms and expresses the self-understanding or self-interpretation of a group or community. If White has recourse to literary criticism in his theory of historical writing, it is to demonstrate this re-pressed truth and to reconcile historiography with its humanist vocation, for, as he writes: "history is the humanistic discipline *par excellence.*"[68]

But perhaps White's greatest contribution to twentieth-century thought is his demonstration that history and theory are not antithetical but mutually implicit, that the divide between the philosophy of history and history proper, and between literary theory and literary history, is only apparent—hence the great synthesis that defines White's work: that between Northrop Frye's archetypal *formalism* and Erich Auerbach's figural *historicism*. For if one can say, with Fredric Jameson, that "all apparently formal statements about a work bear with them a concealed his-torical dimension of which the critic is not often aware,"[69] one can also say that within historicism lies a concealed formalism.

ACKNOWLEDGMENTS

1. "Collingwood and Toynbee: Transitions in English Historical Thought" appeared in *English Miscellany* 7 (1957): 147–78.

2. "Religion, Culture, and Western Civilization in Christopher Dawson's Idea of History" appeared in *English Miscellany* 9 (1958): 247–87.

3. "The Abiding Relevance of Croce's Idea of History" appeared in *The Journal of Modern History* 35, no. 2 (June 1963): 109–24.

4. "Romanticism, Historicism, and Realism: Toward a Period Concept for Early Nineteenth-Century Intellectual History" appeared in *The Uses of History: Essays in Intellectual and Social History*, ed. Hayden White (Detroit: Wayne State University Press, 1968): 45–58.

5. "The Tasks of Intellectual History" appeared in *The Monist* 53, no. 1 (January 1969): 606–30.

6. "The Culture of Criticism: Gombrich, Auerbach, Popper" appeared under the title "The Culture of Criticism" in *Liberations: New Essays on the Humanities in Revolution*, ed. John Cage and Ihab Hassan (Middletown, CT: Wesleyan University Press, 1971): 55–69.

7. "The Structure of Historical Narrative" appeared in *Clio* 1, no. 3 (1972): 5–20.

8. "What Is a Historical System?" appeared in *Biology, History, and Natural Philosophy*, ed. Allen D. Breck and Wolfgang Yourgrau (New York: Plenum Press, 1972): 233–42.

9. "The Politics of Contemporary Philosophy of History" appeared in *Clio* 3, no. 1 (October 1973): 35–54.

10. "The Problem of Change in Literary History" appeared in *New Literary History* 7, no. 1 (Autumn 1975): 97–111.

11. "The Problem of Style in Realistic Representation: Marx and Flaubert"

appeared in *The Concept of Style*, ed. Berel Lang (Philadelphia: University of Pennsylvania Press, 1979): 213–29.

12. "The Discourse of History" appeared in *Humanities in Society* 2, no. 1 (Winter 1979): 1–15.

13. "Vico and Structuralist/Poststructuralist Thought" appeared under the title "Vico and the Radical Wing of Structuralist/Poststructuralist Thought Today" in *New Vico Studies* 1 (1983): 63–68.

14. "The Interpretation of Texts" appeared in *Berkshire Review* 7 (1984): 7–23.

15. "Historical Pluralism and Pantextualism" appeared under the title "Historical Pluralism" in *Critical Inquiry* 12, no. 3 (Spring 1986): 480–93.

16. "'The Nineteenth Century' as Chronotope" appeared in *Nineteenth-Century Contexts* 11, no. 2 (1987): 119–30.

17. "Ideology and Counterideology in Northrop Frye's *Anatomy of Criticism*" appeared under the title "Ideology and Counterideology in the *Anatomy*" in *Visionary Poetics: Essays on Northrop Frye's Criticism*, ed. Robert D. Denham and Thomas Willard (New York: Peter Lang, 1991): 101–11.

18. "Writing in the Middle Voice" appeared in *Stanford Literature Review* 9, no. 2 (Fall 1992): 179–87.

19. "Northrop Frye's Place in Contemporary Cultural Studies" appeared under the title "Frye's Place in Contemporary Cultural Studies" in *The Legacy of Northrop Frye*, ed. Alvin A. Lee and Robert Denham (Toronto: University of Toronto Press, 1994): 28–39.

20. "Storytelling: Historical and Ideological" appeared in *Centuries' Ends, Narrative Means*, ed. Robert D. Newman (Stanford, CA: Stanford University Press, 1996): 58–78.

21. "The Suppression of Rhetoric in the Nineteenth Century" appeared in *The Rhetoric Canon*, ed. Brenda Deen Schildgen (Detroit: Wayne State University Press, 1997): 21–32.

22. "Postmodernism and Textual Anxieties" appeared in *The Postmodern Challenge: Perspectives East and West*, ed. Bo Stråth and Nina Witoszek (Amsterdam: Rodopi, 1999): 27–45.

23. "Guilty of History? The *longue durée* of Paul Ricoeur" appeared in *History and Theory* 46, no. 2 (2007): 233–51.

CHAPTER ONE

Collingwood and Toynbee

Transitions in English Historical Thought

{1957}

It is generally held that, unlike the German and Italian historians, English historians have neither produced a self-conscious philosophy of history nor divided into various schools representing conflicting interpretations of the nature of historical investigation. As A. J. P. Taylor is fond of saying: "In England there are no schools of history; there are only individual historians."[1] Another historian, Herbert Butterfield, contends that English historiography is dominated by one grand school of interpretation, a school which he calls the "Whig interpretation of history."[2] Whether there is indeed no school of historical philosophy in England or one grand school, it is only recently, under the impact of two World Wars and a depression, that English historians have taken to the investigation of the problem of historical knowledge. The two most important representatives of this new movement are R. G. Collingwood and Arnold J. Toynbee. Their work, seen as a totality, is one concerted attack against positivism or scientism in historical thought. Collingwood began his attack from the viewpoint of Continental historicism as represented in the thought of Wilhelm Dilthey and Benedetto Croce. Toynbee completes a cycle begun by Collingwood by abandoning positivism, attacking historicism, and embracing a concept of history that can only be termed theosophic. Both take their point of departure from the conviction that historical knowledge can be used for the formulation of a general philosophy of history upon which cultural values that have suffered as a result of scientism in modern Western thought may be reestablished.[3]

English historiography, unlike English philosophy, remained true to the historiographical precepts of the eighteenth-century empiricists David Hume and William Robertson. Hume's philosophy was based upon ideas that precluded all discussion of "theory, all examination of cause, all doctrine of 'true Being' behind 'phenomena.'"[4] Robertson, working out of a philosophy similar to Hume's, established historiography as an empirical science, holding that the realms of philosophy and history, fact and fancy, science and conjecture, must never be merged. Robertson's position was stated in a letter in which he argued: "It is not by theories and conjectures that history decides with regard to the state and character of nations. It produces facts as the foundations of every judgment which it ventures to pronounce."[5] Only that which was ascertainable from the documents was to be admitted as historical evidence; "interpretation" on metaphysical grounds was to be avoided at all costs. As Robertson phrased it: "If we push our inquiries concerning any point beyond the area where written history commences, we enter upon the region of conjecture, fable, or uncertainty. Upon that ground I will neither venture myself, nor endeavor to conduct my readers."[6]

This point of view led to the establishment of a peculiar kind of English historicism, a historicism that studied historical events in their individuality because empiricism precluded the examination of the "connections" between events. Thus English empirical historicism, unlike the idealistic historicism of Germany and Italy, which studied individual events as manifestations of a unique and creative human spirit, developed in the wake of English scientific thought.[7] Adherence to a strictly empirical view was the only factor in its development that prohibited it from lapsing into complete Comtean positivism and the attempt to establish "laws" of historical change.

The relation of English historical thought to science was consummated in the nineteenth century.[8] G. N. Clark expressed the viewpoint well when he wrote:

> It seems to me that no historical investigation can provide either a philosophy, a religion, or a substitute for a religion. If in this I express only a personal opinion, I think I should have the general consensus of the working historians with me if I confined myself to the simpler conclusion that we work with limited aims. We try to find the truth about this or that, not about things in general. Our work is not to see life steadily and see it whole, but to see one particular portion of life, right side up and in true perspective.[9]

Guided by such a view, English historiography has steered a middle path between Crocean historicism, which allies history and philosophy, and Comtean positivism with its desire to construct "laws" of historical change. It has also managed to avoid the pitfalls of theological or metaphysical interpretations of history such as those of Saint Augustine, Bossuet, and Hegel. In a recent monograph, the philosopher Patrick Gardiner pointed out that there are questions to be asked *in* history and questions to be asked *about* history; historians ask the former and philosophers that latter.[10] Yet, until the appearance of Collingwood and Toynbee, few philosophers had found it apposite to ask questions *about* history, and attempts by historians to do so were met only with derision.[11] Nonetheless, under the impact of what has come to be termed "the crisis of modern Western civilization," English thinkers have turned more and more to the study of history for an explanation of the European and the English *Untergang*.

This renewed interest in the philosophy of history springs from the inability of scientistic philosophy to deal with contemporary moral issues. Collingwood began his inquiries into historical knowledge in an attempt to counteract this scientism in philosophy.[12] Scientism had come to dominate English thought in the early decades of the present century through the attempt of logical positivists and analysts to make philosophy as purely objective and empirical as science itself. The fanaticism with which English philosophers embraced logical positivism may be explained historically by viewing it as a reaction to the Hegelian idealism that dominated English philosophical thought in the latter part of the nineteenth century.

Under the leadership of Green, Bosanquet, Bradley, Wallace, and others, idealism had held unquestioned sway in English universities for over two decades. But gains made in the physical sciences in the late nineteenth and early twentieth centuries revealed what seemed to many to be striking limitations in that philosophy. In England, logical positivists held that idealism, when extended to fields such as physics, mathematics, and biology, frequently resulted in sheer nonsense.[13] The inability of Hegelian thought to accommodate the kind of knowledge derived from the physical sciences (except as a polar opposite) led to a general reaction to all forms of idealism and ultimately to the defeat of idealism in England.

By 1903–1904 the attack against idealism had turned into a rout. Bertrand Russell, formerly a Hegelian, now held that the world as discovered by the natural sciences was not only self-sufficient but "intellectually satisfying," and he accused the idealists of being "less anxious to understand the world than to convict it of unreality in the interests of a suprasensible real world."[14] Metaphysics was held to be largely concerned with pseudo problems, for the positivists claimed to be able to "demonstrate conclusively by logical analysis the purely empirical reference of all significant propositions."[15] Russell and his followers argued that the role of philosophy was not to construct a worldview that encompassed and illuminated art, science, morals, religion, and politics. Instead, philosophy was identified with logic, and its major role was held to be that of policeman of science: the scientist would discover and investigate the real world; the philosopher merely reserved the right to subject scientific propositions to the test of logical consistency.[16] The physical sciences had become the paradigm of all knowledge.

Carried over into the field of ethics, such scientism resulted in complete skepticism. Russell's colleague, G. E. Moore, in his celebrated *Principia Ethica* (1903), gave the classic statement of the new philosopher's view of ethics when he wrote: "If I am asked 'How is the good to be defined,' my answer is that it cannot be defined, and that is all that I have to say about it, disappointing though this answer may appear."[17] And from this conclusion Moore argued: "It will follow that unless new reasons never urged hitherto can be found, all the most striking results of philosophy have as little claim to assent as the most superstitious beliefs of the most ignorant savages."[18] Such a statement did, as its present-day adherents hold, constitute a "revolution in philosophy," for, in effect, it denied the efficacy of philosophy itself.

Collingwood's first philosophic work was, like that of Bradley, concerned with the attempt to keep philosophy from being identified with empirical psychology. In particular, he opposed the claim made by psychologists of his time that psychology was the true science of mind and was, therefore, capable of dealing with subjects such as logic and ethics. It was the acceptance of the psychologistic concept of mind that had led, according to Collingwood, to the moral skepticism of Moore and Russell. In his first book, *Religion and Philosophy*, Collingwood sought to point out that, whereas psychology was perfectly competent to deal with the physiochemical aspects of mind, it erred when it held that such physiochemical manifestations constituted mind completely. The psychology of knowing differed from the philosophical theory of knowledge in that it treated judgment—the act of knowing something—as merely an event in the mind, a physiochemical event, and, unlike philosophy, psychology did not go on to determine the "relation of this mental event to the 'something' known, the reality behind the act which the mind, in the act, apprehends."[19]

The psychologist regards mind as a complex of mental events, whereas the philosopher sees it as a system of knowledge. The confusion of the one view with the other sprang from the acceptance of the empiricist canon that reason and will—the *functions* of mind—were in reality only sensation and appetite. The identification of reason and will with sensation and appetite implied, for Collingwood:

> the systematic abolition of all those distinctions which, being valid for reason and will but not for sensation and appetite, constitute the special subject matter of logic and ethics: distinctions like that between truth and error, knowledge and ignorance, science and sophistry, right and wrong, good and bad, expedient and inexpedient. Distinctions of this kind form the armature of every science; no one can abolish them and remain a scientist.[20]

Hence, the triumph of scientism in philosophy could only result in the description of mind in terms of physiochemical processes, and such description would necessarily lead to the abandonment of ethics as a *prescriptive* science. Under the canons of a strictly scientific ethics, the philosopher could only say: "Moral philosophy is only a theory of moral action; it can't therefore make any difference to the practice of moral action . . . I stand here as a moral philosopher; I will try to tell you what acting morally is, but don't expect me to tell you how to do it."[21]

The moral skepticism that the triumph of scientific philosophy had brought about was, for Collingwood, merely one aspect of a general decline in Western thought. The separation of philosophy from life was the result of the triumph of the psychologistic concept of mind, for the psychologist could only construct abstract generalizations of how the mind *would act* given certain conditions. Psychology could not go on and tell the mind how it *should* act in the situation in which it found itself. With modern existentialists such as Karl Jaspers and Gabriel Marcel, Collingwood held that philosophy must be reunited with the problems of life from which scientism had divorced it. Under the canons of such a view, a philosophically relevant reflection might be defined as one that "captures that ontological import of our experience and throws open a door for communication among the joint participants in existence."[22] The moral crisis that followed upon World War I was described by Collingwood in the following terms:

> The reason why the civilization of 1600–1900, based upon natural science, found bankruptcy staring it in the face was because, in its passion for ready-made rules, it had neglected to develop the kind of insight which alone could tell it what rules to apply, not in the situation of a specific type, but in the situation in which it actually found itself.[23]

But, humanist that he was, Collingwood did not believe that the failure of nerve occasioned by the First World War and its aftermath could be dissolved by merely more goodwill and human affection. In his view, what was needed was not more piety but more knowledge of human affairs and how to handle them. To the end of establishing a humanistic science of human affairs, therefore, Collingwood embarked upon his systematic investigation of the relation holding between mind, culture, and history. The fruit of these inquiries was a comprehensive philosophy of mind similar to that of Kant, a concept of history similar to that of Hegel, Dilthey, and Croce, and a completely original theory of culture. Upon the bases of these investigations Collingwood launched his attack upon traditional English historiography.[24]

Collingwood's philosophy of history hinges upon his concept of the relation between mind and nature. According to Collingwood, the world of nature evolves and develops through at least three stages: physical nature, animal nature, and human nature. Like Whitehead, Alexander, and Bergson, he holds that each stage contains the previous stage through a process of sublation. This means that each successive stage in natural development is qualitatively different from the one that preceded it. It is the last stage, human nature, where mind appears self-consciously. In man, the natural process reaches a new stage of development in which all previous stages are contained implicitly as sublated.[25] Therefore, man is part of nature but in a new stage, and this stage is made what it is by the appearance of self-conscious mind. This unique quality of mind gives to man's development a peculiar character, a character that requires a unique discipline for its study. The study of man's development insofar as it is a manifestation of a mind unique in the universe is the study of history. The study of mind's manifestations in the physical organism is the proper competence of psychology; and psychology only errs when it asserts that the physiochemical manifestations of mind are mind *in toto*.[26] Thus, purposive thought, the function of self-conscious mind, forms the criterion for the differentiation between history and nature as well as the criterion for the distinction between historical knowledge, on the one hand, and scientific knowledge, on the other. In *The Idea of History*, Collingwood writes:

> No doubt nature contains, undergoes, or even consists of process; its changes in time are essential to it; it may even (as some think) be all that it has or is; and these changes may be genuinely creative, no mere repetitions of fixed cyclical phases but the development of new orders of natural being. But all this goes no way towards proving that the life of nature is a historical life or that our knowledge of it is historical knowledge. The only conditions on which there could be a history of nature is that the events of nature are actions on the part of some thinking being or beings, and that by studying these actions we could discover what were the thoughts which they expressed and think these thoughts ourselves.[27]

Thus historical events are differentiated from natural events by virtue of the existence of thought as an essential element in their genesis.[28] An event is not historical unless (1) it is a product of some kind of reflective or purposive thought and (2) that thought becomes "encapsulated" in some cultural artifact that can be known by a historian living after the event itself.[29] Historical knowledge attempts to "reconstruct" the thought behind the artifact. Thus envisaged, historical knowledge is the individual mind studying cultural creations (artifacts) in order to determine the thought processes of the mind in the past that led to the creation of the artifact in its unique aspects. Analysis of Collingwood's criticism of Croce will aid us in understanding this idea.

It will be recalled that for Croce history and nature were part of the one spirit and the one history; nature was merely "history not written by us."[30] Historical knowledge is not, therefore, to Croce knowledge of the human as opposed to knowledge of the natural world: "It is simply the knowledge of facts or events as they actually happen in their concrete individuality."[31] The distinction between history and nature as the difference between spirit and matter is artificial. Historical knowledge lies at the base of all knowledge for Croce, because events must be apprehended in their individuality before one can generalize about them. One attempts, therefore, to study nature in the same way that one studies history, that is, "by thinking oneself into" the life of the event under consideration.

Croce states that in order to understand Neolithic man, one must try to "become" a Neolithic man. Similarly, if one wishes to know a blade of grass, one must attempt to "become" a blade of grass. If one cannot, in the second case, become a blade of grass, then one must be content with "analyzing its parts and even arranging them in a sort of ideal or fanciful history."[32] The analysis of the parts and their arrangement in a sort of ideal history is science. Thus, the differentiation between historical knowledge and scientific knowledge results from the success or failure of the intuitive powers of the investigation; it is not the result of an essential difference between the objects of knowledge themselves.

Collingwood begins his critique of Croce by asking whether the articulation or growth of a blade of grass is really the same as that of a human being. And he answers:

> I am not so sure. And when we come to a crystal, or a stalactite, my skepticism reaches the point of rebellion. The process by which these things form themselves appears to me to be a process in which, through no lack of our own historical sympathy, we look in vain for any expression of thought. It is an event; it has individuality; but it seems to lack that inwardness which, according to this passage by Croce, is made (and, I think, rightly made) the criterion of historicity. The resolution of nature into spirit seems to me incomplete, and not at all proved by the converse fact that spirit, by being handled scientifically instead of historically, can be resolved into nature.[33]

Thus, for Collingwood, unlike Croce but similar to Whitehead, Bergson, and Alexander, the human spirit is seen to be a qualitatively different stage in the total process of natural development, and the fact that both mind and nature *may* be viewed scientifically does not prove that they are not essentially different. Self-conscious mind, the peculiar attribute of human nature, emerges in the late phases of natural development, and historical knowledge alone is competent to deal with its unique aspects. One of Collingwood's students has summarized the view more than adequately when he writes:

> It is the earlier phases of the process of evolution that we identify as nature and study through the natural sciences (though we also acknowledge a sense in which nature embraces the whole of the process). But at the stage where mind emerges as human personality capable of consciously organizing a life lived in cooperation with other persons, the continuation of the process becomes history— the process in which the human mind develops itself by its own conscious effort . . . The study of history is the study of *res gestae*: the study of men's choices as they combine to constitute the organization of their social life and to facilitate the growing awareness of human nature and the world in which it is set.[34]

Now, it may be pointed out that Collingwood is seeking to rigidly define the criteria for establishing the historicity of events, and the assignment of those criteria hinges upon his assuming that human thought is in some sense unique. He is willing to admit that certain forms of thought are found in the lower animals, forms such as perception, memory, and instinct. But these do not qualify as determinants of historicity for they are neither self-conscious nor do they produce cultural artifacts. Insofar as they appear in human beings they are not so much manifestations of his humanity as functions of his animal organism. Therefore, it is only self-conscious or purposive thought that qualifies as the creator of historical events.[35] All other events are natural events and are most profitably studied by scientific methods. Only events that grow out of mind exercising its peculiar functions— reason and will—are historical events and are to be studied by historical method.

The distinction is made easily enough, for cultural artifacts are created only by mind exercising its unique functions. Purposive thought is "encapsulated" in these cultural artifacts (giving each its unique aspect—as over against natural objects, which are uniform), and thus thought is preserved through time for examination by the historian of later periods. Hence, culture is seen to be the objectification of thought, and the study of culture by the historian is ultimately seen to be the study of mind. Thought, history, and culture are all connected in an essential way. The individual acting organism creates artifacts for the accomplishment of its ends; these artifacts are *cultural* artifacts, distinguished from *natural* artifacts by the thought encapsulated in them; the accumulation of these artifacts constitutes the records of historical development. The disciplines by which the individual mind studies these cultural artifacts scientifically are archaeology and anthropology; the process by which it knows these artifacts as products of mind is historical knowledge. Therefore, the growth of historical knowledge results in the growth of our knowledge of mind. Knowledge of all other minds by individual minds is philosophy, or mind knowing mind; and with the growth of knowledge of mind man becomes civilized. Thus historical knowledge is the base of philosophic knowledge and the tool by which man becomes civilized through awareness of his own uniqueness.[36]

The relationship between mind and culture was developed by Collingwood in his *Speculum Mentis* (1924). This work may be studied from three viewpoints: it may be seen as a general theory of knowledge, as a theory of culture, or as a speculative philosophy of history. For Collingwood, a theory of culture and a theory of knowledge are merely two sides of the same coin. He believes that mind has two aspects: subjective and objective (or reflective and expressive). Culture is held to be the objective or expressive manifestation of mind, while knowledge is mind studying its own creations in order to know itself. Progressive enlightenment of mind concerning its own being is the measure of civilizational growth. As mind becomes more conscious of its own essential nature, new and more subtle forms of thought emerge. The history of these forms of thought is the history of man in time as he seeks to define his own humanity.[37]

The components of culture are, according to Collingwood, reflections of the categories of mind. They are art, religion, science, historical knowledge, and philosophy. Each category differs by virtue of its place on a spectrum running between pure expression and pure reflection. Thus, art is identified with pure imagination and philosophy with pure contemplation. But while the categories constitute the "rungs of Collingwood's epistemological ladder," the emergence of each of the categories in culture constitutes the record of man's growing self-consciousness.[38] For even though in each category of expression the mind seeks truth, it is only in the last two stages that the true object of knowledge, mind, merges as the identifiable object of true knowledge.

In art, science, and religion, only parts of total reality are seen, and these parts are taken to be the whole of truth. In art, it is never inquired whether or not its vision of the world is real or fanciful.[39] Religion, being uncritical faith and mythological thinking, is more reflective than art for "it asserts what it imagines, that is, it believes in the reality of the figments of its own imagination."[40] Science is distinguished from the first two forms of thought, not because it is rational but because it is *consciously* rational. Yet science also is limited in its search for truth, for it takes the real object of knowledge to be the material world of facts, and it supposes them as instances of general laws of physical change.[41] In so doing science overlooks the real object of knowledge, the unique aspect of the universe that is mind. Science, in denying that products of mind such as myth, symbol, and imagery are real forms of knowledge, thus limits itself by refusing to admit to its ken those aspects of mind not commensurate with its own vision of reality.[42] As Collingwood writes in *Speculum Mentis*:

> We found that the real world was implied, but not asserted, in art; asserted, but not thought out, in religion; thought out, but only subject to fictitious assumptions, in science; and therefore in all these we found an ostensible object—the work of art, God, the material universe—which was confessedly a figment and not the real object [of knowledge].[43]

Now it is obvious that the first three forms of thought (art, religion, and a certain crude science) exist even in the most primitive human societies.[44] It is only in civilized societies, however, that historical thought exists, that is, it is historical self-consciousness that distinguishes civilization from primitive culture. Only when man becomes able to distinguish between the individuality of the products of his own creativity does history begin. Prior to that time all is prehistory; man is caught in the same eternal present as the animal. But the consciousness that minds in the past did things differently lifted man out of the cycle of nature and projected him onto a stage of historical development in which nature merely serves as a background. Here man becomes aware of the various potentialities of his mind, and thus historical self-consciousness is also the birth of philosophic knowledge. In philosophy, the individual mind seeks to understand mind by studying it in all of its manifestations; but philosophy can only generalize about mind with the aid of history, for in history alone is mind known in its individual instances.

In historical knowledge concrete thought is apprehended, though in all its forms, both rational and imaginary; and no aspect of mind is denied being apposite to the formation of a true and total picture of mind. Hence, the emergence of historical consciousness is merely the emergence of "absolute mind" to consciousness, the point at which mind turns back upon itself and begins to contemplate its own nature—an activity that is impossible in nature because nature (even though it may be creative and developmental) is not conscious of its own activity. But the self-conscious mind incorporates all previous forms of its existence by sublation and thus knowledge of itself is knowledge of the world as a whole.

In a similar manner, historical knowledge rises superior to all previous forms of knowledge (art, religion, and science) because of its willingness to affirm that all previous forms of knowledge are *valid* activities of mind itself. And just as mind incorporates all previous forms of existence into itself by sublation, historical knowledge incorporates all previous forms of mental experience into itself by sublation. Historical knowledge is the doorway through which mind, observing itself in its manifold aspects, comes to knowledge of itself—that is, philosophical knowledge. From this point of view, Collingwood is forced to hold that science itself is merely "a point of view." He writes:

> From a strictly scientific point of view science is the only form of thought, and history does not exist at all. From the historical point of view science does indeed exist, but only as an element within the body of history itself, as a mere weapon or tool of historical thinking. The quarrel between history and science is whether generalization is a means of knowledge itself.[45]

The quarrel between science and history is over the proper object of knowledge— whether mind is to be relegated to another aspect of man's physical existence or is to be considered a new and qualitatively different aspect of reality, different from physical and animal nature and therefore requiring a discipline for its study that is qualitatively different from science.

If man is to know mind, it is necessary that he know it in all of its unique instances, myth and science included. Thus, science itself must be seen historically, as *another* aspect of knowledge not as *the* form of knowledge. Only then can the mind in regarding itself fully, know itself fully, that is, philosophize.[46] Through historical knowledge, the intuitive re-living and reconstruction of all past intellectual experiences through the study of cultural artifacts, the various phases of man's development are cognized. Once historical knowledge has shown to man the vision of mind in action—in art, religion, science, historical thought, and philosophy itself—the individual reflects upon this vision and comes to know himself by knowing how his own mind is an aspect of the absolute mind.[47]

Thus envisaged, the development of human awareness from pure expression (art) to disciplined self-awareness (philosophy) is the reflection of mind's growing self-awareness in time. That whole process Collingwood calls civilization. It is the process by which mind attempts to approximate some ideal of fulfillment that it vaguely senses and gives voice to in cultural expression. And he asserts that this late phase of human development points to an even later phase in which, through self-knowledge, all minds are united in the fully realized absolute mind. History, therefore, is the story of man's definition of his own humanity, and this is merely one phase in the total definition of Being seeking its own fulfillment. Collingwood agrees with the Jaspers who could write:

> My outline is based upon an article of faith: that mankind has one origin and one goal. Origin and goal are unknown to us, utterly unknown by any kind of knowledge. They can only be felt in the glimmer of ambiguous symbols. Our

actual existence moves between these two poles; in philosophical reflection we may endeavor to draw closer to the origin and goal.[48]

Beyond history mind will conceivably move to a new stage of development.[49] As Collingwood himself wrote: "The absolute mind, then, unites the differences of my mind and other peoples', but not as the abstract universal unites; rather as the concrete universal of history unites. The absolute mind is the historical whole of which mine is a part."[50] Thus the ghost of Hegel reappeared to haunt the historiographical scene in England.

It is from this metaphysical position that Collingwood attacked positivism and empiricism in historical investigation; for he holds that while it is perfectly permissible to view mind as a part of animal and physical nature, to view it in only that way is to deny its peculiarly human aspects. In order for human minds to know past minds in their characteristic function, it was necessary that they be studied in their individuality—not as instances of general laws. We should approach the historical artifact with the intention of recreating the thought of the human mind that created that artifact. When we have done this, we will be said to *know* the object historically, not to have merely perceived it scientifically and catalogued it under the Humian terms of time, space, and resemblance.[51] This historical knowledge will then serve as a base for philosophic contemplation of mind itself and thence to self-knowledge; for:

> if what the historian knows is past thoughts, and if he knows them by rethinking them himself, it follows that the knowledge he achieves by historical inquiry is not knowledge of the situation as opposed to knowledge of himself. In rethinking what somebody else thought, he knows that he himself is able to think it. And finding out what he is able to do is finding out what kind of man he is. If he is able to understand, by rethinking them, the thoughts of a great many kinds of people, it follows that he must be a great many kinds of man. He must in fact be a microcosm of all the history that he can know. Thus, his own self-knowledge is at the same time, knowledge of the world of human affairs.[52]

It is also by making thought the criterion for historicity that Collingwood claims to be able to distinguish between history (*res gestae*) and pseudo-history. Narratives by the geologist, paleontologist, and astronomer had, in the late nineteenth century, taken on the aspect of historical narratives through the popularity of evolutionary concepts in these sciences. But while nature might be viewed as developmental, it did not follow that it was historical, for historical events are only those events that grow out of purposive activity:

History and pseudo-history alike consisted of narratives, but in history these were narratives of purposive activity, and the evidence for them consisted of relics which had been left behind which became evidence precisely to the extent to which the historian conceived them in terms of purpose, that is, understood what they were for; in pseudo-history there is no conception of purpose, there are only relics of different kinds, differing among themselves in such ways that they have to be interpreted as relics of different pasts which can be arranged on a time scale. I expressed this new conception of mine in the phrase: All history is the history of thought.[53]

Collingwood held that if the historian were to realize that the real object of knowledge in historical investigation was mind, then he would be able to free himself from the limitations of "scissors and paste history"—a view of history that confused knowledge with the multiplication of perceptions of previous states of being. By ceasing to view historical artifacts scientifically and by beginning to view them historically—that is, by seeking to discover the thought processes that had led to their creation—historical knowledge could make a genuine contribution to man's knowledge of himself. If historical artifacts were regarded as somehow alive in a way that nature was not, it would become obvious that the purpose of history was "to inform about the present, insofar as the past, its ostensible subject matter, was encapsulated in the present and constituted a part of it not at once obvious to the untrained eye."[54] Thus envisaged, historical knowledge takes its place beside and is yet liberated from science as a "self-explanatory, self-justifying," autonomous and self-authorizing form of thought.[55] To Collingwood, history stands revealed as "the science of human affairs."

Now, it is obvious that Collingwood's rejection of scientific historiography hinges ultimately upon (1) his distinction between nature and mind, (2) his identification of culture with the categories of mind, and (3) his assertion that purposive thought is the assignable distinctive criterion for the differentiation of nature and history. Identification of historical knowledge with philosophy and his resolution of historical knowledge into intuition are valid only if there is an essential difference between mind and nature that renders necessary different disciplines for their study. If nature is not divisible into the three stages designated by Collingwood, his concept of history is not valid. Let us state succinctly the concept of historical knowledge that we attribute to Collingwood above and then note the criticisms that may be brought against it.

Collingwood holds that scientific knowledge is incapable of dealing with ethics because it regards mind solely as an aspect of the natural world and cannot inculcate the kind of insight needed to tell the individual what law to apply in the existential social situation. He therefore makes a distinction between generalized scientific knowledge and historical knowledge (knowledge of the individual) and seeks to show that only the latter can be used to construct a science of human affairs. But he distinguishes between other forms of knowledge that seek knowledge of the individual, such as art and religion, by holding that historical knowledge has as its object mind, whereas art and religion and science each have as their objects only one aspect of the world. But since mind is the last stage of the natural development, the stage at which nature becomes self-conscious, it contains all previous natural stages as sublated; and, therefore, knowledge of the mind constitutes knowledge of the world. Historical knowledge is related to philosophical knowledge by virtue of the fact that the historical imagination apprehends mind in individual situations through the reconstruction of thought, while philosophy is mind generalizing about mind from the evidence provided to it by history. Historical knowledge thus has as its object the study of human actions that reveal mind in its characteristic functions—exercising reason and will. The proper study of a historical artifact consists in penetrating behind the object to the realm of "intellect," "thought," "reflection," or "purpose" that caused the artifact to be formed in just the way that it was.

The existence of this realm of thought gives to historical events a dual character that distinguishes them from natural events; historical events have both an "internal" and an "external" character. Whereas we can understand a natural event scientifically when we have perceived its various parts and located it in space and time or shown it to be an instance of some general law, we can understand a historical event only after we have reconstructed and re-thought the thoughts that passed through the mind of the person who created the artifact. This does not mean that historical artifacts may not be studied externally, but this external examination is the task of philology, archaeology, and (in the case of institutions) sociology. We have re-created the thought of the person who created the historical artifact when we can say that we understand exactly why the object was made in the way that it was. We thus re-think the thoughts of many different kinds of people and thereby gain knowledge of mind in general.

In the first place, it may be noted that Collingwood's philosophy of history does not so much seek to revolutionize historical thought as to strictly define the "historical." It was his aim to turn the lines of historical inquiry away from the *cul de sac* of atomistic empiricism—in which events were merely noted—as well as from the positivist tendency to resolve history into sociology. But instead of really establishing the autonomy of historical knowledge, as he claimed to have done, Collingwood succeeded in avoiding empiricism and positivism only to identify historical knowledge with philosophy. From the point of view of the historian it may be inquired whether the identification of history with philosophy is any more satisfactory than its identification with sociology.[56]

Secondly, the identification of history with philosophy certainly does not create a "science" of human affairs, for the criterion for the establishment of truth is, for Collingwood, purely relativistic, existing only in the mind of the individual historian. There exists no reference outside the mind of the historian by which propositions may become the common property of the society that Collingwood hoped to serve. It is undeniable that to "know thyself" is laudable, but in making the individual mind the sole judge of the desirability of any given social action it is difficult to see how Collingwood can avoid the very activism that characterized Giovanni Gentile's philosophy and fascist thought.[57]

Thirdly, one might ask how one attains the "historical imagination." Collingwood holds that it is a category of mind that is developed more or less in different individuals. But if this is so, then why is it that different cultures produce completely different views of history? Certainly the Hindu concept of history is completely different from that of the West. Does it follow that the Western version of history is more nearly true than that of the East? How are we to judge? Collingwood's apparent Western humanist bias would have led him to assert that our view of history is superior to that of the Hindu, but the assertion alone is hardly enough to convince us. On the other hand, if the visions of history entertained by various societies are equally valid, then it is difficult to see how a "science of human affairs" that is valid for all human beings, Eastern and Western, can be constructed on the basis of historical knowledge.

Fourthly, one might challenge Collingwood's division of mind into compartments as well as his differentiation between the outside and the inside of events. Even if one grants that mind is nature become self-conscious, we are far from agreeing as to the essence and structure of mind itself. Furthermore, the kind of psychology attacked by Collingwood has largely been superseded in our own time by Gestalt psychology; and Carl Jung's investigations begin with assumptions concerning the relation between mind and body that are not unlike those advocated by Collingwood.[58] Yet Jung does not have to conceive of historical knowledge as autonomous and self-sufficient in order to study mind on the one hand and body on the other.

Finally, it may be noted that one can hold an emergent theory of mind without having to revert to Hegel to explain its development. Certainly it is not obvious that mind contains all earlier stages of natural development as sublated. With the followers of John Dewey, one can assume the position of naturalistic humanist without following Collingwood into his metaphysical labyrinths. Mind may be a part of nature, the part in which nature becomes self-conscious, but such self-consciousness may be only the adjustment of the organism to the environment and nothing else. The teleological undercurrents of Collingwood's philosophy that lead him to speak of an "Absolute Mind" towards which individual minds tend comes too near to prophecy to be taken seriously.

Nonetheless, Collingwood's work was important. A century of painstaking scientific historiography has certainly not brought us any closer to agreement on major historical problems. While it has clarified problems of philology and chronology and while such progress may satisfy the archivist, no historian should be content with the solution of merely these kinds of problems. Therefore, in challenging the merits of scientistic history, Collingwood objectified a pressing problem for his colleagues in England and forced them to consider the epistemological problems ignored since 1900.

Secondly, it must be admitted that in the world of quanta, relativity, and evolution, Collingwood's philosophy of history is certainly much more commensurate with what we know of nature than is that of his empiricist critics. In an age in which matter has dissolved into energy, it may not be completely beside the point to demand, as Collingwood did, whether it is not time to change our concept of historical events as the physical scientist has changed his concept of physical events. Certainly, the empirical view of history was itself historically determined; and as the spirit asks new questions of history—questions prompted by the destruction of all ideologies and all Utopias at the hands of science itself[59]—it is not inconceivable that the answers given by history will have to be framed in new terms. It is possible that Collingwood's concept of history will in the future be one of those that historians will have to consider as the demand for answers from history becomes more violent. There is already evidence of the Englishman's interest in philosophy of history in the amount of attention given to the publication of Arnold J. Toynbee's *A Study of History*. If the fall of the Roman Empire demanded a "meaning" from history and was rewarded with Saint Augustine, the fall of the British Empire has given us Arnold Toynbee. With Toynbee's appearance a cycle is completed; for in the last volumes of his work, the historicism of Collingwood gives way to the theosophy of history.

Toynbee began his historical research out of motives strikingly similar to those of Collingwood: he was disillusioned with the results of World War I and hoped to find in history some clue to the establishment of a science of human affairs. It was Toynbee's purpose to discover laws of historical change in order to be able to analyze history in the same way that the physical scientist analyzed nature. This knowledge of history was to be used by man to aid him in directing history toward creative rather than destructive ends.[60] His method was to be strictly empirical and the end envisaged was the construction of positivistic laws. In a word, civilizations were to be treated as biological entities presented with the problem of adjusting to their environment during the course of their life cycles and these civilizations were to be studied scientifically.[61]

Upon the appearance of Toynbee's first three volumes in 1934, Collingwood subjected them to criticism. He held that Toynbee had erred because he failed to recognize the difference between the life of nature and the life of history. He objected to Toynbee's arbitrary division of human society into distinct and concrete categories. Collingwood noted that according to Toynbee:

> We are not allowed to say the Hellenic civilization has turned into Western Christendom by a process of development involving the accentuation of some of its elements, the fading away of others, and the emergence of certain elements within itself and the borrowing of others from external sources. The philosophical principle involved in saying that would be the principle that a civilization may develop into new forms while yet remaining itself, whereas Toynbee's principle is that if a civilization changes it ceases to be itself and a new civilization comes into being.[62]

Obviously Toynbee's categories could not be applied even to animal organisms that, in growing from birth to maturity to old age, do in fact change their characteristics while remaining themselves. Why are we not allowed to say, asked Collingwood, that civilizations shade off one into the other? Because Toynbee viewed civilizations as the scientist viewed natural phenomena, a view that saw the individual as constituted in such a way as to be cut off from everything else by a sharp boundary distinguishing clearly what is within from what is outside.[63] Such a view of civilizations is possible only if the life of societies is regarded, like that of a stone, as a natural life and not as the mental life that it is.

As noted above, for Collingwood civilization was a process, a mental process in which mind came to know itself by identifying all its aspects. The relationship, therefore, of Western civilization to Hellenic civilization is a mental relation, not a natural one; and it must be studied historically, not scientifically. Collingwood writes:

As a matter of fact, Western civilization has formed itself by doing exactly this, by reconstructing within its own mind the mind of the Hellenic world and developing the wealth of that mind in new directions. Thus, Western civilization is not related to Hellenic civilization in any external way. The relation is an internal one. Western civilization expresses, and indeed achieves, its individuality not by distinguishing itself from Hellenic civilization, but by identifying itself therewith.[64]

Thus, for Collingwood, in history the division between various civilizations is arbitrary, for history itself is the development of absolute mind as it comes to recognize and identify itself with its manifold expressions. Toynbee's reaction to Collingwood's criticism, developed at length in the ninth volume of Toynbee's *Study*, does not however attack Collingwood's concept of the relation between civilizations so much as deny that the essence of civilizational growth is intellectual.[65]

Toynbee begins (erroneously) by noting that Collingwood errs in instructing the historian "to ignore all strands of experience but the intellectual one."[66] Such a view, Toynbee holds, is a peculiarly Western one and springs from the Western notion that knowledge derived from science is more valid than that derived from intuition and revelation. To argue that thought is the sum of history constitutes for Toynbee "an idolization of thought"—"the philosopher's sacrifice on the altar of his professional patriotism."[67] Hence Toynbee holds that Collingwood's concept of history is an idolatrous one because, in Collingwood's epistemology, religion and art do not occupy a place equal to that of philosophy, but inferior to it. For Toynbee, Collingwood's view of history and knowledge shuts out the wisdom to be derived from religious experience and substitutes the worship of man's own mind for the worship of the Creator. Therefore, Toynbee's final objection to Collingwood is that he refuses to admit that the world is not self-sufficient, that a Creator bears some essential relation to Creation, and that the historian must consider the nature of the relation between God and the world before the meaning of history will be revealed. Thus Toynbee moves the driving force of historical development one step beyond that envisaged by Collingwood, and in place of mind as the object of historical knowledge Toynbee substitutes God. Whereas Collingwood sees historical development as the progressive self-realization of mind, Toynbee sees history as the progressive creativity of God. And whereas Collingwood sees knowledge of history as progressive self-knowledge of the human mind, Toynbee sees it as a progressive movement toward the "Beatific Vision." Toynbee states his view thus:

The meaning behind the facts of history towards which the poetry in the facts is leading us is a revelation of God and the hope of communion with Him; but in the quest for a Beatific Vision that is visible to a Communion of Saints we are ever in danger of being diverted from our search for God to a glorification of Man; and this sin of associating the creature with the Creator precipitates the man-worshipper into a continuing fall from idolatry through disillusionment to an eventual deprecation of Man which is almost as excessive as the adulation to which it is the inevitable sequel. . . . When *Dominus illuminatio mea* is taken in lieu of "Man is the measure of all things" as man's key to the riddle of Human Life, the vanity of man is transfigured in this divine light.[68]

Thus Collingwood is attacked by Toynbee "the positivist" not because of his intuitionism nor because he conceives of historical events as different from natural events, but because he fails to see that the internality of events is not thought, or mind, but the relation of human events to the search for God. Instead of mind as the motive force in history, Toynbee sees it as God. This conclusion results in a complete denial of Toynbee's earlier positivism. In the years between the publication of his first three volumes and the last four, Toynbee has made a complete reversal in his position. The final outcome is a philosophy of history not unlike that of Schelling in the last stage of his development. Philosophy, history, and theology have all been related in Toynbee's mind in such a way that the result is a material philosophy of history that approaches the theosophic.

As Schelling attacked Hegel for the latter's "negativism" (the inability of the dialectic to account for the transition of God from potentiality to actuality), so too Toynbee attacks Collingwood and all humanist philosophies of history for their refusal to examine the relationship between the world and the Creator.[69] Like Schelling, Toynbee is forced into irrationalism by his desire to incorporate the religious motif into his philosophy of history. As a result of this development, Toynbee's youthful empiricism no longer satisfies him. He now argues (as did Collingwood) that strict empiricism leads one to study the facts of history in such a way that their true meaning cannot be discovered.

In the seventh volume of his work, published nearly twenty years after the first volume, Toynbee asserts that the purpose of the study of history is to link the world to God. History itself is seen to be one phase of God's creative development (again a Schellingian notion), and historical events are seen to be significant only in the extent to which they reveal the drama of man's search for God in time. The historian's angle of vision is held to be only one among many, but "it makes a distinctive contribution of its own to Mankind's piecemeal vision of reality."[70] In answer to the question "Why do people study history?" Toynbee answers: "In order to feel after God and find Him." Historical knowledge is merged with religious knowledge (just as for Schelling philosophy had become identified with theology), for, according to Toynbee:

> History's contribution is to give us a vision of God's creative activity on the move in a frame which, in our human experience of it, displays six dimensions. The historical angle of vision shows us the physical cosmos moving centrifugally in the four-dimensional frame of Space-Time; it shows us Life on our own planet moving evolutionarily in a five-dimensional frame of Life-Time-Space; and it shows us human souls, raised to a sixth dimension by the gift of the Spirit, moving, through a fateful exercise of their spiritual freedom, either towards their Creator or away from Him.[71]

Thus, historical knowledge becomes a vision of reality that, like Collingwood's concept, assumes that all other forms of knowledge are contained within it. The physical sciences are limited to the world of Space and Time. The biological sciences may study the world of Life-Space-Time insofar as such a world responds to laws of natural change. But it is only in history that these sciences are synthesized with the peculiarly human modes of experience, art, and religion, in order to inquire into the "gifts of the Spirit." It is by linking these "gifts of the Spirit" to the development of Nature that a total vision of God's purpose is revealed to us. History, in providing a six-dimensional vision of reality, unifies all knowledge by linking it to the search for God. Thus, only history can provide the impulse for "Science and Religion [to seize] their opportunity of drawing nearer to God by jointly seeking to comprehend God's protean creature the Psyche . . . for the Subconscious, not the Intellect, is the organ through which Man lives his spiritual life for Good or Evil."[72]

One of the results of Toynbee's transition from positivism to theology is the reorientation of his theory of historical change. Historical development is now envisaged by Toynbee, as it was by Schelling in his *Philosophie der Mythologie* (1842), and *Philosophie der Offenbarung* (*Philosophy of Revelation*, 1842–43), as the crucible in which the great religions emerge. Toynbee asserts that the study of history can enlighten us only insofar as it brings us closer to universal religious experience. He writes: "It was the historical function of civilizations to serve, by their downfalls, as stepping stones for a progressive process of revelation of always deeper religious insight."[73] And again: "[Civilizations] have forfeited their historical significance except insofar as they minister to the progress of Religion."[74] This means that instead of cyclical developments of individual civilizations as the pattern of historical change, we are now presented with a linear development in which civilizations may be catalogued according to the intensity of their religious experiences. Supposedly such development leads from mystery religions and mythology to the great histori-cal religions (Christianity, Confucianism, Hinduism, Islam) and to a final revela-tion. Here mankind will be transported to a higher development out of time when the unity of all truth has been made manifest.[75] It is difficult to see how such a view cannot be called theosophic, for, as Toynbee himself writes:

> God's presence and participation transfigures a precarious Brotherhood of Man into a Communion of Saints in which God's creatures are united with one an-other through their union with the Creator . . . "Vere Jersualem est illa civitas"; for, in this full and perfect communion, man is reconciled with man, and Man-kind with non-Human Nature . . . While the philosopher is shaking his head, the saint breaks out in jubilation:
>
> *Altissimu, omnipotente, bon Signore*
> *Tue so le laude, la gloria e l'honore et omne benedictione . . .*[76]

Now, both Collingwood's "idealism" and Toynbee's Gnostic theosophy, if they conflict on specific points, are in agreement when they attack positivism and em-piricism as inadequate to answer the questions asked of history by modern Western man. Recent comment seems to indicate that some of the points raised by Col-lingwood have led to reexamination of ideas long held indisputable in English historical thought.[77] Toynbee has put himself beyond criticism on empirical grounds by his frank avowal of an irrational position, but even Toynbee's appeal to the spirit has not been met with total dismay.[78]

What is most significant in the work of both Collingwood and Toynbee is that they represent a crack in the armor of a historiographical tradition that has, here-tofore, avoided all connections with Continental historicism and philosophy of history. In the history of German historiography, the way from Hegel to Schelling led to Schopenhauer and Nietzsche.

Perhaps, as A. J. P. Taylor has commented, we stand upon the brink of a Byzantine historiography in England today.[79] On the other hand, it may only be that English historians are examining their craft with a view to adjusting it to ask the questions demanded by a troubled time. They can learn from the Continental historiographi-cal tradition, which in Karl Jaspers has produced a historian who can write:

> A view of history creates the area out of which our consciousness of humanity is aroused. The picture we form of history becomes a factor in our volition. The manner in which we think of history sets the limits on our potentialities, or sus-tains us by its implications, or lures us away from reality.[80]

Both Collingwood and Toynbee seek to make their vision of history a universal view of humanity; for in this age of crisis they would hold, as Jaspers does, that

> a universal view of history and consciousness of one's present situation mutually sustain one another. As I see the totality of the past, so I experience the present. The deeper the foundations I acquire in the past, the more outstanding my participation in the present course of events. Where I belong and what I am living for I first learn in the mirror of history.[81]

Religion, Culture, and Western Civilization in Christopher Dawson's Idea of History

{1958}

The main stream of English historical thought takes its source in the "scientistic" atmosphere of the Enlightenment, more specifically in the philosophic preconceptions of Hume's empiricism. Throughout the nineteenth century the majority of English historians were distinguished from their Continental counterparts by their unwavering loyalty to the idea that the empirical physical sciences constituted the paradigm of all knowledge. Unlike the French historians, however, the English historian was unwilling to follow his scientific ideal to its logical conclusion in order to attempt to construct general laws of historical change. Unlike the Italians, he was unwilling to subsume history under a general concept of art and surrender himself to the intuitive communion with the past as an aesthetic experience. And unlike the Germans, he eschewed any tendency to identify history and philosophy and adamantly refused to search for a metaphysical cause, pattern, or meaning in the historical process.[1]

Having remained true to the empiricist ideals of Locke, Hume, and Mill, the English historian has occupied a twilight world between science, on the one hand, and art, on the other. In his general view, history is not a process at all but a series of self-contained events of varying size and complexity that must be studied empirically and described impressionistically. The method of investigation is objective, the mode of exposition artistic. His characteristic medium is the historical equivalent of the familiar essay. The empirical element in his psychology has discouraged any attempt to probe beneath the surface of individual and institutional motivation. As a result, his work produces an intellectual effect not unlike that received visually from an impressionist painting: it tends to be a brilliantly executed technical exercise, abounding in charm and frequent insight (an accomplishment in itself, to be sure) but lacking in depth and philosophical self-consciousness. In Benedetto Croce's terminology, it may be considered chronicle or even "scholarly history"; it does not manifest genuine historical judgment. Invariably the reader is left with the burden of deciding which is more important, the contact with the past events or the virtuosity of the narrator.[2]

Recently a tendency has been manifested among English thinkers to leap the bounds imposed by the long empiricist tradition. In the years between the wars, R. G. Collingwood subjected this tradition to a scathing critique in the light of Crocean idealism. Arnold J. Toynbee's massive *A Study of History* was a monument to the failure of the empirical method to frame the sort of questions and give the sort of answers that the modern world must ask of its own past. Toynbee admitted the inability of the empirical method to deal with the problems posed by universal history in his last four volumes. Here he abandoned empiricism in order to embrace a religious ideal as the criterion of historical investigation. Thus, the first revolts against historiographical empiricism in England resulted in history's being merged with philosophy, on the one hand, and with religion, on the other. England seemed on the way to experiencing the "crisis of historicism" that dominated German thought in the nineteenth century. The only agreement among the rebel historicists was on the point of denying the efficacy of empirical methods in historical analysis.[3]

While Collingwood approached his problem in the light of philosophical idealism and Toynbee worked within the framework of a Protestant pietism, the attack against traditional English historical thought was mounted in the Catholic camp by Christopher Dawson. Since the appearance of his first book in 1928, Dawson has worked with amazing consistency toward the formulation of a philosophy of history that would accommodate both the findings of modern social sciences, such as anthropology, and the presuppositions of Thomism. In a sense, Dawson's life work may be seen as an attempt to construct a philosophy of history that will unite in a single system the modern concept of secular progress with the medieval notion, first stated clearly in Saint Augustine, of history as *Heilsgeschichte,* or history of salvation.[4]

A similar endeavor by Protestant thinkers in Germany had resulted in disaster. Ernst Troeltsch had ended his sociological investigations of the European religious tradition by denying the universal applicability of Christian principles. In the thought of Max Weber a similar effort had resulted in the affirmation of the total break between the world of fact, on the one hand, and the world of value, on the other.[5] Dawson may be seen as taking up the problem where the German thinkers left off; he hopes to show that the Catholic natural law tradition provides for the solution to a problem that, considered under the canons of Protestantism, is insoluble. Unhampered by the Lutheran idea of total depravity and seeing history in Thomist terms, Dawson seeks to modify the Augustinian concept of universal history, which denies the importance of the material world, and demonstrate the necessity of Roman Catholicism as the only bridge between man's natural exigencies and his divine obligations, between the world of fact and the world of value.[6]

Dawson's historical essays and his theoretical works are complementary of each other. As a historian, his fame may be said to rest on three works: *The Age of the Gods* (1928), a study of the formation and breakdown of the archaic civilizations of the ancient Near East; *The Making of Europe* (1932), a study of the genesis of European civilization; and *Progress and Religion* (1929), an analysis of the rise and fall of modern European secular culture.

Seen as empirical demonstrations of his general system, *The Age of the Gods* and *The Making of Europe* deal with a single theme: the impact of the nomadic warrior cultures upon the sedentary peasant civilizations of the Mediterranean basin. It is the conflict and fusion of these cultural "types" that, in Dawson's view, result in those miraculous flowerings of civilization that are axial in world history. His *Medieval Essays* (1953) is an analysis of Europe's "classical age," while *Progress and Religion* deals with an instance of breakdown and decline of the classical form. It is from an analysis of the Western European "type" of civilization that Dawson deduces the principles that inform his tracts of the times: *Understanding Europe* (1952), *Essays in Order* (1940), *The Modern Dilemma* (1932), and *Beyond Politics* (1939). His theoretical works may be seen as applications of principles deduced from his study of Western civilization to the broader field of world history. The principles themselves are succinctly stated in *Religion and Culture* (1947) and in his collected essays recently published under the title *Dynamics of World History.*

For Dawson the basic unit of historical study is the culture, and he defines a culture as:

> a common way of life—the particular adjustment of man to his natural surroundings and his economic needs. In its use and modification it resembles the development of a biological species, which . . . is primarily due, not to a change in structure, but to the formation of a new community, either with new habits, or in a new and restricted environment.[7]

In its conception and development, therefore, a culture is like nothing so much as a biological organism: "it is the result of an intimate communion between man and the region in which and from which he lives."[8] Thus, the formation of a culture is not only a historical event; it is also a biological event. For if the communion be-

tween man and the particular environment endures without change for a sufficiently long period, "it will produce not merely a new way of life, but a new type
of man—a race as well as a culture."[9]

Obviously there are overtones of Herder here, and Dawson is conscious of them.
Herder, with precisely this theory of the relation between man and nature and race,
had inaugurated the line of thought that had dealt the death blow to natural law
theory and cosmopolitanism in all its forms. Herder had, on the basis of such a
view, shown the way to irrationalism and ultimately to historicism, the archenemy
of the natural law ideal.[10] Dawson now takes up the problem at the point where
European thought, on his account, went off the track. He will try to set it right
again by producing a revised natural law theory that does justice both to the social
and the physical sciences and to the claims of theology as well.[11]

Herder's nineteenth-century European successors had tended to split the natu-
ral-historical process in two or to unify the two processes within either a common
natural frame (thus reducing history to nature and studying it by the means of
sociology) or a common historical frame (as Hegel had done). Dawson stresses the
similarities between nature and humanity but also emphasizes important differences. He holds that human culture is distinguished from the communal life of the
social animals and insects by a special element of self-consciousness. It is human
thought that removes human culture from the level of instinctive necessity that
rules in nature and infuses it with the creative *élan* of moral purpose. Hence, for
Dawson, a culture is really the point of nexus of our independent factors: a genetic factor (race), a geographic factor (natural environment), an economic factor
(function or occupation), and a psychological factor (thought). Therefore, any
given culture must be seen as a fourfold community: it is "a community of work
and a community of thought as well as a community of place and a community of
blood."[12]

Cultural change may result from transformations occurring in any of the four
moments of the cultural configuration. According to him, the various determinis-
tic philosophies of history, such as those of Hegel, Marx, and Spengler, err in trying
to reduce all cultural change to functions of changes occurring in only one of the
four moments.[13] It is Dawson's merit to have stressed the necessity of viewing historical change pluralistically, and insofar as he actually does so his work is of the
highest quality, doing justice to the true multiplicity of historical forms of thought
and action. He seemingly sees history as the interplay of the four moments, each
of which acts on every other and all effecting thought, resulting in the evolution of
ever higher forms of historical being. Cultures, like human organisms, may be
changed by a number of factors:

In reality, a culture is neither a purely physical process nor an ideal construction. It is a living whole from its roots in the soil and in the simple instinctive life of the shepherd, the fisherman, and the husbandman, up to the flowering in the highest achievements of the artist and the philosopher; just as the individual combines in the substantial unity of his personality the animal life of nutrition and reproduction with the higher activities of reason and intellect. It is impossible to disregard the importance of a material and non-rational element in history. Every culture rests on a foundation of geographical environment and racial inheritance, which conditions its highest activities. The change of culture is not simply a change of thought, it is above all a change of life.[14]

Thus, by stressing the material and non-rational elements in culture and history, Dawson gives the lie to the idealists.

But once he has given the material element in culture its due, Dawson hastens to stress the importance of the spiritual element. He argues that "a culture is a spiritual community which owes its unity to common beliefs and common ways of thought far more than to any uniformity of physical types."[15] The distinctive mark of a culture would seem to be, therefore, the values informing it. This element of value centers on the culture's "vision of Reality," the index of its "inner life," which is the carrier of "the life of Reason."

For Dawson, there is a level of consciousness in man that qualitatively distinguishes him from animal nature. So too with culture:

It is this inner aspect of a culture which constitutes its most distinctive features. The unity of a culture involves not only a certain uniformity in social organization, but also a continuous and conscious social discipline. . . . There is a common conception of reality, a view of life, which even in the most primitive societies expresses itself through magical practices and religious beliefs, and which in higher cultures appears in a fuller and more conscious form in religion, science, and philosophy. . . . It is the active and creative element in culture, since it emancipates man from purely biological laws which govern the development of animal species, and enables him to accumulate a growing capital of knowledge and social experience, which gives a progressive control over his material environment.[16]

It is the inner life, formed by self-conscious mind, that liberates man from the exigencies of a purely natural existence. It is the creative element in culture, for it produces those "visions of Reality" that inspire man to break the cycles of natural change and project himself upon the developmental, progressive stage of material *and* spiritual history.

A given culture develops in relation to its ability to intuitively conceive a vision of reality proximately close to the nature of objective reality itself. In the very earliest cultures this vision of reality was formed by trial and error contact with a strange and ominous Nature. Without the commitment to this vision of reality there can be no progress, no development. Civilizations are cultures which, prompted by radical changes in the life of Nature, were forced to change their ways of life, or perish. Originally, they were driven to conceive a "vision of Reality" willy-nilly, as pure acts of faith, and some of these were truer than others. This first movement of analysis of the world surrounding man resulted in the differentiation between primitive culture and civilization, for having once made the creative response to environmental change and committed himself to the task of discovering the nature of Reality, man was thrust upon the path to civilization, the self-conscious development in higher forms of thought of the investigative faculty.

The first "response" (in Toynbee's terminology) or "breakthrough" (in Jaspers's) resulted from environmental changes that followed upon the last glacial recession. Here we have the emergence of the two basic "types" of cultures that have broken with the primary vision of the world implied in food gathering and hunting societies. These two types are the nomadic cultures of the steppes and the farming communities of the river valleys, each based upon a different "vision of Reality."[17] Further challenges presented to the nomad, particularly in the third and second millennia BC, resulted in the great migrations of the horse peoples out of the steppes, their conquest of and assimilation by the sedentary, peasant civilizations of the river valleys. This in turn presented a new challenge to the river valley civilizations, a social challenge this time, that necessitated another reformulation of the "vision of Reality" and further advance in mankind's picture of total Reality. And all of this was made possible by Reason, the unique element dominating the "inner life" of man:

> The existence of Reason increases the range of possibilities in the fulfillment of the instinctive purpose. The old impulse acting in a new environment, different from that to which it was originally adapted, may be not merely a decadent survival, but a stepping stone to some new conception of reality. Thus there is a continual enlargement of the field of experience, and, thanks to Reason, the new does not simply replace the old, but is compared and combined with it. The history of mankind, and still more of civilized mankind, shows a continuous process of integration which, even though it seems to work irregularly, never ceases. For Reason is itself a creative power which is ever organizing the raw material of life and sensible experience into an ordered cosmos of an intelligible world, a world

which is not a mere subjective image, but corresponds in a certain measure to the objective reality. A modern writer has said: "The mind of man seems to be of a nature to assimilate itself to the universe; we belong to the world; the whole is mirrored in us. Therefore, when we bend our thoughts on a limited object, we concentrate faculties which are naturally endowed with infinite correspondences. . . ." We cannot shut our eyes to the significance of this steadily growing vision of Reality, which is at once the condition and the result of the life of human society.[18]

Thus we have arrived at the traditional idealist division of the world into mind and matter and the view that history is the field upon which those two forces make contact. But belying his assertion that mind is a stage of nature, that stage upon which nature achieves self-consciousness, Dawson manifests a typically Hegelian view of the relation between history and nature. Even though he might admit that nature is not merely cyclical, but is genuinely developmental, he removes the cycles to the plane of history itself and then posits a super-history that is the carrier of the life of Reason. Thus, even if both nature and super-history are creative and developmental, history itself, the life of man in time, is cyclical and can be studied as the rise and fall of sociological types. As he wrote in his critique of Spengler in *Religion and Progress:*

> Nevertheless, though culture is essentially conditioned by material factors, these are not all. A culture receives its form from a rational or spiritual element which transcends the limits of racial and geographical conditions. Religion and science do not die with the culture of which they formed part. . . . There are, in fact, two movements in history; one of which is due, as Herr Spengler shows, to the life process of an individual people in contact with a definite geographical environment, while the other is common to a number of different peoples and results from intellectual interaction and synthesis. . . . Only by taking account of both these movements is it possible to understand the history of human development, and to explain the existence of that real element of continuity and integration in history which alone can justify a belief in human progress.[19]

It would seem, therefore, that the contact of cultures in time and space, the usual plane upon which history evolves and is studied, has a secondary function in Dawson's scheme. These contacts merely initiate the changes that are genuinely creative, those that take place in the "inner lives" of cultures. While individual civilizations rise and fall due to changes in either race or environment or thought (or all three), the life of thought (or Reason) continually augments itself.

Thus Dawson does justice to the task of the historian, who must judge the facts,

and he provides him with an incentive to find the justification behind every historical individuality, that is, those factors that brought it into being and that, therefore,
justify its existence in its peculiar form. But he does not end his judgment there;
instead, he refers the coming to be and passing away of the individual manifestation of the spirit to an abstract principle, Reason, that overarches history and gives
him an absolute criterion for judging any given culture in its light. It is now necessary for us to see how Dawson articulates this idea in his view of history as action
and see whether his view can do justice to a view of Reason that is genuinely
historical.

ว€

At this point one might profitably compare Dawson's theory of culture with that
of another modern English idealist, R. G. Collingwood, as expounded in his
Speculum Mentis, a book written at about the same time as Dawson's *The Age of
the Gods*.

In Collingwood's thought, the life process is seen as an infinitely differentiated totality that develops through three stages: physical nature, animal nature,
and human nature. The last stage, which contains all previous stages as sublated,
is marked by the emergence of self-conscious mind (as in Dawson), and history is
seen as the articulation of mind in time. This history is constituted by the life
of thought as it realizes the categories for interpreting and knowing the world of
which it is part. The various categories of thought are given concrete form in the
progressive emergence of higher forms of self-consciousness as cultural forms.[20]

Art is identified with imagination; religion is conceived as the assertion of the
reality of the products of the imagination; and science is seen as the organization
of the physical world for practical human ends. Each of these forms of thought
contains implicit error insofar as each mistakes a part of reality for the whole. Art
makes no distinction between the products of its imagination and objective reality;
religion asserts the reality of a particular vision of reality unself-critically and ir-
rationally; while science denies both art and religion to be forms of knowledge by
asserting only the physical world's existence, thus offending the justifiable demands of the spirit. Each is a qualitatively different form of thought insofar as each
represents higher forms of self-consciousness. None—neither art, nor religion, nor
science—can offer a true picture of reality, for each denies the existence of some
part of it in the interests of its own claims to be the final form of truth.[21]

It is only with the emergence of historical thought that a total view of human
knowledge becomes possible, for only in history are all manifestations of mind—
art, religion, and science—included, embraced, and justified as products of an
infinitely creative human spirit. Humanity itself is justified and dignified by the

realization that all of its products are precious and apposite to the construction of a total view of the total life process. It is at this point that historical knowledge, knowledge of mind, is merged with philosophy, the science of mind as creative spirit.[22]

It is not our purpose to subject Collingwood's view of history or his metaphysics to analysis here. Collingwood is his own best exponent and we have examined his work elsewhere.[23] His theories are attractive to the historian because they embrace a Crocean denial of all transcendence and give the central place in epistemology to historical thought, the knowledge of the individual. It is a theory, therefore, pre-eminently humanistic in its orientation and violently opposed to any monism that might reduce historical multiplicity to the status of illusion in the interest of an abstract principle. What concerns us here are the respective places given to religion in the thought of Collingwood and Dawson.

For Collingwood, as it must be for any humanist, religion is not error, it is only half-truth. It is thought removed one step from artistic creation, which artistic creation we might liken to Dawson's intuitive "vision of Reality." Religion differs from art only (and most importantly) in the element of thought that enters into its constructs in the form of assertion. A religious vision is an imaginative vision of reality buttressed by an act of will that asserts the truth of that vision. Art makes no such assertion, being unconcerned with whether its vision of reality is true or false, concerned only with its beauty or ugliness. A religious vision is derived in the same way as the artistic but becomes critical in the first degree by the assertion that the vision is true. But religion offers no rational means of establishing the truth of its assertions over against the claims of any other imaginative vision that might equally well claim to be true. This is that negative moment in religious thought that engenders its own criticism on the basis of its lack of conformity to the facts of the material world. Religion must criticize itself because, in asserting the truth of its own propositions, it implies the falsity of at least one other set of propositions constructed by a similar imaginative act but then denies the capacity of reason to decide between the two claims. Religious truth, having raised the critical question, then attempts to throttle reason by denying its criteria of judgment or by lapsing into some stop-gap theory of the double truth or (as in Thomism) by arguing that faith and reason are unified in faith (which completes the circle).[24]

Hence, for Collingwood, religion is a necessary moment in the development of thought—for individuals as well as cultures, both of which go through a "religious phase"—but it is a form of error that must be transcended if mind is to arrive at a total vision of the proper object of knowledge, which is not God but mind itself.[25]

Needless to say, it is at this point that Collingwood and Dawson part company.

In Dawson's implied theory of knowledge the part assigned to history by Colling-wood is supplanted by religion. For him, historical thought is not a peculiar form of knowledge; it is a method of gathering materials, which are then submitted to religion for their proper interpretation.[26] It is this aspect of Dawson's thought that makes him more acceptable to the practicing historians of England who, trained in the empirical tradition, can agree with him that history merely observes the facts and leaves for other disciplines the task of interpreting them (if they are to be in-terpreted at all). Unlike Dawson, Collingwood had attempted to raise historical thought to the dignity of a self-justifying, independent, and autonomous form of thought, one that contained implicitly the artistic, religious, and scientific mo-ments, but which transcended their limitations by seeing the world as a totality of distinct elements, each of which had its own proper raison d'être and that denied judgment by any partial or one-sided view of reality. Dawson apparently leaves historical thought in its old servile dependency upon empirical science but in real-ity resolves it into sociology, on the one hand (as the analysis of historical types), and theology, on the other (as the analysis of the life of Reason). Thus the three levels of meaning implied in any of Dawson's historical reconstructions: an empiri-cal meaning (the objective existence of the historical individual); the typological meaning (the individual seen as a type, as the instance of a general social law); and the "inner meaning" (the individual seen as one stage in the growth of religious consciousness). A basic problem, of course, is justifying the removal of religion to a place beyond either the first or second meanings and granting it a special place of its own. Dawson seeks to justify the special place given religion in his idea of his-tory on the basis of history itself.

❧

Dawson argues that the religious moment and human history emerge at the same time, that, indeed, one is the function of the other. He states, for example: "[Reli-gion] is as old as human consciousness . . . and we can no more go behind the re-ligious stage of history than we can go behind the origins of language or the social life itself."[27] The religious consciousness is the awakening of humanity to itself, not (as for Collingwood) an imaginative vision that seeks to fill the gaps in man's knowledge of the universe or a series of rituals meant to placate hypostatized natu-ral forces. Yet it is that too, seen objectively and insofar as it constitutes in its early phases imperfect visions of the supernatural reality that it envisions. But if the first visions of the supernatural forces controlling the universe were misconceived hy-postatizations of natural forces, the impulse in man to hypostatize those forces testifies to the reality of their existence: "The whole religious experience of man-kind—indeed, the very existence of religion itself—testifies, not only to the sense of the Transcendent, but to the appetite for the Transcendent which can only be satisfied by immediate contact—by a vision of the Supreme Reality."[28] And Dawson deduces from this historical generalization the primacy of the religious moment in the formation of any given culture's vision of reality, and, therefore, the primacy of the religious moment in history itself:

> From the beginning the social way of life which is culture has been deliberately ordered and directed in accordance with the higher laws of life which are religion. As the powers of heaven rule the seasons, so the divine powers rule the life of man and society, and for a community to conduct its affairs without reference to these powers, seems as irrational as for a community to cultivate the earth without paying any attention to the course of the seasons. Through the greater part of mankind's history, in all ages and in all societies, religion has been the guardian of tradition, the preserver of the moral law, the educator and teacher of wisdom.[29]

That religion itself is influenced by culture Dawson does not deny, but he argues that we must never exclude the alternative relation, "that culture is molded and changed by religion," for

> while in practice the religion of a people is limited and even conditioned by culture, in theory—and even in the theory of the primitive himself—culture is a deliberate effort to bring human life into relation with divine reality and into subordination to divine power.[30]

Thus, for Dawson, historical time is bifurcated. Culture is really subject to changes that emanate from two different sources, one material and the other spiritual, and the great changes in world civilization come about either as a result of conflicts between cultures in space or as the result of some prophetic "breakthrough" into a super-temporal realm—contact with Divine Reality—which gives the culture a new vision of reality and sets it off on a new and radical course.[31] For Dawson, these visions of reality are determining, and he therefore concludes that "religion is the key of history . . . It is impossible to understand a culture unless we understand its religious roots."[32]

Let me emphasize once more, however, that in Dawson's stated view not all cultural change is religious change nor is religion free from cultural or material influences. But since religion is the prime expression of a culture's view of reality, the moral commitment to a vision of reality, it alone provides that spark that sets the culture into motion; it alone is the one true index to the culture's "inner vitality." Or, as he wrote in "Civilization and Morals,"

it seems to be the fact that a new way of life or a new view of Reality is felt in-
stinctively before it is comprehended intellectually, that a philosophy is the last
product of a mature culture, the crown of a long process of social development,
not its foundation. It is in Religion and Art that we can best see the vital intention of the living Creature . . .

[For] the same purposeful fashioning of plastic material which is the very
essence of culture, expresses itself also in Art. The Greek statue must be first
conceived, then lived, then made, and last of all thought. There you have the
whole cycle of creative Hellenic thought. First Religion, then Society, then Art,
and finally Philosophy.[33]

In the religious moment, therefore, the form or mold of the culture is set, and the
development then progresses to the self-consciousness of philosophy. Art, thus envisaged, is merely the expression of the religious values of an age, philosophy their
conscious expression in rational terms, and society itself the practical life based
upon its assumption. But given such a view of culture, it is necessary that Dawson
see every historical event in terms of its religious significance. And this in turn
demands a criterion for discovering which religion is true in an ultimate sense, for
otherwise there would be as many valid views of history as there are religions. On
the basis of an examination of the history of religions, he hopes to show how Christianity satisfies all the requirements of an ultimate religion. Here he joins hands
with Scholasticism and, despite his sociological wrappings, shares both its merits
and shortcomings. In the process of constructing his view, however, we are given
many insights not into history of religion but into how a Scholastic view of religion
may be turned into a criterion of historical interpretation.

Dawson organizes his world-historical frame in terms of the religious experiences of the various higher civilizations. Civilization is distinguished from primitive culture by virtue of the fact that in the latter there is no distinction between
man, nature, and God in any substantial sense. Civilized life emerges with the
discovery of the laws of natural process, a discovery of the river valley cultures in
the arid subtropical zone, and this discovery was, according to Dawson, a religious
not a scientific discovery. As he writes in *The Age of the Gods*:

The primitive condition of food-gathering and hunting peoples does not necessarily imply reasonable purpose or any reflective vision of Reality. Consequently
it does not imply civilization. The dawn of true civilization came only with the
discovery of natural laws, or rather with the possibility of man's fruitful cooperation with the powers of nature.[34]

But for him, the appearance of a new technology, new forms of economic and social organization, or the appearance of science (over against religion) do not mark the emergence of civilization; all of these already imply the new vision of Reality, a religious vision, as their necessary presupposition. The institution that marks the appearance of civilization is not a socioeconomic one, the city, but a religious one, the priesthood that grows out of the shamanate.[35]

This is because the priest, unlike the shaman, "must be a man of intellect, and his influence brings a new principle of order into the whole life of primitive man."[36] It is the priesthood that is the repository of the wisdom of the culture, that sets up and directs the ceremonial year (based upon the agricultural year), and that embraces "the whole social and intellectual life of society." Therefore, the ritual order that informed the archaic civilizations of the river valleys was at once "the reflection and fulfillment of the cosmic order," for "it coordinated the order of the heavens with that of the seasons, and by its ceaseless round of sacrifice and prayers assisted the powers of nature to function."[37] These cosmologically oriented civilizations lasted until the middle of the second millennium BC, at which time they succumbed to the hand of the invading barbarian horse peoples from the steppes and deserts.

It was this intrusion of the horse peoples, with their worship of sky-gods and high moral conceptions, that forced a reformulation of the vision of reality upon which the older river valley cultures had been built. The failure of the cosmologically oriented civilizations stemmed from the fact that they had been too completely bound up in the ritual life and, because they had formed a vision of reality based upon their own limited environmental and social experience, had not conceived the possibility of radical social change itself. The destruction of the older, stable order led to a bifurcation in man's vision of reality and a tendency to juxtapose the age of change and conflict with the earlier age of tranquility:

> And thus there arose a sense of moral dualism, an opposition between that which is and that which ought to be, between the way of man and the way of the Gods. . . . The sacred order was no longer a ceremonial system, but a moral law of justice and truth.[38]

Therefore, in accord with Toynbee, Jaspers, and Mumford (and others), Dawson describes the first millennium BC as an "axial age" marked by the discovery of the bifurcation of the world, the juxtaposition of the spiritual order (or moral order) and the natural order.[39]

But the dialectical reaction to archaic materialism was too extreme. The result was a universal tendency to flee this world in order to prepare for or serve the next. In India, China, and Greece, as well as in the Near East, the reaction was characterized by excesses that were "equally injurious to religion as a social force" and to material culture, for: "The condemnation of matter and the body as evil, the flight from nature and the world of sense, the denial of the reality of the world, and the value of the social order—all appear to make any real synthesis between religion and culture impossible."[40] Among the Jews, the tendency toward the spiritualization of the social life found its most radical expression, and in Jewish prophetism the religious moment was cut loose from association with any particular material culture.[41]

The free-floating character of Jewish religious life had both advantages and disadvantages. On the one hand, it led to the discovery and investigation of a moral law in history; on the other, it led to a negation of the importance of material forces in the life of man and thus tended to discourage the impulse to conquer nature with methods and tools proper to that conquest. But in Christianity—which in Dawson's terms must be seen (1) as historical individuality, (2) as a dialectical synthesis of two types of religious experience, that of the river valleys and that of the Jews, and (3) as the highest form of religious experience—all the older forms of religious experience are transcended through sublation. In the conception of Jesus as the Incarnated God all the old myths are at once explained and given new meaning in a reestablishment of the dynamic relation between man, nature, and God, for here:

> the Absolute and the Finite, the Eternal and the Temporal, God and the World were no longer conceived as two exclusive and opposed orders of being standing over against one another in mutual isolation. The two orders interpenetrated one another, and even the lower world of matter and sense was capable of becoming the vehicle and channel of divine life. . . . The world process was conceived not as an unchanging order governed by the fatal law of necessity, but as a divine drama whose successive acts were the Creation and Fall of Man, his Redemption and his glorious restoration.[42]

Through the media of the Roman Empire and classical culture this new vision of reality became the common property of the Mediterranean world by the fourth century AD. That unity was torn asunder by a new wave of horse peoples who came out of the steppes and deserts surrounding the Mediterranean basin. Only in Western Europe were conditions "just right" to allow this synthesis to flower in its most perfect form; only here was there "an organic synthesis of religion and culture."

At this point it is obvious whence Dawson derives his criteria for evaluating all religions, and, since "religion is the key of history," his criterion of historical discrimination. From the historical evidence concerning the religious history of mankind, he deduces the reality of the two worlds that these religions assume. The first stage in man's quest for a vision of reality commensurate with objective reality places him in a position to discover the character of the natural world. The second stage forces him to realize that an earthly order can never be a perfect approximation of the Divine Order. This stage is characterized by a tendency to reject the world. But man can never reject his animal nature any more than he can deny his spiritual aspiration. The dialectic moves back to a point midway between the two extremes of affirmation of nature and rejection of nature, to Christianity, the only one of the world religions that finds salvation in man's devotion to God through self-transcendence in social service. Thus, religion is shown to be the prime moment in cultural development; Christianity is identified with Religion itself; and Western civilization is, by implication, identified with Civilization itself. After Christianity has been founded, all that remains for the historian of culture is to record its development, articulation, triumphs and tribulations as it develops in time and expands (or contracts) in space.

✺

In *The Making of Europe* Dawson shows the development of Christianity in the three cultural areas enclosed by the limits of the Roman Empire. The three cultural complexes that flourished in the Roman imperial subsoil were the Greco-Persian (heir to the older Mesopotamian archaic culture), the Semitic (heir to the older Egyptian archaic civilization), and the Greco-Roman (heir to classical civilization). In each of the three cultural areas, Christianity underwent transformations in the light of the indigenous ideas.

In the Byzantine Empire, Oriental and Persian elements triumphed, religion became an adjunct of the State, and theology exhausted its creative power in "meaningless speculation" concerning the nature of the Godhead. This destruction of the purity of Christianity did not satisfy the Semitic elements in the Near East and the result of this dissatisfaction was the Islamic revolt, a reversion

> to a simpler type of religion, which felt no need for any incarnation of the divine or any progressive transformation of human nature. The bridge between God and Man was broken, and the Divine Omnipotence once more reigned in lonely splendor, like the sun over the desert.[43]

Thus, in Islam, which Dawson sees as a Christian heresy, the prophetic element in the religion triumphed, destroyed the stabilizing priestly element, and subordinated the state to a purely Semitic conception of the social life that cut the nerve of creative social effort. In Byzantium, the Persian conception of religion and culture triumphed; Caesaropapism resulted, and the religious moment in culture became subordinated to political interests, thus destroying the creative prophetic element in the religion.[44]

Only in the West were conditions such as to allow a truly organic development of Church-State relations. Here dynamic tension was maintained between the organ through which man organized himself in this world, the State, and that by which he prepared himself for the next, the Church. It was the existence of this balance between man's spiritual aspiration and his political needs that gave to Western civilization its peculiar vitality and allowed a progressive deepening and articulation of the Christian vision of reality in the light of an ever-changing social and natural environment. Naturally, the period in which this organic relationship was conceived and grew to maturity must be considered the most creative of all ages.[45] This is why Dawson regards the Middle Ages as the "classical period" of Western civilization, and, indeed, of the world.

ॐ

According to Dawson, the Western Church was saved by the barbarian invasions, which, if they destroyed the Roman state, allowed the free development of a new Germanic-Latin culture under the aegis of the Church. Western Europe was, "in a very special sense a religious creation, for it was based on an ecclesiastical not a political unity."[46]

The period of the "Dark Ages" was a period of fusion in which four cultural traditions met and were mixed together in the crucible of the universal Church. Celtic, Germanic, Latin, and Oriental (Christian) ideas came together in different degree in different parts of Europe to create the various national cultures within the super-culture that was Europe and Christianity. Under the hammer blows of Slavic, Arab, and Viking invasions, the Christian peoples of the West gradually forged the new view of reality that distinguished them from their enemies and neighbors.[47]

The geographical and cultural center of the new civilization was that part of Europe in which Nordic and Latin elements met as equals: in Gaul between the valleys of the Loire and the Rhine, where fusion took place first and most completely. Here occurred the fusion of Latin classical civilization and Germanic tribal culture under the direction of a Christian episcopacy and priesthood, and here the first political expression of that new cultural unity, the Carolingian Empire, flourished. Out of this vital center flowed those institutions which later flowered in the thirteenth-century cultural synthesis.

These institutions Dawson holds to be peculiarly European. Their passing would therefore constitute the passing of Europe. These institutions were: Christian Aristotelianism, the universities, the communes and free cities of the Rhine and North, the representative system of estates, Gothic architecture, the religious orders, and chivalry.[48] All were held together in a common frame and given a common direction by Roman Catholicism with its international priesthood, liturgy, language, and worldview. The period of the so-called Dark Ages was an incubation period, a period of organic fusion; it was only in the eleventh and twelfth centuries that the new culture flowered. And

> when the social revival of Western Europe began, the new development was inspired by religious motives, and proceeded directly from the tradition of the spiritual society. The struggle of the Investitures and the international supremacy of the reformed Papacy were the visible signs of the victory of the spiritual power over the feudal and barbaric elements in European society. Everywhere men became conscious of their common citizenship in the great commonwealth of Christendom. And this spiritual citizenship was the foundation of the new society.[49]

Real danger lay in the fact that the victory of the Church over the State might result in the creation of a great Church-State, after the pattern of Islam, with the Pope as Commander of the Faithful. This would have opened up the West to the social instability that had plagued the Arab world since the Islamic revolt. This danger was averted by the Franciscan revival, the attitude of which toward human nature "marks a turning point in the history of the West."[50]

Dawson finds the source of Franciscan pietism in the Augustinian tradition, but there is a difference. In Saint Francis's teachings:

> There is no longer any separation between faith and life, or between spiritual and material, since the two worlds have become fused together in the living reality of personal experience.[51]

The powers of nature that had at first been "divinized and worshipped" and then in turn rejected by man as he realized the transcendent character of the Spiritual, are now brought back into the world of religion:

> It is the end of the long period during which human nature and the present world had been dwarfed and immobilized by the shadow of eternity, and the beginning of a new epoch of humanism and interest in nature.[52]

This new attitude was given philosophical expression in Thomism, which consciously attempted "to break with the old established tradition of oriental spiritualism and Neo-Platonic idealism, and to bring man back into the order of nature."[53] In Thomism, therefore, the Christian development reached philosophical self-consciousness and Western civilization had reached its ultimate intellectual attainment.

By Dawson's own lights, considering his belief that cultures go through four phases (religious, political, artistic, and philosophic) and given the fact that he considers Christianity the highest of all religions, it would seem that the ideal cultural complex had been attained. No further development would seem possible; any change would have to be decline. In fact, he argues that at the very moment in which the West attained cultural self-consciousness, centrifugal forces were working within to destroy its unity. These forces were not religious, nor were they indigenous to Christianity. Furthermore, they penetrated into and corrupted the papacy itself. What were they, and whence did they come?

Dawson traces the decline of this ideal culture, this classical age, to the intrusion of "alien" elements into the West. These elements strengthened the barbarian strains in the West before they had become *thoroughly* assimilated and came to the West from the East via the Crusades.[54] Contact with Byzantine Caesaropapism strengthened the state idea inordinately, even to the point of tainting the popes and leading them into the attempt to vie with the state for supreme political power. Contact with Islam resulted in the strengthening of the rebellious prophetic element (which led to heresy), on the one hand, and the strengthening of a secular philosophical tradition, on the other. In sum, contact with the East led to the rise of an aristocratic, courtly, and secular culture, the vernacular and nationalist literatures, the Greco-Arabian philosophical tradition, and the great heresies that motivated the lower classes in their revolt against the priestly authority. All of these ideas cut at the roots of the sacramental society ruled by the international papacy, and the medieval unity was torn asunder by a force "which made itself felt alike in culture and religion, political and ecclesiastical organization."

In southern Europe, the movement against an international unity was not anti-Christian but anti-Germanic (or anti-Gothic), and it manifested itself in an attempt to return to the older classical civilization that predated the Christian. Hence the rise of Renaissance humanistic civilization.[55]

In northern Europe, the movement of national awakening had to find a different form of expression, since there existed no higher civilization behind the medieval; there was only the pagan world of tribal barbarism. With Luther, the Nordic element cut itself loose from the vital center and the ideals that informed it and expressed itself in a rejection of everything that was Latin in the spiritual and institutional life of the folk. Of Luther, Dawson writes:

He embodies the revolt of the awakening German national spirit against every influence that was felt to be foreign or repressive; against asceticism and all that checked the free expression of the natural instincts, against the intellectualism of Aristotle and Saint Thomas, against the whole Latin tradition, above all against the Roman Curia and its Italian officials which were to him the representatives of Antichrist and the arch enemies of the German soul. "The Lutheran Reformation," wrote Nietzsche, "in all its length and breadth was the indignation of the simple against something complicated." It was a "spiritual Peasant Revolt."[56]

Thus it was Lutheranism that eliminated the philosophical and Hellenic elements from Christianity and accentuated everything that was "Semitic and non-intellectual." Luther "took Saint Paul without his Hellenism and Saint Augustine without his Platonism." The result was not a return to Apostolic Christianity, which was Luther's aim, but an accentuation of "purely occidental elements" in religion that merely hastened the very secularization against which the Reformation was in rebellion. Here Reformation and Renaissance worked toward a common end of eliminating religion as a vital force in the cultural life. This secularization, expressed quintessentially in a science and technology freed from all moral restraints, produced a culture that was "infinitely superior to that of the thirteenth century on its physical side" but "was inferior in that it no longer embraced the whole of reality."[57] Modern secular culture severed the relation between man and supernature, took the physical world to be the only reality and thus destroyed that urge to moral commitment that alone could provide for a unified, continuous, and creative social life. The inevitable result of such a freewheeling science was the chaos and self-destruction of European civilization that, having lost its direction, its common aim, destroyed itself in an orgy of animal, national conflict.

The intellectual class that displaced the priesthood as the directors of society (first the humanist, then the physical scientist) could not offer an ideal that transcended animal will and brute self-interest. In the disappearance of this priestly class Dawson finds the immediate cause of Europe's decline:

It is . . . questionable whether a culture which has once possessed an institution of this nature—I mean a spiritual class or order that has been the guardian of a sacred tradition of culture—can dispense with it without becoming impoverished and disoriented. This is what has actually occurred in the secularization of Western culture. . . . For the intellectuals who have succeeded the priests as the guardians of the higher tradition of Western culture have been strong only in their negative work of criticism and disintegration. They have failed to provide an integrated system of principles and values which could unify modern society, and consequently they have proved unable to resist the non-moral, inhuman, and irrational forces which are destroying the humanist no less than the Christian tradition of Western culture.[58]

Dawson concludes, therefore, that the instability of modern Western civilization is a result of the divorce of traditional culture and traditional religion.

Nor does the destructive impulse end with this divorce, for the characteristic of modern amoral science is to destroy not only the link between man and supernature but between man and physical nature itself. The economic and social changes of the last century, according to Dawson, have produced a revolution in that relation between man and physical nature that had existed from the beginning of humanity itself. In the manner of Lewis Mumford he writes:

> They have destroyed the biological equilibrium between human society and its natural environment. Hitherto in every European society the higher urban civilization has been a comparatively light superstructure which rested on the broad and solid foundation of rural society. [The peasant life] was a reservoir of human material, from which the culturally active elements of the cities and the ruling classes could derive new life and energy. There was a continual movement of the population from the country to the towns, and from the lower to the upper strata of society, which served to replace the human material that had been exhausted in the strain of an artificial way of life and a more intense form of social activity. . . . Everywhere the conditions of life are becoming more and more artificial, and make an increasing demand on men's nervous energies.[59]

Thus man, estranged from the spiritual element by modern secularism, has also become estranged from the creative source of nature itself. He lives in an artificial world of his own creation in which the springs of creativity dry up from lack of contact with his spiritual and physical roots. The restoration of Christianity of the medieval type "would provide Europe with the necessary spiritual foundations for the social unification it so urgently needs" and for which it will search in vain within the confines of a modern secular worldview. Even in 1954, in considering the problems posed by the creation of a global civilization, Dawson repeated this formula for the cure of Europe's ills:

> The creative development of the [European] inheritance depends on the vitality of the spiritual forces which inspired the achievement of European culture, the religious tradition of Christianity, and the intellectual tradition of Humanism;

and these are still alive today. They live inside and outside Europe: on the one hand, in the Catholic Church, and on the other, in the Western tradition of science and scholarship and literature. And it is to these two powers that we must look for the creation of the new civilization which will unite the nations and the continents in an all-embracing spiritual community.[60]

It was Dawson's avowed aim to construct an idea of history upon the Augustinian model that would overcome the limitations of that model by providing a place for material as well as spiritual culture. Has he succeeded in this task? I think not.

In the first place, it is obvious that what he has given us is an abstraction of the history of religion from ca. 4000 BC to ca. AD 1400 in the Mediterranean world, as Christianity emerged out of that spiritual melting pot. Here material culture itself serves only as the negative moment that incites the dialectical process to its next stage of development.

Yet Dawson is not consistent here, for he is unwilling to admit that the dialectic may proceed beyond the point reached by Christianity at a given stage of its development: the medieval. Here he arrested the dialectic, something that even Hegel himself had not dared do. Instead of the Prussian state, Dawson gives us the Catholic Church as the "carrier" of all that is genuinely spiritual in the West. Beyond that point of development any variation is "decline." Genuine progress may continue only within its confines.

Having identified Civilization with merely one of its manifold manifestations, he must point to all the achievements of Western culture as products, not of individual or communal human creativity, but as either expressions or residues of this special religious complex. This allows him to see all social dislocations as falls from this peculiar type of spiritual ideal, as functions of the West's abandonment of the institutionalized religion that characterized it at one stage of its development. In such a view, the sociological and historical facade of Dawson's ornate cultural history falls away, and we are once more in the world of Saint Augustine in which all the achievements of men are denied except as either carriers or negative moments in the development of the religious dialectic.

Concerning Dawson's construction of sociological "types," at first sight it seems sound enough. Natural religion is not far removed from modern sociology of religion: it is as old as Philo (if not older) and has its Christian consummation in Thomist social philosophy. But it is a fundamental tenet of true sociology that the construction of a type is based upon an empirical examination of all species of a genus and an abstraction of their common characteristics. The criterion of discrimination may vary, but all the instances of the genus should be included in the type. In constructing his archetype of "culture," Dawson takes not all instances of the type, but all save one. He argues that because all previous civilizations have been informed by a particular kind of religious belief, then any secular culture we may find is not a variant species of the genus but a sport, or a decline from the pure and only admissible type. For him, a civilization may be considered healthy only if and when it conforms to a type that existed at a given time and place. In fact, it must be informed not with religious ideals but with religious ideals of a peculiar sort—those that presuppose a highly developed ritual order based upon the seasonal cycles of the subtropical and temperate zones and that are directed by a priestly caste. Those that have not developed such a priestly caste he dubs primitive; those which have rejected them he calls decadent.

In reality, Dawson's sociology of culture is not that at all but a sociology of religion. It is not even that: it is a sociology of religion of a particular time (4000 BC– AD 1400) and a particular place (the Mediterranean world). The merits of Dawson's work derive from his acute study of the history of religion that he finds in this time and place, but he transforms it into the criterion for judging every other religion that he finds. Hence, his distinction between the "inner vitality" and the "external form" of a religion is admitted only in his study of Mediterranean religion, for "inner vitality" in his terminology can only mean "approximation to Christianity."

This brings us to a criticism of Dawson's idea of history. In *The Idea of History* Collingwood wrote: "A truly historical view of human history sees everything in that history as having its own *raison d'être* and coming into existence in order to serve the needs of the men whose minds have corporately created it."[61] To see any human creation, religion included, as an aberration or a sport is anti-historical. The idea of the sport is to sociological or historical analysis what the idea of "chance" is to science. Its use is an admission of analytical failure. We arrange the multifold reality that is history into types and study them in order to heighten the knowledge of the individual by contrasting it with the general. But the type itself is always constructed arbitrarily; it is always made up of a finite group of individualities that we have brought under scrutiny solely in order to find the general characteristics common to them all. Dawson dissolves religions into types when studying everything but Christianity. At this point he reverts to history in order to emphasize its individuality and then converts this historical individuality into a hypostasis of a religious sort by which he judges all other historical entities. Then within Christianity he follows the same process: true Christianity is found in only one of its stages, in the priestly-sacramental, medieval type of Christianity. This allows him to see Greek Orthodoxy as an abortive form of Christianity, Islam as a deviation, and Protestantism as a decline. It also leads him to assume that Judaism stopped developing with the prophets, who are now given the traditional Christian role of being merely the *praeparatio* of Christianity. In his schema there is no appreciation at all of post-biblical and Talmudic Judaism. And whereas he attributes to the religious views of Islam and Judaism the failure to produce a high material culture and to Protestantism all the evils of the modern Western world, the evils and shortcomings of medieval culture are not attributed to its religious vision but to "the intrusion of alien elements." Thus we see that Dawson's conception of cause, which at first seemed pluralistic, is pluralistic for a purpose. He finds the "cause" of the backwardness of the Near East not in material underdevelopment itself but in the religious vision; he finds the "cause" of modern ills in Protestantism; but he finds the "cause" of medieval society's ills not in its religion but in its abandonment of or failure to adopt Roman Catholicism. When a given society fails, it is because of the inadequacy of its vision of Reality; when Roman Catholic culture fails, it is the result, not of the inadequacy of the ideal that informs it, but of individual men.[62]

Again, aside from the fact that it is highly dubious that the life of primitive man "implies no reasonable purpose," it is dubious that Dawson can justify seeing all changes in the view of Reality as religious changes. In primitive societies, religion often serves the purpose that technology does in modern society; or better, among primitive peoples there is an attempt to dominate and control by a special sort of technology (magic) those areas of life that are not controllable with an underdeveloped technology.[63] The cultural life of man has always consisted of a mixture of two orders, a technical order, on the one hand, and a moral order, on the other. The differentiation between primitive culture and civilization may be said to be the difference between a world in which the moral order occupies the prime position and one in which the technical order occupies it.[64] For the first few millennia of his existence, man's technology remained relatively unchanged; his world was made up of forces that he could not comprehend and that were, as a result, hypostatized into governing mysterious or spiritual forces. Religion had the task of discovering the nature of these forces and keeping them placated. It is this to which Dawson refers when he speaks of a priesthood that "assisted the powers of nature to function."

But so, too, does the shaman help the powers of nature to function. Even though he may not work within the frame of a sophisticated cosmological vision such as that which informs the priesthood, he works within a field of knowledge that presupposes a repeatable cause-effect pattern as the necessary basis of his magic. Thus, while it may very well be true that a civilization becomes possible only when man discovers order in nature, there is no reason to call this discovery religious rather than technical or scientific. It was drainage of the swamps in Egypt, their irrigation by a complex system of canals, and planting at the proper time of the year that allowed the growth of civilization in the Nile valley; no amount of ritual would have worked that miracle. And while it is true that the directors of that process may have been priests, they were priests who had also become scientists.

It has been shown by Gordon Childe that one may write the history of the emergence of civilizations in the river valleys in purely materialistic terms.[65] But Childe errs as far in his monism as Dawson does in his; neither does full justice to the multiplicity of human creativity. Civilization might well be defined as the product of the intrusion of the technical order into an area formerly controlled and interpreted by the moral order.[66] It was at this time that in man's vision the cosmic order was broken in two. From this moment, we watch the progressive retreat of the moral order, the progressive diminution of the moral order. For thousands of years, the priesthood held the two orders together in a common cosmological frame and formed the common sacred intellectual tradition. But this common frame could be maintained only so long as the technical order did not produce a cosmological conception that was fundamentally antagonistic to the mythology that sustained the older moral order and its priesthood.

The various religious conflicts that characterize human history from ca. 1750 BC to AD 1750 may be said to stem from the impulse of the technological order to free itself from the limits imposed upon it by a mythology inherited from the primitive period and modified in the light of the first great technological revolution (ca. 4000–1500 BC). It succeeded only in the West during the eighteenth century. Here rational philosophy subjected the older mythology to a scathing critique in terms of the new cosmology constructed by a liberated science. With the destruction of the older cosmology went the power of the ritualistic priesthood whose claim to authority had been founded upon the older earth-centered, animistic cosmology and cosmogony. In fact, as Jaspers and Toynbee have argued, world history may be profitably conceived as moving through three phases: prehistoric or primitive culture, the civilizations based upon the limited worldview of the cosmologically oriented civilizations of the river valleys, and the current civilization in process of formation, which is based upon a non-geocentrically oriented cosmology. The task of modern religions, it would seem, is not to cling tenaciously to the older geocentrically oriented cosmology and its attendant rituals, but to forge a new worldview in which the moral precepts of which the older religions were products are reinterpreted in the light of the new cosmology.

The disappearance of the older cosmologies and their attendant rituals and priesthoods is not an occasion for despair. It does not mean that the moral order has been destroyed. It has been weakened due to the unwillingness or inability of a religious intelligentsia trained in the older mythology to reinterpret its moral precepts in terms amicable to the new cosmology. Part of that adjustment demands the abandonment of an earth-centered sacramental order. In that readjustment, a religion tied too securely to the old order must suffer, while the very religions which, in Dawson's terms, had erred in cutting themselves loose from a closely circumscribed and limited view of nature and the cosmos—such as Judaism, Buddhism, Hinduism, and Islam—might conceivably offer the proper ethical precepts to an age that has transcended the Nature of the earth.

If the Roman Catholic or, indeed, any ritual has lost its meaning in the modern world, it is because its symbols were too dependent upon one small part of the universe for their meanings. Those symbols were discovered and divinized out of an experience that took place in the Mediterranean basin. As modern science dissolves the world of nature into energy and man transcends earth-nature, he must move into a different symbol world as well. Art has already made the transition, or at least is experimenting to that end, and religion must soon follow. It is interesting to note that to the Hindu, who can, in Radhakrishnan's phrase, "find God in a test-tube," the new science of Max Planck, Albert Einstein, and Niels Bohr presented no difficulties."[67] This is because it was never, as Christianity had become, linked to a ritual that derived its meaning from a ceremonial year based upon the seasonal changes and workings of a world circumscribed by the arid subtropical and temperate zones of the planet Earth. It seems to indicate that in the formation of a new religious ideal, if Christianity is to survive, it must abandon the older ritual order or at least modify it radically; this does not mean that the kernel of the Christian ethic, as contained in the Sermon on the Mount, will have to be abandoned, only its historical accretions. If it is argued that Christianity without its historical accretions is not Christianity, I can only say that such a view confirms the anti-Christian attitude that identifies that religion with a given culture. If, in fact, Christianity is so limited, then it deserves to pass with the culture that gave it birth. In a world unified by modern technology, such cultural ethnocentrism is as outmoded as the tribal blood cult. Any attempt to maintain the older ritual order is as foredoomed to failure as Dawson's desire to maintain a Europe within the confines of a ritual order that in the thirteenth century had its good reasons but has since then succumbed to the judgment of history.

One final word about Dawson's conception of European civilization. That the medieval unity of which he writes so eloquently never really existed in fact is shown by Dawson's attempt to account for the reasons for its passing. The only reason he can find is "the leaven of oriental influences" of which Europe never purged itself and that were strengthened and given new life by Christian contact with the Orient during and after the Crusades. Christian contact with the Orient led to the articulation of disruptive elements such as the vernacular literatures (which militated against the international cultural unity imposed by the Church), a lay aristocratic tradition (which militated against the authority of the priesthood), and Greco-Arabic philosophy (which struck at the philosophical synthesis constructed by Saint Thomas). All of these disrupted the medieval unity by their secular and individualist tendencies, until both orientalism and medievalism itself were destroyed in a revolt against religion during the Renaissance and Reformation.

But surely there is something amiss here. How could one conceive Europe without thinking of its lay culture, its vernacular traditions and the Greco-Arabic philosophic tradition that lies at the base of modern science? Had Europe been purged of these elements it would not have been Europe at all, but merely an infinite prolongation of the thirteenth-century synthesis, a state of suspended animation that would have nipped in the bud the growth of those dynamic elements that characterize Europe quintessentially.

Does it really follow that Europe is not Europe without the religion that characterized it at one stage of its existence? The principle involved in saying this denies that a thing can change and still remain itself. Why should the thirteenth century be considered Europe's "classical age"? Why not the eighteenth? Or the nineteenth? Why should there be a "classical age" at all? In purely historical terms, there cannot be; as Leopold von Ranke said, every age stands immediate to God, each has its own proper raison d'être. In sociological terms a "classical age" might be admitted as an abstraction, but it is also assumed that this abstraction does not exist in actuality but is only an analytical tool. Therefore, what gives the character of moral imperative to Dawson's "classical age," the implied judgment on the West that decline from or change from the thirteenth-century ideal is the cause of all its difficulties? Does not abandonment of the thirteenth-century social ideal in itself point to the inadequacies of that ideal? For Dawson, such a judgment would be decisive were he dealing with any religion other than Christianity of the Roman Catholic type.

But Roman Catholicism is not, for him, either a historical individuality or a sociological abstraction; it is the one, true religion; it is Religion itself. He has split the time process into two spheres and finds in the Church the point at which the two spheres make contact. Hence the society informed by that institution takes on eternal significance.[68] This allows him to hypostatize Roman Catholic Christianity as an eternal archetype, and any deviation from it is not due to the institution's inadequacies, but the fault of those who abandon it—therefore, decline. To point to this deviation as the "cause" of the West's current dislocations is to imply that men are less moral today than they were in that happier, earlier age. It constitutes a return to the myth of the golden age that plagued the Egyptians after the Old Kingdom, the Greeks after Hesiod, and the Romans after the Stoics.

It might equally well be argued that if there are more anxieties in the modern world than in the medieval (and this is highly dubious), it is because man has come to realize that any given solution to a given problem (in religion as well as culture) can never be an eternal answer to all problems. Modern man must, whether he will or not, assume responsibilities for his own actions rather than have them exorcised by a priesthood claiming contact with the one, true God. If earlier societies seemed better adjusted or more harmonious than our own, it is because State and Church acted together to destroy individual responsibility rather than encourage it. For good or for evil, modern science has broken through these older compulsives and offered to man responsibility for everything he does. It is a terrifying gift but one eminently worthy of its recipient. To ask man to deny that gift in the interests of "peace of mind" is an insult. Religion must offer, like science, philosophy, and history, a truth that admits the possibility of revision. Having done this, it will have no need of sedatives.

CHAPTER THREE

The Abiding Relevance of Croce's Idea of History

{1963}

||||||||||||||||||||||||||||||||||||||||||||||||||||||||||||||||||||||||||||||||||||||||||||||||||||||||||||||||||||||||||||

The enemy is metaphysics.

—SETTEMBRINI IN THOMAS MANN'S *Magic Mountain*

In one of his many acute moments, Erich Auerbach remarked: "To write history is so difficult that most historians are forced to make concessions to the technique of legend."[1] He could easily have extended his generalization to include every form of social theory and criticism as well. The social theorist who does not realize that legendary modes of thought will inevitably intrude themselves into his narratives is either epistemologically naive or is concerned solely with trivial questions. The fall into legend is the price science pays to myth for the use of language. Hence, whether a particular age may be considered "scientific" or not depends less upon its actual contribution to knowledge than upon the attitude with which it confronts its innate propensity for mythic modes of thought. Historians of Auerbach's generation regarded the use of legendary techniques as a forced concession; in our own time, such techniques are often willfully, and respectably, embraced as a welcome liberation from the irritating restraints of rational inquiry.

Myth, fable, and legend loom increasingly large in the social thought of our time, not only as objects but also as a means of inquiry. This is why those who possess a peculiar sensitivity to the complexities of human life and seek to warn us against the diabolical powers of myth seldom receive a disinterested public hearing, much less public recognition of their true worth. It is therefore fortunate that intel-

This paper was written while the author was a Social Science Research Council Faculty Fellow in Italy. A shorter version of it was presented at the December 1961 meeting of the American Historical Association. My friend and colleague Wilson H. Coates read it for me when I was unable to attend the meeting, and I should like to thank him for it.

ligences capable of living without the solaces of myth are also usually immune to the narcotic of popular acclaim. Indeed, consistent mythophobes often shame us by their apparently natural self-sufficiency, and we are frequently tempted to forget them or to deify them so that we may be saved from having to emulate them. But it is fitting that we remember them on set occasions, especially after they have retired to the neutral ground of past history, so that we may be reminded that human knowledge is the product of a dialogue between hero and chorus and that human life itself is an eternal struggle to realize for the many that awesome self-sufficiency that, as yet, has remained the enviable privilege of the exceptional few.

Benedetto Croce has now been dead for ten years. His long life was lived in an atmosphere of honors and outright idolization, on the one hand, of hostile criticism, isolation, and threats of physical violence, on the other. Yet through every vacillation in the public's appraisal of his contribution to modern thought, he provided Italy, and indeed all of Europe, with a living example of an intellectual who could remain consistently concerned with the vital problems of his time without surrendering either his humanity or his critical integrity. Gilbert Murray once likened him to Tolstoy and then went on to point out that Croce's strength of character had been more remarkable than Tolstoy's, because he had eschewed the consolations of religion and had derived his guiding principles from the study of man alone.[2] Whatever we may think of Croce's judgments on particular occasions—I have in mind his qualified support of Mussolini in the early days of fascism—his life and work, considered as a whole, remain a monument to most of what was good and vital in the humanistic culture of old Europe.[3]

Modern Italy's debt to him cannot be questioned. He, more than any other, taught his generation how to study and moved it off the dead center of cultural provincialism. But he was much more than an intellectual force in the forging of modern Italian culture; he was a moral force as well. As his friend and critic, Guido De Ruggiero, put it at the end of the last war: "If among us only a fraction of the cultivated classes capitulated before the enemy, while the major part maintained intact the values of the Western tradition, in contrast to what happened in Germany, much of this is due to Croce."[4] The debt owed him by contemporary European culture at large is more difficult to specify. Perhaps it is contained solely in the fact that, during the years between the wars, when most of Europe was yielding to the fascination of a simple solution for all of its complex social problems, Croce, virtually alone on the Continent, continued to launch his work as social critic from that arduously won high ground between arid intellectualism, on the one hand, and puerile sentimentalism, on the other. In an age of simplicist creeds, Croce continued to remind Europe that human nature was a problem rather than a datum;

and in an age of easy enthusiasms, he repeatedly pointed out that every new idea might serve as an instrument of liberation from an imperfect humanity but that, if carelessly handled, it could as easily become an instrument of oppression as well.

But if any of this is true, how are we to account for the antagonism that meets every attempt to introduce Croce's name into the discussion of contemporary social problems? Ten years after his death, Croce's reputation has fallen as low as it is ever likely to fall, both in Italy and abroad. Among contemporary historians, philosophers, and social theorists, his fate has been similar to that of Thomas Mann among contemporary literary critics: most will admit the essential nobility of his spirit, but few find what he has to say relevant to the problems of the time. The younger Italian intellectuals tend to view him as a burden, as a "cultural dictator" who, through his sustained opposition to "scientism" in social thought, prevented the Italian intelligentsia from confronting realistically the peculiar problems of mass culture and industrial society.[5] In the world of English scholarship, he is often branded as a mystic and a reactionary and dismissed as unimportant except as a representative of late nineteenth-century neo-Hegelianism.[6] In the most recent survey of the intellectual history of Croce's own generation, H. Stuart Hughes's generally perceptive and judicious work, *Consciousness and Society*, Croce himself appears as the Jovian exponent of an antiquated humanism, a humanism crippled by its hostility to science and blinded by its want of a "sense of tragedy."[7]

It may be recalled that the same sort of criticism was often leveled against Goethe, with whom both Croce and Mann are frequently compared. And it may also be recalled that Goethe suffered a similar eclipse immediately after his death in the last century. Germans of the period of national unification and expansion found greater satisfaction in the contemplation of the more "practical" Schiller and the more "realistic" Heinrich von Treitschke. We have only recently come to realize that this repudiation of Goethe was less an evidence of a growing realism in Europe than a first step in the identification of realism with anti-humanism. It may well be asked, therefore, whether the current, almost universal, rejection of Europe's last great representative of the Goethean frame of mind does not reflect a similar false identification in the culture of our own time. The ultimate purpose of this essay is to pose that question. Its immediate purpose is to isolate the vital center of Croce's thought, to point out once more its essential worth, and to establish the relevance of his contribution to the contemporary cultural dialogue in the face of its assumed, but by no means proven, inadequacy.

It will not be necessary to linger over the accidents of birth that allowed Croce to assume the role of arbiter of Italian culture for the greater part of this century.[8] It is more important to recall that, unlike another patrician-philosopher of an earlier generation, Jacob Burckhardt, Croce never surrendered to the temptation to withdraw from an active struggle to create a better world in order to enjoy the benefits conferred by his birth. Throughout his life, he dedicated himself to a purification and advancement of that liberal tradition that Burckhardt had condemned as sterile and doomed. Social position and inherited wealth, however, did free him from the distractions of a professional academic career. Unlike those contemporaries with whom he is most often compared (Henri Bergson, Max Weber, Ernst Troeltsch, Friedrich Meinecke, Freud), Croce was not and did not aspire to be an academician. Thus he was relieved of the burden of having to appear to speak to eternity on every occasion, which allowed him to turn his full attention to the exercise of his powerful personality on the more vital plane of active social polemic. In fact, Croce was not even formally trained and cannot be said to have belonged to any particular philosophical school. The many-sided character of his thought may have resulted from the fact that he was the last great autodidact in the Western humanistic tradition, a successor to his earlier "amateur" compatriots, Petrarch and Machiavelli, whose respective positions on the relation between culture and politics he attempted to synthesize.

If Croce rose above the small fascinations of the university lecture room, he was equally immune to the grander temptations of the political podium. Yet his distaste for politics never hindered him from assuming the burden of public office when his eminence as a social philosopher thrust him onto the political stage. It took remarkable courage for a man of his temperament to descend into the political arena, and it required even greater courage to take responsible stands on vital political issues when the fashion demanded extremist postures in place of reasonable compromises. The nature of modern society makes it difficult to be both a humanist and an academician simultaneously, no matter what the official academic myths may tell us, but it is much more difficult to remain a humanist while serving as a practical politician. Croce's essentially humanistic outlook prohibited him from being either an effective pedant or a successful politician. But his "failure" was a testimony to his true greatness. That greatness lay in the charisma of a mind unafraid to see life in all its complexity and unashamed to scandalize the public by a concern for the humanity involved in every lost cause. Croce refused to be influenced by the public fad of the moment. In the face of every pressure, he went his own way writing about the life of the mind and the sphere of action with a noble disinterestedness that his opponents castigated as reactionary and his friends damned as "Jovian" but which he himself saw as a necessary combination of realism in the analysis of social problems and idealism in the prescription of solutions for those problems.

Croce became a formal philosopher in spite of himself. His original and his lasting interests were historical. But he was transformed into a philosopher by his sensitivity to the moral dilemmas of his time and by his awareness that no man can be a moralist—at least an effective moralist—without making clear to himself the deeper bases of his own ethics. He had been shocked out of his narrow, youthful antiquarianism by the apparent failure of liberalism at the time when it should have been rejoicing over its greatest successes and planning for the future. He saw the difficulty as a failure of liberal theory to keep pace with practice.

In the late nineteenth century, liberals had begun to doubt the truth of assumptions that had once sustained them in their struggle against prejudice, obscurantism, and authoritarianism. Mechanistic psychology had broken down the distinction between mind and matter; utilitarian ethics had come to regard the distinction between reason and will less as a necessary assumption than as a fusion, one that could be cleared up by the reduction of reason to sensation and will to appetite. Whether justified or not, these reductions dulled the conceptual tools with which liberals had traditionally circumscribed the real world of human affairs and ascribed moral responsibility in it. This in turn had led to a loss of nerve among liberals, reflected their growing confusion over the very nature of liberty (as in Lord Acton) and their inability to take action in the name of liberty when action was called for (as in Max Weber). In later years, Croce looked back upon the last quarter of the nineteenth century as "prosaic" yet "skeptical and dissatisfied" and found the cause of its doubt and anxiety in the fact that

> [t]he practical activity that was encouraged and aided by the liberal spheres was no longer joined to a lofty understanding of this activity, one capable of appreciating its full meaning and of recognizing its inestimable value; and so the religious and ethical impulse was weakened, the capacity for inventing and transforming the requisite concepts was diminished, the inner life of the conscience was mortified, that life in which alone suffering and sorrow and anguish can be gathered into purifying travail and converted into consoling and revivifying forces.[9]

He realized that the times required a new statement of the liberal ideal, one broad enough to encompass the findings of the modern sciences of matter, mind, and society, yet capable of transcending by sublation the fascinating half-truths of the great anti-liberal ideologies, of which determinism, vitalism, and idealism were the generic representatives.

The essential problem, as he saw it, was to find some ground common to mind and matter, prior to and encompassing both, a ground upon which the traditional concept of mind could be joined to the newly articulated concept of matter in such a way as to present them as distinct functions of a single process. Such a synthesis would reestablish the dignity of those ethical distinctions necessary to the liberal worldview and restore the confidence of liberals in their own highest ethical traditions. He believed that such a ground could be provided by history, the humanistic conception of which constituted, in his view, not only the methodological premise of every genuine science, but the greatest single contribution of European culture to human self-knowledge.

But he could not naively present the humanistic conception of history as an answer to critics of liberalism because most of them based their cases upon their own peculiar conceptions of history, each of which claimed to reveal the "real" basis of human life and the "true" goal of social action. And although each of the various anti-liberal ideologies deduced a different theory of action from its own particular vision of "reality," all agreed that the liberal era was coming to an end. The reaction of the disheartened liberals to these attacks had been to retreat into their own brand of conservative historicism, the myth of the essential changelessness of the current social dispensation.

The liberal-bourgeois myth of changelessness was as offensive to Croce as the various brands of anti-liberal historicism because, in his view, modern Western civilization was distinguished from all others by its acceptance of the idea that change was the essential characteristic of life and by the conviction that the variety of history alone provided the challenges by which man, in responding to those challenges, defined his humanity and realized his potential spirituality. In short, the essential cause of the dilemmas of liberal Europe was the loss of a sense of history. This loss opened the way to the conviction that history was less a product of man than a field of subhuman or superhuman forces—or what was worse, no forces at all. The problem thus confronting him was resolved into that of reeducating Europe to its lost sense of history. This alone, he believed, would provide the basis for a rebirth of vital ethical awareness and alone lead to a regeneration of an otherwise potentially moribund culture. Between 1893, the date of his controversial essay, "History Subsumed under a General Concept of Art," and 1906, the year of his essay on Hegel ("What Is Dead and What Is Living in Hegel's Philosophy"), Croce aggressively confronted the major anti-liberal theories of history while systematically defining his own position in his studies for his *Aesthetics* and his *Logic*. In an essay on the state of Italian historiography, written for the *Revue de synthèse historique* in 1902, he named positivism and naturalism as his main targets and portrayed his own work as the representative of an anti-mechanistic tradition of social criticism that had begun with Vico.[10] Against the current scientistic historicism he argued that history, while a form of knowledge, was less a science than an art. When forced to specify what he meant by art, he was constrained to adopt an idealist terminology, but he specifically denied that he could be called an idealist in the traditional sense of that term. He had been drawn to Hegel's early writings, to the *Phenomenology of Spirit* and the *Encyclopedia*, but like Marx he had wanted to stand Hegel "on his feet," which meant to him seeing the World Spirit as nothing but the spirit of man.[11] As he wrote in his autobiographical sketch of 1913: "My conception of the world has often been called . . . 'Hegelanism' or 'Neo-Hegelianism'; but it could as well be called . . . 'Neo-Positivism,' 'Neo-Kantianism,' 'Neo-Value Theory,' 'Neo-Vichianism,' and so on."[12]

Actually, like most of his generation, Croce had been simultaneously attracted and repelled by the major philosophical currents of his time, attracted by the insights they offered for an understanding of modern society but repelled by their monism. Unlike many of his contemporaries, however, he did not reject the anti-liberal ideologies out of hand—because he believed that every system of thought sprang from some legitimate human impulse and therefore served to illuminate the problems connected with the realization of that impulse. And so he confronted all of them sympathetically yet critically; on one occasion he was even referred to in a Marxist journal as "Comrade Croce." To him, the great anti-liberal systems at least directed one's attention to history *as a process*, which helped to dissipate the pernicious myth of social stasis. Moreover, each spoke on behalf of some aspect of human life that a complacent or deluded bourgeoisie preferred to forget or deny. In a society that increasingly tended to view the social life as an undifferentiated continuum, without qualities, variation, or unique forms, Marxism pointed to the pressing problems generated by the industrial revolution and aided in the political education of the masses; vitalism drew attention to the eternal irrationalities in human life; and idealism reminded men that there were still higher goals to which they might aspire.

But in the end, Croce believed, the various forms of materialism as well as traditional idealism failed, for they all manifested a crippling insensitivity to what he intuited as a uniquely human dimension in life. Not that he pretended to be able to specify the ultimate nature of that human dimension; in his resistance to every form of facile reductionism he resembled Nietzsche, for whom he felt a deep sympathy and in whom he recognized, long before most of his generation, the last great manifestation in the nineteenth century of the spirit of Goethe.[13] All of the major anti-liberal systems began, he argued, with an awareness of some aspect of the great dilemmas of the human condition, but in the course of their inquiries they lost sight of man and never returned to a consideration of his unique problems. The materialists reduced every human action to physical process and therefore discussed animal drives when they pretended to be dealing with human decisions. Idealism passed too rapidly through humanity in order to seize that realm of the spirit that it imagined existed, not in the minds of men, but apart from them or above them, thereby inevitably condemning the specifically physical side of human existence to a lower or inferior status. In short, the great worldviews of the late nineteenth century were all based on *partial* visions of the world and were slaves to metaphors provided by those partial visions. All of them erred when they tried to specify the real nature of human life. Was it therefore possible, Croce asked, that they erred in trying to specify it at all? And the answer to his question foreshadowed that of a similarly concerned Spanish thinker who was worrying about the same problem at the same time. With Ortega y Gasset, Croce affirmed: "Man has no nature, what he has is . . . history."

Therefore, in his systematic, as distinguished from his critical, works Croce attempted to frame a concept of history that would depend upon no single metaphor for its characterization but would point to a level of being so complex as to defy equation with any analogue in nature, technics, or pure thought. History was to be considered a unique category. In an early essay he had written: "Society is not an original element, it is not a primary function, it is not a form; it is simply a product of the human spirit."[14] In a later work he deepened and expanded that insight to include both humanity and history. In *History as Thought and as Action* (1938), he wrote: "The two propositions: 'Humanity makes itself in its history,' and 'The presupposition of this history is humanity,' are usually presented as distinct and often contradictory, and yet they must form, and in fact do form, a single proposition."[15]

For Croce, the historical process was a part of the world process, but it was also a transcendence of the material phase of that process in precisely the degree to which man transcended his simple animal nature. Humanity he therefore defined as that part of the world process that self-consciously seeks to know itself and mold its environment into forms not given by simple physiochemical combination. Croce believed that this view of human nature was justified, not because man was an emissary from another world, as the traditional religions taught, but because the historical record provided living evidence of individuals who, through thoughts and actions more noble than anything displayed to human understanding by the lower animals, were in fact creating, or at least striving to create, a world that could be called "spiritual" in a purely humanistic sense. And he concluded that the capacity to see history in this light was a measure of one's humanity. History written from this viewpoint had to be a history of human liberty; it would at once describe and promote the liberty of which it was the story.

This did not mean that one was justified in seeing life as totally free or inevitably easy; in fact, it implied that the freest lives were the most burdensome, if not the most tragic. Man was governed to a large extent by what Christian theologians called his "lower nature," but this lower nature was not a penalty imposed on him by some mythical Fall. It constituted rather the tools by which man came to know the world of sheer matter and worked upon it in order to realize both his necessary and his freely willed ends. In turn, the so-called spiritual nature of man was not a scintilla of the divine imprisoned in matter; rather it constituted those faculties that allowed man to establish contact and communicate with other men in uniquely human ways. Thus envisaged, the historical life was neither a reward nor a burden but merely a process in which men do their work or play their game to the end of defining their own proper nature. Physical nature and the specifically human nature work together in man to provide the possibility, though not the inevitability, of the transcendence of mere physical necessity through the exercise of a unique human responsibility in particular, morally pregnant situations. Thus, the physical, biological, and psychical sides of human nature had to be considered each as an essential, but by no means totally determinative, moment of the historical life. As Croce put it in his general study of history and historiography (1915):

> By liberating itself from servitude to an extramundane will and blind animal necessity, by freeing itself from all transcendence and all false immanence (which is a kind of transcendence), thought begins to conceive history as the work of man, as a product of human intelligence and will; and we arrive at that form of history called humanistic.[16]

In *The Theory and History of Historiography*, which constitutes the final volume of his "Philosophy of the Spirit," Croce brought together and fused those partial visions provided by the various forms of materialism and idealism into a comprehensive theory of history. He envisaged history as a field upon which the various moments of the life of humanity (investigated in his systematic philosophical works under the categories of the aesthetic, the logical, the ethical, and the vital) acted as functions of a single autonomous process.[17] In this process, each moment served now as the positive impulse, directing human life in the service of its particular needs, now as the negative impulse, offending the needs of other moments through extravagant claims and thereby activating them in defense of their own needs, thus turning them into positive impulses. This constant disequilibrium and rebalancing of the various moments of human life led to that growth of human knowledge and control over the physical world apprehended naively in the Christian conception of history as salvation; in its liberal middle-class counterpart, the conception of history as material or economic growth; in positivism as the growth of scientific knowledge; and in vitalism as the movement of vital force.[18]

The reciprocal action of these moments of the life of the spirit could be observed in the practical realm of politics and economics as well as in the life of the mind. Revolutions, whether political, economic or intellectual, were generated out of this field of countervailing forces when excesses in one sphere found their limits and their negations in the other, equally valid but temporarily slighted, spheres of thought or action. A revolution, Croce held, is always touched off by some reaction to an excess of a specific sort, but it will succeed only if it is capable of identifying the specific principle that it represents with the cause of liberty in general, and it will be creative only so long as it maintains such identification. When the specific interest of the carrying group of a revolution triumphs over and absorbs to its own purposes the general principle of liberty, it degenerates into tyranny and is rightly opposed by the conscientious citizen. Classic examples of the degeneration of liberating movements into tyrannies may be seen in the history of Christianity and in the history of the French Revolution. Both began as protests against tyranny in all its forms and spoke on behalf of oppressed humanity in general, but each became an ideology in the service of narrowly circumscribed interest groups, the former serving to justify the tyranny of the Church over the civil life, the latter of the mob over the individual. Not even liberalism was immune from this danger. The identification of the principle of liberty with laissez-faire economics was a case in point and was one of the causes of the liberal bad conscience against which Croce was fighting.[19] In short, history in general, like history in its particular periods and individual movements, could not be seen as a simple ascending line or expression of homologous forces; it was rather a subtle interplay of different sides of human life, each with its own raison d'être and valid claims on the individual, each necessary to the maintenance of a creative and growing humanity.

However, Croce did not mean that we should regard either the mechanism here described or the individual moments of the human spirit as metahistorical forces of which human actions are only reflections. Neither the mechanism nor the individual moments have any existence apart from human beings, and we encounter and study them only in the actions of human beings. In short, when we speak of the moments or the process as a whole, we are using a theory to aid us in our research, not positing the existence of "higher" forces that stand over or beyond humanity and direct its life. For the whole historical process, like the wholeness of humanity, "has no being except in the making of it, and the making of it is never a making in general but a determinate and historical task."[20]

History so conceived, Croce argued, provided a criterion for distinguishing between "true" historical analysis and all forms of pseudo-history. In true histo-riography, physical, biological, and psychological necessity appear, not as gover-nors of life, but as *opportunities* for the living of a peculiarly human life; therefore, they are of interest to the historian only insofar as they serve as the occasions for responses that, for good or for evil, indicate more than mere animal capability in man. Insofar as they do not call forth specifically human responses, they have no place in historical accounts but are properly relegated to those technical treatises especially set up to study man as a "human animal." In short, Croce argued, "his-tory is about what man does, not what happens to him."[21] This having been said, it remains to guard ourselves against slipping into an unconscious dualism in which mind and matter confront each other as separate and hostile principles. Actually, according to Croce, mind and matter shade off one into the other, for both "in a homogeneous manner, belong to the single spirituality and the single history."[22]

True historical insight, then, demands tact or a sense of decorum that allows the historian to mediate within himself between the demands of the antiquarian, chronicler, metaphysician, and engaged social being. He must be able to recognize the degree to which man is a slave to passion and animal necessity, but his ultimate interest will always be individual persons or events insofar as they manifest the capacity for morally responsible decisions. The task of the true historian is to de-scribe the encounter between man's various projected ideals of life and the social-physical world operative around and within himself that that ideal is meant to explain, contain, and order. And therefore, when properly narrated, history be-comes the equal in transforming power to tragic poetry, inspiring fear and pity when it forces contemplation of an aspiring humanity cut down in its every effort to realize its projected ideals, but also inspiring pride and emulation of heroic vir-tue when it shows a defeated humanity repeatedly returning to the battle for its own proper freedom.

Here history and philosophy become one, for just as every philosophical inquiry must be based upon historical awareness and must use historical techniques for the ordering of its materials, so historical inquiry itself shows the impossibility of ar-riving at any *simple* formula for deciding where good and evil lie in any particular historical event or for predetermining choices in future existential situations, and hence eternally generates new philosophical inquiries. History confirms our aware-ness of a moral sense in man but no particular moral code (except of the highest generality) can be derived from its study.

If history teaches anything at all, it shows us that moral decisions must be made with something less than complete knowledge of the situations in which they are called for and with as little knowledge of the ultimate effects of those decisions upon the surrounding world. But at the same time history alone (and here it surpasses both philosophy and art in its powers of moral suasion) provides us with *living* models of human beings willing to act within the limits thus given and teaches us that, potentially at least, we too possess a similar courage. Great historical works act on the mind of the reader like those Platonic dialogues that end on a seemingly ambivalent note but that really intend that the problem exposed and the dialectic begun live on in the mind of the reader, becoming part of his moral consciousness and being consummated, not in mere reflection or contemplation, but in an action proper to the situation in which the reader finds himself. Thus conceived, historical knowledge may grow out of any question about real men and events, and it assumes philological competence, logical acumen, and critical common sense for the gathering and preliminary organization of the materials. But it goes far beyond these minimal requirements, demanding above all a sustained recognition of the manifold complexity of human life, a tact that inspires caution before every attempt to contain that complexity in verbal generalization, and the courage to live a morally responsible life in the face of the ambiguities that a history so construed implies. Thus in *Historiography and Moral Ideality,* which he wrote just three years before his death, Croce said:

> True historiography can never serve as "master of life" in the sense of providing us with practical schemes for actions to be realized, but only as an inspiration to acts of moral and religious elevation, those kinds of acts which transport man into the presence of God . . . and make him aware of his duty to work at his own job, however small it may seem, in the continual creation of the world to which he belongs and which belongs to him. Historiography . . . is preparatory and not determining.[23]

Only a history thus conceived could serve as a basis for that communication and cooperation (and, failing these, that toleration) among men that make civilized life possible.

The usual complaint against Croce is that he went too far. In his anxiety to erase every trace of determinism, vitalism, and idealist metaphysics from historical analysis, his critics maintain, he ended by endowing the whole historical process with all the attributes once ascribed by Saint Augustine to the Church, by Hegel to Reason, and by Marx to the modes of production. In short, he ended by idolizing History itself. Such an attitude toward the past must lead, we are told, not to action in the name of a specific ideal, but to the contemplation of history's infinite variety as an end in itself. History thus conceived endows every product of human activity with an aura of sanctity and thereby prohibits any "artificial" transformation of it by the reformer. All the reformer can do is wait and hope that history goes the way he would like to see it go. Second, Croce's critics maintain, this sense of awe and respect for historical events and personalities sounds suspiciously like a remnant of the medieval attitude toward Creation in general; it effectively prohibits the empirical study of history and denies the possibility of framing general causal laws descriptive of its processes.

Finally, it has been held, not even Croce was true to his own principles. In his theoretical works he ranted against all metahistory; in his historiographical works, however, he introduced all sorts of metaphysical entities (the Spirit, the Goddess Liberty, etc.) that reign as hidden arbiters of seemingly free human actions.[24]

There is some justice in these criticisms, but they need not blind us to Croce's positive contributions to the contemporary cultural dialogue. The charge that Croce's idea of history is unscientific or antiscientific begs the question, since it was Croce's purpose to investigate both the possibility and the desirability of history conceived as a science. Moreover, it obscures the fact that Croce, in denying the possibility of a scientific history, was not denying the role or importance of science for the investigation of physical nature in its simpler levels of organization. Nor was he arguing that history is not a form of knowledge. He was merely pointing out that history provides us with a kind of knowledge different from that provided by science. With those who were using the word "science" to mean "knowledge in general" Croce had no immediate quarrel; he was merely asking if there are not different kinds of knowledge. Those who answer in the negative are then left with the task of providing a conception of science that will either include the kind of knowledge we receive from art or will exclude it. If they include art as a form of knowledge, then they must abandon the attitude of the naive empiricist and the positivist; and the question of the nature of historical knowledge is once more reopened. If art is excluded from their concept of science (conceived as knowledge in general), then they merely reveal their ignorance of art and cannot be expected to show greater wisdom in any discussion about the nature of history.

To be sure, in his earlier writings Croce spoke of science in late nineteenth-century terms. In his discussions of the nature of history his enemies were men like Hippolyte Taine and Herbert Spencer. Against them, he was concerned to show that, although historical knowledge might use the techniques of empiricism and positivism, it was much more than either of these. However, in saying that history had more in common with art than with the physical sciences, he was not just throwing history into the sphere of the irrational, the mystical, and the totally subjective; for at the same time he was opposing the commonly held concept of art as mere pleasure or narcotic and trying to elevate it to the status of knowledge. He believed that history differed from science in the kind of questions it asked of its materials and in the kind of communication that was possible between men and men, on the one hand, and between men and animals or plants or rocks, on the other. He believed it was possible to know things about men that one could not know about animals and plants, because in men the element of motive was an important part of understanding movement and action. This meant that the historian was less interested in *describing* his objects of study than in *understanding* them, and by "understanding" he meant recognizing and sympathizing with the processes of consciousness called for in every human action. And while it was possible, he believed, to speak of a "science of description" (which in fact existed for the historian as philology and chronology), to speak of a "science of understanding" did not make sense. "Understanding" resulted from a kind of communication that is possible between human beings only outside of the mechanical rules of all methodologies, whether the conventional ones, such as rules of etiquette, or avowedly "scientific" ones, such as those rules of laboratory method constructed specifically to destroy intimate contact between the investigator and his object of study.

Croce's argument with the scientific historians was similar in its general character to the arguments between psychoanalysts and empirical psychologists or, better still, between conventional moralists and linguistic analysts who define ethics as the study of ethical language, not moral action. Talk of a "science of history" was as meaningless to Croce as talk about a "science of morality," for just as a discussion of moral actions assumes the moral sense as a precondition of their existence, so historical understanding assumes a preexisting sense of the human. Just as "moral sense" is in that tact that shows which "rule" to apply in a particular situation, so the historical sense directs the attention of the historian to those elements in the historical record that are reflective of our humanity. For those who lack this "sense of humanity" and insist on seeing only the similarities between the lower forms of animal life and human life, Croce has nothing to say. He can only use his critical ability to show that when they pretend to be talking about men, they are really talking about something else, such as a rock, a plant, or a microbe. Their type of history illuminates our understanding of man only insofar as this "something else" happens to be present in the action under study.

As for the charge that Croce was inconsistent, attacking metahistory in his theoretical writings and practicing it in his historiography, it could be answered that he never intended his works to be read *in vacuo*. Most of his historical productions were collections of lectures or occasional pieces that had been delivered and were meant to be heard in specific social situations. Croce once said that he had never aspired to write one of those "definitive" works of historical scholarship, because, in the first place, he did not believe that definitive works were possible, and because, second, he believed that, in order to be adjudged "definitive," a historical work had to be too narrowly defined in scope and too neutral in its social attitudes to influence history as well as describe it.

All of Croce's historical works are more properly designated as moral tracts than "pure" scholarship, and this was completely consistent with his conception of historical understanding as the preparation for morally responsible action. Since, in Croce's view, true historical investigation was always inspired by some moral concern, it could be brought to completion only in an attempt to influence social decisions. Thus his studies of the past are always conceived as instruments for illuminating the present.

This did not mean that the historian was to be merely a propagandist for the currently prevailing cause. In fact, the contrary was the case. He saw the historian as defender of a balanced social life. This meant that from the higher vantage point to which his discipline had led him, the historian must always return to the world of action and through his writings encourage now one tendency in his society, now another. Long before Albert Camus had popularized a similar idea in *The Rebel*, Croce had held that it was the chief task of the historian to speak out for that side of thought and action suffering from neglect and abuse at the hands of the *simplificateurs* who are always a threat to our humanity. For Croce's abiding enemy was fanaticism, whether the fanaticism of belief (which is the surrender of responsible judgment to supposedly "eternal" rules) or the fanaticism of unbelief (which is the surrender of the will to a slothful skepticism). At one point in his *History of Europe in the Nineteenth Century* Croce quotes Goethe approvingly: "Every fanatic should be nailed to the cross at thirty, because he who has been under an illusion, when he comes to his senses, turns into a knave."[25] Croce resembled Goethe in many respects and not the least in his distaste for what Erich Heller has called the "plebeian" elements in modern intellectual fashions—"elements of either self-abasement or rational conceit, of excessive curiosity or psychological tactlessness, and a sniggering suspicion of the absence of meaning in anything that evades definition or experimental proof, and above all, a disregard for those intangible qualities that make the world a noble habilitation."[26] And like Goethe, Croce has been an enigma to those who would categorize his attitudes under terms that reflect their own inherent lack of faith in man: terms like self-interest, greed, and cowardice.

Croce's historical works were a sustained warning to Europe against the dangers of simplicism in thought and fanaticism in action in their constant repetition of the conviction that even the highest ideals become arid and oppressive when they are pushed to the outer limits of their potential development. Thus, both his *Theory and History of Historiography* and his *History as Thought and as Action* were written as antidotes to the fascination of Utopian programs, simplicist political theories, and monistic conceptions of man, society, and human history. The inevitable and necessary ambiguity of every moral act is the main theme of both his *Lives of Adventure, Faith, and Passion* and his *History of the Kingdom of Naples*. In these works, Croce sought to depict men undertaking actions in the half-light of moral awareness, showing, on the one side, the ineluctable forces working to reduce man to nature and, on the other, the eternal resurgence of the human spirit out of defeat to confront ever more realistically the world that is both its master and its enemy. At the same time, these works seek to show that it is possible to live a life that is both heroic and civilized, even in the absence of total knowledge or divine power. The very ambiguity of moral action frees us to change direction in the light of every new, qualifying experience, allowing us to live by an ethical ideal that is both self-assertive and self-critical.[27]

The History of the Baroque Age in Italy and *The History of Italy from 1871 to 1915* affirm Croce's belief that liberty is never given to an individual, a culture, or an epoch without limitations but must always be reaffirmed and reconquered in every concrete labor. The former book is a study of a culture built upon the human capacity for self-deception, while the latter is a study of moral failure resulting from the inability of the Italian people to make the transition from high revolutionary ideals to those plain, workaday tasks that might have consolidated the gains made in revolution. All his historical works reflect Croce's conviction that the grandeur of the modern conception of liberty lay in its rejection of every hope for a final solution to human problems. The end of history lay, not in the realization of some specific system of ideas or institutions, but in the urge in man "to draw breath more freely . . . [to] grow deeper and broader."[28]

Marxist critic Georg Lukács has seen in all of this nothing but the reactionary irrationalism of a decadent and parasitical bourgeois confronted with the harsh realities of the imperialist era.[29] Lukács's hostility toward Croce is understandable. It may be recalled that Lukács was the model for the fanatic Naphta in Mann's *The Magic Mountain,* while Settembrini figures many of Croce's humanistic convictions. But unlike Settembrini, Croce was no "organ grinder," no uncritical admirer of traditional humanism and conventional middle-class values. He knew that no institution or idea could serve as an eternal solution to the constantly changing problems of a creative humanity. Ultimately, even the liberal ideal itself was subject to the corroding hubris of success, and at the height of fascist power in Italy he turned to an examination of the failure of liberalism in his *History of Europe in the Nineteenth Century* (1932). This book, dedicated to Thomas Mann and in more than one respect a historical handling of the theme of *The Magic Mountain*, is not at all, as has been charged, an uncritical tribute to nineteenth-century liberalism. Nor is it a sanguine assertion of the inevitability of liberalism's triumph, which would have made it a kind of historiographical *Divine Comedy*. It is rather a study of the failure of liberals to create a world in conformity to their own laboriously articulated and heroically affirmed ethical ideal, which makes of their story a tragedy.

Throughout his great study of liberalism, Croce sets the liberal ideal over against the historical reality as it is lived it a given moment in order to remind us that even in success the good is frequently evil and the evil good. In short, his tragic vision is Sophoclean, not Aeschylean; and it is Sophoclean optimism that allows him to end his work, not on a note of despair, but in a mood of hope qualified by a realistic respect for mankind's capacity to choose the baser side in particular situations. His history of Europe ends in 1915, not because he was unable to "explain" fascism—that he could have done as easily as any of his contemporaries—but because for him the idea about which he was writing reached at that moment a point of critical decision. He knew that World War I constituted a failure of liberals, and from his own experience he knew that the challenge presented by the war had been too much for his own generation to cope with. It therefore remained for the next generation to choose between the ideal that had been betrayed and the easy faiths that claimed to transcend that ideal but were in reality merely manifestations of the betrayal.

There was a great humility in Croce's willingness to forgo the part of lawmaker or prophet, even in the most critical situations, and to content himself with the more difficult role of reminding his readers of their obligations in the definition of their own destinies. Like one of those Platonic dialogues, his *History* was meant to be finished in deeds, not words, deeds of our own choosing rather than deeds inspired by the beauty of words. Thus he concluded his work:

> All this, rapidly outlined, is not prophecy, for that is forbidden to us and to everyone for the simple reason that it would be vain, but a suggestion of what paths moral consciousness and the observation of the present may outline for those who in their guiding concepts and their interpretation of the events of the nineteenth century agree with the narrative given of them in this history. Others, with a different mind, different concepts, a different quality of culture, and a different temperament, will choose other paths, and if they do so with a pure

mind, in obedience to an inner command, they too will be preparing the future well. A history inspired by the liberal idea cannot, even in its practical and moral corollary, end with the absolute rejection and condemnation of those who feel and think differently. It simply says to those who agree with it: "Work according to the line that is here laid down for you, with your whole self, every day, every hour, in your every act; and trust in Providence, which knows more than we individuals do and works with us, inside us and over us." Words like these, which we have often heard and uttered in our Christian education and life, have their place, like others from the same source, in "the religion of liberty."[30]

CHAPTER FOUR

Romanticism, Historicism, and Realism

Toward a Period Concept for Early Nineteenth-Century Intellectual History

{1968}

The simultaneous emergence of Historicism and Realism out of the Romantic movement during the second quarter of the nineteenth century has necessarily raised the problem of the relationship between them. The inquiry into the problem has thus far, however, proceeded along the two lines that are least likely to produce any significant agreement on the nature of that relationship: the determination of formal similarities and differences between them and the search for influences of one on another. The search for direct influences of Historicism on Realism, and the reverse, has drawn a blank; and the attempt to relate these two movements to the one that preceded both of them, Romanticism, has also failed. The outstanding representatives of French Realism—Stendhal, Balzac, and Tocqueville—were generally indifferent to the principal work of the German historicists, Hegel in philosophy and Ranke in historiography. If German Historicism "influenced" French Realism it did so at such a remove as to be indistinguishable from that general interest in history that the Romantic movement fostered all over Europe during the first quarter of the nineteenth century. Michelet and Victor Cousin tried to popularize German thought in France in the 1820s and 1830s, but there is no evidence that either Stendhal or Balzac took notice of their efforts; and although Tocqueville studied Schelling, Fichte, and Hegel, he rejected all three as too doctrinaire for his taste.

The failure of the search for influences has quickened interest in the alternative approach to the study of the relationships between these three cultural movements. This other, formal or comparative, approach authorizes the historian, first, to con-

This essay was originally presented at the Joint Session of the American Historical Association and the Association for the History of Science, American Historical Association Meeting, San Francisco, December 1965.

struct models of cultural movements that are superficially similar; then, by descending to particulars, to show how they differ in detail; and, finally, to account for these differences in detail by referring to differences in the social environments within which the movements respectively arose. The most important advocates of this approach are the Marxist critic Georg Lukács and the humanistic philologist Erich Auerbach.

Both Lukács and Auerbach view early nineteenth-century literary Realism as a movement that combined the romantic conception of the Promethean personality with a new sensitivity to the "demonic" nature of social process that emerged with the French Revolution and that found its highest expression in Historicism. And both, like their heir Harry Levin, interpret Stendhal and Balzac as "disillusioned" Romantics. This disillusionment is expressed in their sensitivity to the intractability of the social sphere by human will or reason. Their art is "realistic" inasmuch as it encompasses some consideration of the category of the social as an irreducible factor in the historical process; and since this sensitivity is by their lights also the main characteristic of German Historicism, they are allowed to conclude that Realism is in some sense a product of the combination of the Romantic theory of personality with the Historicist theory of social irreducibility.

But when all has been said, neither Lukács nor Auerbach is able to explain why the combination of the Romantic conception of personality with the heightened sensitivity to the autonomy of society produced Realism in France and failed to do so in Germany. Both have pointed to the special social, political, and economic conditions that obtained in Germany in the nineteenth century and have argued that until social conditions changed to approximate those that obtained in France during the middle decades of the century, a fully self-conscious Realism was impossible. And both find proof of their analyses in the fact that, when these conditions did change, Realism flourished, as the appearance of Thomas Mann's *Buddenbrooks* in 1901 shows. But until Realism became possible in Germany, German intellectuals had to remain satisfied with a fractured version of it, that is, Historicism.

Thus envisaged, Historicism is nothing but an abortive form of Realism, which is in turn a worldview reflective of the ideological needs of the middle class. By this account, Realism and bourgeois hegemony go hand in hand. Only if you combine the Romantic conception of personality and the social experience of the Revolutionary age with the special needs of the ascending bourgeoisie do you get Realism; the same mixture in the context of social reaction or stagnation results in Historicism. Auerbach does not put it quite so starkly as Lukács, but his argument is substantially the same.

The principal difficulty with the argument is that it obscures the originality and richness of Historicism. But it also does an injustice to early nineteenth-century Realism. As Lukács and Auerbach set it up, we must view Historicism *and* Realism as different phases of a larger intellectual drama that reaches its culmination only in the twentieth century, when a special order of consciousness, called "true" Realism emerges. For Lukács, this true Realism is nothing but socialist class consciousness, while for Auerbach it is that fully articulated representation of the world, both internal and external, that appears in the novels of Joyce and Proust.

There can be no doubt that this broadened perspective with which Lukács and Auerbach have provided us has many virtues; but its weaknesses are manifest and crucial. For in neither case does it lead the student of early nineteenth-century intellectual history *into* Historicism and Realism. On the contrary, it leads him *away* from them: *out* to the social and political milieu and *forward* to the modern, "true" Realism that everything in Western culture has been straining to become since the beginning. Finally, this Olympian perspective on nineteenth-century intellectual history blurs fundamental differences between Romanticism, Historicism, and Realism. That this is so can be seen by Auerbach's tendency to define Historicism in one context in such a way as to render it indistinguishable from what he calls Realism in another. And the same can be said about the attempts to relate Romanticism to both Historicism and Realism. By Lukács's strange dialectical gymnastics, the novelist Walter Scott is turned into the most "Realistic" writer of his generation—a judgment that historicists like Hegel and Ranke would never have accepted and that Balzac took great pains to deny.

There is genuine confusion here, and part of it stems from the use of the comparative method for analyzing relationships between cultural movements *that occurred at roughly the same time and approximately the same places.* Since the movements being considered usually draw upon a common fund of organizing metaphors, are fashioned out of responses to the same kinds of problems, and are addressing the same kinds of public—the general similarities will tend to swamp all differences in detail. The historian is inclined, then, to concentrate on the similarities and to deduce from them the existence of a pervasive Zeitgeist, or to overweigh the significance of whatever differences in detail that he turns up in his research and to fall prey to a kind of particularism that denies any unity to the thought of the age whatsoever. The current split between the followers of René Wellek and the heirs of A. O. Lovejoy over the nature of the Romantic Age is a case in point, and similar splits between Platonists and Aristotelians exist in the literature on Historicism and Realism.

What seems to be needed for dealing with the problem of relating contemporaneous and contiguous cultural movements is a different analytical model, or system of notation, from those generally used (the formalist approach, on the one side, the hunt for influences, on the other). I am therefore going to discuss the relationship between Romanticism, Historicism, and Realism in terms of a metaphor developed by the philosopher Ludwig Wittgenstein in his discussion of "language games." I shall try to show that with this metaphor we can contemplate the construction of a period concept for early nineteenth-century intellectual history that neither projects us into the doctrine of the Zeitgeist nor requires that we abandon the hunt for general characteristics altogether.

In the *Philosophical Investigations* Wittgenstein considers the charge that he has failed to provide a definition of the "essence of a language-game, and hence of language," the subject of his philosophy. Wittgenstein's defense is that, when he speaks of "language-games," he is not suggesting that "these phenomena" have a single thing in common, "which makes us want to use the same word for all—but that they are related to one another in many different ways." It is "because they are *related* to one another in many different ways . . . that we call them all 'language.'" Therefore, if one asks "What is common to them all?" or assumes that "There *must* be something common, or they would not be called 'games,'" one would be approaching the problem of definition in a self-defeating way. For, he points out, if you *look* at various examples of all the things called games, "you will not see something that is common to *all*, but similarities, relationships, and a whole series of them at that." In fact, you see a "complicated network of similarities and crisscrossings: sometimes overall similarities, sometimes similarities in detail." And then Wittgenstein concludes:

> I can think of no better expression to characterize these similarities than "family resemblances"; for the various characteristics between members of a family: build, features, color of eyes, gait, temperament, etc. etc. overlap and *crisscross* in the same way.—And I shall say: "games" form a family.[1]

Now, in this paper I shall exploit the metaphor of family resemblance by considering Romanticism, Historicism, and Realism as a "family" of "cultural games." I shall do this by taking the metaphor more literally than Wittgenstein did. That is, I shall argue that Romanticism, Historicism, and Realism not only *resemble* each other as members of a single family, but that they are *related* in the way that members of a family are, that is, genetically.

Like a family, at least, like a good nineteenth-century bourgeois family, Romanticism, Historicism, and Realism are generationally affiliated, and they live in the same, or similar, social neighborhoods. They share certain common problems, agree on the ways of categorizing the data that must be accommodated in any successful solution of those problems, address similar publics, use the same literary genres for presenting their solutions to the public, and employ similar stylistic devices for staging their achievements. And they differ from each other in the way that members of families over a period of two or three generations will do: that is, by the dominance and recession of certain characteristics shared by them all. And if we pursue the family metaphor further, we shall see that we have a way of determining when this family dies out, or is replaced in its neighborhood by another: that is, when the family traits that characterize it are supplanted by others.

Time requires that I concentrate on merely one problem shared by representatives of these three movements: the problem of historical change. Early nineteenth-century thinkers were concerned, in a way that eighteenth- and late nineteenth-century thinkers were not, to determine in what sense their own age constituted an advance over, or a decline from, the immediately preceding age. It is not too strong to say that they were obsessed by the problem of determining what had been gained, or lost, during the Revolutionary epoch. They may have ultimately disagreed over the worth of the post-Revolutionary period, but all agreed that the determination of the value and main drift of their own lived present was a problem worthy of the most serious inquiry, meditation, discussion, and analysis.

Moreover, in their attempts to close with this problem, early nineteenth-century thinkers and writers distinguished between three different *kinds* of data that had to be accommodated in their solutions to this problem: (1) the data of physical-natural process, (2) the data of individual human consciousness, and (3) the data of social process. Of these three kinds of data, those of physical-natural process offered special theoretical problems. Early nineteenth-century thinkers could not agree over whether nature should be conceived mechanistically or vitalistically, for in the first half of the century the principles by which biological matter is organized were still not known. Thus, Ranke and Balzac tended to view nature vitalistically, while Stendhal and Tocqueville inclined towards a mechanistic notion of it. Hegel vacillated between the two views. But *that* nature constituted a specific causal force in the determination of the physiognomy of historical epochs was a conviction shared by Romantics, Historicists, and Realists alike. In the designation of nature as a specific causal force, early nineteenth-century thinkers do not, of course, depart from their Enlightenment counterparts. Where they differ—and what makes them members of a specific family—is in what they set beside that primal force as having an autonomy similar to it.

Here Romanticism makes its distinctive contribution. For all of the thinkers mentioned thus far regarded individual human consciousness as a causal force in the historical process. Moreover, they shared a common conception of the nature of the human psyche from which this force emanated. All of them had assimilated something of Rousseau's notion of the structure of human consciousness, either directly from him, or indirectly as transmitted by Kant through the second and third *Critiques*. That is to say, all admitted the primacy of the emotions in the disposition of natural energies in mankind. They assumed that sense perceptions entered into consciousness only as colored by a host of personal and private conditioning factors. Thus, they tended to believe that the individual actor in the historical drama did not so much "perceive" as "construct" the reality against which he moved on the basis of needs and desires that were purely personal and subjective. All tended to believe, therefore, that individuals were effectively isolated within subjective visions of what the world is and what it ought to be. In their view, men inhabit what are putatively different worlds. And while they may have disagreed over why they "see" the world differently, *that* individuals see it differently they never doubted for a moment.

Stendhal, of course, is the master of all those who, in the early nineteenth century, examined the implications of this fact of human consciousness. His novels are beautifully articulated set pieces in the analysis of the conflicts between individual consciousness and external reality. In his novels he dwells with exquisite subtlety on the phenomena of pre-dramatization of situations by the individual subjective consciousness: anticipation, retrospective rationalization, and perverse misconceptions of the situations in which the protagonist finds himself. But he is no more subtle than Hegel who, in a more abstract way in the *Phenomenology of Mind*, does the same thing for culture at large. For Hegel, as for Stendhal, desire (*Begierde*) is the immediate impelling principle of individual action *and* thought. And for both, the conflict between individual consciousness and the non-conscious world of society and nature constitutes the central problem of human inquiry. In this, they are both the heirs of Romanticism, and specifically of Rousseau.

Where Stendhal and Hegel differ is in their conceptions of the possible gains to society involved in the conflict between the individual and the external world. Julien Sorel's self-chosen death at the age of twenty-three is supposed to inspire in Stendhal's readers an awareness of the absurdity of social existence; in Hegel, that same death would have been seen as necessarily contributing to humanity's ever-growing consciousness of itself. Stendhal tells us that we become human only through our conflict with society, but that our humanity slips our grasp somewhere in the process of socialization. By contrast, Hegel affirms again and again that the socialization of man is always a positive force in history. Whether the individual lives his life as a dutiful citizen or as a rebel, the carriers of collective human consciousness—the state and culture—are served. Here is the parting of the ways, where Historicism and Realism part company with Romanticism. If what I have said about Stendhal is true, we might want to distinguish his attitude from that of the Historicist and the Realist alike—and resolve the dispute over whether or not he was fundamentally a Romantic by pointing to his conviction that the individual is *always* the victim, never the beneficiary, of society. This is an attitude characteristic of Romanticism, but it is as alien to a Realist like Balzac as it is to a Historicist like Hegel.

In short, Romanticism, Historicism, and Realism differ in their expectations about the resolution of any conflict between the individual and the social world in which he lives. But they share one important attitude toward specifically social phenomena, which allows us to declare them individual members of a single family of cultural games. They all consider social forces to be relatively autonomous factors in the historical drama. The Romantic regards social forces as negative factors in the life of mankind; the Historicist regards them as positive factors; while the Realist regards them as capable of acting both positively and negatively. And it is these differing senses of the autonomy of social forces in the historical process that distinguishes them one from another, even while making them members of a single family of cultural games.

By this I do not mean to suggest that eighteenth-century thinkers were not concerned with social problems. But most of them tended to consider social problems as subsidiary aspects of other kinds of problems, such as the nature of God (as in Leibniz), the nature of the physical world (as in Montesquieu, Holbach, and Helvetius), or the nature of human consciousness (as in Hume and Kant). On the whole, Enlightenment thinkers regarded the commendable aspects of their own societies as functions of essentially harmonious natural processes; the deplorable aspects they tended to see as residues of primitive misunderstandings of how nature really worked. Therefore, they were inclined to feel that if they cleared up the problem of the nature of the physical world or explicated properly the relationship between the knowing subject and the object given in sense perceptions, they would provide solutions to most social problems *by the way*. Thus society as such was not a problem for a thinker like Kant, and neither was history.

Rousseau constitutes a significant exception to these generalizations: for Rousseau, society was a problem in the way that neither nature nor individual consciousness was. He regarded social existence as paradoxical, not to say absurd, which no amount of merely intellectual progress could alleviate. Rousseau taught his contemporaries that the social problem would have to be handled by social means, by a radical transformation of society itself. This is what makes him a pre-

Romantic and a proto-Realist at one and the same time. His links with Historicism are less clear. His belief that the social stage of human development might someday be transcended in the realization of a genuine community, the community suggested in *The Social Contract,* points to a trans-historical state that the Historicists did not, on the whole, admit the possibility of. Like Vico, the Historicists tended to believe that man was irredeemably condemned to society in the same way that he was condemned to history.

But Romantics, Realists, and Historicists alike agreed with Rousseau that social existence brings as many liabilities as benefits to the task of winning an integrated humanity. They differ in the degree of optimism with which they approach the task: for the Romantic, nothing is essentially changed by the hero's agon with society. At least, nothing new is created that can be publicly confiscated; at the most, the individual gains some new insight into a purely private human essence. Thus Stendhal's hero, Julien Sorel, a romantic personality *par excellence,* is allowed a momentary glimpse of an ideal integrity—in his prison cell, while awaiting his execution—before being hurled back into the maw of a nature that Stendhal believes to be as powerful as it is purposeless. Hegel and Ranke, by contrast, assimilate individual suffering to the conquest of the universal ground from which both individual and society spring. For both of these German thinkers, the ground of history becomes more fully known to humanity as a result of social conflict.

Balzac and Tocqueville can be called Realists with some accuracy by virtue of the way that they assign gains and losses in the total historical process. Both feel that in spite of the self-seeking, self-delusion, duplicity, and dissimulation that characterize man's life in society, history in general wears the aspect of a "Human Comedy." There are more than enough reasons not to believe it, Balzac tells us, but men *are* sometimes made better by society. And even though the assertive individual is destroyed by his society more often than not, there are enough instances of men prevailing over their societies to credit the belief that men can change their societies *from time to time.* So too Tocqueville reiterates his conviction that history is no blind alley into which men have been driven by a perverse nature. He sees history as moving ahead by a two-steps-forward, one-step-backward rhythm; and in the end, he feels, human freedom and dignity will prevail.

In their conception of the essentially comic issue of history, then, Balzac and Tocqueville resemble the Historicists Hegel and Ranke and differ from the Romantics. Where they part with the Historicists is in their reluctance to identify progress with the rise or enrichment of any specific institution, class, group, or nation. They are more realistic in their assignment of causal efficacy and benefits in the historical process because they are more pluralistic in their conception of both. In this, they differ not only from the Romantics and Historicists of their own time but from the self-styled "realists" of the later nineteenth century whose "realism" always entailed a monistic reduction of the phenomena of history to the status of function of some more primal, metahistorical ground.

My point, then, is that Romanticism, Historicism, and Realism do resemble each other, and in ways that distinguish them as *early* nineteenth-century cultural movements. Their essential similarity is to be found in their conception of the *kinds* of causal forces operating in the historical field. They differ in virtue of the value-systems by which they assign general human significance to those forces. Thus, for example, we might want to say that a self-consistent Romanticism *recognizes* that history is a field whereon forces that are natural, human, and social meet, interact, and conflict; and that it assigns primary causal efficacy to nature, which it conceives as a dark, overpowering, energic fund. But at the same time, the Romantic *cherishes* and thereby encourages any individual who, against all reason, still tries to transcend the limits of a merely natural existence. Romanticism values social institutions only insofar as it can interpret them as manifestations of arcane natural forces or as expressions of individual human will; on the whole, however, it regards social institutions, ideas, and values as barriers to be overcome, bastions against the free expression of nature and individual human will. Thus, we might say that, for the Romantic, the *hierarchy of causal efficacy* has nature at its apex, and descends from nature through the individual to society; while the *hierarchy of valuation* by which these forces are affirmed or denied runs from the individual, who is most highly cherished, down through nature to society. The characteristic tensions of Romanticism are caused by the conflict between what it perceives reality to be (the apprehended order of causal efficacy in history) and what it wishes were the case (the ideal order of valuation).

We could then go on to say that a self-consistent Historicism regards nature as a neutral or passive force in the determination of specific historical configurations; for the Historicist, nature supplies the "material" or milieu within which individuals and societies arise. Ranke, like Herder, sees social institutions as being continuous with the natural milieu in which they arise; but continuous in a way that a plant is continuous with its environment—the soil, light, and air that sustain it and to which the plant itself contributes and into which it "fits" as a circle "fits" into the space around it with perfect accommodation. So, too, for Hegel the "spirit of a people" is defined as nothing more than the *interaction* of people organized into communities with the nature that sustains them. Nature is not, then, to the Historicist, a primary causal force in history; it is merely a basis or stage upon which history unfolds. The primary active forces are two: men and social institutions, that is, entities endowed with varying orders of consciousness and will, purpose, *telos*. But since individual men come and go, while social forms abide, the Historicist assigns a higher value to the latter than it does to the former. Both Hegel and Ranke find the meaning of history in the growth of human consciousness as it becomes objectified in social, political, and cultural (i.e., collective) forms.

And this is why Historicism lacks the characteristic tensions of Romanticism. For the Historicist, the order of causal efficacy in history *corresponds* to the scale of valuation by which he assigns significance to the historical process: *what is* and *what ought to* are perfectly consonant in every situation he contemplates. This sense of consonance gives to thinkers like Hegel and Ranke an aspect of impunity in the face of every social dislocation and every individual human tragedy. Instead of seeing the agon between the individual and society in tragic terms, as the Romantic tends to do, the Historicist resolves all apparent conflict in history by endowing social forms with a similar but higher order of consciousness to that found in individual men. For the Historicist, every historical conflict has a "comic" issue because consciousness-in-general (*Bewusstsein überhaupt*) inevitably benefits from any expenditure of human energy.

The "realism" of Balzac and Tocqueville resides in their unwillingness to specify a single causal determinant or a single beneficiary for every historical situation. They want to distinguish between different kinds of causal forces, and they want to say that different gains and losses are met with in different epochs of history and in different situations. As for the way in which they affirm or repudiate *what is*, they are pluralists here also. Sometimes they will recognize the validity of nature's claims on men and institutions; at other times, they will dwell with Sophoclean sympathy on some deed suggestive of human nobility; and at still other times, they will confirm the needs of society against both natural exigency and human aspiration.

In sum, early nineteenth-century Realism is not to be differentiated from Romanticism and Historicism either by the kinds of problems that it admits for consideration in its philosophy of history or by the rubric of causal forces that it postulates as underlying the historical process. And it is not to be distinguished from these by its interest in *individual* phenomena per se; this interest in the richness and diversity of phenomena it shares with both Romanticism and Historicism. Realism gathers these phenomena into categories of analysis similar to those utilized by the Romantic and the Historicist. But Realism descends to a level of inquiry that permits it to discriminate between the causal forces at work in specific situations, while Romanticism tends toward monistic reduction of them, on the one side, and Historicism tends toward dialectical reconciliations of them, on the other.

All three movements were progeny of the conflict between Enlightenment ideals and the realities of history revealed by the Revolutionary experience. All of them were especially sensitized to the "demonic" quality of social forces, their intractability by human reason and will, which the Revolution had made manifest. But whereas Romanticism deplored this revelation and Historicism submitted to its implications, Realism tried to assimilate it to what the Enlightenment had revealed about nature, on the one hand, and what Romanticism had revealed about the human psyche, on the other. All of them recognize that this "demonic" quality of society had found expression in the release of new classes onto the stage of world history, and each of them attempted to provide a script to anticipate the role that these new classes would play in the future. And all contributed to the understanding of how the bourgeoisie and the proletariat would actually comport themselves later on. Their differences are shown in the degrees of objectivity that each attained to in its analyses of these new classes. Romanticism vacillated between idolization of the new classes and damnation of them. Historicism accepted the emergence of the bourgeoisie as an accomplished fact and then tried to halt history in place to prevent the release of the class behind it, the proletariat. The great Realists, basically conservative as individuals, tried to distance both the middle and the lower classes and to assign virtues and vices to them with equity. Realism, therefore, rather than Romanticism and Historicism, contributed most to the formation of a genuinely objective social science in the second half of the century.

What gives the aspect of a family to these three cultural movements is their agreement on what constitutes the basic problems of historical description and analysis; they also agree on the ways that reality must be catalogued in order to be comprehended; and they agree as well on the urgency of their analytical tasks. The father of this family was Romanticism: it was the most restive, the most creative, and as it grew older, the most dissatisfied with its own achievement. The first offspring of this rebellious sire, Historicism, was more eager to accommodate itself to the world as given by common experience, less interested in innovation and adventure, a natural inheritor of the family business. Realism, a younger child born to privilege and its accompanying hypersensitivity, tried to combine the aesthetic sensibility of the father with the common-sense wisdom of the older brother. But the legacy that Realism left to European intellectual life was too complex, too sophisticated, for easy assimilation by the generation that grew to manhood in the 1850s. The next generation rebelled against the hard complexity of the Realist worldview and expended its energies in the search for the *single* principle by which all of the diversity of the historical process could be explained. Naturalism, Symbolism, Positivism, Social Darwinism, and Vitalism all sought to reduce the complexity of the Realist worldview to simple formulaic clarity. These form a new family. It was only at the end of the century, after these monisms had been exhausted, that the achievement of Realism was fully recognized. At this time, European intellectuals made a concerted effort to retrieve the complex historical vision that Realism had willed them. Only then did Hegel, Tocqueville, Balzac, and Stendhal come into their own. But by then it was too late. The task of the fourth generation was foreclosure and the tone of its "neo-Realism" elegiac.

CHAPTER FIVE

The Tasks of Intellectual History

{1969}

Intellectual history—the attempt to write the history of consciousness-in-general, rather than discrete histories of, say, politics, society, economic activity, philosophical thought, or literary expression—is comparatively new as a scholarly discipline; but it can lay claim to a long ancestry. It is arguable that intellectual history has its remote origins in the sectarian disputes of ancient philosophers and theologians, who, by constructing "histories" of their opponents' doctrines, sought to expose the interests that had led them into error or to locate the precise point at which they had strayed from the path of truth or righteousness. An especial interest in the history of thought and expression is, of course, characteristic of transitional ages in the lives of cultures; it arises when received traditions in thought and mythic endowments appear to have lost their relevance to current social problems or their presumed coherency, as in the Hellenistic age or the late Middle Ages. During such times, thinkers may try, by means of what is usually called "historical perspective," to gain some purchase on their cultural legacy and to distinguish between "what is living and what is dead" within it.

Karl Mannheim, the sociologist of knowledge, maintained that as long as social stability underwrites belief in the "internal unity" of the world, the "multiplicity of ways of thinking" that conventionally exercises professional philosophers will constitute no real problem for the ordinary intellectual or academic scholar. As long as a dominant social group's way of viewing the world operates sufficiently well to contribute to the maintenance of the group's power, then other, subordinate or recessive groups' ideals and ideas will generally be perceived as mere curiosities, as outright errors, or as heresies to be suppressed—not as possible alternatives; and the intellectual leaders will be little inclined to treat them as objects of serious philosophical or historical investigation. When, however, major social or cultural changes undermine the authority of the dominant group, and thereby bring under question its characteristic worldview, many other thought-systems may begin to appear to a great many people as equally feasible ways of approaching reality. Then thought and the status of thinking can become matters of general social concern rather than the exclusive problem of professional philosophers. At such times, intellectual history, inquiry into the ways men have differently perceived their world in the past, becomes a legitimate, if not compelling, enterprise; and historians, turning from a consideration of what *actually happened* in the past, begin to consider seriously what men in the past *thought was happening* and the ways in which their perceptions of events influenced their responses to the problems confronting them.

In other words, over and above the general interest in the past that characterizes historically oriented cultures such as our own, we can distinguish between professional historians' interest in "history as action" (things done, *res gestae*) and their interest in "history as thought" (man as a feeling, thinking, willing entity, culture as a product of consciousness). And it could be argued that the former tends to predominate in the historiography of ideologically self-confident periods, while the latter comes to the fore in times of cultural stress and social tension. To be sure, interest in the history of thought in itself is not indicative of the onset of a cultural crisis. Self-confident ages such as the Renaissance and the Enlightenment were fascinated by the history of their distinctive forms of ratiocination, and it would be difficult to conceive a humanistic civilization in which the history of thought was not an important scholarly activity. It is only when intellectual history, history *as* thought or history *as* consciousness, begins to supplant history as action as a principal form of historiography—as in Germany at the end of the last century or in France today—that we can legitimately inquire whether a crisis in a social establishment and a loss of nerve in its academic servitors may not be under way. The ideological complementarity of philosophical idealism to social conservatism has been remarked often enough to make it a commonplace. It may well be that intellectual history has the same ideological role in historiography that idealism has in philosophy; and that the advent of one signals the imminence of the other. Intellectual history centers attention on man's highest faculties—his reason, his will, his emotions—but, curiously, it conduces to the kind of pessimism found in Schopenhauer and the kind of reconciliation with things as they are (*rebus sic stantibus*) that one associates with Croce.

The pessimistic and accommodationist tone of intellectual historiography is in part a function of its subject matter. Since human apprehension of the world always outstrips comprehension of it, histories of consciousness would appear fated to come out as stories of human failure in a way that histories of action are not. This fatality they share with their counterpart in the novel, the *Bildungsroman,* or novel of education, in which the full development of the protagonist's faculties is usually paid for by his death or destruction—as in Stendhal's *The Red and the Black* and Mann's *Magic Mountain*. And like the *Bildungsroman*, the tone of intellectual historiography tends toward the elegiac rather than the epical. Only when the protagonists of intellectual histories are abstractions such as Hegel's *Weltgeist* or Croce's *libertà*, rather than the thoughts and aspirations of individual human beings, do they attain to a genuinely heroic stature. This may be because abstractions never die, but like Sophocles' Oedipus or the souls in Dante's Purgatory, always get a second chance.

Histories of consciousness inevitably take on the aspect of chronicles of frustrated hopes, unrealized plans, or unfounded aspirations. Hegel recognized as much when, in both the *Encyclopedia* and the *Aesthetics*, he made histories of thought and art secondary forms of historiography, twice removed from the real world of politics, society, and economics, where in his view tragic aspiration was alone possible. His intuition was sound. Intellectual histories, like histories of philosophy, offer unlimited possibilities for critical second-guessing. It is much easier for the historian to find the flaw in the logic or perceptions of past thinkers than to second-guess men of action who were trying to deal with social, political, or economic affairs, change their fates, or better their conditions.

As historical reading, intellectual history is rather like vicarious sex: neither satisfying nor, ultimately, very helpful as a guide to action. Still, it induces a certain post-coital kind of melancholy. Committed to the notion that consciousness is more interesting than *praxis*, that the way men conceived their world is as instructive as their actions against it, intellectual history substitutes for the color of the marketplace, the battlefield, and the parliament, the odor of the study, the library, and the academic hall. When this odor pervades the historiographical profession of an age or culture, it may not mean that something is dead; but it certainly means that something has changed. It may suggest, as the advent of idealism in philosophy does, that men have become less interested in transforming their world than in enjoying the privileged positions they occupy in it. It may even be that the advent of intellectual history as a predominant form of historiography signals the appearance of times when dominant classes wish to freeze society in its present state or to deny either the possibility or desirability of social change of any sort.

If such is the case, then the conceptual antithesis of intellectual history in historiography is dialectical materialism. And indeed, in the Soviet Union, where dialectical materialism is enthroned as historiographical orthodoxy, there has been very little interest in intellectual history. We need not speculate on whether this situation reflects a felt confidence in the capacity of the Soviet social system to meet whatever challenges its enemies might offer to it or whether it is a result of a general adherence to the Marxian theory that socially significant thought always follows after (and is established by) changes in the modes of production. A dialectical materialist is understandably interested less in what men thought was the case in different times and places than in the relationship between the sociopolitical superstructure and the modes of production. For a consistent dialectical materialist, what men thought was the case is always a function of a perfectly comprehensible relationship between an individual's place in the sociopolitical order and the interest he has in sustaining or changing the current modes of production. This is not to say that he will have no interest in the history of thought at all; it is just that what men think and why they think it is not a *special problem* for him, as it is for anyone without his explanatory system.

As a historian, a dialectical materialist may cherish those individuals who "correctly" foresaw the way history was tending at a particular time and who took a "proper" position on the main social issues of their day. In principle, he should have no difficulty in regarding ideologically burdened thinkers of the past with detachment and even with sympathy, since the reasons for their conscious or unconscious distortions of reality have been rendered transparent by the Marxian analysis of the ubiquity of the class struggle throughout history. But since he possesses what he thinks is a perfect criterion for judging what is "progressive" and what is "reactionary" in any social situation, either past or present, the ways by which men arrive at their views on particular social issue is less interesting to him than what they did to implement those views in the sociopolitical order of their own times, the ways they sustained or changed that order, and the extent to which they dominated or were dominated by it.

This may seem strange: that a dialectical materialistic historiography, which is supposed to presuppose a strict determinism, should be led to concentrate on "history as action." In reality, dialectical materialism views history primarily as process, rather than as either action or thought; but precisely for this reason the Marxist historian is more concerned with the ways in which men *adjust to or dominate* reality than he is with the ways in which men *perceive* reality. It should be remembered that Marx himself often defined the modern task of philosophy to be the transformation, rather than the interpretation, of the world. The key to men's interpretation of the world, he located in the interest they had in supporting or changing the inherited social system. The explanation of their success or failure in these operations Marx saw as residing in the objective possibilities of society as determined by the modes of production at a given time and place. There was, then, nothing problematical about the relationship between thought and social reality for Marx.

Marx's communist successors have, of course, approached the kinds of problems dealt with by Western intellectual historians by way of Lenin's *Materialism and Empiriocriticism* (1908), which has a place in the communist canon as a definitive refutation of "idealism" in all its forms, including neo-Kantianism, and as the final word on the problem of consciousness's relation to external reality. During the 1920s and 1930s a number of Marxist intellectuals tried to go beyond the simplistic ideas contained in this polemical work (Georg Lukács, Karl Korsch, Ernst Bloch, and others). Lukács especially, in his *Geschichte und Klassenbewusstsein* (*History and Class Consciousness*, 1923), tried to insert a Hegelian awareness of the relation between consciousness and praxis into Marxist historiography. Above all, he was concerned to recognize the extent to which literary and philosophical intelligences rose above the limits of consciousness of the class to which they belonged and the capacity of minds that, because of their threatened nature in declining or disintegrating social situations, were driven to perceptions of social reality far superior to those of many self-designated dialectical materialists. Lukács, however, was criticized by Nikolai Bukharin and Grigory Zinoviev, the arbiters of thought in the Communist International, and accused of idealist deviationism; eventually he himself suppressed his book. Nonetheless, the insights contained in it continued to dominate his studies of literary history (*Goethe and his Age*, *Studies in European Realism*, and *The Historical Novel*), in which such bourgeois artists as Goethe and Walter Scott and such "reactionaries" as Balzac are granted a range of vision and profundity of understanding of what he calls "social reality" far beyond anything that conventional Marxists are likely to grant them. Of course, the test of such qualities lies in the extent to which they approached or fell away from Marxist perceptions of history; but the correlations Lukács makes between consciousness and society in the nineteenth century are truly impressive and for the most part convincing in their broad terms.

Lukács's example and above all his theory of historical consciousness as set forth in *History and Class Consciousness* have inspired many contemporary Marxist historians to try to discredit the two principal approaches to intellectual history that flourish outside Marxist circles: a kind of sublimated idealism, on the one hand and, on the other, a kind of Darwinian conception of the history of ideas in which whatever has survived in Western thought is taken to have its own sociological justification and to require no further analysis of its ideological weight in the social struggles of the community under study.

The principal immediate predecessor of contemporary Western intellectual historiography, that *Kulturgeschichte* (cultural history) that arose during the middle decades of the nineteenth century and of which Jacob Burckhardt was the outstanding practitioner, was manifestly reactionary in its political posture. Burckhardt's approach to the subject was impressionistic in method and typological in its manner of presentation, programmatically anti-scientific and self-consciously aestheticist in its desired effects. This aestheticist approach had a scientistic counterpart in the *Geistesgeschichte* of Wilhelm Dilthey, whose principal heirs were Max Weber and Friedrich Meinecke. Dilthey brought to his study of the history of ideas a lingering respect for Positivism, which required him to pay lip service to the ideal of a science of society, based on a combination of sociology, psychology, and Rankean historicism, to which *Geistesgeschichte* was supposed to contribute as the basis for a scientific theory of mind. But like Burckhardt, who vested the motive power of history in an ineffable Schopenhauerian will, Dilthey fell back on the conception of *Erlebnis*, a kind of Germanic *élan vital*, which was incomprehensible in its machinations as it was supposedly fertile in the production of new cultural forms. Both movements reflected a pervasive need in late nineteenth-century thinkers to reassess the main achievements of Western culture in the light of social developments inaugurated by the French Revolution, that is to say, to assess the value of traditional European culture, on the one side, and the relative worth of mass democracy, on the other.

Although both *Kulturgeschichte* and *Geistesgeschichte* have been interpreted as late counterparts of Hegel's phenomenology of mind, in reality they are more understandable as part of the effort mounted by social conservatives to meet the threat presented to them by neo-Positivism in philosophy and by Marxism in politics. The irrationalist conclusions of Burckhardt and Dilthey effectively denied the possibility of a *science* of consciousness. Their efforts to turn thought to the study of consciousness as an independent element of cultural life, worthy of the same consideration as that lavished by earlier historians on political, social, and economic phenomena, had the effect of historicizing consciousness itself, of removing it from the position of dominance that it had enjoyed in Hegel's system, but also of disengaging it from the socioeconomic matrix in which Marx had embedded it in his work. If it also had the effect of undermining the authority that Kant and Auguste Comte had vested in science, by relegating it to the status of one among many possible worldviews, this seemed a small enough price to pay for discrediting Marx's claims for a scientifically sanctioned socialism.

Late nineteenth-century theorists of consciousness—among whom Bergson, Croce, Max Weber, and Emile Durkheim must be numbered—could not agree over the precise nature of that "spirit" they took to be their object of study; but they agreed uniformly over the limited power of science to define reality and the inadequacy of Marxism as a program for changing it. The intellectual histories written by their followers and descendants were uniformly designed to show consciousness's ultimate independence from all mundane concerns, its intrinsically transcendental origin and goal, and its anchorage in some ontological ground beyond or below social phenomena and impervious to reason's power of understanding. This side of contemporary intellectual historiography is properly viewed as part of the general neo-Idealist revival that took place at the beginning of this century, and it has a distinct ideological role even if this has not been the conscious intention of its practitioners. Above all, most of contemporary non-Marxist Western intellectual historiography has given up the attempt to define precisely the relation between consciousness and society. Underlying much of it is the tacit conviction that the decisive factor in this relation is one of structural similarity rather than causal connection. Thought and action are conceived to exist in a relationship of what Wilhelm Windelband called *Zusammengehörigkeit* (which is perhaps best translated as "mutual implicativeness"). The rule of *adequatio rei intellectus* undergirds most of this historiography; thought is conceived to be always adequate to its object, and the Marxist problem of "false consciousness" is not permitted to arise at all. Whence the essentially encyclopedic, typological, or (to use a term borrowed from cultural anthropology) "synchronic" character of much of the best Western intellectual historiography.

The work of three recognized masters of intellectual history may be noted by way of example: that of Ernst Cassirer, Johan Huizinga, and A. O. Lovejoy. Their organizational principles are uniformly typological: the "modes of thought" of Cassirer, the "forms of thought and expression" of Huizinga, and the "unit-ideas" of Lovejoy. All three specialized in the study of great, global trends or epochs; but on the whole they avoided the problem of intellectual historical dynamics. They tended to view the history of consciousness as an intramural or domestic affair within consciousness itself. They did generalize from their intellectual or cultural historical data to wider, cataclysmic transformations of consciousness—such as the emergence of *logos* out of *mythos* (Cassirer), one major idea-set such as Evolutionism out of another such as the Chain of Being (Lovejoy), or the modern cultural "game" out of the medieval "game." Of the three, only Huizinga was interested in the relation between ideas and socioeconomic structures, and then only because of what he believed to be the ludic capacities of human beings to ignore or to override their imperatives. Like Cassirer and Lovejoy, Huizinga was fascinated by consciousness's capacity for self-transcendence; and while he did not specialize in the construction of genealogies of thought, as Cassirer and especially Lovejoy did, it was the continuities of consciousness rather than its disjunctions and transformations that commanded his attention as a scholar.

Outside of Marxist circles the only serious challenge to the approach to intellectual history practiced by Cassirer, Lovejoy, and Huizinga has been that deriving from the impact of psychoanalysis on literary history. Lionel Trilling, Northrop Frye, Stephen Marcus, Noel Annan, Leslie Fiedler, and many others have successfully utilized psychoanalytical (Freudian, Jungian, and post-Freudian) insights in their efforts to explicate texts and to link them to the cultural experiences of the groups in which they arise. In addition, the works of a classicist, Norman O. Brown, and a practicing psychiatrist, Erik Erikson, have enjoyed a certain "underground" vogue among the younger historians of the current generation. But although the work of historians trying to utilize depth-psychological concepts, such as Philippe Ariès and Peter Laslett, has generally been accorded an open hearing among professional historians on both sides of the Atlantic, psychoanalysis as an instrument of intellectual historiography remains generally suspect. Most historians resent what they regard as the "reductionist" tactics of the Freudians as much as they fear the same tactics in the Marxists. They seem equally "monistic" to a profession that has never had a firmly consolidated explanatory theory or a single, uniformly agreed upon canon of causal laws.

History has always attracted the eclectically minded, and its professionally recognized achievements have generally been products of many explanatory models rather than of monolithically consistent systems of theories. Epistemologically and methodologically, the professionals have remained captive of a pre-Newtonian (more specifically, Baconian) conception of the scientific side of their work and of a pre-Symbolist (that is, Realist) conception of its proper form of representation. While recognizing intellectual history as a possible field of specialization, therefore, the profession has on the whole admitted only an extension of its conventional objects of study, not a change in methods. Instead of chartularies, diplomata, diaries, state papers, and business records, the intellectual historian concentrates on philosophical and religious works, artistic and literary monuments, and social and political tracts—and wherever it seems profitable, biographical and social-historical materials that might contribute to some oblique illumination of why it was that certain works appeared or became popular when and where they did. For the professionally recognized intellectual historian, the task has remained—as it was for Ranke—the reconstruction of the past "as it really was," the past being the intellectual, or spiritual, tone of an age rather than its political or social institutions.

The attempt to provide a comprehensive picture of the "climate of opinion" or "intellectual concerns and achievements" of the past has inevitably led historians into fields where specialists in, say, the history of philosophy or the history of literature, have already staked out claims and mined the ore to be found there in their own ways. And it has led to charges of amateurism and philistinism against intellectual historians who have no training in a conventional discipline but claim only a knowledge of history-in-general. The charge of philistinism is usually directed against the efforts of historians to "reduce" a datum in one area of intellectual endeavor to a "reflection" of an accomplishment in some other area, as when, for example, a poem of Milton and a painting by Rembrandt are seen as manifestations of a worldview having its most perfect expression in a scientific tract by Leibniz. Similar resistance has met the conventional intellectual historian's proclivity for analogies and superficial similarities, the explanatory value of which appears problematical at best.

Defenders of intellectual history as a special field of historiography usually reply that the historian is preeminently a generalist, a synthesizer, or a coordinator of findings in many different fields, and that he properly tries to provide "the general picture" that inevitably gets lost in the construction of many specialized studies. This defense loses in persuasiveness, however, the more professional philosophers succeed in exposing the conventionalist nature of most historical explanations and the virtual impossibility of ever arriving at anything like scientific rigor in historical representation. It is also weakened by the fact that specialists in literary or philosophical history (such as Erich Auerbach and J. H. Randall) have apparently found it easier to utilize the work of historians in the construction of their specialized histories than historians have to confiscate the work of specialists in literature and philosophy in constructing their "general pictures" of the "spiritual climates" of ages and groups. The exception to these generalizations is to be found in the work of those intellectual historians who have concerned themselves with the history of social and political thought. Here their specialized knowledge of the social and political institutions of the ages they study has paid off in a host of monographs and general studies that show a commendable synthetic power and representational fullness. And of course, historians trained in the more philologically oriented fields of study, such as classical, medieval, Byzantine, Islamic, and Renaissance studies have been forced—both by the nature of their documents and their philological interests—to give more attention to intellectual history for a longer time than their counterparts in modern and contemporary historical studies; and they have shown a correspondingly greater power of synthesis as a result. For the modern period, however, the most fruitful work in intellectual history has been done by nonhistorians, those trained in philosophy, literature, or art, rather than by historians as such.

The reasons for this situation are not far to seek. The specialist in a discrete field of intellectual work can move out into contiguous areas guided by the particular problems arising within his own area of competence. He can use studies of the sociopolitical milieu selectively and merely point to those areas of the milieu illuminated by his findings rather than try to construct a comprehensive "picture" of the entire age, culture, or group under study. The general historian, by contrast, must appeal to some theory of connection by which the various spiritual manifestations of an age can be brought into relationship with the institutional and customary comportment of the age, an appeal that he is reluctant to make, *given the essentially antitheoretical bias that prevails in the profession at large.* Moreover, it is relatively easy (it is at least conventional) to derive from what men did the possible reasons they had for doing it; it is much more difficult to derive, from a consideration of what the leading intellectuals of an age were thinking, the rationale behind the actions of ordinary men. The former tactic can at least make appeal to common sense or human nature or some such fiction sanctioned by ordinary usage; the latter requires, first, the construction of the general thought patterns of an age, and then, the derivation of the actions of the men of that age from the patterns thus postulated. Marxism or some form of sociological determinism has the advantage here, for in the conviction that the course of ideas must follow the course of institutions (as Vico put it), it has a rule for making the necessary transitions between thought and action. But "sociologism" has become as much a *bête noire* to the professional historian as Marxism, with the result that he has been forced into a kind of diluted idealist conception of the history of ideas that lacks both the vigor and clarity of its Hegelian variety, and with which he is equally ill at ease.

Whether he likes it or not, the intellectual historian is forced to decide whether the thought of an age illuminates the action, or the reverse. Of course, one need not choose monolithically between the two alternatives, but unless he fails to make the choice *pari passu* in the construction of his narratives, the historian runs the risk of excessive ambiguity or equivocation of judgment. As a specialized subbranch of history-in-general, intellectual historiography must have some criterion for determining which data can be constituted as evidence and which can be eliminated. Yet, the more general the criterion, the flabbier the resulting narrative; the more specific the criterion, the more idiosyncratic the product.

Those intellectual histories that have come under the most severe attack at the hands of the professional historians are those that claim to represent the general spirit or dominant worldview of a whole culture, such as the Hellenic, or a whole age, such as the Renaissance. For every intellectual history purporting to establish the essentially humanistic bases of Greek civilization, there are fifty general historians prepared to document evidences of its essential theism. And so too for the Renaissance, the Baroque, the Enlightenment; for concepts such as Mannerism, Idealism, and Romanticism; or for an emotive atmosphere, such as the "optimism" of the Enlightenment or the "pessimism" of the late Roman Empire. Intellectual historiography seems to progress by the conflict between specialized monographers and general synthesizers, just as other branches of historiography do; but it seems more prone to controversy, because its categories touch, not only upon the "essences" of different ages and groups, but upon the "essence" of human nature as well, in a way that social, political, and even economic history do not. This is perhaps why some of the best work in contemporary intellectual history has been done by specialists in the histories of art, science, and literature, who have availed themselves of the late developments in experimental psychology and, above all, of the learning theory of the Gestalt, or structuralist, school.

The achievements of E. H. Gombrich, Thomas Kuhn, and Lucien Goldmann in the history of art, the history of science, and the history of literature respectively may be cited as examples of this new trend. The work of Gombrich and Kuhn is especially interesting for its wealth of mesoscopic generalizations, the kind that are productive of new questions and suggestive of new lines of research. In their general approach, both tend to be somewhat more "Popperian" in their conceptions of what history can accomplish than Goldmann who, although he is a student of Jean Piaget, is still given to more grandiose, Hegelian and Marxian generalization than Anglo-American scholars are inclined to tolerate. Still, Goldmann is a major figure in intellectual historiography, and his work gives hope of the development of a revised Marxist approach to the subject that may be able to deal with problems that Gombrich and Kuhn leave untouched, or touch upon only in passing.

Gombrich and Kuhn have studied what is really a common Western intellectual tradition: the attempt to "represent reality *realistically*," that is, empirically and in sets of coordinated conceptual systems that have built-in criteria for their disconfirmation and successive revision and evolution. The essence of Western art for Gombrich and of Western science for Kuhn is to be found in the intrinsically unstable relationship between the "making" and "matching" aspects of consciousness's response to its milieu. Gombrich stresses the interplay between received conventions of pictorial "encodation" and the impulse of the artist-genius to contrive new systems of encodation and to impose them on his public. Kuhn is concerned with the ways by which the "normal science" of an age or generation becomes progressively exfoliated in specialized areas of research, through the necessity of dealing with the "anomalous cases" turned up in experiments, and the aggregation of a set of such cases that requires abandonment of the worldview (or "paradigm") authorizing the "normal science," causing a "scientific revolution" thereby.

Both Gombrich and Kuhn make appeal to the model of the binary computer, with the feedback mechanism that requires that each successive "matching" of a picture of the world-reality be followed by yet another "making" of the picture. The "remaking" is, in Gombrich's theory, the occasion for the production of a new artistic style; for Kuhn, it is the occasion for the creation of a new discipline and a qualification of the theoretical canon sanctioned by the established "paradigm" or worldview. Moreover, for both of these historians, genuine revolutions in sensibility—such as the creation of realism in Greek art, or the Copernican-Newtonian synthesis in the seventeenth century—are results of an overloading of a received mechanism of encodation beyond its capacity to function at all. The overloading gives rise to what amounts in Kuhn's metaphor to a quantum-leap in sensibility, in which the "anomalous cases" of the old "normal science" are taken as primary data in the constitution of a new "paradigm" and with it a new "normal science." Such a reversal or inversion took place in science in the seventeenth and again in the early twentieth century, Kuhn argues; and such a reversal seems to be occurring in contemporary art, according to Gombrich.

The important contribution of these theories lies less in their designation of when a "revolution" in sensibility occurs than in the kind of research tasks they suggest to other workers in their fields. Instead of leading *out*, to general questions of the world-historical course of human consciousness or the nature and destiny of man, as the older idealistic conceptions of intellectual history do, Gombrich's and Kuhn's approach leads *into* the subject, to concentration on the relations between theories and procedures within specific disciplines and stylistic conventions and to the dynamic interaction and mutual influences of conflicting thought-styles. By focusing study on the relationship between theory and practical applications of thought-styles, Gombrich and Kuhn direct research away from the construction of genealogies of ideas alone and toward the development of sophisticated sociologies, psychologies, and anthropologies of consciousness in its concrete manifestations and dynamic historical dimensions. Their approach can be applied to the various branches of intellectual history conventionally pervaded by ideological preconceptions, such as political, economic, and social thought, and even, though with somewhat more difficulty, to the history of philosophy and religion.

This decision to concentrate on the production of mesoscopic generalizations in intellectual history does have a price, however; and it is paid for by the manifest incapacity of the method to deal with the great, cataclysmic shifts in worldview that are the main inspiration for undertaking intellectual historical study in the first place. The fact that Gombrich can account for the crystallization of the stylistic tradition he studies only by an appeal to a Greek "miracle" and that Kuhn is forced to fall back upon a mysterious quantum-leap in sensibility to explain what happens in a scientific revolution marks the limits of their approach. Of course, their acceptance of the limitations of their approach may only signal their recognition that no approach can deal with all problems and their desire to halt intellectual history somewhere short of the metaphysical speculations that all too often give it the coloration of ideological special pleading. But a Marxist could argue that this apparent modesty and good sense are nothing but a kind of special pleading of its own, a reflection of bourgeois reluctance to link the history of ideas to the socioeconomic infrastructures that alone make understanding of transitions *across* different epochs and traditions possible.

Such in fact has been the charge raised against both the older idealistic conception of history of ideas and the new anti-sociological French school of structuralism by neo-Marxists such as Henri Lefebvre and Lucien Goldmann. Both of these thinkers have developed theories of intellectual history within the context of and against the prevailing structuralist historiography that took shape in France between the World Wars, that was inspired by the historians Marc Bloch and Lucien Febvre, that has found theoretical defense from the anthropologist Claude Lévi-Strauss, and that has been represented by the contributors to the journal *Annales* (the organ of the VIth Section of the *Ecole Pratique des Hautes Etudes* in Paris, directed by Fernand Braudel) as well as by the literary historian Roland Barthes and the psychologist-historian Michel Foucault.

Marc Bloch and Lucien Febvre represented a movement to integrate all of the social sciences under the rule of a programmatically eclectic historicism in such a way as to allow the reconstruction of the flavor, the fabric of consciousness and action, which gave to specific past ages a unique lifestyle. Lucien Febvre led the way in intellectual history with his *Le problème de l'incroyance au XVIe siècle: La religion de Rabelais* (1942). The third part of this work was devoted, in the words of Braudel, his student, to "the 'mental apparatus' of the period—the words, the feelings, the concepts that are the infrastructure of the thought of the century, the basis on which everything was constructed or could be constructed, and which may have prevented certain things from being constructed." This approach has been cited by Lévi-Strauss as one of the inspirations of structural anthropology, an anthropology that all but ignores what it calls the "diachronic" (or developmental) aspects of society in the interest of constructing a "synchronic" picture of the channels through which human comportment runs and the structures it creates in all of its forms of expression. The emphasis placed on "the words, the feelings, the concepts" that are conceived to be, in Braudel's words, "the infrastructure of the thought of the century," has driven the followers of this school to structural linguistics (as developed by Ferdinand de Saussure, Roman Jakobson, and others) for models to suggest lines of research and metaphors for presenting their findings. The resulting searches for "significative" structures, structures of meaning and relationship, that give to a thinker, a group, an age, or a whole culture a distinctive lifestyle, have resulted in the imaginative and influential products of Michel Foucault and Roland Barthes.

Foucault's *Histoire de la folie à l'âge classique* (*Madness and Civilization*, 1961) and *Les mots et les choses: Une archéologie des sciences humaines* (*The Order of Things: An Archeology of the Human Sciences*, 1966) and Barthes's *Michelet par lui-même* (1954) and *Sur Racine* (1960) are less histories of thought or even of practices than virtuoso "readings" of the relevant established documents in the effort to see how far one can utilize Marx, Freud, Sartre, Hegel, Durkheim, and most anyone else the historian happens to be acquainted with, in the "unearthing" of the "structures" that make specific styles of thought and action possible. These are genuinely "underground" histories of thought or sensibility, owing as much to the example of Nietzsche's *Genealogy of Morals* as to anything; that is to say, they are searches for the kind of psychological data that gets obscured in repression in the hope of piercing through or uncovering the "lived reality" of which formal thought and expression are only sublimations.

In his *Histoire de la folie*, Foucault examines attitudes toward sanity and the insane as a way of determining what the "age of reason" *really meant* when it characterized itself as such. The positive content of the terms "sanity" and "reason" in the classical age is provided only by an account of the age's designation of what was "insanity" and "unreason"—and, above all, by the way that the self-designated "sane" treated the insane. But Foucault is not writing institutional history either; he contributes nothing new to our knowledge of how the insane, the indigent, and the criminally deviant were incarcerated. His interest is in the "structure" of "confinement" in all its manifestations; and he finds a common structure perduring in the history of Western man from the late seventeenth through the early twentieth century. This structure was marked by a kind of "communication" between the confined and the confiners throughout all the changes that took place in the definitions of what or who was insane during that time, and which has disappeared, in his view, in the totalitarian atmosphere of the twentieth century.

Barthes uses the same approach on the biographical level in his study of Michelet, whom he characterizes as "un réseau organisé d'obsessions" (an organized network of obsessions). The format of the work is itself important, even though it was dictated in part by the format of the series, "Ecrivains de toujours," to which it was a contribution. There is no narrative line attempted at all; rather, relevant texts from Michelet's writings are brought together under structural rubrics: "Michelet mangeur d'histoire," "Mort-sommeil et mort-soleil," "Fleur de sang," "L'Ultra-sexe," and so on, each with further structural subdivisions, and each preceded by Barthes's remarks on the relation of one structural set to another. One purpose is to show that there is a structural *continuity* throughout Michelet's lifetime, a continuity that is provided by psychological obsessions rather than by conscious thought; the thought achieves its unique form by the relationship obtaining between the structures. The advantages of this approach are impressive; it permits the linking up of Michelet's historiographical works with his nonhistoriographical activities—especially his essays on botany and zoology, which have hitherto found no place in historians' studies of him—in shared structures of signification; and it allows Barthes to account for Michelet's original popularity and later obscurity by an original convergence and subsequent divergence of his and his publics' "obsessions." To be sure, this kind of intellectual history has been criticized as overly *précieux* and modishly responsive to Parisian intellectual fads, as irresponsible with respect to the texts and the academic scholarship on the subjects dealt with, and, above all, as sharing the same "synchronic" bias as Lévi-Strauss's studies of primitive cultures (as in *La pensée sauvage* [*The Savage Mind*]). The attack has been mounted from the academic right as well as from the Marxist left. But the approach has found favor in the powerful *Annales* coterie and gives evidence of rising rather than falling in the immediate future.

The intellectual historian who has spanned the gap between the "synchronic" and the "diachronic" structuralists is Lucien Goldmann, a student of Piaget, a historian of philosophy and literature, and a Marxist of the Hegelian (or, more precisely, early Lukácsian) persuasion. Goldmann's work ranges over the whole of Western thought and expression from the seventeenth century (on Pascal and Racine) through the twentieth (on André Malraux). He calls his approach "genetic structuralism" to distinguish it from the ahistorical varieties noted above. The problem of intellectual history, as Goldmann sees it, is to treat major literary and philosophical creations, not in terms of their *contents* (since here the artist or thinker is able to exercise the greatest freedom of choice), but in terms of the "structures of the world of the work" that are "homologous with the mental structures of certain social groups." The group, Goldmann maintains, "constitutes a process of structuration that elaborates in the consciousness of its members affective, intellectual, and practical tendencies towards a coherent response to the problems presented by their relations with nature and their inter-human relations."[1]

The mental categories here postulated exist, Goldmann argues, only in a vague and incompletely formulated way in the group as a whole, achieving a rigorous coherency only in the work of the most advanced thinkers and writers; these create an "imaginary world" the structure of which "corresponds" to that "towards which the whole group tends." The problem, therefore, is to determine the "constituent elements" of the "imaginary worlds" of the writers of an age and to indicate the social groups to which these worlds relate by structural homology.

The important point is that the work of any given thinker or writer is not significantly illuminated by his relation to the "age" in general, although the discovery of generally shared ideas and problems is a necessary basis for further analysis. Nor is any "reflective" conception of intellectual activity, which searches for a "representation" of historical data in the work under study, adequate to the task of relating a thinker to his age and, *what is just as important*, to subsequent ages in the culture to which the thinker belongs. This can only be done by working *from* the most intimate knowledge of the texts constituting the thinker's corpus, *through* biographical information, *to* ever widening circles of social involvement, in such a way as to explain all of the "facts" agreed upon by the specialists working in the field. The method to be used for this operation Goldmann calls "successive approximation," by which a work is inserted in a totality of experience in which the object and its milieu are related both "comprehensively" and "explicatively." That is to say, the elucidation of a distinctive structure of an intellectual creation "constitutes a process of *comprehension* when its insertion into a larger structure is, in regard to it, a process of *explication*." And by way of example as to how this operation proceeds, Goldmann offers his own epoch-making work: *Le dieu caché: Etude sur la vision tragique dans les* Pensées *de Pascal et dans le théâtre de Racine* (*The Hidden God: A Study of Tragic Vision in the* Pensées *of Pascal and the Tragedies of Racine*, 1955).

In *Le dieu caché* the analysis of the shared "tragic structure" of Pascal's thought and Racine's drama is viewed as an operation of "comprehension," which appears to correspond to the *Verstehen*-technique of German sociology or the New Criticism in literary studies. The "explication" of this tragic structure is achieved by its "insertion" into the history of radical Jansenism in seventeenth-century France— the construction of this history being a "comprehensive," that is to say, conventional historiographical, operation. The insertion of radical Jansenism into the history of Jansenism in general, by the revelation of their structural homology, is an "explication" of the former and a "comprehension" of the latter. And so on, in increasingly wider circles of social existence, from Jansenism to its place in the history of the seventeenth-century *noblesse de robe*, from the *noblesse de robe* to its place in the history of the French aristocracy, and from the French aristocracy to the history of French society as a whole in the age under study. The important point for Goldmann is that research should expand outward, *from* the texts *to* the social groups to which they are structurally homologous, rather than inwardly, *from* the texts *to* the psychoanalytic investigation of their authors. The tactic is sociological, and specifically Marxist, but Goldmann's Marxism is of the Hegelian variety of the early Lukács, which means that he is sensitive to the enormous variations in consciousness met with in different writers and thinkers and to the possibilities of clear perceptions of reality in reactionary, no less than in progressive, thinkers. He does not pretend that class origin or allegiance explains everything in the texts, nor is he interested in "explaining away" the genius of those who opposed the values for which Marxism militates. On the contrary, he explains the marvelous diversity of French thought and letters in the late seventeenth century by the fact that, for a while, the monarchy stood above, and mediated between, the various classes, representing no one of them exclusively; this, in Goldmann's view, provided the objective conditions within which thinkers and writers of all the different classes could give full and open expression to the visions of the world, the "*univers imaginaires*," aspired to individually by them. Taken all in all, Goldmann's work is a hopeful sign of a revival of interest in intellectual history by Marxist scholars and evidence of a continuation of that interest in the history of consciousness that flowered, only to be crushed, just after World War I. And in my opinion, it offers the best suggestions for dealing with those cataclysmic transformations—those revolutions in sensibility—that the structuralism of Gombrich and Kuhn, on the one side, and of Foucault, Barthes, and the *Annales* group, on the other, have avoided trying to analyze in any sociologically significant way.

Any attempt to assess the objective scholarly value and future of intellectual historiography as a special field of study—different from but inclusive of philosophy, literary history, the histories of art, science, and religious thought—must necessarily be subjective and, within the limits of this paper, seemingly unfair. I have already indicated my own feeling that an especial interest in intellectual history reflects a more general crisis, either in humanistic scholarship or in society as a whole; and I am certain that its current vogue will continue for as long as the present "Hellenistic" mood persists as a dominant feeling among Western scholars and intellectuals. There are hopeful signs that intellectual history may yet be able to provide that "synthetic picture" of the "spiritual climate" of an age, or a group, or a whole culture that its practitioners have claimed to provide in the past. But it will be able to do this only by abandoning the older forms of historiography inherited in their crude forms from the main scholarly traditions of the nineteenth century. Neither Hegelian idealism, Rankean empiricism, Comtean positivism, nor Marxian sociologism in their nineteenth-century forms has been able to provide the methodological rules leading to an intellectual historiography satisfactory to professional historians in the conventional fields of study. It may well be that general histories of thought, or ideas, or of consciousness will never gain the acceptance among professional historians that they have enjoyed among intellectuals in general. But if intellectual historiography is to deliver what it has promised for so long, it will do so only by following out the twofold path marked for it by scholars like Gombrich and Kuhn, on the one side, and engaged social theorists like Goldmann, on the other. Their work avoids the pitfalls of metaphysics as well as the arid deserts of simple chronicle and genealogy. Rather than being opposed, they are complementary of one another. Gombrich and Kuhn have given us models of how to write the histories of genres, styles, and disciplines; Goldmann shows us how to unite them on the broader canvases provided by social, political, and economic historians. If professional historians can purge themselves of the rage that seems to arise in them every time the name of Marx makes its appearance, intellectual historiography may well gain that "grounding in social reality" that it has long lacked and that Goldmann has shown us how to win.

CHAPTER SIX

The Culture of Criticism

Gombrich, Auerbach, Popper

{1971}

The disciplines that constitute the central core of the humanities—history, literary and art criticism, and philosophy—are as old as the subject matter they investigate. But the humanities conceived as a distinct area of study, with their unique aims, methods, and cultural function, have existed only since the Renaissance. At that time the humanities became disengaged from what might be called the divinities, just as various forms of social practice, such as politics and economic activity, became liberated from the religious restraints formerly placed upon them during the Middle Ages. It was only after the Renaissance that scholars could openly give themselves over to the study of cultural artifacts as specifically *human* creations and suppress the impulse, as old as thought itself, to view everything in the world as a mere epiphenomenon of more basic metaphysical and religious realities. The residues of the original religious loyalties lingered on far into the modern period, but by the middle of the nineteenth century, the theoretical bases for the complete demystification of the world had been worked out, and sufficient reasons had been articulated for belief in the human origins of everything in the world that was not a part of the natural order. History, criticism, and philosophy could therefore proceed to the task of secularizing culture in a radical way, that is to say, by finding the root of every cultural artifact in human reason, will, or imagination alone, without having to postulate the existence of any noumenal ground by reference to which every putatively "spiritual" creation was to be "explained."

The humanities played a crucial role in the global process of demystification of culture, which culminated in the foundation, at the end of the nineteenth century, of the social sciences. But their participation in this process obscured the essentially conservative nature of their characteristic operations. For although the humanities shared with the embryonic social sciences a common a- or anti-religious attitude, so too were they anti-Utopian in their inherent political orientation. As students of the products of human thought, reason, and will, humanists were deeply suspicious of the Utopian visions that often underlay and authorized a given artist's or thinker's impulse to bring under question the world as given in the current social dispensation. It was this opposition to the dream in the name of which men dared to demand something better than the hand dealt them by genetic or social forces that appeared in the humanists' claim to stand as mediators between the powers engaged in the social and cultural drama. Humanists defined their cultural roles as custodial and critical; their task, as they saw it, was to mediate between the old and the new, between "life" and "thought," between the "imagination" and "reality," between the producers of culture, on the one side, and the consumers of culture, on the other—in a word, between genius and the publics that genius sought to order, direct, and fashion after its own Utopian visions.

By the end of the nineteenth century, the humanists had blocked out a special preserve of their own, located somewhere between the position occupied by religious rebels like Martin Luther and Girolamo Savonarola and that held by radical secularists like Machiavelli and Hobbes. Their patron saint was of course Erasmus, and after him Montaigne, men whose personal integrity was assured by the attitude of irony that allowed them to see all sides of every question but in the end to bow to authority in the public sphere as the sole alternative to anarchy. This ironic attitude was elevated into a value under the name of "detachment," which dissolved the tensions created by a sense of membership in the common humanity, on the one side, and a sense of belonging to an elite group, on the other. This ideal of detachment was then, in turn, retrospectively justified by the pretended discovery of an indissoluble tension between the realm of culture and that of society. Thus the humanists characteristically took their stand on a middle ground between "art" and "life," between *ethos* and *kratos*, and took refuge in their own Utopian dream, which they called by the name "autonomy of culture." Thus, for example, that late Erasmian and master of irony, Northrop Frye, draws a distinction between two kinds of criticism—one "historical," which always "related culture only to the past," and the other "ethical," which "relates only to the future"—only to dissolve their differences in commitment to that "liberty" that must begin with "an immediate and present guarantee of the autonomy of culture."

As I see it, the so-called crisis in the humanities about which we hear so much these days stems from the realization on the part of humanists that this "autonomy of culture" is under attack, not only from the political Left and the political Right, but also from within culture itself, from those artists and thinkers whose creative activity supposedly requires that autonomy as its necessary precondition. From both the extreme Left and the extreme Right of the political spectrum come recurrent demands for an art, science, and philosophy that are engaged, relevant, or, more generally, "socially responsible." The conventional claim to detachment in scholarship, the ideal of an intelligentsia that is "free-floating," the concept of the "disinterested" scientist, and the idea of an art for art's sake—all these have lately been criticized as mere means of defending privileges of specific social groups. Much of modern art is created precisely out of a need to destroy the distinction between art and life, just as much of modern social thought is directed at the dissolution of the distinction, formerly believed to be inevitable and ineluctable, between social thought and social practice. The rise of a mass audience for both art and thought, an audience that is greater in numbers and power than anything previously known to historical experience, an audience created by mass education and sustained by mass media, has created a demand for a new kind of culture. The consumers of this new culture deny the claim to extraordinary authority in the determination of what may count as legitimate art or thought; they question the necessity of a special group of scholars whose specific task is to exercise custodial and critical functions for an audience that views its own opinions as authoritative in matters of thought and expression, no less than in matters of social practice.

Call this new public whatever you wish: pop, youth, body, drug, or nonlinear—the fact is that it constitutes a large, rich, and increasingly powerful constituency that shares with the avant-garde artist a distrust of the very category of the artistic, and with the Utopian radical thinker an indifference to the benefits of historical consciousness as we have cultivated it up to now. This means that by virtue of this new public's dedication to the cult of the casual, the immediate, the transitory, the unstructured, and the aleatory, the avant-garde has an important new ally in its traditional attack upon the critical and custodial operations of the humanities. Thus the sense of crisis in the humanities, the sense of being in a revolutionary situation, is more than justified: humanists have to face the prospect of a foreclosure on their most highly valued operations. Small wonder that, in spite of all the evidence to the contrary, humanists should suddenly appear as the most eloquent defenders of the notion that, not only is a real revolution in culture and society undesirable, it is impossible as well.

The humanities are divided today, among themselves as well as between themselves and the avant-garde in art and thought, over whether the cultural upheaval we are witnessing throughout the world is revolutionary or not, and if it is, whether the revolution represents a progressive or retrogressive force in civilization. Creative artists and social radicals have no doubt about the desirability of a revolution and are convinced that whatever comes out of it will be better than what is replaced. Some sociologists regard pop culture as a revolutionary movement, the first genuinely mass cultural movement in human history, with potentialities for creative development every bit as strong as its potentialities for destruction. Marshall McLuhan has given popularity to the idea, setting pop culture within the larger context of a dialectic between culture and electronic technology and supporting the belief that the revolution in culture heralds the advent of a new kind of consciousness necessary to the creation of a new kind of community. And even within the humanities there are avant-gardists, or at least liberals, who, in their devotion to the principle of creativity, are willing to encourage both the avant-garde and its pop audience in their work of clearing the boards of traditional forms—not because they believe the boards can actually be cleared and a true nonformalist cultural convention can be realized, but because they recognize that the avant-garde, from the early nineteenth century at least, has always declared itself against art and literature as a preparation for the articulation of its own vision, which can always be seen, after the fact, as a further development of, rather than a radical break with, what had come before.

But in general these liberal critics do not constitute a majority in the humanities, and their ranks have dwindled as the revolution has intensified or at least as it has moved out of the coffeehouses into the universities. The liberal critics have tended to join the larger group of traditionalists in the humanities, who have stood firm against the contemporary avant-garde and, even while continuing to study them, have consistently denied that the current radicalism in art and social thought can have anything but a harmful effect on civilization.

An impressive tradition of criticism has thus taken shape during the last generation, inspired as much by its experience and fear of totalitarianism as by its dedication to traditional humanistic culture; the representatives of this critical tradition are E. H. Gombrich in art theory, Erich Auerbach in literary history and criticism, and Karl Popper in what I shall call scientific criticism. They do not constitute a formal school, but their influence is pervasive throughout the humanities, and anyone working in any of the fields they have tilled cannot avoid coming to terms with them. They represent the best work of the last generation on that ground between cultural and social criticism which, it seems to me, the humanities are indentured to occupy in the times in which we live.

This tradition of criticism and historical analysis represents an attempt to provide a definitive defense of naturalistic realism in Western art and literature and to maintain the vital historical link between realistic art, liberal-humanitarian social principles, and humanistic ethics. Its defense of realism as an artistic and literary equivalent of those values that have made progressive development possible in Western culture, in contrast to the stagnancy of non-Western archaic cultures, is so well argued and so oppressively documented that consideration of it may help to illuminate the specific nature of the current avant-garde's revolutionary posture and the nature of the resistance to that revolution that is contributing to the sense of crisis in the humanities at the present time. For the defenders of realism see, as the avant-garde itself sees, that much more is involved in the current cultural revolution than an assault upon tradition, or perception, or reason, or even book culture. The revolution includes such an assault, but it goes much deeper than this. For it also includes an attack upon what is increasingly recognized as the idea that binds realism in the arts to liberalism in society and to progressive developments in science—that is to say, the idea of fictive truth, the notion of a twilight realm between absolute conceptual certitude, on the one side, and the chaos of unprocessed sense data, on the other, that sense of provisional certitude that makes the *orderly* and *incremental* development of our knowledge of reality possible. What the avant-garde in art and the radical Utopians' social thought bring under attack is the concept of the fictitious; and it is this aspect of their attack that makes them so much more radical than the avant-gardists and revolutionaries in times past.

The avant-garde is not simply opposing traditional forms, whether the emphasis is placed on the word *traditional* or on the word *forms*. The avant-gardists themselves say they represent, not a revision of the old—and they insist that they will not be assimilated to it—but a radically new kind of cultural and social experience, one that permits them to believe that the gap between the possible and the real, the gap where fiction has thrived heretofore, can at last be closed. This Utopian dream they justify by appeal to a material situation in which the condition of scarcity, which has hitherto driven artists and visionaries back finally to some compromise with the notion of a fractured humanity, no longer has to be viewed as an inevitable condition for mankind and hence is no longer an ineluctable limitation on cultural creativity and innovation.

This sense of a new material ground for culture and society is reflected in the language of rebellion against both culture and society itself, not in their present incarnations only, but as specific forms of human relationship. Radical writers speak of a literature directed at the dissolution of language; their painters create self-destructive art objects; their dramatists dream of a theater without dialogue; their choreographers envisage a dance without gestures; their composers conceive of a music without sound; and their social commentators speak of the possibility at last of a genuine transcendence of historical existence and the advent of apocalypse, the dissolution of society in the interest of community. Everywhere we find the advocacy of the worth of the casual over the contrived, the bodily over the mental; the triumph of the gestural, the graphic, the random, the aleatory, as against the verbal and structural, and so on.

The will to formlessness. Does it also herald the advent of chaos? Is it—as Buckminster Fuller puts it—an earnest of Utopia or an intimation of Armageddon? The old guard in the humanities knows that more is involved in the avant-garde's attack upon form than a simple artistic or intellectual experiment; for them, what is involved is the fate of progressive civilization itself. They are inclined to see the recognized pioneers of contemporary art and thought, from Picasso to Robert Rauschenberg, Schoenberg to John Cage, Artaud to Alain Resnais, Joyce to Nathalie Sarraute, Yeats to Allen Ginsberg, Freud to Norman O. Brown, and Max Weber to Hebert Marcuse, as repudiating the very principle that has made progress in society, art, and thought possible in modern civilization. The new avant-garde represents to them an attack upon the worldview that produced a culture that was both scientific (hence orderly) and humanistic (hence liberating)—the culture that was created by the example of a music without sound; and their social commentators speak of the possibility at last of a genuine transcendence of historical existence and the advent of apocalypse, Greek transcendence of the anxiety-ridden world of the savage, on the one side, and the oppressive mythic formalism of archaic higher civilizations, such as the ancient Egyptian and Mesopotamian, on the other.

According to Gombrich, Popper, and Auerbach, modern, enlightened, and progressive civilization is sustained by a set of moral and intellectual commitments, first envisaged by the Greeks, that have their characteristic expressive forms in the traditions of humanistic realism. All three believe that this set of commitments arose from a genuine revolution in sensibility, a revolution that Gombrich calls "the Greek miracle," which was opposed during the Middle Ages but was taken up once more and was elaborated and refined, between the fifteenth and nineteenth centuries in Western Europe, in such a way as to make any further revolutions in sensibility either impossible or undesirable—impossible because the realistic tradition appears to possess powers of resistance to radical transformation and undesirable since, if any radical transformation were to occur, it would lead, because of the very nature of consciousness itself, to a regression to earlier, infantile, savage, or archaic forms of imaginative oppression.

In Gombrich's influential *Art and Illusion: A Study in the Psychology of Pictorial Representation*, the Greek miracle is presented as having consisted above all in the discovery of the possibility of provisional truths, of fictive possibilities, of approximative realities. The discovery of the realm of fictive reality created a kind of distinctively human psychic space, between the rigidifying strategies of the mythic imagination, of the sort that led to Egyptian king-worship and the closed society of the slave-subject, and the terrifying world of uncontrolled imagination that presumably imprisoned man originally in a savage condition.

Gombrich links this discovery of fictive possibility to the notion of a narratively structured time, which permitted the conception of the *significant moment,* on which the artist—whether painter, sculptor, or writer—could center his attention for the purpose of determining the possible relations obtaining between objects caught in that moment, without appeal to universal explanatory principles or absolute conceptions of causal relationship. That is to say, realistic art, from the Greeks onward to the end of the nineteenth century, contents itself with the careful and progressive matching of hypotheses about what might actually occupy a defined field of perception of that ground on which the field has been constructed, by appeal to the authority of perceptions, on the one side, and to areas already secured by prior mapping operations, as recorded by tradition, on the other. This ability to bracket a temporal moment, in turn, leads to the creation of a specifically historical consciousness by its implicit suggestion of the moments preceding and the moments following it. In the arts, it ultimately leads to the conquest of a perspectivally structured, or autonomous, space—a space whose reality is confirmed by the sensed internal consistency of the empirically discoverable relations between objects occupying it, and not by appeal to some sustaining transcendental principle, such as eternity or infinite being, as the mythic imagination requires. These two conquests, that of narrative time and that of perspectival space, together with historical consciousness, liberated the imagination from the mythic search for eternal and absolute truths and committed it to the much more mundane, but humanly more profitable, task of controlled information-gathering. At the same time, it led to the search for a principle of rational entailment by which new bodies of information could be assimilated to the older, secured ones contained in tradition.

But there was more to this miracle. The triumph of realism depended upon a mastery and cultivation of the techniques of illusionism, the discovery of a way of using fictions to mediate between what men desired or hoped might be the case about reality and the way things actually were or are in fact. It was the use of fictions in literature, of controlled illusions in art, of provisional schemata (or hypotheses) in science—the use of the notion of the provisional or merely possible, in place of the necessary or merely inevitable—that has permitted every new structuring of reality by each successive generation of artists, thinkers, and scientists to develop toward an ever more precise understanding of the true nature of the external world and which has led, in modern Western civilization, to the attainment of whatever control men now have over it.

The dialectical interplay between (1) traditional wisdom or lore, (2) fiction, hypothesis, or provisional schema, and (3) perception, broke that tyranny of thought and imagination over sense that consigned men to a servitude to their own illusions in the archaic civilizations of the ancient world and, at the same time, dissolved the power that sense exercised over thought in primitive culture. And Gombrich rightly discerns that the avant-garde art of our time is a threat to humanistic-scientific or realistic civilization precisely because it denies, at one and the same time, the authority of tradition, of thought, and of sensory perception in such a way as to destroy the mediative role that the "fictive" has played in the promotion of a humanistic cultural endowment. For him, this threefold denial, however noble the Utopian impulses behind it, however motivated by an understandable urge to know reality directly—this attempt to take reality by storm, to seize it immediate and pure, and to liberate it from the constraints of merely fictive truths and provisional generalizations—all this is an attack upon civilization. It can lead, in his view, only to a regression into myth and to the creation of the kind of totalitarian society that arises whenever myth takes command, as in Germany during Nazism.

So too, for Auerbach. In his magisterial *Mimesis: The Representation of Reality in Western Literature*, he shows that the principal achievement of Western literature has been the full development of the potentialities of *mimesis*, the realistic representation, or verbal imitation, of an action. This achievement Auerbach regards as a product of the progressive liberation of literature, both from the tyranny of unprocessed sense data and from that overprocessing of it, to the point of its near extinction, in mythic thought. He grants a more important role to Christian ideas in the development of literary realism than Gombrich is inclined to do with respect to pictorial realism. But the conclusion with respect to the most important achievements of Western literature is much the same: historical realism results from the controlled interplay of human consciousness with a shifting social and natural milieu. It alone, of all literary traditions, has promoted the progressive charting of the elements in that milieu through the testing of different stylistic fictions, concepts of reality, and paradigms for dictating the nature of relationships that might bind objects together to constitute them as a comprehensible domain. The history of literary realism has been a story, in Auerbach's view, of the gradual elimination of mythical powers as explanatory concepts in social and psychological matters and the cultivation of social, natural, and psychological forces as rationally comprehensible intrahistorical forces in their own right. All of which adds up, in his view, to the gradual discovery of the realm of history as the temporal domain in which man has his proper habitat, just as he has his proper spatial habitat in nature and his proper spiritual habitat in an internally differentiated society. Abandon the historical frame—as Joyce does—and you court disaster.

And so too, finally, for Popper, who has labored long and arduously to demonstrate that science provides no absolute truths, neither for nature nor for society—to show that true science is inductive in method, that its tactic is to generate disposable hypotheses, and that it aims legitimately only at the construction of an expanding, yet ever more elegant and comprehensive, set of probability statements about the "true" nature of reality. For him, Western science, like Gombrich's Western art and Auerbach's Western literature, triumphs by giving up the hope for final truths and absolute knowledge in its investigation both of nature and society, while still carrying forward the careful and controlled charting of reality in an evolutionary, or piecemeal, way. It is this willingness to suppress the desire for absolute certitude that protects Western culture, Popper believes, from totalitarianism. Totalitarianism always follows close upon the dissolution of belief in the ultimately provisional nature of every generalization. It is the inability to live with provisional truth that generated the fallacies of philosophy of history in Marx and Toynbee and that inspired or justified the tyrannies of Nazism and communism in the interwar period.

For these great critics, then, realism in thought and art is intimately tied in with the open society; and the abandonment of realism, which has characterized so much of avant-garde thought and art of this century, leads inevitably, in their view, to the dissolution of the one cultural protocol capable of promoting orderly development, safe evolution, and expanding control by man of his world, both natural and social. For this reason, the avant-gardists appear, to these three authorities as well as to most other humanists, to be indulging in a luxury that is either insane in its motivation or criminal in its intent. Popper, in fact, in *The Poverty of Historicism* and *The Open Society and Its Enemies*, looks upon every radical social theory as both a mistake and a crime. He views even the social-scientific attempt to predict future courses of social change as an error; to him all this is nothing but prophecy masquerading as science. He views all philosophy of history—all metahistorical generalization—as nothing more than personal whim passing for wisdom. Since the best we can hope for in the way of social knowledge is *provisional* truth, the best we have a right to demand of society is *gradual* transformation. He concludes that liberal, piecemeal planning, or what is now called "fine tuning" of the social mechanism, is the only scientifically responsible political program imaginable and that every form of Utopian dreaming is a threat to civilization.

And so too, for critics like Gombrich and Auerbach, with respect to the arts. Neither of them can make much sense of anything that has happened in painting since Cézanne or in literature since Proust. Gombrich disapproves of the Cubists because they tried to frustrate perception rather than refine it. Auerbach finds Joyce and Kafka disturbing because, for them, the mapping of external reality had given way to interior psychic probes. Now perception is subordinated to and made captive of the psyche, and the psyche itself is released from the control of tradition, which has always ultimately exercised some direction in previous literary movements, however much they were committed to the justification of the claims of the imagination against both sense and reason. The surfaces of the external world, so laboriously charted over the last three thousand years, suddenly explode; perception loses its power as a restraint on imagination; the fictive sense dissolves—and modern man teeters on the verge of the abyss of subjective longing, which, Auerbach implies, must lead him finally to an enslavement once more by myth.

Of course I am not suggesting that the humanities are dominated by all or any of these three great critics. But attitudes like theirs predominate in them. Gombrich, Auerbach, and Popper are merely somewhat more philosophically self-conscious than many of their colleagues, and they have been—as a result of their experience of Nazism—driven to articulate their understanding of the relations between the humanities and a particular form of society more self-consciously. Whatever their differences with their colleagues on specific points of fact or theory, they share with most critics and scholars in the humanities certain ground assumptions that are now falling under attack by both the avant-garde and the new public. One assumption is that only evolution, not genuine revolution, in the arts is possible. A corollary of this is their belief in the authority of tradition as a control on what will be permitted to count as a creative advance in thought and art. For all three, received tradition serves both as a source of new hypotheses about the nature of reality and as a determinant of the mental set of the individual artist or thinker who wants to make something other than a simple cry or grunt.

This is not to say that they are reactionaries, either in their cultural or their social attitudes. In fact, as I have tried to indicate, they know and appreciate the importance of experimentation and the desirability of innovation in both culture and society. As I said, they take it as self-evident that Western civilization is unique in its capacity to change without falling into anarchy and to resist precipitous change without hardening into totalitarianism. But this means for them, as it does for most humanists, that what might count as a permissible worldview in both art and thought has to be, finally, reconcilable with that knowledge of reality contained in the previously secured strategies of realistic representation; that is to say, what could count as art, science, or social theory for them has to be in principle assimilable to the lore of the realistic tradition by something like logical entailment or technical consistency.

That means that all Utopian visions have to be ruled out. For realism is a product of a decision, unique in world history, to put off Utopian assaults upon reality, to defer any form of thought and action based on a passionately held conviction of the way things *ought* to be. Realism, in their view, is the cultural expression of a society that, because it is technologically innovative, can look forward to the overcoming *at some time* of the condition of scarcity and the division of men into classes that now characterize it, but that cannot really conceive that this Utopian condition of genuine affluence might ever truly be attained. Because the experience of Western society has always been an experience of hierarchically distributed privileges and responsibilities, realism in thought necessarily consists in the discovery of internally differentiated and hierarchically ordered natural and social structures, even though it recognizes that the contents of these hierarchies have changed throughout time and space and might become more open, that is to say, internally more mobile, in specific situations of affluence from time to time.

The crucial question, however, is this: Do art and thought need to be hierarchical in what they allow perception to find in the world and language to represent? If that were not the case, then we might be able to understand the current attack by artists on art, by writers on language, and so on; we might be able to show the essentially Utopian content of the art they produce and link up the avant-garde in art with the radical wing of contemporary social movements.

What Gombrich, Auerbach, and Popper have seen in the new art and thought of this century is a repudiation, not only of a way of *viewing* reality, but also of the reality that that way of viewing was committed to find and map. The repudiation of realism appears as a repudiation of an external reality that is seen to be internally divisible *ad infinitum* and unifiable only in *theoria* never in *praxis*. The form of reality, in short, shares the attributes of the artistic and intellectual traditions that were developed in the West alone for its mapping and gradual conquest. Both the reality and the cultural traditions created by the attempt to map it are conceived to be *syntactical* in nature, by which I mean that both reality and the sole possible strategies for its encodation are regarded as homologously *hierarchical* in principle.

The word *syntactical* comes from two roots that when combined mean "to arrange together." Grammarians use the word *syntax* to refer to the rules of certain languages by which the elements of those languages are defined and their arrangement in certain acceptable combinations to constitute sentences is carried out. But the connotations of the notion of syntactical strategies are further ranging: syntactical linguistic conventions generate rules of combination by the tactic of subordination and stress. The important point is that a syntactical linguistic strategy permits the growth of vocabulary and the evolution of concepts of combination and therefore the mapping of new contents of experience; but it requires that, whatever the contents of language, those contents be organized in a relation of subordination and domination. It may well be that such linguistic strategies prevail in cultures that, like the Greek, are dynamically hierarchical, that is to say, hierarchically organized at any given time but, like their languages themselves, constantly changing the verbal contents that occupy the positions of subordination and domination. Auerbach uses the term *syntactical* to characterize the literary style of Homer and goes on to make the triumph of syntactical culture the mark of progress in the development of literary realism. This is certainly the kind of thing that Popper has in mind when he lauds the open society of the West over the closed societies of Asia and modern totalitarianism. That is to say, he envisages as the ideal those societies that are open to talent but in which only the individuals who have talent are presumed to deserve positions of privilege and responsibility, in contrast to those societies that simply confer privilege by right of birth or by adherence to some abstract or presumably timeless principle of selection.

But the term *syntactica*—whatever its use among grammarians—helps us to understand the revolutionary nature of much avant-garde art, pop culture, and current social rebellion, as well as the originality of the current avant-garde when compared with previous ones. For the current artistic rebellion, like the current social rebellion, is programmatically opposed to syntactical strategies for representing and organizing the experience of the world, on the one side, and for structuring society, on the other.

What the innovative artists and thinkers of this era have rebelled against is the very principle of a syntactically organized vision, the consciousness that requires the organization of reality into relationships of subordination and domination. The rebellion against perspective in art and against narrative in literature, like the rebellion against historical consciousness, reflects the feeling that hierarchical modes of relationship are no longer the fate either of perception, of representation, or of society.

As Auerbach himself tells us, the grammarians have a word that might be used to characterize the stylistic conventions being developed to figure such a world; they call them *paratactical*. Paratactical conventions try to resist any impulse to the hierarchical arrangement of images and perceptions and, as the roots of the word *parataxis* indicate, sanction their "arrangement together, side by side"—that is to say, indiscriminately, by simple listing in sequence, in what might be called a democracy of lateral coexistence, one next to another. As you can see, the term *paratactical* could be used to describe what aleatory music is about; it certainly applies to the Happening, to much of pop art, and to the techniques of *nouvelle vague* (new wave) cinema and the *nouveau roman* (anti-novel). It represents a class of stylistic conventions ideally suited to the representation of a world in which hierarchy, subordination and domination, tragic conflict, and psychic scarcity are conceived to have been transcended. The avant-garde is not interested in the substitution of a new syntactical convention for the older ones, and it is not trying to purge our vision of tired preconceptions so that we can reconstitute society and culture as yet another structure of subordination and domination.

The avant-garde of this century envisions the possibility of realistically conceiving a world in which hierarchy, whether open or closed, has finally dissolved because the condition presupposed by these two models of society, the condition of material scarcity, is no longer a tragic inevitability. The avant-garde insists on a transformation of social and cultural practice that will not end in the substitution of a new elite for an old one, a new protocol of domination for the earlier ones, nor the institution of new privileged positions for old ones—whether of privileged positions in space (as in the old perspectival painting and sculpture), of privileged moments in time (as one finds in the older narrative art of fiction and in conventional historiography), of privileged places in society, of privileged areas in the consciousness (as in the conservative, that is to say, orthodox Freudian psychoanalytic theory), of privileged parts of the body (as the genitally organized sexual lore insists is "natural"), or of privileged positions in culture (on the basis of a presumed superior "taste") or in politics (on the basis of a presumed superior "wisdom").

The practitioners of the humanities know about paratactical styles, and they fear them, not the least because they deny the need for "critics." In fact, Auerbach associates them with archaic, or myth-dominated, cultures and with those periods of crisis in Western thought and art when the need for transcendental certitudes or the solaces of religion, or simply a boredom with formal disciplines, has asserted itself against the dominant realistic tradition—such periods as the fourth century AD in Rome, the seventeenth century in Western Europe, and, of course, our own age since about World War I. And they are probably correct in their belief that all previous paratactical deviations have finally ended as little more than ground-clearing operations, preparations for the crystallization of new syntactical conventions, as when mannerism eroded Renaissance formalism only to give place to neoclassicism. In short, paratactical conventions in thought and art have been recessive or subdominant strains in Western culture, at least since the Renaissance. And all previous mannerist movements are probably correctly viewed as manifestations of imperfectly repressed religious feelings or reflections of a mythic belief in fate or destiny that may still be present with us all. But—equally—it may well be that this conception of the historical function of the paratactical imagination is inadequate for an understanding of the current cultural rebellion against tradition, fiction, and perception and the combination of them that has sustained realism throughout its long history. And for this reason: the paratactical style is an intrinsically *communal* style, rather than a *societal* one; it is inherently democratic and egalitarian rather than aristocratic and elitist, and it is possible that the rebirth of parataxis in art and thought in this century does not represent the fall back into myth or the advent of a new totalitarianism so much as the demand for a change of consciousness that will finally make a unified humanity possible.

For although there is much that is merely exotic and perhaps even pathological in contemporary avant-garde art and Utopian thought, what is characteristic of its best representatives—from Joyce and Yeats on down to Resnais, Robbe-Grillet, Cage, Merce Cunningham, Samuel Beckett, and the rest—is a seeming ability to live with the implications of a paratactical consciousness: a language of linear disjunctions rather than narrative sequences, of deperspectivized space, and of definalized culminations without any need for that mythic certitude that has always attended the flowering of such a consciousness in the past. And this may indicate that the current avant-garde is able to take as a fact what every previous one had to regard finally as only a hope—that is, that the condition of material scarcity is no longer an inevitability and that we are at last ready to enter into a Utopia in which neither myth, religion, nor elites of taste and sensibility will be able to claim the right to define what the "true" aims of either art or life must be.[1]

CHAPTER SEVEN

The Structure of Historical Narrative

{1972}

In this paper I will discuss three topics: (1) the nature of narratives in general; (2) the relation between story, plot, and argument in different kinds of narrative history; and (3) the ways in which the emplotment of a set of events can endow them with different, though by no means mutually exclusive meanings. I will, therefore, be talking more about the place of historiography in narrative than about the place of narrative in historiography. For historiography is a species of the genus narrative, rather than the reverse; and one point I want to make is that the distinction between narrative history, on the one side, and non-narrative history, on the other, is less illuminating than it might appear to be at first glance. In fact, as currently used, the distinction between narrative and non-narrative history obscures more than it clarifies. The term *narrative history* is often used to distinguish histories that "tell stories" from those that do not, stories being understood as stories with a beginning, middle, and end. In my view, the criterion for the distinction rests on a scant knowledge of stories in general and the different ways they can be used for different dramatic, and even explanatory, effects.

On the other hand, there is another distinction that is not much used in the discussion of historical narrative but which, in my view, could be profitably revived. It is the distinction between story and plot. This distinction is not very useful for contemporary literary critics, for reasons that I will note shortly, but I think that it can be usefully made for purposes of analyzing historical narratives, and that it will help us understand the different functions of story, plot, and argument for the achievement of different "explanatory effects" in different kinds of historical narratives. And I will suggest that what we honor as a classic historical narrative, long after we have adjudged its story naive and its argument invalid, is the subtlety

This paper was originally presented to a Conference on Philosophy of History at the University of California, Davis, November 26–27, 1971.

of the emplotting procedures used in it to make of the events it describes a comprehensible *dramatic* unity.

ᐅ

Let me begin by talking generally about three examples of historical narrative: Leopold von Ranke's *History of Germany during the Age of the Reformation*, Alexis de Tocqueville's *Democracy in America*, and Jacob Burckhardt's *Culture of the Renaissance in Italy*. These works represent different kinds of historical narratives. Each tells a story, each can be said to have a plot, and each has an argument to make about its subject: German *history*, American *democracy*, and Renaissance *culture* respectively. But these three elements—story, plot, and argument—are used differently in each of the three works, with the result that each is definable as a verbal structure radically different from the other two. And the question is, would we want to call any of them a true narrative history to the exclusion of either or both of the other two?

The temptation to try to do so is inspired by conventional usage and reinforced by recent philosophical arguments. Ranke's *History of Germany* manifestly conforms to the notion of what a proper history of the specifically "narrativist" sort ought to be. In the first place, it tells a story with a beginning, middle, and end. Secondly, its subject is an entity that is undergoing a process of change from one condition to another while remaining identifiably what it was all along. And third, it "explains" what happened during the process of change, not so much by appealing to universal causal and relational laws (though it does make such appeal from time to time) as by "showing" how one thing led to another, or how one set of events engendered another set, or how one situation became an occasion for a response on the part of the actors in the drama that no one in that situation could have predicted on the basis of the knowledge that he might have been expected to have had at that time.

By contrast, Tocqueville's *Democracy in America* appears to have very little story in it. Certainly, it has no story with a beginning, middle, and end. It can be said to have a kind of beginning, consisting of a background sketch of how democracy was born in Europe, was transferred to America in the seventeenth century, how it took root here and flourished; and it can be said to give us a kind of extended middle of a story, that is to say, an account of the institutions and forces in play in American democracy at the time of the writing of the book. But it certainly does not provide us with an ending to that story. True, it blocks out a number of possibilities for ending the story in the near or remote future. But actually these are not so much endings of the story being told as ways of anticipating what the next phase of democratic development in America might be. If there is a story in Tocqueville, it is a peculiarly open-ended one. How it will all come out in the end, he leaves, he repeatedly tells us, to the decision of those who might read his history; it is up to his readers to provide by their actions an ending to the story he has begun. Do we want to say that, although Tocqueville explains many things during the course of his history, he does not explain anything by telling a story about it or that, in fact, he is not telling a story, in any important sense, at all?

It seems to me that what we have are two different kinds of stories, one whose ending is provided by the known outcome of a particular set of events and another whose ending is still unknown or is perceivable only in its general outline. The story told by Ranke ends in the past of the prospective reader, that told by Tocqueville in the reader's own present. The provision of a definite ending in the former may account for the relative absence or unimportance of the formal arguments advanced in it. While there are many generalizations about human nature, society, and civilization in Ranke's work, these generalizations do not really have to be taken as causal laws or universals functioning as major premises in nomological arguments in order for the reader to gain an impression that he has understood what was happening in Germany between the late Middle Ages and the end of the Wars of Religion. As a matter of fact, as I shall argue later, these generalizations are not so much theories as fixed motifs that provide the continuities of his storyline; whatever theories Ranke has about human nature and society can be separated from the story he tells and ignored as components of arguments without any loss of understanding of the story he is telling about the evolution of early modern Germany. The kind of understanding we get from following his story is different from the kind of understanding we might get from following his arguments. We can dissent from the argument while assenting, in such a way as to increase our comprehension of the facts, to the story itself.

But in Tocqueville's work, the reverse appears to be the case. Without the theories, Tocqueville's work is neither very significant nor very interesting as history. He has theories galore: about social structures in general; about democratic social structures as against aristocratic ones; about the relation between social structures and culture, on the one hand, and about social structures and political systems, on the other; about the role of religion as a mediating force between social groups, technological endowments, and natural environments; and so on. If his story is open-ended and unsatisfying, his theoretical apparatus is, if anything, closed and almost oppressive in the demands that it makes on our ability to follow an argument. Is Tocqueville telling a story at all?

In my view, he is. He is only telling a different *kind* of story (a story with a beginning and an extended middle but no ending); but more importantly, he is *using* story for a different purpose than that for which Ranke was using his story. Specifically, he is using story to illuminate and carry an argument. The meaning of the story he is telling is not to be found in the ending, "the way it all comes out," but in the argument that it figures and sustains, "the point of it all." The difference between these two works as stories is similar to that pointed out by Northrop Frye with respect to Henry Fielding's *Tom Jones, the History of a Foundling* and Jane Austen's *Sense and Sensibility*. The titles of these works, Frye says, indicate differences of emphasis and purpose in the stories that will be told in them. They invite different kinds of questions about them. The former invites what Frye calls "plot-questions," the second "theme-questions." The first directs attention to plot-articulation ("How does it all come out in the end?"), the second to thematic elaboration ("What is the point of the story?"). We might say the same thing about Ranke's *History of Germany* and Tocqueville's *Democracy in America*. The title of the first indicates that the story told will figure a plot; the title of the second suggests that the story will figure a theme. The first sets up expectations and provides satisfactions of one sort, the second sets up different expectations and provides satisfactions of a different sort.

The fact that one is *primarily* about processes or changes of a sequential or diachronic sort and that the other is *primarily* about a stable or continuous condition that can be apprehended as a synchronic structure has nothing to do with their status as narratives. It is a matter of emphasis; what is dominant in one is subdominant or recessive in the other. Whereas Ranke sets the changes he depicts in his story against a putatively changeless background of human nature, national ideas, and certain kinds of power relationships, Tocqueville achieves his narrative effects by constantly contrasting what appear to be surface changes in his subject to the stable set of structural relationships underlying them and making of them a comprehensible totality. Ranke tracks changes against a background of changeless relationships; Tocqueville delineates changeless structures behind a surface agitation. The subjects of primary interest do not make one a narrative and the other a non-narrative account. As R. G. Collingwood was fond of pointing out, any historian worthy of the name wants to tell how *this* came out of *that* while remaining recognizably *what it was* throughout the entire process of change. Narratives can be about changes-in-continuity or continuity-in-changes indifferently. And it makes as little sense to try to distinguish between narrative and non-narrative history on the basis of subject-matter as it does to try to base such a distinction on the presumed presence of a "story" in one and its presumed absence in another. As a matter of fact, both of the works under consideration not only have stories, they have plots as well; and both "explain" what is happening in the storyline by the progressive emplotment of their stories in such a way as to make them recognizable as stories of a particular type. And I will argue shortly that historical narratives achieve a secondary explanatory affect, over and above whatever arguments they advance, by the progressive identification of the story they tell as belonging to a certain *class* of stories. In short, in historical narrative, plot "explains" not the events in the story but the story itself, by identifying it as a certain *kind* of story.

The different functions of story, plot, and argument in historical narrative can be illustrated by consideration of a third example of narrative history, Burckhardt's *Culture of the Renaissance in Italy*, which is often cited as an example of non-narrative history. Incidentally, the work is subtitled, "An Essay," which would seem to confirm the view, now become quite conventional, that the work is not meant to tell a story and that one ought not expect a history of the conventional narrative sort at all. And on the face of it, this view is more than justified, for Burckhardt's work appears to have no story, no plot, and hardly even an argument. Although it has an opening, it certainly has nothing that could be likened to Ranke's openings, which are manifestly beginnings of the stories that are to follow through recognizable middles to manifest conclusions. And although Burckhardt's book does end, it would be more accurate to call its ending a termination rather than a conclusion. For, on the face of it, the story Burckhardt tells is even more open-ended than Tocqueville's. The latter at least gives us, at the end of Volume II (Chapter VIII) of his work, a "General Survey of the Subject." Burckhardt's last chapter, which is a general account of "Morality and Religion" in Renaissance Italy, terminates with a two-sentence paragraph that can be called neither a summary of an argument nor a synopsis of a story. He simply says: "Echoes of medieval mysticism here flow into one current with Platonic doctrines and with a characteristically modern spirit. One of the precious fruits of the knowledge of the world and of man here comes to maturity, on whose account alone the Italian Renaissance must be called the leader of modern ages."[1]

What do we have here? I suggest that it is merely another instance of a statement of a motif that is repeated throughout Burckhardt's work, almost *ad nauseam*, and that gives to the work its notoriously monolithic character. If anything, Burckhardt's history is even more thematic than that of Tocqueville. Whereas Tocqueville figures many themes in his history, Burckhardt appears to be interested in figuring only one, that of individualism, and in collecting as many instances of it as he can find under the conventional categories of historiographical analysis: the state, religion, society, and culture. There is even less argument in the work than there is in Ranke's *History of Germany*; the theoretical content is almost nil. It is certainly not crucial for our comprehension of the "meaning" of the events he portrays. Nor can the "meaning" of those events really be discerned in his depiction of them *seriatim*. This is one of those works that one can begin anywhere and leave off at any point along the way. The "point" of the story is present from the very beginning. It is that there existed an age of peculiarly intense individualism in Italy during the fifteenth and early sixteenth centuries; it manifested itself in all aspects of society and culture; it resulted in the creation of objects of lasting beauty and interest; and it is now ended. Take it or leave it. Let him who has eyes to see with look on the glory of the age and weep. So much and no more.

We can extract a *kind* of argument from this book if we read it along with other works in Burckhardt's corpus, where he elaborates a general theory of the relation between culture, on the one side, and the state and religion, on the other. This theory tells us that when the state and religion exhaust one another in a contest for the control of society, culture flourishes as the expression of individual talent. When, however, one of the great "compulsive" institutions—the state or the church—succeeds in establishing its hegemony, individualism dies out. But Burckhardt is not so much arguing in defense of this "theory," as simply pointing to the instances of individualistic expression to be found in the time and place under study—which is what makes those endless debates over his "theory of the Renaissance" so tiresomely beside the point. His subject is not, as his title suggests, the Renaissance, it is rather the theme of individualism. And he is less interested in analyzing it than in simply logging in instances of it that he finds in the record. This is why the work is for many so boring to read; it has about as much story in its manifest content as an encyclopedia. But it does have a story of a sort, the kind of story that is all middle, which incidentally is recognizable as a story of a *certain* sort, the kind of story that we associated with Ironic plot-structures.[2] These are stories that "go nowhere" precisely because they are intended to frustrate expectations that there is anywhere to go in either a significantly moral or a significantly epistemological sense.

Burckhardt's story depends for its explanatory effects upon the contrast between the individualism of an earlier age and the conformity and dullness of his own, a contrast that the reader can be expected to provide out of the combination of his own experience and the countless instances of individualism given in Burckhardt's book. The ceaseless repetition of the same motif, the motif of individualism, which makes this book such a monolithic thematic performance, tells a story that figures a plot-structure in which beginnings and endings are as unimportant as the major premises and conclusions in his arguments. Burckhardt's is a world of mere data, in which things are just what they appear to be, that is to say, without any ultimate meaning save their own existence. It is the world that is figured in Schopenhauer's philosophy and Kafka's art. The meaning of the story told about it derives from its frustration of our normal expectations of Romantic, Comic, or Tragic stories and from its denial that theories can be combined with evidence to produce conclusions with any scientifically compelling authority.

Thus, with Burckhardt we have a third kind of historical narrative. Ranke's history takes us from somewhere specific through a well-marked peripety that issues in a specific ending in a known past. We might call this kind of narrative *processionary*. Tocqueville's takes us from a well-defined beginning to an ambiguous middle, which is Tocqueville's own present, but provides us with no particular ending. And since he is obviously more concerned to figure a structure than to describe a process, we might call this a *structuralist* narrative. And finally, we have Burckhardt's history, which has neither beginning nor end, but is all middle or peripety; it neither describes a process nor figures a structure. It simply positions us before a body of data thematically organized, which is to be savored as by a connoisseur, as an "interesting" effluvium the origins of which are as obscure as its final fate is melancholy. We might call this kind of narrative *impressionistic*. No doubt this third kind of narrative is, in one sense, the most sophisticated, for it depends for its effects upon the reader's provision of the correct meaning of the events depicted. The reader must recognize that he is in the presence of a time and a condition that he himself has lost beyond recall. The meaning of Burckhardt's "story" is the meaning of all Ironic elegies: this once was, but is no more. Its meaning is the plot that underlies and makes of the story told a particular *kind* of story. Ranke tells Comic stories in all his histories; Tocqueville tells Tragic stories in both of his; Burckhardt tells stories meant to figure a condition in which "the more things change, the more they are the same," Ironic stories in which things are "explained" by being represented as what they *appear* to be, no more and no less.

❧

Now, I do not have time to defend my "readings" of these three examples of historical narrative, but I hope that by my summary characterizations of their structures I have suggested the possibility of making two points about historical narrative in general.[3] One has to do with what we mean by "narrative" and the other has to do with the difference between the kind of explanatory effect we might get by story-elaboration and the kind we might get by plot-articulation.

The point to be made about narrative is quite simple; and I hope that it is not simply reactionary. It turns upon the literal meaning of the term etymologically considered. The word derives from a root (*gnâ*) which appears in Latin, Greek, and Sanskrit alike as connoting the sense of "knowing, the known, the knowable." It was not until the seventeenth century that the term *narratio* began to be used synonymously with *historia,* which derives from a Greek root meaning simply "inquiry" and which is used by Aristotle to denote inquiry into matters of fact as against examinations of matters of belief or opinion. In Roman usage, *narratio* had a quite specific meaning; it was used to designate a part of an oration in which an account of the facts that led up to and necessitated the speech itself was given. It was that part of the speech in which the agreed-upon background of a case under dispute was recalled to memory, to set the stage for the dispute itself. This accords with late medieval usage in which the term *narratio* designates the claim or plea that lawyers argued in court.

One can see quite easily how, in the atmosphere of religious conflict that prevailed throughout Europe in the seventeenth century, the two aspects of *narratio*— that which had to do with a truthful account of the facts and that which had to do with a claim or plea or argument—could be combined with the ancient sense of it as a "knowing" account to produce its synonymy with what "history" was supposed to provide. The important point is that in the concept "narrative history" the literal meaning and usage direct attention, not to the "story" being told as a "fiction," but to the knowledge-ability of the person telling the story. In short, literally speaking, the term "narrative" qualifies the term "history" in an *epistemological* not an aesthetic sense. It does not suggest that the account being given has to be cast in a story form, much less that it has to be cast in the form of a story with a recognizable beginning, middle, and end. What it does suggest is that the verbal representation will be recognizably that of a "knower," an account of the facts by one who "knows" what the facts are, an account that is not "made" (*factum*) or "feigned" (*fictum*) but rather "found" or "discovered" in the facts themselves (*inventum*). Properly used, the term "narrative" denotes an account of something that is known or is knowable, or that was once known and has been forgotten and therefore can be recalled to mind by the appropriate means of discourse. It presupposes a "knower," who tells or informs us of what he knows; and it is this presupposition of a "knower" present in the discourse that is the true basis of the distinction between narrative verbal structures, on the one side, and non-narrative verbal structures, on the other.

We might say, then, that a narrative is any literary form in which the voice of the narrator rises against a background of ignorance, incomprehension, or forgetfulness to direct our attention, purposefully, to a segment of experience organized in a particular way. In realistic narrative representation—as against mythic or legendary representations—the narrator is both present and absent: present as a means of communication, absent as a means of communication that is transparent and does not block access to the segment of experience whose organization it is his purpose to reveal to us. It is the presence of an identifiable narrative voice that permits us to credit such "realistic" representations as a history and a certain kind of novel as "objective" accounts. Because we can recognize the directive function of the narrative voice, we can take account of it as one way among others of organizing the data being represented.

The narrative voice is absent in most dramatic representations, in the lyric, and in a sense in myth, legend, and folktale. Dramatic representations simply display their data, organized in a certain way to be sure, but perceivable in a host of different ways by the audience, which narrative forms like the realistic novel and the epic are not. As for myth, legend, and folktales, the voice in them is a collective voice, which is why we do not waste our time inquiring into their purpose as representations but speak rather of their "functions" in different cultural situations. Myths, as Claude Lévi-Strauss says, come precisely from "nowhere"; in this they resemble the chronicle. What we miss in the chronicle is the narrative voice that orders the materials syntactically and then directs our attention to the materials thus ordered in such a way as to gain retrospectively characterizable effects, theoretical, moral, or aesthetic as the case may be. In order to get these effects, the narrator may or may not tell a story; and if he tells a story, it may have a beginning, a middle, and an end, or it may not. The narrator may organize his account of the facts conceptually, as Tocqueville did, or, like Burckhardt, so order them as to undermine previous conceptualization of them or suggest that no conceptualization of them is possible.

The important point is that, by taking the literal meaning of the term "narrative" and stressing it, we highlight the relationship between the narrator's voice and its purpose in directing our attention to evidence organized in a particular way. This permits us in turn to speak, not about explanation and representation in narrative history, as if these were in some sense separate operations, but rather about a whole range of explanatory effects that we get from good historiography. And what I want to suggest is that in good narrative history what we respond to specifically is the narrator's voice as it directs our attention to three different levels on which explanatory effects can be achieved: story, argument, and plot, respectively.

Let me stress again that I am not saying that the Hempelian analysis is not useful for identifying and assessing one level on which most historians operate. But it is not the only one, and it may not even be the most important one. Of course, one hopes that the arguments contained in a narrative as explanations of the events depicted in the story will be convincing; but it is not necessary that this be the case in order for a narrative history to get the effect of having explained something important. In fact, it is not even necessary that there be arguments in a history to permit it to provide the semblance of endowing the events contained in the story with a meaning. Let me, therefore, speak briefly about the relations between stories and plots in narrative history, and explain further why I think they provide different kinds of explanatory effects from one another, and different kinds of explanations from anything that we might want to call a nomological or covering law or regularity explanation.

First, let me register my awareness that the story-plot distinction is not very popular among literary critics, and for good reasons. There are just too many kinds of fictional narratives in which story-elements and plot-elements are indistinguishable, and more than a few in which we can see stories without plots or plots without stories. But the distinction between stories and plots in the analysis of historical narratives seems to me a useful one for two reasons. First, most historical accounts are still cast in some variant of the modes of nineteenth-century narrative or discursive prose. This means that we can usually distinguish quite easily between story and plot, on the one side, and between story and argument, on the other, in the way that we do for most realistic novels and for essays of the sort that Kierkegaard and Nietzsche write. Second, however, while it is sometimes difficult to distinguish between story and plot in some kinds of verbal fictions, in history we have one way of doing so that is unique to this literary form. In histories, unlike novels, the events that make up the storyline are not (or are not supposed to be) products of the historians' imaginations but must be attested to by evidence, or at least are supposed to be plausibly inferable from what the documents explicitly say.

I am not saying that the storyline *is* the same thing as the events contained in it; a set of events arranged chronologically is not a story at all, but only a chronicle. In order to be transformed into a story, a set of events must be organized in such a way as to inspire a certain type of question in the reader, such questions as: "What happened next?" or "How did that come about?" Answers to these questions have two dimensions, a factual one, consisting of mere information, and a conceptual one, consisting of the patterning of events into motif-clusters. The organizational pattern provided by motific-tactics of encodation is open-ended; it can go on indefinitely. This motific organization is necessary because historical events are not *as such* openings or closings of processes or even immediately recognizable as transitions. This is true even of the births and deaths of individuals. For example, the death of Diocletian, though manifestly a closing event in the life of Diocletian, is, as a historical event, *either* an opening or a closing of a process, depending on how the individual historian chooses to use it. It may serve as part of a closing motif in a history of pagan Rome or as part of an opening motif in a history of medieval Christendom. Motific organization, then, is an aspect of story elaboration; it provides a kind of explanation, the kind that Louis Mink may have in mind when he speaks of historians providing "comprehension" of events in their stories by "configuring" them.

Motifs mark off phases in a story; they organize data centripetally, so that the reader can tell when he is leaving one phase of a story and is entering upon another. The repetition of a motif makes up a theme, which establishes continuities in the story by throwing the reader's attention backward and forward, *across* the disjunctions established by motific organizations of a non-repeatable sort, and in such a way as to suggest that, beneath the changes shown on one level of the story, there is *something* that remains the same. On the level of storyline, this "something that remains the same" is usually some aspect of human nature or of the human condition that the historian can assume that his reader will recognize. His reminding of the reader of it provides also a kind of explanation of the events depicted in the story. We might call this "thematic configuration." But like motifs, themes too are infinitely extendable. In themselves they do not tell the reader when he can stop asking "What happened next?" or "How did that come about?" and finally say to himself, "Oh, *now* I see what was *really* happening all along." That point is signaled, not by the elaboration of story, but by the articulation of plot. Plot-structures function as "relational crytograms" by which we identify the various phases organized as motifs and as themes as components of a particular *kind* of story.

In narrative histories, in short, plot-structures bear a relationship to story-elements similar to that which theories bear to evidence in arguments. But there is a difference. Whereas the theories appealed to in a historical argument to explain the evidence do so by subsuming evidence under something resembling a causal law, plots explain the evidence organized as a story by identifying that story as belonging to a certain class of stories. This secondary explanation, which is an explanation of the story, not of the events in the story, is moral or aesthetic in nature, but not subjective or purely personal for all that. It is culturally provided in the archetypes of storytelling that a culture recognizes as different ways of telling stories about certain kinds of events in order to get different kinds of emotional effects.

It was his belief that plots explained stories in the way that causal laws explained sequences of events that led E. M. Forster astray when he examined the plot-story relationship in his *Aspects of the Novel*. Like Henry James before him, Forster thought that plots explained events; he did not see that they explain stories, and that they explain them by "categorizing" a given "configuration" of events in a specific story. It is plot-structure, not story, that tells the reader of a history when to stop asking: "What happened next?" and to say: "Oh, *now* I see what was *really* happening all along." That "really" may apply to either argument or plot-identification, but we can still respond, in ways that imply we have "understood" the story being told in a historical narrative, to plot-structures, long after we have abandoned the arguments of a given historian who claims to have explained "what happened" by appeal to universal causal laws, or something that passes for such laws.

What appears to happen in the following of a historical narrative when we feel justified in saying something like "Oh, *now* I see what was *really* happening after all," is rather like what happens when a person who has both lexical and grammatical competence in a foreign language finally grasps the rules of syntax that permit him to formulate, and to understand, sentences uttered in that language.

In short, in histories there appear to be three levels of comprehension. On the first level, there are what might be called lexical elements, the atomic events defined in a particular way on the authority of the documents or some kind of evidence and ordered in a rough chronicle. On a second level, we have the provisional ordering of these events into motific clusters and thematic continuities, which provides a kind of grammar of historical events of this set. And then there is a third, syntactical level, on which themes and motifs are related as either components of an argument or as phases of recognizable, traditional story-models. The different levels of organization give to historical narratives different aspects as an explanation of the events in the chronicle. Motific and thematic organization gives one kind of explanatory effect, argument another, and plot-structure, once it becomes recognizable, yet a third.

I have said that plot-structure functions as a "relational cryptogram" by which, not the events in the story, but the story itself is encoded in a particular way. Here I draw upon E. H. Gombrich's studies of realistic representation in art. My point is that plot functions in much the same way that rational cryptograms do in visual representations to assure that images will be "read" as representing one set of relationships and not another. In paintings of a certain sort, Gombrich says, we employ a specific rational cryptogram so as to be able to decode correctly patches of paint that *might* be read as images of a small man standing next to a large man if the appropriate clues for reading it otherwise were lacking. But if we have enough clues, we do not read the two patches as a small man standing next to a large man, but as a man of a certain size standing *behind* another man of a certain relative size. The syntactical rules being appealed to here have to do with the problem of representing proportion in perspective on a two-dimensional plane. The ancients apparently did not understand such rules, but modern Western painters have applied them as a matter of course in their paintings since the Renaissance. And the viewers of those paintings have applied them as a matter of course, even without being aware that they have been applying them, when they have read a given picture as a representation of a three-dimensional field on a two-dimensional plane instead of reading it as patches of paint on a two-dimensional field.

There are similar, culturally provided rules for storytellers in any culture; and historians invoke such rules as a matter of course to give the general form to their narratives, to reveal what was "really happening" in their narratives, beneath or behind the stories they have been telling, all along. Plot-structures charge the phases of a story with different affective valences or weights, so that we can read the change in continuity (or the reverse) figured in the story as a consummation, a culmination, or a degeneration—that is to say, as a drama with Comic, Tragic, or Ironic significance, as the case may be. These are the modes of the basic plot-structures of Western historiography. These are the general meanings of any narrative history of genuinely classic scope and profundity in our historiographical tradition. They are what we recognize as the "timeless" contents of many great historical works whose factual information we have long since adjudged inadequate and whose theories of human and social processes we have long since abandoned.

※

All this helps, I hope, to illuminate the "place of narrative in historiography," or rather the place of historiography in narrative prose in general. And I hope it helps to illuminate a question raised by Louis Mink, in a recent article, namely: what does it mean *to have followed* a story, or what kind of knowledge can we be said to have gained from *having followed* a story. Mink suggested that what we gain from having followed a historical story is comprehension of a particular sort. He called this "configurational" comprehension, which he distinguished from the "theoretical" comprehension that we gain from having followed a scientific argument and the "categoreal" comprehension that we gain from having followed a philosophical demonstration. This mode of "configurational" comprehension he likened to the kind of knowledge we employ when we "grasp together" the movements of a dancer in such a way as to recognize it as a dance rather than as a set of random motions. And he suggested that this "grasping together" of a set of events as a "configuration" is what we are called upon to do when we follow a story in either a novel or a history. What I have tried to do is distinguish *within* the historical narrative three different levels of comprehension that can be simultaneously appealed to by historians who are truly in command of the materials they deploy in stories. On the story-level proper, we might speak of "configurational" comprehension of a set of events. On the level of argument, we might speak of "theoretical" comprehension of them. And on the level of plot, we might speak of a "categoreal" comprehension, though not of the events in the story so much as of the story itself.

These distinctions permit us to revise somewhat the notion of the disposition of the evidence in the body of the narrative on which the conclusions are based. Mink suggested in a 1965 article entitled "The Anatomy of Historical Understanding" that the conclusions of historical narratives were not "detachable" from their demonstrations in the same way that the conclusions of scientific arguments were detachable from their proofs or as logical conclusions were detachable from their demonstrations.[4] And he suggested that if, on having read a particular historian's work, one still did not see how his conclusions followed from his disposition of evidence, one would have no other recourse than to re-read the work in its entirety, since the conclusions were little more than a synopsis of the story told in the body of the narrative.

What I have suggested is that while this may be true of the story-level of a narrative, it is not true of either the argument or the plot-level. The Hempelians are right to insist that historians' arguments must stand or fall by the tests of adequacy that we apply to any scientific argument. And the narrativists, who oppose Hempel's suggestion that the sole import of a historical account is to be found in the adequacy or inadequacy of the argument embedded within it, are right to suggest that the telling of a story provides a kind of explanation that is different from, though not necessarily opposed to, the kinds of explanations that we can extract from historical narratives by nomological analysis. What both appear to have overlooked, however, is a third kind of comprehension that we get from any historical narrative worthy of the name, that is to say, comprehension of the ways that traditionally provided modes of storytelling function to inform us of the ways that our own culture can provide a host of different meanings for the same set of events. It is here, I think, that Collingwood's "constructive imagination" is really active in the best historical work. This, rather than either storytelling itself or argument, is what we mean by interpretation. And it is the place where narrative capability pays off most profitably in the great historians, past and present.[5]

CHAPTER EIGHT

What Is a Historical System?

{1972}

The title of this paper is misleading. For it suggests that I have an answer to a problem that has been debated, with inconclusive issue, by historians, philosophers, and social theorists for over one hundred and fifty years. It is also misleading because I propose primarily to tell what biological systems are *not* rather than what historical systems consist of. And this might seem presumptuous, given that biologists are so much better qualified to speak on these matters than I am. But it seemed better to err on the side of presumption in the interest of encouraging debate than to stifle discussion by re-rehearsing the trivia of my own discipline's internecine squabbles. In order to do our work, we historians frequently have to act *as if* we knew what a biological system was, the point at which the biological level of integration shades off into the historical level, and the ways that the two levels are related to one another. It would have been cowardly not to have admitted this at this gathering and to have avoided the issue altogether. And so, in the interest of possible clarification and at the risk of possible self-annihilation, I have decided to set forth what I believe to be some crucial distinctions between biological and historical systems, at least as they appear from the vantage point of the historian. If it turns out that these distinctions are not justified from the standpoint of biologists and philosophers of science, so much the better. We only discover the error of our ways by testing them in the presence of those best qualified to judge them.

This preliminary gesture to specialized competence having been made, I would like to begin by noting what seems to be a commonplace to investigators working at the transition points between the different levels of integration to be dealt with. It is true that while historical systems can be profitably described in part by biological modes of representation and explanation, the reverse does not seem to be the

[As White mentions in his preface to this volume, this essay was originally given as a lecture at a conference in 1967, though it did not appear in print until 1972.]

case. That is to say, although we *often* talk about sociocultural systems as if they were strictly analogous to biological systems, we only *occasionally* treat biological systems as if they were analogous to sociocultural systems. For example, we may choose to treat the growth of a nation, a political institution, or even a socialized human being as if it had undergone the same kinds of processes of germination, maturation, and development as a tree or a forest or an animal organism; but when we try to characterize the evolution of a plant or an animal society, we do not ask *all* of the same questions about it that we do about nations, institutions, or human beings. This is because the life-history of a biological system is *in principle* exhaustively describable in terms of the laws of genetic inheritance, variation, and mutation that govern such systems plus the boundary conditions obtaining in that milieu in which the organism lives. We do not normally invoke the concepts of choice, purpose, or intent when describing the responses that biological organisms or entire species make to stimuli coming from their environments. Of course, we *can* invoke such concepts for narrative purposes, as ways of presenting our findings about such systems in common language; but they are not necessary for the scientific understanding of the systems in question. In the analysis of historical systems, by contrast, we cannot do without such terms; we need them to account for a whole range of sociocultural data, especially those data that suggest that man *as a social being* can and often does choose self-destruction in service to some ideal value or culturally provided norm of comportment rather than yield to the laws of adaptation and survival that ought to govern him as mere *mammal.*

It is a characteristic of sociocultural systems that they sometimes seem to choose, self-consciously and programmatically, *not* to survive, if survival entails abandonment of the lifestyle constituted by their dedication to ideal values, goals, norms, or aspirations. Thus, for example, the devotee of the Japanese code of Bushido responds to the culturally induced sense of shame that particular kinds of failure require him to feel by committing suicide. From the standpoint of his membership in a genetic line of descent, this act of suicide is non-adaptive. From the standpoint of his group membership, however, it is *adjustive,* as psychologists use that term, for it removes the stimulus causing the irritation felt as shame; and moreover it is adaptive in sociological terms because it affirms the values that make of the Samurai class a specific group among all the other groups to which the individual might possibly belong if he chose to do so. Thus, in this case, social adaptation seems to run counter to the imperatives of biological adaptation. And we can imagine a situation in which all of the adherents of the code of Bushido might feel compelled to commit suicide *en masse,* in which case an entire genetic population might be wiped out in the interest of affirming the ideal values that make of this population a distinct social grouping. I do not think that animal populations make such gestures by which, in choosing their own self-destruction, they at the same time affirm a set of values without which life itself would appear to be not worth living. Suicide in the interest of ideal values, then, would seem to be one possibility open to sociocultural systems that is not open to most biological systems. And it would be interesting to know whether this is in fact the case.

But it could be argued that the behavior of such a social group is understandable on the analogy of the laws of natural selection. It could be said that the code of Bushido is analogous to a set of genetically inherited characteristics, that the code, even though provided by education and indoctrination, functions as a habit; that habits function in the same way that instinct does; and that the *Bushi* who conforms to the standards of behavior required by the code is *acting* in the same way that an animal *reacts,* which is to say automatically or mechanically. We might want to say that those *Bushi* who do *not* honor the code, but who, in a situation in which they might be expected to commit suicide, instead decide to go on living and to cease being *Bushi* by this decision, represent a kind of species variation. When a significant number of individuals who might be expected to act in conformity to the code, choose instead to improvise another code, in which shame is not adjusted to by suicide, we might liken this to a species mutation; and we could view the new group as a new species characterized by its treatment of survival as a value higher than mere conformity to a social code. The growth of this mutation could then be accounted for by pointing to changes in the *Bushis'* environment, to such socially significant factors as industrialization, urbanization, secularization, and the effects that these have on traditional social units, such as the family, religion, and traditional military castes. And then both the behavior of those adherents of the code who committed suicide and of those who chose to change their way of life would be strictly analogous to the behavior of animal populations adapting or failing to adapt to changes in their natural environment.

In fact, when historians are in their more scientific frames of mind, this is the way they account for such ruptures in sociocultural systems. The sociocultural system is treated as *a genetic endowment* circumscribing specific kinds of behavior for the individuals indoctrinated into them. When such systems dissolve, their dissolution is explained by the fact that they were not programmed for the kinds of responses required by their environments. The social units that split off from the original group, abandon its ideals, and constitute themselves as a new group by modifying their behavior in such a way as to permit survival and reproduction of their kind, are treated as types of species variations with mutational capacities. The old group is said to have "died" and the new group to have been "born."

But what gets obscured by this mode of representing historical transitions is the fact that sociocultural systems do not actually have a "life" except insofar as individuals honor them as appropriate systems for living a distinctively *human* life. Sociocultural systems are constituted and dissolved by the choices of individuals, which choices are conscious precisely in the degree to which indoctrination into them requires systematic repression of instinctive modes of behavior in order to create specific habits of social comportment. Whatever the genetically provided constitution of the individual, he is asked to alter it in some way and to merge his aspirations with those of the group; and he is *forced* to alter them by programs of education and indoctrination that work on the individual's consciousness more or less directly.

In the course of his socialization, then, the human individual is asked to accept as his own a set of ideal values that are determinative of the characteristics of the group's lifestyle. This lifestyle has to be *re*-presented and *re*-accepted by each new generation of individuals born into it. And there is no way of predicting in advance of the event whether a new generation will accept the lifestyle offered to it as the sole appropriate way of achieving a distinctively human life by the previous generation. Even if changes in the environment could be predicted with perfect accuracy, it would be impossible to predict whether a given generation would abandon its inherited lifestyle or affirm it, even in the face of its own imminent self-destruction. When individuals who have been given the same education as their progenitors no longer confirm the values that gave the parent group its distinctive lifestyle, the sociocultural system does not so much die as simply dissolve. Whether the choices were dictated by environmental pressures or by personality characteristics received by genetic endowment is irrelevant. Sociocultural systems do not have lives of their own; they exist solely as a function of the choices of individuals to live their lives this way and not another, regardless of what the environment would seem to require for survival. And when individuals cease to choose a given way of life, this way of life ceases to exist.

Now I suspect that the kind of choices that I have been referring to here have their analogues in biological systems. And it might well be that the difference I am suggesting between historical and biological systems depends upon the vantage point taken for observing them, depends in short on whether we look at the matter from the standpoint of the *object chosen* or from the standpoint of the *choosers*. But it seems to me that there are good reasons for distinguishing between sociocultural systems and biological systems by invoking the concept of *conscious* choice to describe the operations of the former. For the fact that sociocultural systems always come equipped with programs of education and indoctrination suggests the extent to which they are implicitly recognized to be *un*natural by the individuals who are promoting them. Indoctrination into the group requires that the individual's genetic endowment be shaped and molded, augmented and channeled, so that patterns of behavior demanded of him as a social being be regarded as more desirable than those patterns of behavior that are natural to him. The process of sociocultural indoctrination itself presupposes that the individual *could* choose not to accept the proffered system or code, that he might be inclined naturally to reject it, and that he might be able to find perfectly adequate reasons in the economy of his psychic existence to abandon it altogether. In short, the life of a sociocultural system is only as strong as its power to convince its least inclined potential member that he *ought* to live his life as a human being *this way* and not another.

One of the reasons why genetic explanations appeal to historians is that we are interested in processes of *sociocultural change or continuity that extend over many generations.* When a given generation chooses to abandon the system or code proffered it by its parents, we are not inclined to say that the rebellious generation is exercising a freedom of choice, but that *the system itself* has entered a crisis. If in the course of the crisis the individuals in the system choose to reconfirm the system, we say that the *system* was healthy, that it had adequate survival capacities for that time and place. If the generation fails to reconfirm the system, we say that it was sick, that it was overripe or decadent, and that in the end it simply expired.

Thus, we are inclined to speak of the "death" of Roman civilization and the subsequent "birth" of medieval Christian civilization, as though these systems were living organisms, with indeterminate life spans to be sure, but as having theoretically calculable capacities for survival that made it possible for them to adapt to certain environmental conditions and not to others. We conventionally speak of medieval Christian civilization as having taken shape in the "womb" of Roman culture, of having "grown to maturity" in its "bosom," and of then having freed itself from it when it reached "maturity," as if civilizations were organic individuals with received ontogenetic capabilities, phylogenetically affiliated with their predecessors. And in fact our interest in sociocultural processes justifies our use of these terms, for the human individuals that comprised these systems did not have the temporal endurance that the systems themselves had.

But we are inclined to overlook the fact that the language that we borrow from the ontogenetic and phylogenetic processes of organic systems merely provide us with metaphors for characterizing *long-range* temporal processes, processes that occur only on the macro-temporal scale of historical evolution. If we shifted our perspective to the micro-temporal scale, to the scale marked by hours, days, and years in the life of the individual, rather than use that marked by centuries and millennia, we should not be able to discern any *process* at all. We should lose sight of both continuities and significant changes in the historical system, swamped as we would be by the plethora of atomic facts that have no pattern whatsoever. So we shift to the macro-temporal scale in order to see both long-range continuities and long-range transformations in sociocultural systems and to discern a plan or pattern of growth and decline. This gives us a bit of comfort in the face of the possible meaninglessness of the whole sociocultural enterprise.

But we gain meaning only by sacrificing awareness of the essential evanescence of every sociocultural system, only by obscuring the extent to which any such system rests upon fictions that are turned into lived realities by the individual's choices of them as the sole possible way of living a human life, of realizing his personal aspirations, of achieving his goals as a *human* being. And we also lose sight of the fact that when a generation chooses *not* to honor its received sociocultural endowment as *its* way of realizing a distinctively human life, we are in the presence, not of a crisis in the system, but of a crisis in the lives of human beings who must now choose another way of life. Revolutions in historical systems do not occur automatically; they are manifestations of widespread discontent with both the received social-system and the system of education and indoctrination by which men are made into social beings. And as thus envisaged, no sociocultural system can be said to "die"; it is simply abandoned. Nor are new sociocultural systems "born"; they are constituted by living men who have decided to structure their orientation toward their future in new ways.

The points at which old systems are abandoned and new ones are constituted are the most difficult for historians to deal with, precisely because they do not lend themselves to analysis by appeal to genetic models of explanation. The compulsive power of sociocultural systems cannot be discerned at this time; and it cannot be discerned because the systems themselves are in process of being abandoned and constituted by the choices of men. Our mechanistic biases make us loath to recognize the constitutive power of these choices. And so we look for the "survivals" of the older system and the "nascent" forms of the emergent one. Because we do in fact know that medieval Christian civilization was in process of being formed between the third and eighth centuries AD, we treat its nascent forms as if they were self-generated, or as if they were generated by phylogenetic processes.

But the abandonment of Roman civilization and the constitution of medieval Christian civilization were not genetic necessities. Roman society did not die because it had exhausted its genetic potential; for that survival potential was the same so long as men continued to act as if it were adequate to their needs. It might have lasted much longer than it did in Western Europe, as it did last in Byzantium. But in fact men abandoned it; and then chose another system which they not only *felt* was more adequate to their needs but which they *treated as if they had genetically descended from it*. In fact, the Christian past was a segment of the total historical past, which included a Roman pagan segment, of Western European men. What happened between the third and eighth centuries was that men *ceased to regard themselves as descendents of their Roman forebears and began to treat themselves as descendents of their Judeo-Christian predecessors*. And it was the constitution of this *fictional* cultural ancestry that signaled the abandonment of the Roman sociocultural system. When Western European men began to act *as if* they were descended from the Christian segment of the ancient world; when they began to structure their comportment *as if* they were *genetically* descended from their Christian predecessors; when, in short, they began to honor the Christian past as the most desirable model for creation of a future uniquely their own, and ceased to honor the Roman past as *their* past, the Roman sociocultural system ceased to exist. Or at least it was reduced to the status of a recessive characteristic in the ideal ancestry of the new system, the dominant characteristics of which were provided by the fiction that the system was a genetically provided legacy of Christian antecedents.

What I am suggesting here provides an important qualification on my distinction between biological and historical systems, on the basis of the choosing capacities of the latter. I am suggesting that historical systems differ from biological systems by their capacity to act *as if they could choose their own ancestors*. The historical past is plastic in a way that the genetic past is not. Men range over it and select from it models of comportment for structuring their movement into their future. They choose a set of *ideal ancestors* that they *treat* as *genetic progenitors*. This ideal ancestry may have no physical connection at all with the individuals doing the choosing. But their choice is made in such a way as to substitute this ideal ancestry for their actual, genetically provided but socially undetermined, modes of comportment. And they act as if they were more obligated to this ideal ancestry than they were to their actual progenitors.

Thus envisaged, the process of socialization can be characterized as a process of *ancestral substitution*, as a request for individuals to act *as if* they were actually descended from historical or mythical models in preference to any model that might be provided by genetic inheritance. That retroactive ancestral substitution is an essential ingredient in the constitution of historical systems is signaled by the fact that every society recognizes the kinds of conflicts it causes in the individual and tries to provide ways of sublimating them. The conflict between the individual's obligations to his genetic progenitors and his obligations to his culturally provided ancestral models stands at the center of Greek tragedy, Judeo-Christian ethics, and

Roman law. In the end, every individual, before he is fully socialized, in whatever system, is forced to make at least a partial substitution of the culturally provided set of ideal ancestors for his actual progenitors; and to structure his comportment on models found in the former, in ways often detrimental to the health and even the survival of his genetic line.

No such choice is required in biological systems properly so-called, I should think. Biological systems are always functions of all or parts of their genetic endowment plus whatever forces have worked upon their immediate progenitors to increase or decrease their adaptive capacities in their present. Trees, forests, animal populations and cells *may be* conceived as the effect of selective *causes* operating in their pasts; but only human beings are asked to selectively choose their ancestry retrospectively. No father can require that his son treat him as his ideal father, even though he can demand that he treat him as his real father. Fathers bestow sonship on their progeny by the simple act of insemination; they become fathers in the biological sense thereby. But anyone who has had a son will know how tenuous is this merely biological claim on fatherhood, how difficult it is to turn it into the ideal fatherhood required by the son to act in his society as a putatively free agent, or to overturn it and reject it if he needs to do so.

In fact, social fatherhood is only bestowed by the sons, and it is bestowed by the choices men make of models of comportment offered by the sociocultural system. When a whole generation fails to find in the culturally provided repertory of possible ideal ancestors any who sanction satisfaction of what they consider to be justifiable needs, revolutions are in the offing for that system—through no fault of the system. The disaffected members of the rebellious generation will begin to ransack the system's historical record for possible ancestral models hitherto acknowledged as having only questionable worth as ideal models. Failing to find in the historical past of the system any ancestor to which the reverence that imitation indicates can be given, the generation may recur to the historical records of other, even contending systems, import models of comportment from these systems, and demand that their contemporaries honor them as their ideal ancestry. If they succeed in incorporating this alien ancestry into the officially sanctioned repertory of possible models for the system, a revolution or a reformation has in fact occurred. We might see these revolutions and reformations *as variations or mutations in the system*; but they are inconceivable without the act of retrospective ancestral constitution that gives them their specific contents. Thus, Luther and his followers bestowed ancestry on a group that had lost it during the course of the Middle Ages, and set the Reformation in process thereby. Lenin, by contrast, imposed a completely new set of ancestral models on Russian society, and consolidated a revolution thereby.

The history of Russia written by a socially assimilated Russian historian prior to 1917 would not have had to contain any reference to Karl Marx and other European socialists to count as a full and adequate representation of Russian evolution. After 1917, however, any history of Russia that did not place Marx and the European socialists in the main line of ancestral descent of the society in process of formation would be regarded as incomplete. And rightly so; for what the Russians did in 1917, among other things, was to reconstitute, retroactively, but in a degree that was mutationally significant in a sociocultural sense, the historical ancestry from which they chose to act as if they had descended. Once this *ideal* ancestry was established, it could be treated *as if* it were the *real* ancestry of the Russian people; and it was such insofar as the Russian people structured their comportment in terms of their understanding of their presumed obligations to their adopted ancestral models.

This retrospectively provided ancestry *appears* as an actual genetic constitution to individuals fully indoctrinated into the system that has chosen it as a legitimizing agency. Once constituted *and accepted by a group as a genetically provided past*, this past *is* the past for that group as a sociocultural entity. And no amount of "objective" historical work pointing out the extent to which this *chosen* ancestry is *not* the *real* ancestry can prevail against the choosing power of the individuals in the system. This is because as an adherent of the Russian sociocultural system, the individual *is* a descendent of what he has chosen to be descended from. His behavior is understandable only if this *choice* is taken into account.

A recent disciple of Freud has said that in psychotherapy the problem is less to come to terms with our *real* fathers than to find our *true* fathers. The same can be said of sociocultural systems. When a set of "true" ancestors are found to which many individuals can give the reverence of imitation for structuring their lives in their present, a sociocultural system is formed. This system takes precedence over the genetically provided biological system without which, to be sure, even the capacity to indulge in this fiction would be unimaginable. But the process of retroactive ancestral constitution, of abandonment of culturally provided ancestral models, and the search for new models of comportment by which the satisfaction of secondary needs can be achieved, this process stands at the heart of the historical system. Eliminate it and historical systems would not exist at all.

As a kind of coda to these incoherent ramblings, I would like to say something about history-writing, and more specifically, about the relation of historians to the process of retrospective ancestral constitution that I have put at the heart of the historical system. If I understand Erwin Schrödinger correctly, he characterizes life as a reduction of positive entropy in particular time-space locations through a borrowing ("sucking") of negative entropy from the immediate environment. Historical accounts that establish the putative genetic connections between sets of chosen ideal ancestors and the sociocultural systems using them to legitimize their goals or ends serve a similar function retroactively. Historians try to provide both the sufficient and the necessary reasons for any achieved sociocultural complex being what it is and not something else. They put "life" (in the Schrödingerian sense) where formerly there was only chaos. They do this by establishing putative genetic connections between an achieved present and past sociocultural systems. Men seem to require an ordered past as much as they require an ordered present. They want to believe that what they have in fact created could not have been otherwise. And historians assure them that this was so; out of the chaos of individual choices, the historian finds the order that even the choosers could not have seen. As they are *lived*, then, historical systems seem to move *forward*, into the future; as conceived and justified, they appear to *back* into it. Our anxiety in the face of the unknown drives us to embrace the fiction that what we have chosen was necessary, given our past. But the *historical,* unlike the biological past, is not given; it has to be constructed in the same way and in the same extent that we have to construct our sociocultural present.

In choosing our past, we choose a present; and vice versa. We use the one to *justify* the other. By constructing our present, we assert our freedom; by seeking retroactive justification for it in our past, we silently strip ourselves of the freedom that has allowed us to become what we are.

CHAPTER NINE

The Politics of Contemporary Philosophy of History

{1973}

Both the intellectual and social pressures of our time have conspired to make of history a serious philosophical problem where before it could be regarded primarily as a technical exercise. Earlier, we were at least socially justified in thinking that historical investigation consisted of the excavation of buried segments of the cultural past, eternally fixed and immutable, comprehensively describable in principle, and relatable to our present by reference to finite sets of causal generalizations. Now we see that our reconstruction of a socially useful past is but another side of our encounter with our received social order and a function of the projects we set for our social future.[1]

This is to put the matter hyperbolically. Less melodramatically, it might be said that one of the most striking features of Western thought during the last generation is its apparent rediscovery that history might be a problem and not merely a set of puzzles, each of which was to be solved by an individual researcher, the several solutions to which were to be synthesized by simple aggregation. This discovery is part of a general reassessment of the whole sociocultural process that has been going on in the sciences and the humanities since the end of the last century. It has special implications for the professional historian, for it brings with it a specific suggestion that the way we look at history and the uses we make of it are potentially too dangerous to leave to the cultivation of academic historians alone.

Of course, these generalizations are more or less apt as we move from the Americas to Continental Europe or as we move from one discipline to another. On the whole, British and American thinkers have tended to concentrate on the epistemological and methodological problems raised by our attempt to study the past, and, in the matter of history's relation to the social sciences, have, in general, been more concerned to analyze existing practices than to bring about changes. The Continental Europeans, by contrast, have tended to merge such questions with more fundamental, anthropological, or even ontological concerns and to see both historical existence and historical consciousness as aspects of the more general problematics of Western cultural development. As for attitudes in the different disciplines with respect to the philosophy of history, there can be little doubt that historians bring a different cargo of affective predispositions to the debate over history from that of philosophers or social scientists.

The historical profession likes to think of itself as a guild; it might more aptly be likened to a tribe. Certainly the rites of passage through which one must pass share more with tribal initiation ceremonies than they do with admission procedures in the craft-guilds. Novice historians cannot realistically expect to take their profession by storm, in the way that a young scientists or artist can hope to do. Becoming a historian is a process in which not only a great deal of information must be logged in but also a whole set of specific folkways, customs, and mores must be introjected. In large part, this subculturally provided "second nature" consists of a set of restrictions on the kinds of questions the novice historian may ask of the past and the ways he may formulate them, rather than a set of procedural rules that tell him how to distinguish between true, false, and anomalous answers to the questions he poses to his documents.

History is not a discipline that self-consciously seeks to frame new questions for its data so much as ask familiar questions of new bodies of materials. History does not advance in the way that the sciences do, incrementally and dialectically; rather, it seems to work towards the production of the "classic" or "model," towards what Northrop Frye calls that "feeling of definitive revelation" that we experience in the reading of a great poem or the hearing of a great piece of music. Professor Louis Mink has argued, correctly I believe, that *what* the historian says is in many respects inseparable from the *way* he says it, that the historian's conclusion is really little more than a synopsis of his prior disposition of his evidence and that the conclusion of a given work of historical reflection is not detachable from the arguments by which it is arrived at, in the way that scientific conclusions are detachable from their demonstrations. If Mink is correct, it would follow that historians' conclusions cannot be synthesized in the same way that scientists' findings are, that they cannot be assimilated to ever more comprehensive and at the same time ever more elegant sets of generalizations, and that, therefore, historians' findings are arrived at by cognitive operations that have more in common with poetry than they have with science.

The kind of training historians receive would suggest as much. It consists for the most part of exposure to classical models, rather than assimilation of specific procedural rules or corpora of systematically correlated laws or first principles. Which may merely be another way of saying what a leading historian, Professor

G. E. Elton, has expressed repeatedly by both precept and example, namely, that history is essentially a "practice," rather then a body of knowledge or a set of theories. My simile of the tribe requires me to go even further: historiography, I would say, is ultimately a mode of social comportment rather than an intellectual discipline.

Professor Elton might agree with that characterization. He argues that the fundamental distinction to be drawn between the various kinds of historian is that which separates the amateur from the professional. The distinction hinges, in his view, on the difference between those who are continually surprised by what they find in the historical record and those who are surprised by nothing. This would suggest of course that a historian is anyone who has, unlike the poet, lost all capacity for wonder. Professor Elton, however, attributes this absence of wonder to a professional's acquaintance with his materials. Being surprised by nothing, he says, comes from being so thoroughly familiar with one's subject that one not only knows what the documents are saying, but also what they are going to say *next*. Until one acquires this kind of acquaintance, he insists, one will misconstrue both the nature of history and the nature of historical inquiry, whatever one's expertise in other forms of scientific research or philosophical inquiry.

Now, I raise the specter of Professor Elton neither to exorcise nor to deride it. I want rather to use it as a kind of plumb line by which to measure variations among both philosophers and social scientists from what I take to be the orthodoxy of the professional historiographical establishment. For I have no doubt that Professor Elton does speak with the voice of what is usually called "the majority of working historians." His views on the historian's activity are at least *consonant* with the views of the profession at large, at least in the Anglo-American scholarly community.

Since much of the debate over the relation between history and social science takes the form of a testing of territorial claims, or a contesting of colonial prerogatives, it seems fair to use political labels to designate the position held by Elton and his type of historian. In the context within which Elton's self-styled "manifesto," *The Practice of History* (1967), was issued, it is difficult to resist dubbing it reactionary; for he summarily dismisses as beside the point, if not positively dangerous, all of the issues raised by philosophers, social scientists, and political ideologues of the last quarter-century regarding the nature and purpose of historical inquiry. In fact, for Professor Elton, the suggestion that historians might want to revise, or even reconsider, the nature of their enterprise endangers the practice of history in crucial ways. In his view, the historian's right to pursue his studies in virtual isolation from both the society in which he lives and the intellectual community in which he works must be defended "to the knife," as the Italians say. His defense consists in large part in heaping derision upon the use of anything like social science theory in historical explanations and of anything like jargon in the historian's language. "The study and writing of history are justified in themselves," Elton writes, "and . . . a philosophic concern with such problems as the reality of historical knowledge or the nature of historical thought only hinders the practice of history."[2] As for attempts to import concepts and techniques from cognate fields into history, he regards this as both intellectually foolish and socially perilous. For, he says, "since the rashness of the social scientist, treating his theories as facts and intent on applying them in practice, constitutes one of the main dangers to which modern society lies exposed, the study of history may be said to serve a vital purpose when it combats the overconfidence of the men who see the world as categories and statistics, and who think in jargon."[3]

This kind of objection to any rapprochement between history and philosophy, on the one side, and between history and social science, on the other, is familiar enough. It has been current among academic historians since Leopold von Ranke, and it is often used to parody the style of the humanistic pedant or antiquarian by critics of history when they are in their more vicious moods. It is surprising, therefore, that this "reactionary" attitude appears to have found such uniform support among those philosophers of history who might have been expected to challenge it, given the scientific and social pressures to contrive a new historical consciousness over the past twenty-five years.

Perhaps the most famous philosophical defender of the kind of view Elton represents is Karl Popper, who, in his desire to discourage any movement toward socialism or long-range social planning, has tried to show that the very concept of a "social science" constitutes a *contradictio in adjecto*, and that historians quite properly limit themselves to an "interest in actual, singular, or specific events, rather than in laws or generalizations."[4] An exponent of what might be called radicalism in his consideration of the epistemology of the physical sciences, Popper explicitly defends as a methodological principle in history the "popular idea that to explain a thing casually is to explain how and why it happened, that is to say, to tell its 'story,'" and castigates those who "despise old-fashioned history and wish to reform it into a theoretical science."[5] The physical-scientific (or hypothetico-deductive) model of explanation is not appropriate to the treatment of either historical or even social scientific problems, Popper suggested; and those who tried to use it in history or social analysis were as misguided as those who, like Plato, Hegel, and Marx, had confused history with metaphysics and sought to subordinate the former to the latter to create metahistory and its political counterpart, the closed (or totalitarian) society.

The position of the positivist Popper and that of the old-fashioned historicist Elton converge, then, or at least share common ground. Both believe that history must be kept pure of any impulse to claim social scientific or philosophical authority, that "old-fashioned history" has a right to a place among the legitimate forms of knowledge in the modern world, and that the social utility of this conventionally modest form of inquiry lies beyond serious challenge. For both, "old-fashioned history" is a healthy counterweight to a potentially dangerous tendency on the part of social scientists to claim more authority than their actual achievement thus far warrants. It is almost as if these two thinkers viewed the intellectual community as a spiritual counterpart to the nineteenth-century balance-of-power political system. They certainly appear to believe that each discipline must pursue only those projects that offer no danger to any of the others and that the various disciplines ought to work in such a way as to assure the continued survival of them all.

Now, this *cordon sanitaire* conception of history as a discipline flies in the face of some important considerations. One is that, except for a brief period beginning roughly around 1850 and continuing down to the present, historians have usually confessed quite openly the religious, metaphysical, ethical, and political—that is to say, the ideological—motivations behind their survey of history. It is only since the academization of history, which occurred at a time when both the intellectual and political fashions required professions of disinterestedness and objectivity, that historians have felt compelled to lay claim to an *autonomous* role among the disciplines. In fact, in the century in which historians have claimed autonomous status, neither historians themselves nor philosophers have succeeded in defining what it is that makes of history an autonomous *mode* of inquiry. The only distinction that history is generally agreed to enjoy is a concern with the remote, rather than with the immediate, past.

To this consideration I would add another, namely, that both Marxist critics of "straight" or bourgeois history and sociologists of knowledge such as Karl Mannheim, have agreed that the way one looks at history, that is to say, the conceptual principles one appeals to for determining what will count as a satisfactory explanatory strategy, is a function partly, if not completely, of more general ideological commitments. On this even the older "idealistic" philosophers of history (I use this term because it is conventional, not because I believe it to be accurate as a description), such as Benedetto Croce and R. G. Collingwood, agreed. Collingwood never tired of insisting that the way one looked at history was a function and a measure of the kind of man one was; Croce, in his later thought especially, abandoned the view that history was a subcategory of aesthetics and linked it up with ethics as the basis of a distinctively humanistic conception of the world. In this respect, the "idealists" join hands with their "tougher-minded" Existentialist and Positivist counterparts. Neither Jean-Paul Sartre nor Popper denies the connection between one's perspective on history and one's ideological, specifically political, interests. Both view the search for laws in history as a manifestation of a socialistic inclination—though with different feelings about the desirability of such a linkage to be sure. Sartre maintains, with Popper, that history-in-general has no meaning, but then goes on, against the view held by Popper, to insist that men should (indeed, inevitably must) give it a meaning through the choice of a perspective— reactionary, conservative, liberal or radical, as the case may be. Such at least is one of the messages of his *La critique de la raison dialectique*.[6] Popper, by contrast, insists that the causes of human freedom and security can be served only by a steadfast refusal to discern the meaning of history, the laws governing history's processes, and a repudiation of the impulse to plan history's course *for anything but the immediate future.*

The real dividing line between the philosophers would seem to lie, then, somewhere between those who want to use history to curb the impulse to totalistic (or metaphysical or ethical) generalization and those who want to use it to cultivate that impulse. Although all are agreed that the way we view history, the expectations we bring to the study of history, and the kinds of satisfactions we get from it, are in some way tied up with the kind of person we are and the place we occupy or desire to occupy in our society or the kind of society we might want to see constructed in our own immediate future, we appear unable to grant that a *world-transforming* vision can appropriately be brought to the study of history. This is, I am convinced, the true basis of the distinction drawn between "straight" history and "metahistory" by the current generation of Anglo-American philosophers of history, a distinction that, in its way, is as spurious as that drawn between "straight" history and "chronicle."

The current generation of Anglo-American philosophers of history, who think of themselves as "critical philosophers of history" in order to distinguish themselves from those who do "metahistory," appears to be divided into two main groups. The one group, following C. G. Hempel, have in general insisted on the nomothetic nature of all legitimate explanation, or at least the desirability of nomothesis, and appear to envision either the transformation of history into a full-fledged social science or its assimilation by the social sciences. The other major grouping, in reaction to this view and drawing, in different ways, on the thought of Collingwood for inspiration, have tried to establish the possibility of other, non-scientific but not necessarily anti-scientific, modes of explanation that might operate in history. What in fact historical explanations do consist of is not agreed on, though the work of Arthur C. Danto points to the possibility of a synthesis of the many views represented by this group (among which may be listed Alan Donagan, William Dray, W. H. Walsh, Patrick Gardiner, W. B. Gallie, and others). On one point, however, there is virtually universal agreement, not only among the representatives of this group but also between the group and the Hempelians: and that is that "metahistory" or speculative philosophy of history, the attempt to determine the *Weltplan* or universal laws of historical process, is an offense against philosophy, science, and proper history alike.

Although the Hempelians tend to be somewhat more prescriptive, in their insistence that history either serve or become transmuted into a social science, than their Analytically oriented counterparts, who appear to be satisfied with analyzing what historians actually do rather than trying to draw up programs for them, even the Analytic philosophers fail to find in "metahistory"—the work of thinkers like Hegel, Marx, Croce, and Spengler—any of the virtues that they claim to find in the work of the ordinary historian. There is an inconsistency here, I feel, similar to the inconsistency that one finds in Popper's defense of "old-fashioned" history.

An epistemological radical in scientific matters, Popper adopts an attitude of epistemological reaction in his consideration of any attempt to advance historical learning by the scientization of it. This inconsistency is, of course, politically motivated, or at least has specifically conservative (or possibly liberal, in the nineteenth-century sense) implications. While granting that we ought to search for universal laws of physical causation, he denies that the search for universal laws of the social process can be justified *even in principle*—though it is obvious that his most important reason for so arguing is his (no doubt justified) distaste for the actions of totalitarian political leaders who appear to have been motivated by metahistorical visions. This same view is subscribed to, though for somewhat different reasons, by both Hempel himself and Maurice Mandelbaum, both of whom see history as serving the modest role of data gatherer for the more sophisticated social sciences, the sophistication of which, incidentally, appears to be manifested in their "realism" as against the "prophetism" of the "metahistorian."

The anti-Hempelians, by contrast, have produced conceptions of historical explanations that serve for some as an alternative to and for others as a complement of the hypothetico-deductive model used in the physical sciences. It is difficult to summarize the general conclusions about historical explanation arrived at by this group, not only because they eschew technical language, carry on lively debates among themselves over fine points of logic and language, and tend toward almost exclusive use of the throwaway, understated style of Oxford common rooms, but because they too, like the "old-fashioned historians," claim to be doing little more than observing and analyzing established practices rather than prescribing or urging. If I understand them correctly, however, they would agree to something like the following: historians explain past events or sequences of events by breaking down macro-entities into micro-entities and then arranging them along a timeline, and constituting them as a story, thereby producing an account of "what happened" that is, as Gallie puts it, "followable after all." They make a story out of a series, in turn by an appeal to the different kinds of generalizations that a literate lay audience would recognize as an appropriate way of linking up micro-entities so as to make the micro-entity originally calling for explanation comprehensible to it. Among the kinds of generalizations appealed to by the historian, whether he is writing a narrative (diachronic) or cross-sectional (synchronic) account, may be physical scientific or social scientific laws, conventionally held conceptions of what constitutes rational activity, truisms, commonplaces, metaphysical, religious or aesthetic propositions traditionally held to be true by the society for which the historian is writing, or simply commonly honored rules of description. The important point seems to be, however, that what counts as "straight" history" as against "metahistory" is determined by whether the historian is making appeal to that which his prospective audience can legitimately be expected already to know, or whether he is trying, behind the apparent effort to tell what happened as it actually happened, to do something else: namely, change the way his audience normally thinks about human nature, society, or the process of historical change itself.

My own view is that this distinction between "straight" history and "metahistory" is itself ideologically loaded. It is a valid distinction, but not because "straight" history is a legitimate and "metahistory" an illegitimate form of intellectual activity, but because, as currently employed at least, it functions to discredit culturally innovative forms of reflection on history. For by "straight" history is meant, in most cases at least, that form of historical writing that does not, in the course of constructing its account of the past, make appeal to anything but what might be called the "common wisdom" of the group for which it is written as the source of generalizations by which the phenomena under study are to be explained. This implicit appeal to the *consensus gentium*, manifested in the professional historian's distaste for jargon or any technical language and reflected in the philosopher's uniform distaste for any "metahistory" (which could almost be defined by its tendency to try to substitute special language for ordinary educated speech), is the mark of "straight" history as against every form of "metahistory."

The objection, for example, to Marx as a historian and the basis of his condemnation as a "metahistorian" lies less in the fact that he is wrong or mistaken than that his particular terminology conduces to social "error" (i.e., rebellion). Strip

Marxism of its terminology, or translate Marx's principles of historical explanation into non-Marxist terms, for example, into "ordinary language," and they are shorn of their force as parts of a *revolutionary* view of history; and they become simply mistaken, confused, contradictory, etc. The proof of this can be seen in the fact that, in the Soviet Union, it is precisely dialectical materialism that represents what its philosophers would call "straight" history, while the Western European and American equivalent, that is, the professional historians' conventional operations, are regarded as ideologically tainted, confused, contradictory, etc. To espouse a radical vision of history is to be willing to use radical language, a language that, by its very nature, brings under question the conventions of ordinary educated speech of the society under attack. And the same thing can be said of a reactionary vision of history and its attendant linguistic conventions. "Old-fashioned" history, as Popper (and Marx, not to mention Nietzsche) saw quite clearly, can serve certain of the ideological needs of the conservative-liberal bands in the political spectrum. Anyone who wants to change his society in radical ways, whether toward the left or the right, will not necessarily have to articulate a metahistorical vision; he may, for instance, like Norman O. Brown, improvise an ahistorical, mystical, or transcendental one—the kind of vision of history that "dropouts" from a society would find congenial. But anyone who wants to change society in *politically* radical ways will be forced to articulate what the philosophers call a "metahistorical" system.

I am suggesting that the term *metahistorical* is really a surrogate for "socially innovative historical vision." What the philosophers and the historians themselves call "straight" history is the historical vision of political and social accommodationists, whether of those who want to change nothing (conservatives) or those who want to change details while leaving the basic social structure untouched (liberals). It is quite true that "metahistorians" tend to use the prophetic voice and permit, when they do not attempt, legislation for the future. But this is precisely what we mean when we speak of radicals, I should think; and it seems to me that the objection to using a vision of a desirable future to give the form to one's account of past and present would bear weight only for those to whom the present is basically satisfactory as it is. And by the "present," I mean the *social* status quo.

Professor William Dray has distinguished between "ordinary" history and "speculative philosophy of history" on the basis of the latter's tendency to go beyond the empirical data-collecting or social scientific generalizing stages of inquiry and to pass beyond "the question of 'pattern' to that of 'mechanism,'" which, in his view, is a violation not only of history but of philosophy as well. Citing Marx as an example of this transgression of what "ordinary historical inquiry" consists of, Dray accuses the speculative philosopher of history of offering "less a law, yielding scientific explanations, than a kind of schematic *model* showing how all acceptable explanations in the field must go." Such schemata are, Dray maintains, "held with much greater conviction than any available evidence would seem to warrant; and they are usually bound up with some general conception of the nature of man and the world."[7]

This last remark seems to suggest that "ordinary historical inquiry" is not "bound up with some general conception of the nature of man and the world" and that conventional historical accounts do not ordinarily make appeal to generalizations that might be "held with much greater conviction than any available empirical evidence would seem to warrant." Yet if, as Positivists as well as many Analytic philosophers maintain, conventional historical explanations, whether cast in the narrative or the cross-sectional form, do make appeal to culturally provided commonplaces, socially sanctioned truisms, or established opinion about the nature of rational human actions, I find it difficult to see how we might easily distinguish between the activities of the "ordinary historian" and the activities of the "speculative philosopher of history." The *scale* of their respective products may differ, and the latter may be more explicit about the principles of selection and explanation being applied to the data he is offering as evidence in support of his interpretation. But apart from these purely quantitative factors, I fail to see how the operations of the ordinary historian differ in principle from those of the speculative philosopher of history, even with respect to the matter of the attempt to predict the future. It seems just as questionable to me to maintain, even implicitly, as the "ordinary historian" characteristically does, that the forces at work in the past or the present will be different in the future as it is to assume a uniformitarian posture and to seek, by reflection on past and present historical processes, to discern the general form that the future will assume.

Historians, Professor Dray has said in a well-known article, ask "why" questions and "what" questions. Sometimes they want to know *why* certain things happened as they did, and at other times they want to know *what* a given set of events "amounted to." At one time they may want an *explanation* of what they already know to have occurred, as when they ask: "What were the causes of the French Revolution?" At another time, however, they want merely to know how they ought to envisage or conceptualize a given set of occurrences that, at first glance, appear to make very little sense or have no apparent connection. In the former instance, they will try to provide an explanation, using either narrative or nomothetic techniques, that will permit their readers to say, at the end of their account: "Ah yes, now I see why the French Revolution occurred," and silently (or openly) add: "That is in accordance with my (commonsensically or social scientifically provided) notion of why revolutions occur." In the latter case, the audience will be introduced to the protocols for using a general term, such as "revolution," as for example when the historian points out that events a, b, c, d, e, . . . n, when coming together in pattern x, can be comprehended in conformity to the rule that permits us to apply to that pattern the term "revolution." To the question, then, of *what* was happening in France between, say, 1789 and 1815, the historian, in replying "A revolution was occurring," has in effect introduced his audience to the use of the term "revolution" by showing them how it can apply to the events happening in a specific place at a specific time. As against the mere chronicler, for whom a suitable explanation would be cast in a "when" and possibly "where" form, the historian goes on to ask "why" and "what."

Why does the chronicler not ask "why" and "what" questions? Obviously because the chronicle is a historical record directed to an audience that shares with the chronicler specific answers to all the significant "what" and "why" questions of their common culture. Croce often said that the chronicler was a historian who lacked a problem, by which he meant that he had no questions. He should have said that chronicle is a form of historical writing produced by groups that have canonical answers to all the important questions. Chroniclers need not raise "what" and "why" questions, except in purely ritualistic or rhetorical ways, because they can assume that their audiences are in general agreement among themselves on the problem of "the nature of man and the world." This general agreement over fundamental problems, ethical, religious, metaphysical, is one of the characteristics of traditional, or archaic, societies; and chronicle rather than "history" is their characteristic way of making sense out of the historical process. But they do not produce chronicle because they lack a "metahistorical" vision; their metahistorical vision sanctions chronicle as the appropriate way to construe the past and to relate it to present and future.

But surely the same can be said of "ordinary history." The "ordinary historian" does not have to elaborate the metahistorical bases of his synthesizing operations because he shares with his audience a generally agreed upon set of answers to questions about "the nature of man and the world." What makes an "ordinary historian" is the "ordinary" quality of the answers he has to such questions. By appealing, implicitly or explicitly, to the common wisdom or the publicly sanctioned social science of his generation, the historian provides confirmation of the conservative-liberal canon on the nature of the social process. The metahistorian tries to defend, by appeal to history, ideas about "the nature of man and the world" that conflict with the current common wisdom. More: he tries to convince men to view history in such a way as to bring about the actualization of his informing preconceptions.

I am not suggesting that the difference between "ordinary history" and "metahistory" can be likened exactly to the difference between, let us say, *standard* English and "bad" or "vulgar" English, though there are a number of important similarities here. Aside from the fact that both distinctions arise from the attempt to treat what are essentially *different* linguistic conventions as if they were more or less *proper* forms of communication, both distinctions also have a social hierarchical origin. As Leonard Bloomfield points out: "Children who are born into homes of privilege, in the way of wealth, tradition, or education, become native speakers of what is popularly known as 'good' English. Less fortunate children become native speakers of 'bad' or 'vulgar' or, as the linguist prefers to call it, *non-standard* English."[8] One difference between the "ordinary historian" and the "metahistorian" is that the latter, although presumably conversant with the conventions of ordinary historical discourse, has found them inefficient or inadequate to his purposes, has decided to try and forge new tools that have to be expressed in new language, and embarks upon the task of selling them to the audience as a better, more precise, or more responsible way of looking at the historical process.

But much of the discussion about the difference between "ordinary history" and "metahistory" proceeds as if the practices of the former were authoritative as historiographical protocols without appeal. Most of the objections raised against "metahistory" turn, at some level of the argument, upon the discovery that metahistorians are doing something different from what "ordinary historians" normally do—which is precisely the point for a radical metahistorian such as Marx, or for that matter Hegel. Not only do they seek to rewrite history, they *are seeking as well to change the rules for determining what an appropriate conception of historical inquiry will be.* Marx saw, quite correctly, that you cannot revise the way you look at history without reforming the social praxis of your audience, and vice versa. And the same can be said of radical rightists such as Arthur de Gobineau or apolitical nihilists such as Nietzsche. What they are questioning, when they attack "history" or "historical consciousness," is the way history is viewed in a particular time and place, and all the assumptions about "the nature of man and the world" that the ordinary historian, along with his ordinarily educated and socially accommodated audience, honors as self-evident truths.

When scholars talk about history finally coming into its own in the nineteenth century, what they often mean is that the dominant social groups of European and American culture finally contrived a vision of history consonant with their own felt sense of "the nature of man and the world." Marx and Nietzsche, whatever their differences on other matters, had no difficulty agreeing on that. It was this "objective" history, now called "ordinary history," that came under (premature) attack in the late nineteenth century by "metahistorians" of the extreme left and the extreme right. What made them "metahistorians," however, was not that they held views about "the nature of man and the world," but that they held views threatening to the social establishments of their time, views that, to the conservative-liberal historiographical establishment, appeared not so much mistaken as simply insane. But the dispute between the "ordinary historian" and the "metahistorian" is precisely over who will determine the rules for looking at history in socially responsible ways. Like the concept "schizophrenia," "metahistory" is as much a political designation as it is a label for a disease. Like the concept of reason itself, the concept of "ordinary history" could be said to have a long history of its own. It would be profoundly unhistorical to think that the form that historical reflection assumed in the nineteenth century was the definitive form that it had to take for all time. The question that ought to interest us, I think, is which of the forms of metahistory now available to us bids fare to become the "ordinary history" of the next age—and more importantly, what kind of vision of our past, present, and future do we need to permit us to make transition to a next age.

What I am suggesting is that the uniform opposition, not merely to the specific conclusions arrived at by "metahistorians" but also to their very project, is inspired by a fear among British and American intellectual elites of the revolutionary implications of such projects. One indication of the probable truth of this assertion can be found in the striking difference between the prestige that metahistorians enjoy on the Continent and the almost universal distaste in which they are held in the Anglo-American scholarly community. In Europe, not only a different set of attitudes with respect to the study of history prevails but a totally different set of questions has been raised in the debate over history that has developed there since World War II.

In Continental Europe, speculative philosophy of history is not only very much alive, the kinds of problems it poses and the questions it raises stand at the center of a debate over the purpose of historical inquiry and the cultural utility of historical consciousness. In part, this is due no doubt to the philosophical traditions prevailing on the Continent. Throughout the nineteenth century, European thought remained more metaphysical in its orientation than its British or American counterparts; European thinkers remained much less convinced of the power of science to substitute for metaphysics; but more importantly perhaps, the Continental experience of the two World Wars and of fascism served to give ethical thought and ontological inquiry a different orientation. The most original philosophical movement of this century on the Continent, phenomenology, anticipated the need that would become general throughout European culture in the 1930s and 1940s, the need to rethink the bases of a uniquely human world from the foundations of consciousness-in-general. This philosophical movement was paralleled by a movement among social and cultural critics to question the worth of every institution, every value, every idea inherited from the previous century. And this necessarily led to the questioning of the socially provided common wisdom that conventional historians had silently or overtly appealed to in order to give their accounts of the past plausibility and to weave them into a followable narrative. That common wisdom that both philosophers of history and historians in Britain and America have tended to take for granted as a fund of explanatory principles for narrative history was, on the Continent, not something to be analyzed and, as Ludwig Wittgenstein suggested, left as it was, but on the contrary, something to be destroyed, or revised, or filled with a new content more adequate to a culture threatened by barbarism from within its own confines. At the heart of this common wisdom was the conception of the historical past and its relation to the present social dispensation that the conventional historians themselves had played a major role in constituting. It is not surprising that artistic movements like Dada or Surrealism should share with a philosophical movement such as Existentialism a desire to purify language, which was regarded as sick and in need of therapy, and to discredit both the *raison* of the philosophers and the common sense of the common man alike. And it is not surprising that artists and philosophers alike should see in the strategies of the conventional historian the cause of many of the afflictions from which European civilization was suffering. Sartre's novel, *Nausea,* which combines Existentialist perspective with Surrealistic techniques of articulating its themes, has a historian Roquentin as its protagonist—just as Gide's *The Immoralist* did. In both cases, the cure for the illnesses that afflict the protagonists is signaled by a repudiation of the historian's concerns, by an escape from historical consciousness itself, and a rejection of both the institutions and the convictions that sustain the common man and his common wisdom. A more recent, and systematic, attack upon the common view of history is to be found in the work of Michel Foucault, especially in *The Order of Things* (*Les mots et les choses*).

The experience of Nazism and World War II confirmed for many intellectuals their suspicion that both their society and its sustaining wisdom were no longer worthy of serious commitment. As a result, consideration of the principles on which a serious inquiry into the past and the loyalties that a concerned man in the present ought to give to inherited institutions and ideas came to occupy the center of philosophical interests after the War was ended. A philosopher like Merleau-Ponty found no difficulty in using language of the following sort:

> I am thrown into nature, and nature appears not only outside me, in objects devoid of history, but is also discernible at the centre of subjectivity. Theoretical and practical decisions of personal life may well lay hold, from a distance, upon my past and my future, and bestow upon my past, with all its fortuitous events, a definite significance, by following it up with a future which will be seen after the event as foreshadowed by it, thus introducing historicity into life. Yet these sequences always have something artificial about them.[9]

Sartre himself moved from the adamantly ahistorical concerns of his early philosophy to consideration of the necessity of constructing a speculative philosophy of history, specifically tailored to the need for a new social praxis. A social scientist like Claude Lévi-Strauss is willing lately to question the human worth of any historical conception of human nature and to advance the claims of an ahistorical vision of the world over its historicist alternative, whether the historicism being rejected be of the conventional narrative or the speculatively philosophical type. Thus, he writes:

> We need only recognize that history is a method with no distinct object corresponding to it to reject the equivalence between the notion of history and the notion of humanity which some have tried to foist on us with the unavowed aim of making historicity the last refuge of a transcendental humanism. . . . In fact, history is tied neither to man nor to any particular object. It consists wholly in its method, which experience proves indispensable for cataloguing the elements of any structure whatever, human or non-human, in its entirety. Rather it is history that serves as the point of departure in any quest for intelligibility. As we say of certain careers, history may lead to anything, provided that you get out of it.[10]

In *The Savage Mind* (*La pensée sauvage*), Lévi-Strauss rejects Sartre's envisaged philosophy of history as a form of myth, but not in order to dignify "old-fashioned" history as a strategy for discovering a dimly glimpsed human nature. Historical consciousness itself, in both its ordinary and its speculative forms, he sees as a kind of self-domesticating thought, a thought obsessed by a desire for "continuity," by a desire to "close gaps" and "dissolve differences" found in the anthropological record. He does not deny the form-giving powers of historical consciousness, but he does deny that historical consciousness is necessary to the creation of the most desirable form that human nature may take.

Nor is this questioning of the cultural desirability of historical consciousness absent among professional historians of major distinction on the Continent. Not only did Marc Bloch and Lucien Febvre contribute to the creation of a peculiarly anti-narrative (or synchronic) historiography in the years between the wars, many other, much more respectable historians urged liberation from the morally neutral historicism that prevailed in the academy. Thus, as recently as 1961, the classical historian H. I. Marrou could write without embarrassing anyone:

> If the historian is a man and if he actually reaches the level of history (if he is not a mere academician, busy selecting materials for an eventual history), he will not pass his time in splitting hairs over questions which do not keep anyone from sleeping . . . He will pursue, in his dialogue with the past, the elaboration of *the* question which *does* keep *him* from sleeping, the central problem of his existence, the solution of which involves his life and entire person.[11]

What is at issue here are not methodological questions or linguistic strategies, but pre-methodological and pre-disciplinary concerns: the moral significance of a man's perspective on the past, the implications for his present that this perspective has, the cultural worth of any merely academic interest in materials properly entertainable as constituting the ways we create a future world. It raises all the questions that Elton begs when he says that "the facts known about the past are in control" or when he insists that to be a proper historian one must never think that you can get your questions in one place, such as your own lived present, and then go to another place, such as the past, for facts that might provide insights in how to answer them.

In short, if we place debates in the philosophy of history on the Continent next to those that have taken place in the Anglo-American world since World War II, we are aware of the existence of two very different psychological or moral contexts for them. On the Continent, nothing is taken for granted; everything has been brought under question, even the utility of historical consciousness itself. To be sure, the existence of a lively Marxist tradition in social philosophy accounts in part for this situation. Marx's injunction to change the world rather than merely interpret it is still taken seriously as a possible philosophical task; and neo-Marxists like Lucien Goldmann and Henri Lefebvre have taken the lead in shifting discussions of philosophy of history from the dianoetic to the activist voice.

In reflecting on all this one is reminded of Iris Murdoch's clever characterization of the different moods of French Existentialism and British Analytic philosophy after the War. After noting their common interest in language, not as "mirror and exclamation," but as "an activity in the world among other activities in the world," she then pointed to the different contents of their respective analyses of linguistic phenomena. The "scene" of British Analytic philosophy, she noted, is "an everyday one from which certain conflicts are excluded. The 'world' of [Ryle's] *Concept of Mind* is the world in which people play cricket, cook cakes, make simple decisions, remember their childhood and go to the circus; not the world in which they commit sins, fall in love, say prayers and join the Communist Party."[12] This juxtaposition of philosophical universes was not exactly accurate at the time, and is certainly no longer adequate as a way of differentiating the concerns of intellectuals on the two sides of the English Channel. But it is apt enough as a way of contrasting the different moods within which the analysis of the problem of history proceeded in the two areas from World War II to the present.

I suspect that the Anglo-American mood is changing and that philosophers' interest in the problem of history is itself an evidence of a shift in perspective on the social environment within which "old-fashioned" history could remain sovereign. As a datum of cultural history, the Anglo-American interest in philosophy of history, especially as pursued by such thinkers as Professors Dray, Donagan, and Gallie, suggests that philosophers have become enlivened to the problematical nature of the British and American social systems. And I would predict that, as this awareness of the problematical nature of the two social systems becomes more widespread, they will begin to consider more sympathetically the efforts of philosophers of history of the European sort as legitimate philosophical activities.

In my view, the debate set off by Popper and Hempel some twenty-five years ago has gone about as far as it can go on the lines set down originally for its development. The relation between conventional historical narrative, historical explanation, and social science, has been as well analyzed as it can be within the context of a philosophical tradition that is content to leave the world as it finds it. It is perhaps time now to begin asking whether any intellectual or scholar, any philosopher, social scientist, or historian can afford the luxury of ignoring the "involvement" or "confrontation" or even "relevance" of the sort that militant social reformers are (legitimately) demanding of the academic community all over Western society. I am speaking about the possibility of radical inquiry into the relationship between specific philosophical and historical and social scientific conventions and the social systems in which and by reference to which such conventions are authenticated. With respect to the study of the past, it is perhaps only by a radical questioning of the cultural utility of such study that we shall contribute to the salvation of the human *species* that it is our duty as thinkers to serve.

CHAPTER TEN

The Problem of Change
in Literary History

{1975}

Any discussion of a topic as comprehensive as "literary change" must begin with an identification of the objects conceived to inhabit what might be called the "literary field." It is these objects and the relationships among them that undergo the process of "change" alluded to in the designation of the topic. The determination of the different *kinds of changes* that these objects and relationships sustain and the *laws or principles* governing any given sequence of changes will be the desired result of any systematic analysis of the field.

What are the objects inhabiting the "literary field"? At first glance, this appears to be a question easily answered. We are inclined to say that the literary field consists of all objects that are manifestly "literary" rather than merely "verbal." But the distinction between the specifically "literary" and the generally "verbal" artifact is not apodictically given. In fact, the millennial disagreement over the criteria for this distinction has generated the four principal traditions of literary criticism identified by historians of literary theory: the mimetic, the pragmatic or didactic, the expressive, and the objective.[1] In fact, it is the *problematical nature* of the specifically literary artifact that necessitates literary criticism. If we possessed generally agreed-upon criteria for determining what the specifically literary artifact consisted of, we should have no difficulty in defining the objects inhabiting the literary field. And we should probably have very little difficulty identifying the changes occurring in that field. But because we possess no generally agreed-upon criteria for determining what is and what is not a specifically literary work, we are uncertain as to what objects actually inhabit the literary field and, a fortiori, what changes these objects undergo and the laws or principles that govern the sequence of the field's articulation in time.

Of course, the four principal traditions of literary criticism noted above could be taken to provide an exhaustive list of the *types* of objects inhabiting the literary field. By their different characterizations of the nature of the "true" literary work, the mimetic, pragmatic, expressive, and objective critical traditions, direct us respectively to the historical context, the audience, the artist, and the work itself as elements constituting the literary field. And thus, we might want to say that any comprehensive study of changes occurring in the field would have to take account of transformations occurring in the relationships obtaining among the elements thus differentiated. If we could agree that changes in any one of these elements must cause changes in the modes of relationships obtaining among all of them, we could conceive of a cognitively responsible *historical* analysis of the field in general. This having been done, we could then turn to the problem of identifying the general *laws* governing the sequence of all known fundamental transformations in the structure of the field. This would permit us to delineate the various phases through which the field, considered as a historical structure in a distinctive process of evolution, had passed in its development from its earliest to its most recent manifestations.

Such an analysis would not commit us to a crudely reductive or mono-causal conceptualization of the field. We would not necessarily be forced to say that one of the elements in the field, such as the historical context, the audience, the artist, or the work, enjoys the status of a supreme causal agency of which the other elements are effects or secondary manifestations. In all probability, in fact, we should be forced to conclude that different elements play different roles as agents, agencies, and effects at different times and places in the historical continuum. Nonetheless, if our interests were genuinely systematic, we should be compelled to seek some general principle by which to characterize and thus to account for all types of changes appearing in the field. We should be compelled to seek the *extra-literary* basis of all changes of a specifically literary sort.

It is obvious, of course, that in formulating the problem in these terms we have raised the question of the relationship between the parts of the literary field and the field considered as a whole. Or, to put it another way, we have raised the problem of the relationship between the micro- and macroscopic dimensions of literary practice. On the most microscopic level, a given literary *work* can be seen to be undergoing changes in the several versions produced by its original author, by its publishers, and even by its successive readers. A given *genre* of literary works can be seen to pass through a sequence of changes as a result of experiments performed upon it by a given group, generation, or line of authors and interpreters. These *groups*, generations, and lines, in turn, are themselves undergoing changes, in both their sociological composition and their conception of the functions of the artist in relation to the historical context, the audience, or the work of art itself. The whole *class* of consumers of literary works (audiences) may be undergoing changes, both internally and in their relationships to both the community of artists and the larger sociocultural context. The *context* itself may be undergoing changes that, even if not reflected immediately in works of art produced during the period of their duration, in the artistic communities, or in the structure of audiences, will at some point or other in the whole historical continuum have some kind of effect on all three of these.

How the literary historian might deal with this complex web of changes and continuities will depend in large part on how he decides to cut into the literary field or the point of observation he chooses from which to begin his survey of the field in general. More specifically, the literary historian's conception of the *possible* changes that *might occur* in the field will be determined in large part by his preconception of the crucial relationships presumed to exist among the four elements in the field: context, audience, artist, and work. Of course, the work itself will enjoy a favored place in any preliminary survey of the field, because it is both the prime datum to be explained (the *explanandum*) and the principal evidence to be used to explain what appears to be happening in the field (the *explanans*).

Here, of course, a problem arises, a problem that might be said to reside at the very heart of the problematics of literary history. It is a principle of logic that the same datum or fact cannot serve, at one and the same time, both as the thing to be explained (the *explanandum*) and the explanation of why that thing is what it is (the *explanans*).[2] This dual function of the literary artifact is not a problem for the literary critic in the same way that it is for the literary historian—and this because much of literary criticism can be said to be less interested in explanation than in appreciation or explication. To be sure, appreciative and explicative criticism can be said to contain implicitly some kind of explanation; but at least the appreciative or explicative critic is not primarily concerned to explain in the same way that the scientist or the historian has to be. This is because the non-historical critic can work under the aegis of the fiction of the finished work, the completed object, which is the text he has chosen to analyze (however complex the notion of text may be in a given critic's practice). But the historian, if he be a true historian and not merely an antiquarian or chronicler of discrete events, must be concerned not only with specific literary works but with whole classes of literary works; more importantly, he must be concerned not only with the final form that these works have assumed in the historical record but with the *process* by which they came to have both the forms and the relationships among the forms that they appear to have in different ages or periods.

How a given form of literary work appeared as it did, *where* it did, and *when* it did, these are the problems that historians must solve. Solutions to these problems will determine the range of possible answers given to the more important questions of *why* a given form of literature appeared where, when, and how it did. But these solutions, however hedged about with reservations and qualifications, will presuppose some theory of the relationships obtaining among the other three elements in the literary field; and these relationships in turn will necessarily be construed in the modality of cause-effect relationships—even when, as in the most formalist of "objective" critical strategies, the profitability of relating the work to its context is explicitly denied.

Even when, as in the New Criticism, one is constrained to speak only of the possible "effects" of a literary construction on some imagined "ideal reader," one has tacitly invoked the notion of causality. For the moment one sets a work so analyzed beside another work analyzed in the same way, so as to contrast their respective structures, one has already explicitly invoked the notion of literary *change* and implicitly raised the speculative question of *how* this change was possible and *why* it might have occurred as it did. Even if the causal question is mooted by appeal to the "mystery" of poetic creativity, this appeal still presupposes the existence of *some* causal agent of which the art object is an effect. Difference implies change. Change implies cause. And where there is no discussion of cause, we must suppose a want of analytical rigor or a willed decision to halt analysis short of comprehensiveness in the interest of other, extra-literary or ideological, considerations.

To be sure, investigation of the causes of literary change must confront the same difficulties that historians in general confront in any effort to explain specific occurrences or clusters of occurrences in any part of the historical continuum. The principal difficulty met with in such investigations is that of moving with analytical self-confidence from the micro- to the macroscopic levels of historical happening. This difficulty has been characterized by Claude Lévi-Strauss as an epistemological paradox common to all putatively "scientific" explanation in the human sciences. This paradox states that the *information* conveyed in any scientific explanation must vary in inverse proportion to the degree of comprehension claimed for the explanation. The more information given about a specific phenomenon, the less *comprehension* to be expected; the more comprehension provided, the less data the generalizations constituting the explanation can be expected directly to apply to.[3]

In fact, in an interesting discussion of historical explanations, Lévi-Strauss argues that any historical account of a given phenomenon can be shown to move *arbitrarily* from one level of generality to another, from the minutest biographical data to the broadest characterizations of history-in-general, in the course of its exposition. Transposing his discussion into terms suitable for our subject, this means that any *literary* history will, in the course of its representation of changes in the literary field, move arbitrarily *from* the work *to* the artist *to* the audience *to* the historical context or contexts of the work, and back again, in circles of expanding and contracting generality, in such a way as to alternate the provision of information (data) with the provision of strategies for comprehending it, until such time as an explanation of the phenomenon under study is *conceived by its author* to be complete, or at least *adequate to his purposes.*

If we multiply the categories of Lévi-Strauss's model and change them for purposes of characterizing the levels of generality discernible in the literary field, we can conceive the following model by which to characterize the different kinds of literary history we can expect:

COMPREHENSION (Philosophical History)

The whole historical context.................................
Specific historical contexts ....
The whole literary audience...............................
Specific literary audiences ....
The community of artists..................................   } Historiography
Individual literary artists.................................
Literary artifacts ....
Verbal artifacts in general ....

Level of Generality

INFORMATION (Chronicle)

This model of the various levels on which the literary historian can decide to work provides us with a way of distinguishing between the "philosophical," the "chronicle," and the "historiographical" conceptions of literary change. A Hegelian approach to literary history would be an example of the philosophical form. It would *begin* analysis on the most general level (that of the whole historical context, the essential nature of which was presumed to be known), *descend* to the more specific levels for confirmation or illustrative examples of the general principles of comprehension, and always *return* to the most general level as the terminal point of its analysis. Here literary change is conceived as a part of a larger process of evolution that bears a relationship to the whole as that of microcosm to macrocosm. The analysis of a specific text, of a corpus of works, of the mentality of a given artist or community of artists, or of audiences would consist of the disclosure of the extent to which each mirrors or recapitulates the presumed formal structure and attributes of the totality. This strategy stands in contrast to its Marxist variant, which always *begins* and *ends* with a consideration of a *specific* social context and concentrates on the determination of forms of consciousness revealed in the literary works produced in that context that either mirror, obscure, or disclose an ontologically more basic structure of production, exchange, and consumption.

In Marxist criticism, the literary work is considered as a microcosm of the macrocosm that is the specific historical context, but it is always a flawed microcosm, the flaw in question resulting from the *form* that the work of art is compelled to assume in a given system of commodity exchange. Interpretation consists, as the late Lucien Goldmann always insisted, of the determination of the *place* occupied by artists and audiences in a specific social order, itself a product of a specific system of social relations of production.[4] Both the form of a work and its latent content must be shown to be products of the forms of consciousness *possible* within such a system. "Forms of consciousness" in turn are to be construed, not in individual but in class terms, since it must be assumed that any *purely* personal vision, however insightful, brilliant, or "correct" in its apperceptions, will fail to find an audience capable of responding to it as a publicly sanctioned form of artistic expression. And this because "audiences" are conceived to be nothing but those classes or groups possessed of the capital to permit them to function as consumers of the art commodities produced by artists in a particular time and place.

It should be noted that a Marxist approach to literary history is *historically* more responsible than a Hegelian approach inasmuch as it insists on the structural differentiation of discrete periods in the whole historical process. For the strict Hegelian, any differentiation between one period of history and another is rendered possible only by changes in the *contents* of experience, not by the structural differentiation of successive modes of consciousness. The structure of consciousness is a constant throughout the whole of history; qualitative changes are construed solely in terms of the changing degree of *self*-consciousness that "Spirit" manifests in its march through the world. For the Marxist, by contrast, the structure of consciousness is always a function of the modes of praxis sanctioned by given modes of production and the system of social relations of production raised on their foundations. And since all publicly sanctioned forms of cultural expression, of which "literature" is one, necessarily reflect the modes of social praxis current at a given time and place, the aim of literary history must be to demonstrate how a given literary form is adequate to the representation of the set of lived relationships possible within those modes of praxis. Since the publicly sanctioned forms of cultural expression are always consonant with the possible forms of consciousness of the dominant class, criticism must consist of the effort to disclose the relations of production hidden behind and presented in appropriately "idealized" (i.e., mystified) forms in the art objects of a given time and place. Both these contents of the art object and the various forms of its possible mystification will change in response to changes in the social structures in which both artists and their audiences have relatively well-defined and relatively privileged places.

Yet, if a Marxist approach to literary history appears to be historiographically more responsible than its Hegelian counterpart, by virtue of its effort to ground "literature" in the more concrete world of "society" instead of in the theoretically more abstract realm of Being-in-general, it is not self-evidently true that "society" is historically more fundamental for determining the phases through which "literature" in its evolution passes than "literature" itself. After all, if literature is a form of social praxis, then there is no theoretically more compelling reason for concentrating on the one rather than on the other. The categories of Marxist analysis (division of labor, class struggle, the law of the relation between the Base and the Superstructure) may be adequate for criticizing the ideological content of a bourgeois theory of history, but they offer no special help in our efforts to conceptualize literary history. They are simply too crude. Once we have placed a given literary work within one or another periods of social history (slave, feudal, capitalist), we still lack a means of relating the specifically *literary* aspects of that work to the historical matrix dominated by a given form of social praxis. In part, this is because Marxism as a total system lacks an adequate theory of consciousness to go along with its admittedly powerful theory of social praxis. But also it is because, as a theory of history, Marxism shares a weakness that is common to all other theories of history: a tendency to take as given the "chronicle" of historical events that it is the purpose of "historiography" to analyze, interpret, and represent in a true account of what "actually happened." Like other theories of history, Marxism takes as given a series of events chronologically organized on which its characteristic analytical strategies are to be brought to bear. But in fact there is no chronicle of events that is unambiguously describable on which the historian can bring to bear his analytical strategies. There are simply different chronicles among which historians must choose or that the historian must constitute before the analytical operation is undertaken. The chronicle is a fiction that permits the historian to act *as if* he has a *found* world of data that his theories can then fashion into a cognitively secured body of knowledge. In this, the historian faces precisely the same ambiguous situation as the literary historian, who must presuppose a criterion for distinguishing between the literary artifact, on the one side, and the generally verbal artifact, on the other, and who must decide what will make up the "chronicle of literary events" on which he will bring to bear his historical-interpretative principles in order to make a cognitively responsible "history" out of it. The literary historian, in short, must presuppose a "chronicle" of primitive facts, specifically "literary" in nature, of which he will write a "history." But since he has no absolute criterion by which to distinguish a specifically "literary" from a generally "verbal" artifact, he must constitute his "chronicle" by a choice or decision to treat *this* kind of artifact and not *that* as the "matter" of his chronicle. But this choice will be determinative of the *kind* of history that he will write; for there is no such thing as a "chronicle" *tout court* of anything; there are only "histories" more or less structured.

How would we conceptualize the chronicle of literary events of which we might write a history? Recurring once more to our version of Lévi-Strauss's model of the historical field, we can characterize the chronicle as the events occurring on the lowest level of historical generality. But if we try to imagine what a literary chronicle would consist of, we would have to say that it would be characterized, not by its content, but rather by the categories it employs for organizing data. The chronicle, we would be forced to say, is simply that form of literary representation in which time and space alone function as the fundamental categories both of representation and of explanation. In the literary chronicle, change itself is conceived in terms of a removal to a different place or as an appearance at different times. Whereas in a history, removal to a different place or appearance at different times is regarded as a datum to be explained, in the chronicle events are explained by being assigned to specific temporal and spatial locations. To have determined the temporal sequence of events occurring in a given place and to have represented them in their actual sequence of occurrence is, for the chronicler, to have explained them.

To be sure, the chronicler will usually appeal to a secondary explanatory strategy, to some set of preconceptions about the "true nature of reality" that he shares with his prospective audience. The paratactical style of the chronicle falls short of pure nonsense because it presupposes the capacity of its envisaged audience to apprehend both the significance of the events reported in it and the causal connections presumed to link the events depicted in a comprehensible order of occurrence. A history conceived in the mode of chronicle would, of course, report events occurring on all levels differentiated in our version of Lévi-Strauss's schema, without discriminating among them as causes or effects and without seeking to disclose the "true" story of which the serial order of events was only a figuration. So, too, the inaugural and terminal points of the chronicle are unproblematical, being provided by tradition or authority (*ab urbe condita* or *anno incarnationis*), as the case might be. Oracles or sacred writ indicate what the inaugural point of the great book of the world must be. *Where* to begin is, therefore, no problem. As for an ending, one need only bring the account down to the writer's own present.

In literary chronicles, however, the inaugural point is not given; it has to be constituted by the chronicler. And the inaugural point can only be constituted by a decision on the part of the chronicler to treat some one event or set of events as representing the time and place at which a distinctively "literary," as against a generally "verbal," phenomenon appears in the life of a people, a culture, or a civilization. Once this epochal moment has been constituted, it is then possible to conceive a chronicle of purely "literary" occurrences. But the moment chosen as epochal is important. For what can be included in the chronicle as a distinctively "literary" occurrence will be determined by the extent to which it corresponds or fails to correspond to the paradigm of "literariness" contained in the decision to regard *this event* and not some other as the point at which "literature" makes its appearance in the historical record.

The chronicler of a city, for example, operates under similar imperatives. His decision to write the history of *this city* and not another determines the general nature of the events to be included in his account. Everything that happened before "the foundation of the city" and everything that happens outside its confines that does not affect it is either prehistorical or ahistorical. The city itself marks off the area of the historical from the area of the nonhistorical. By contrast, everything that happens in the city or bears upon or affects the city is potentially mentionable in the chronicle. No hypotactical decisions have to be made with respect to significant as against insignificant events. Everything even vaguely connected with the city is potential evidence; everything known about the city *might* be included in the chronicle. It is only the whim of the chronicler that prohibits his including everything. That or the physical limitations imposed by the materials and energies available to him.

Our imagined literary chronicle, however, does not enjoy the advantages of the city chronicle. For in the first place, we do not know when "literature" began; nor do we know how or where it began. In an imagined, ideal literary chronicle, *every verbal* artifact might be considered as a candidate for mention in its annals; this because the chronicler could draw no distinction between "good" and "bad" literature, or between works that are "truly" literary and those merely appearing to be so. For if these distinctions were drawn explicitly, we should be provided with criteria by which to challenge the chronicler's judgment in placing a given work in one category rather than in another. And we should be projected into endless disputes over the true nature of the literary work that are the justification for such journals as *New Literary History*.[5] Moreover, once such distinctions were made, the clear line of paratactical representation (of one literary event after another) would give way to hypotactical representations, in which some literary works were given dominant and others subdominant or subordinate roles in the "drama" that we should be forced to contrive. We would be required, in fact, to divide the whole set of literary events into agents and agencies, into protagonists and antagonists, and we would be forced to specify the "plot" that would make of their relationship a comprehensible drama of development, rather than remain content with the simple series that the chronicler takes to be the sole possible form that an "explanation" ought to take.

Of course, our imagined ideal chronicle is simply a heuristic device. There is no such thing as an unstructured chronicle. There are only "histories" more or less structured; or rather histories in which the principles of selection of data and strategies of stress and subordination are more or less explicitly provided by their authors. Chronicles do not fail to "comprehend" the "information" contained in them, any more than philosophies of history fail to provide enough "information" to substantiate their "comprehensions" of what was "really happening" in the course of historical time. The dream of the perfect chronicle is as futile as the dream of the perfect philosophy of history. If we are to discover the grounds for belief in an adequate history, of literature, or of anything else, we must cease to operate at the extremities of the polarities: universals and particulars. We must move to the middle sections of the historical field, the areas occupied, not by "the whole historical context," on the one side, and by the "individual literary work," on the other, but the ground on which they meet. For neither the *whole context* nor the individual work can be the subject of a truly historical account. The "history of literature" like the "history of society," must be an account of a multivariant field of causal occurrence. And a literary history must be nothing more nor less than an account both of change in continuity and of continuity in change.

The important task is to determine what is changing and what is continuous in any given period of the whole historical record. This can only be done by studying the component shared by the context, the audience, the artist, and the work alike. This component is *language in general* (not being or consciousness), and any literary history that does not relate changes occurring in any of the four prime elements of the literary field to the more general field of linguistic transformation is fated, in our view, to the obscurantism of ontological speculation, on the one side, or the reductionism of scientistic distortion, on the other.

The dialectic of literary history, then, must be construed as the dialectic between literature (however defined) and language (however conceived). And any history of literature that does not place this dialectical relationship at the center of its problematic will necessarily be driven to false reductions, on the one side, or to false inflations, on the other. For language is the medium that binds the work, the artist, and the audience together in a common mode of praxis that is at once the expression and the reflection of a shared experience of the world. A literary history uninformed by a general theory of language will be thrown open to the more extreme versions of a "mimetic" theory of the literary work, on the one side, or those of a purely "expressive" theory, on the other. But a literary history informed by a general theory of language will have built into it a formal criterion for assigning significance to different literary works as elements of a history that is neither of "being," "consciousness," nor "society," but of that "language in general" that is the distinctive form of a specifically human mediation with the world.

It is at this point that we can profitably consider the linguistically oriented reconceptualizations of the literary field proposed by Roman Jakobson in his essays on stylistics and poetics. Jakobson refines the notion of the literary field by: (1) distinguishing between two functions of the literary work (as mode of *contact* between the artist and his potential audience(s) and as *message* with an identifiable cognitive content) and (2) postulating "the linguistic code" as that medium that links the artist, the audience, and the work together as elements within a larger historical context. His model can be schematically represented in the following way:

In this system, language-in-general is viewed as the instrument of mediation between man and his historical-natural context. A given language permits the generation of a set of codes in which specific kinds of messages can be transmitted from artists (addressers) to their audiences (addressees). It is assumed that all messages have a cognitive content as well as a specific form, the former being given by the artist's experience of the context and the latter being determined by the decision to use one or another of the possible encoding procedures made available by the whole linguistic endowment.

Messages are sent and received in specific forms; specifically "literary" messages are recognizable, however, not so much by their form or content as by their *function*, which is to direct attention to "the message for its own sake." The "set (*Einstellung*) towards the MESSAGE as such . . . is the POETIC function of language,"

Jakobson argues in his essay "Linguistics and Poetics," and it is this "*function which projects the principle of equivalence*" [which is characteristic of all linguistic phenomena] "*from the axis of selection into the axis of combination.*"[6] As such, the specifically "literary" artifact represents a testing of the linguistic code in general or of a specific form of the code as represented by one or another literary convention.

Jakobson's theory may not give us an ironclad criterion for identifying all forms of *literary* expression, nor permit us to distinguish between linguistic phenomena in general and the "literary work" per se; but it at least permits us to regard "literature" in terms of its *function* in a specific historical context, rather than in terms of its *structure* alone, which is the rock on which all idealist theories of literature founder. By regarding the literary work as that form of verbal artifact that tests the combinatory strategies provided by a given linguistic code, Jakobson gives us a ground for apprehending the dialectical relationship between human consciousness and a given historical context in which language itself is the mediating instrument.

Jakobson's formulation thus permits us to view the literary work, not only as a simple mediation between the artist and his audience(s) or between the artist and his historical context but also as a device for testing the instrument of mediation among all of these, language-in-general. In a given period and place in history, the system of encodation and decodation permits the transmission of certain *kinds of messages regarding the context* and not others; and it will favor those genres adequate to the establishment of contacts between different points in the whole communication system represented by language-in-general. *Significant periods of literary change* will thus be signaled by *changes in the linguistic code*; changes in the code will in turn be reflected in changes in both the cognitive content of literary works (the messages) and the modes of contact (genres) in which messages are transmitted and received. Changes in the code, finally, can be conceived to be reflective of changes in the historical-natural context in which a given language game is being played. Writers may experiment with different genres, with different messages, even with different systems of encodation and decodation. But a given product of such experimentation will find an audience "programmed" to receive innovative messages and contacts only if the socio-cultural context is such as to sustain an audience whose experience of that context corresponds to the *modes of message formulation and conveyance* adopted by a given writer.

Literary innovation must be presumed to be going on all the time, in the same way that speech innovation must be conceived to be continuous. But *historically significant literary innovation* is possible only at those times in which the potential audiences for a given form of literary work have been so constituted as to render unintelligible or banal both the messages and the modes of contact that prevailed in some preceding era. Periods of genuine "crisis" in literary history, consequently, must be seen as those in which new systems of encodation and transmission of messages are being constituted, as times when *language itself* has fallen under question, and none of the conventional modes of message formulation and transmission appear to be adequate for naming and classifying the elements of the larger historical-natural context. In such times, it is not so much the *principles of selection* that come under scrutiny as the *principles of combination* themselves; in "crisis" situations, questions of syntax and semantics take precedence over those of lexicon and grammar.

Literary change, as thus envisaged, must be construed in terms of the possibilities contained in language in general for linking words and phrases under different strategies of combination. It is the emphasis on the axis of combination, conceived as the key to the understanding of stylistic variation, that leads Jakobson to the consideration of the poetic tropes as the link between language and literary style.

In Jakobson's terms, the "poetic function projects the principle of equivalence from the axis of selection into the axis of combination;" and if this is the case, it must be asked, what are the possible modalities of combination? As is well known, Jakobson locates those possibilities between the "metaphoric" and "metonymic" poles of language behavior in general. A *particular style* is viewed as a product of a tension between the *cognitive content* of the messages transmitted under the terms of its convention and the *dominant mode (trope) of figurative usage* that "shapes" the message into a specific kind of contact between artist and audience. Accordingly, the study of the dominant tropes provides a clue to stylistic variation in all literary practice; this holds for both poetic and prose fiction. Thus Jakobson writes: "the study of the poetic tropes has been directed mainly toward metaphor, and the so-called realistic literature, intimately tied with the metonymic principle, still defies interpretation, although the same linguistic methodology, which poetics uses when analyzing the metaphorical style of romantic poetry, is entirely applicable to the metonymical texture of realistic prose."[7] And in the famous fifth chapter of *Fundamentals of Language* (written in collaboration with Morris Halle), Jakobson hinted that the stylistic history of nineteenth-century literature (in Europe) might well be written in terms of a swing from one of the poles of linguistic usage to another:

> The primacy of the metaphoric process in the literary schools of romanticism and symbolism has been repeatedly acknowledged, but it is still insufficiently realized that it is the predominance of metonymy which underlies and actually predetermines the so-called "realistic" trend, which belongs to an intermediary

stage between the decline of romanticism and the rise of symbolism and is opposed to both . . .

The alternative predominance of one or the other of these two processes is by no means confined to verbal art. The same oscillation occurs in sign systems other than language. A salient example from the history of painting is the manifestly metonymic orientation of cubism, where the object is transformed into a set of synecdoches; the surrealist painters responded with a patently metaphorical attitude.[8]

The difficulties that arise in trying to use Jakobson's notion of stylistic change as an "oscillation" between the poles of metaphor and metonymy are the same as those encountered in the application of any dualistic system, from the "naive-sentimental" dichotomy of Schiller to the "Being-Nothingness" dichotomy of Heidegger and Sartre. The most interesting "transitional" phenomena cannot be accommodated, except as "mixtures" of the polar types. As for the polar types themselves, they appear to apply only to the more conventional and most banal forms of literary expression produced by a given age or epoch.

But let us suppose that the metaphor-metonymy dyad has the advantage over other dualistic theories of style (such as the "naive-sentimental" and the "Being-Nothingness" dyads) of keeping the attention of the literary historian focused on the linguistic matrix out of which and against which "literature" emerges. At least, Jakobson's theory does not incline us to dissolve the literary artifact into some putatively more fundamental, metaphysical ground that, like "Being," can be filled with any content. In his theory, "literature" is a special case of language behavior and as such is referable to its human users rather than to some imagined power supposedly determining the modes of being in general. Language is, as it were, provided with its own ground, or domain, and treated as what both Vico and Hegel (as well as Marx and Nietzsche) saw it to be, an *instrument of mediation* between human consciousness and the world it occupies.

This instrumentalist conception of language is not, of course, meant to obscure its generative aspect, the capacity of language to "invent" as well as "describe" a "found" world. On the contrary, Jakobson's insistence on the twofold nature of the literary statement, as "Message" on the one side, and as "Contact" on the other, precludes so utilitarian an interpretation of language. For the literary statement considered as "Contact" directs attention to the "Phatic" and "Conative" aspects of linguistic behavior that are the sources of its *constructive* power. Moreover, it points attention to the specifically "poetic" elements of literary statement, the self-referential or reflexive nature of *poesis*. Literary statement *calls attention to itself as message*, in Jakobson's view, thereby raising itself out of the general field of linguistic usage and inviting investigation of the way it *effects* the other elements of the "literary field": Code, Artists, Audience, and Context respectively.

It is this element of "effect" (and capacity to *be effected*) that is crucial for any *historian* of literature. For whatever the validity of the New Critics' and formalists' injunctions to concentrate on the work "for itself alone" as a critical protocol, the plain fact of the matter is that the concept of the *historical*, conceived as a mode of being, cannot be disengaged from the notion of cause and effect—at least, it cannot be so disengaged without the risk of falling into mere impressionism, on the one side, or metaphysics, on the other. In urging the identity of causal analysis with historical understanding of the literary field and its processes, we need not deny the utility of the New Critics' reminders of the baneful effects of the historical, intentional, and affective "fallacies" as a critical prophylaxis. There may be those who do not want a "history of literature" at all. So be it. For those who want an account of the evolution of literary forms more sophisticated than mere chronicle, however, there can be no ignoring of the problem of the relationship between the literary works that make up the chronicle and the various artists, contexts, and audiences that comprise the other irreducible elements of the literary field. This relationship, in order to qualify as a "historical" one, must be construed in the modality of causal connections.

There is not, however, any generally accepted notion of the nature of the causal relationships obtaining among the various elements of the historical field (work, artist, audience, and context) and between all of these and the linguistic Code which, in Jakobson's model, serves as the mediative agency among them all. To raise such questions is to raise the problem of the *langue-parole* relationship that has worried language theorists since Saussure's original postulation of this profitable concept. The relationship between *langue* and *parole* does, however, have the merit of allowing us to characterize with something more than impressionistic categories the nature of "crises" in literary traditions.

By distinguishing between crises in literature, on the one side, and crises of language, on the other, we have a way of differentiating between the kinds of disruptions that attend the supplanting of one dominant genre by another and those that attend a fundamental recasting of the whole "set" toward literature in general. In making such a distinction, we must not be misled by the avant-garde rhetoric of innovating writers who are inclined to regard their particular way of viewing the task of the artist or the appropriate form of the literary work as representing a fundamental revolution in *both* language and literature. The advent of a new dominant genre, the advent for example of the novel in the late eighteenth century in place of the poem or the essay, is not in itself a revolutionary event. If we consistently utilize the political metaphor at the heart of the term "revolutionary," we must say that such a transition represents little more than a "reform." A revolution in the literary field represents a transformation in the relationship between "literature" and "language-in-general." Revolutionary crises in literary history are times when the whole linguistic code is undergoing revisions. Such crises will usually be attended by generic transformations, but times of generic transformation are not inevitably or necessarily times of literary revolution. Revolutionary periods are times in which the linguistic code of a generation or dominant social group of a culture comes under attack and gets revised.

CHAPTER ELEVEN

The Problem of Style in Realistic Representation

Marx and Flaubert

{1979}

Prior to the nineteenth century, the problem of style in literature turned upon discussion of techniques of rhetorical composition and especially techniques of figuration by which to generate a secondary or allegorical meaning in the text beyond the literal meaning displayed on its surface. But the advent of realism meant, among other things, the rejection of allegory, the search for a perfect literality of expression, and the achievement of a style from which every element of rhetorical artifice had been expunged. For Gustave Flaubert, for example, style was conceived to be the antithesis of rhetoric; in fact, he identified style with what he called "the soul of thought," its very "content," to be distinguished from "form," which was merely thought's "body." Realism in the novel, like its counterpart in historiography, strove for a manner of representation in which the *interpretation* of the phenomena dealt with in the discourse would be indistinguishable from its *description*; or, to put it another way, in which *mimesis* and *diegesis* would be reduced to the same thing. Instead of mediating between two or more levels of meaning within the text, which "style" had been conceived to do during the time when "literature" was identified with "allegory," style now became a manner of translating phenomena into structures of discourse, transforming "things" into "words" without residue or conceptual superaddition.

The aim of realism, then, was literariness as against figurative expression, so much so that the difference between the style of Balzac and his successor Flaubert can be marked by the relative paucity of metaphors in the latter as compared with the former. Nonetheless, writers continued to seek to cultivate distinctive styles of representation. There was no thought, as far as I can determine, that the perfection of a realistic mimesis would result in a uniform mode of expression, with every discourse resembling every other. But the criterion for determining stylistic achievement had changed; it was no longer the manner or form of utterance that constituted style but rather the matter or content of the discourse, as Flaubert had insisted. This meant that style had to do with cognitive perspicuity, the insight that the writer had into "the nature of things." To *see* clearly was to *understand* aright, and understanding was nothing other than the clear perception of the "way things are."

But this conflation of understanding with perception meant, obviously, that if allegory had been barred from entering the house of art by the front door, it had found entry at the back. It entered in the form of "history," no longer considered as a construction of the historian's powers of composition, as it had been considered in earlier times when historiography itself was regarded as a branch of rhetoric, but as a domain of "facts" that offered itself to perception in much the same way that "nature" did to the unclouded eye of the physical scientist. The "truth" of the realistic novel, then, was measurable by the extent to which it permitted one to see clearly the "historical world" of which it was a representation. Certain characters and events in the realistic novel were manifestly "invented," rather than "found" in the historical record, to be sure, but these figures moved against and realized their destinies in a world that was "real" because it was "historical," which was to say, given to perception in the way that "nature" was.

Now, arguably, history does not exist except insofar as a certain body of phenomena is organized in terms of the categories that we have come to associate with a specifically "historical consciousness." History does not consist of all of the events that ever happened, as the distinction between merely natural and specifically human events itself suggests. But neither do all human events belong to history, not even all human events that have been recorded and therefore can be known to a later consciousness. For if history consisted of all of the human events that ever happened, it would make as little sense, be as little cognizable, as a nature conceived to consist of all of the natural events that ever happened. History, like nature, is cognizable only insofar as it is perceived selectively, insofar as it is divided up into domains of happening, their elements discriminated, and these elements unified in structures of relationships, which structures, in turn, are conceived to manifest specifiable rules, principles, or laws that give to them their determinate forms.

The dominant view underlying early nineteenth-century historiography was that the structures and processes of history were self-revealing to the consciousness unclouded by preconceptions or ideological prejudices, that one had only to "look at the facts" or let the facts "speak for themselves" in order for their inherent meaning or significance as historical phenomena to come clear. And this view was shared by novelists and historians alike, with the former grounding their "realism" in their willingness to view history "objectively" and the latter distinguishing their work from that of the novelist by their exclusion of every "fictional" element from their discourse. Few commentators (Hegel, Johann Gustav Droysen, and Nietzsche are notable exceptions) perceived that there were as many possible conceptualizations of history as there were ways of fashioning novelistic fictions; that there were as many styles of historical discourse as there were styles of realistic representation: that if realism in the novel could have its Benjamin Constant, its Balzac, its Stendhal, and its Flaubert, realism in historical representation had its Jules Michelet, its Tocqueville, its Ranke, its Droysen, and its Theodor Mommsen, each of whom felt himself to be representing history realistically, letting the facts "speak for themselves," and aspiring to a discourse from which every element of allegory had been expunged. In supposing that history constituted a kind of "zero degree" of reality, against which the fictive elements of a novelistic discourse could be measured, the realistic novelists of the nineteenth century both begged the question of the metaphysical base of their realism and effected an identification of style with content with which modern critical theory continues to have to contend. But this supposition, when examined critically, gives insight into the hidden allegorical elements in every realistic representation and raises the question of the problem of style in a way different from that which takes the form-content distinction for granted.

I propose to examine the problem of style that the project of realism in the novel raises by comparing a novelistic and a historical text produced at about the same time, both of which deal with the same general set of historical events and lay claims to a realistic representation of the events in question, but which are generally recognized as representing virtually antithetical ideological positions and different stylistic attributes. These texts are Flaubert's novel *The Sentimental Education* and Karl Marx's history *The Eighteenth Brumaire of Louis Bonaparte.* No two texts could be more dissimilar when viewed from the conventional standpoint of stylistic analysis that turns upon the distinction between form and content and identifies style with the former. Flaubert's discourse is cool, detached, leisurely to the point of shapelessness in its depiction of what Georg Lukács calls the fragmented world of its protagonist. Marx's discourse, by contrast, is shot through with an irony bordering on open sarcasm and contempt for the personalities, situations, and events he depicts; it manifestly originates in a preconceived judgment, ideological in nature, of the Second Republic, the bourgeoisie that created it, and the "charlatan," Louis Bonaparte, who overturned it. Whereas Flaubert forbears to intervene, in his function as author, in the narrative, permitting his narrator's voice only a few laconic observations on the folly of human desire in a world devoid of heroism, Marx intervenes continually, alternating between the manner of the clear-eyed analyst of events, on the one side, and the ranting ideologue, on the other. If we conceive style, then, as manner of utterance, we would have to mark down Marx as a representative of the ornate and Flaubert of the plain or mixed style, so different are the rhetorics of these discourses, so opposed the attitudes revealed on the level of language alone.

But if we conceive of style as a perceivable strategy for fusing a certain form with a certain content, then there are remarkable similarities to be discerned between the two texts. The manifest form of both works is the mock *Bildungsroman*: in the one case, of a young French provincial seeking love and self-realization in Parisian society in the 1840s; in the other, of the French bourgeoisie itself, seeking to deal with the vicissitudes of its rise to power in a society fatally divided between contending classes, groups, and factions. This means that the content of both works is the drama of a development of a kind of consciousness—personal on the one side, and class on the other. The *Eighteenth Brumaire* is, we might say, "the sentimental education" of the French bourgeoisie, just as *The Sentimental Education* is "the eighteenth Brumaire" of a personification of a typical member of the French *haute bourgeoisie*. As thus envisaged, the respective plot-structures of the two works describe the same patterns of development: what begins as an epic or heroic effort at the implementation of value—personal on the one side, class on the other (although these reduce to the same thing ultimately, inasmuch as Frédéric Moreau, the protagonist of Flaubert's novel, has no values other than those given him by his historical situation)—progresses through a series of delusory triumphs and real defeats, to an ironic acceptance of the necessity of abandoning ideals to the accommodation to realities in the end.

At the end of Flaubert's novel, Frédéric Moreau exists in precisely the same condition that the French bourgeoisie is depicted as having come to at the end of Marx's history, that is to say, as the very incarnation of a cynical acceptance of comfort at the expense of ideals. Even more strikingly, both authors insist—the one indirectly, the other directly—that the final condition in which their protagonists find themselves was already implicitly present in the structure of consciousness with which each embarked upon its "sentimental education." This structure of consciousness is shown to have been fractured from the beginning: fractured as a result of a fundamental contradiction between ideals consciously held at the outset and the conditions of existence in a dehumanizing society, one in which no *human* value can be distinguished from its commodity status. Frédéric Moreau's final rejection of his ideal love, Mme Arnoux, and his recognition that his life had failed at all crucial points correspond precisely with the French bourgeoisie's rejection of the ideals of "liberty, equality, and fraternity" that it had defended since the French Revolution and its acceptance of the cardsharp Bonaparte as the custodian of "order, family, property, and religion."

What is most remarkable, however, is yet a fourth resemblance between the two discourses, what I wish to name as their shared style, considered as a transformational model for marking off the phases in the development of the consciousnesses being depicted and for integrating them across a time series so as to demonstrate their progressive transumption. This model I call *tropological,* since it consists of a pattern of figurations that follows the sequence: metaphoric, metonymic, synecdochic, and ironic; and I identify this tropological model with the style of the discourses being analyzed since it constitutes a virtual "logic" of narration that, once perceived, allows us to understand why these discourses are organized in the way they are both on their surfaces and in their depths. The tropes of figuration, in other words, constitute a model for tracking processes of consciousness by defining the possible modes through which a given consciousness must pass from an original, metaphoric apprehension of reality to a terminal, ironic comprehension of the relationship between consciousness itself, on the one side, and its possible objects, on the other. The tropes of metonymy and synecdoche function as models of transitional phases in this procession of modes of comprehending reality, the former governing the arrangement of phenomena into temporal series of spatial sets, the latter governing its integration into hierarchies of genera and species. The deployment and elaboration of experience under these modes of figuration is what I mean by *style,* a usage that permits us to pay tribute simultaneously to the conception of style as form and style as content, of style as the union of the two in a discourse, of style as both group and individual signature, of style as the process of composing a discourse, and of style as an attribute of the finished composition. Style as process, thus conceived, is the movement through the possibilities of figuration offered by the tropes of language; style as structure is the achieved union of form and content that the completed discourse represents.

Let us begin with a consideration of Flaubert's *Sentimental Education.* Tropological criticism directs us to look, first, not at plot, character development, or manifest ideological content (for this would presuppose that we already had an understanding of these phenomena at least as subtle as that of the author, or a better understanding of them, or that these were not problems for the author but solutions to problems), but rather at the principal *turns* in the protagonist's relationship to his milieu. Flaubert's narrative is divided into four chronological segments, three covering the years 1840–51 and ending with the coup d'état of Louis Bonaparte, and a fourth, comprising chapters 6 and 7 of part 3, which is separated by fifteen years from the last event recorded in chapter 5 of this part. In the last segment, the protagonist, Frédéric Moreau, and the woman he had loved, Mme Arnoux, meet after a fifteen-year separation in order to realize how ill-fated their love had been from the beginning; and Frédéric and his best friend, Deslauriers, meet in order to reflect on how and why their lives had gone wrong from first to last. We have no difficulty recognizing the ironic tone of these two chapters. The three characters in it themselves display the attainment of an ironic distance on their earlier passions, beliefs, ideals, follies, pride, and actions; and, as Jonathan Culler points out in his reading of this passage, Flaubert himself reaches sublime heights of ironic sympathy for the attempts of the actors to ironize their own lives.[1]

Having specified the ironic nature of the conclusion, we might be inclined retrospectively to cast the shadow of irony back over the sections preceding it. And this is legitimate enough, since we must suppose that irony (or what Freud called secondary revision) is the dominant trope of any consciously wrought fiction—and the governing, even if unacknowledged, trope of all "realistic" discourse, insofar as its author supposes that he sees clearer or understands better what was "really happening" than did the agents whose actions he is describing or retailing. But here we must distinguish between the irony of the author and the consciousness he ascribes to his agents and discriminate among the changing modes of relationship, between the protagonist and his milieu, which mark off the significant turns in the narrative. And we may say, following a Hegelian reading of the text, that here we have an allegory of desire, personified in all of the figures but condensed especially in that of Frédéric Moreau, projected into a world in which everything appears in the opaque form of a commodity, to be bought, exchanged, and consumed or destroyed without any awareness of what might be its true, its human value. It is the commoditization of reality that accounts for the melancholy tone of the whole novel, even in those moments of *hysterica passio* that constitute the most sensual scenes in the story. Flaubert has no need to set forth explicitly a theory of the true value of things; the absence of that value or its absence in the consciousness of the agents in his story is sufficiently suggested by the succession of frustrations that he recounts in the efforts of every one of them to achieve a deep union with his ideal object of desire. It is the absence of this human value, we may say, in the face of the oppressive presence of the dehumanizing uses made of others, which is the true subject of the discourse.

But that being given, what are the stages Frédéric Moreau is supposed to have passed through in the process of realizing the discrepancy between aspiration and possibility of achievement that he comes to in the conclusion? When we ask this question in the light of tropology, the structure of and relationships among the first three sections of the book become clearly discernible.

We may say that the first part, which covers the period 1840–45, presents us with an image of desire personified in Frédéric projected in the mode of metaphor, desire seeking an object but unaware of anything but practical obstacles to its gratification. Here the object of desire is first presented to Frédéric in the mystery of Mme Arnoux's *appearance* only, as mere image rather than as image grounded in substantial reality, desire not yet individualized, and sensed to be painfully unattainable—in Frédéric's mind, simply because he is not wealthy enough to pursue it. This is the period of Frédéric's reluctant exile from Paris to the dull life of Nogent, which, in retrospect, will have turned out to be no duller, no more dispiriting than Paris itself. While there, he encounters another potential object of desire, in the figure of the girl-child, half provincial bourgeoise, half savage peasant, Louise Rocque, the ambiguity of whose nature is signaled in her illegitimate birth no less than in the precociousness of the passion she feels for Frédéric from the start. But Frédéric's desire for her is still unfocused, still sublimated in the unconsummated Paolo and Francesca relationship they have and limited to caresses and fraternal kisses on Frédéric's part. This part of the novel, which opened with a leisurely journey by water from Paris to Nogent, ends with Frédéric's inheritance, by pure chance, of the fortune that will permit him to imagine that, by returning to Paris, he will be able to possess whatever he wishes and achieve whatever he likes, spiritual as well as carnal.

Part 2 begins with a journey, not by *paquebot,* but by coach, the rapidity of the sensations of which already signals the disjunctions and discontinuities of the relationships figured in this section. Allow me to call the dominant mode of relationships figured in this section, between Frédéric and his world as well as between the objects inhabiting that world, *metonymic,* not only because the literal meaning of the word, "name change," suggests the shifting, evanescent nature of the play of appearances rather than an apprehension of any putative reality, but also because the mode of relationship supposed to exist between things in the use of this trope is that of mere contiguity. Here desire becomes specified, fixed upon particular objects, all of which are equally desirable but found to be in the possession of them equally unsatisfying, frustrating, finally unpossessable in their essence. Kierkegaard would call this *desire* "desiring" (insect-like), as against *desire* "sleeping" (plant-like); *desire* carnal, but desire conscious of itself as desire, and rising to the level of technical competence and cunning in pursuit of object—like Don Juan in Mozart's opera, seeking the universal in the particular. Which means that all particulars become possible objects of desire, irrespective of any considerations of intrinsic value. The image of desire is now endowed with material substance, is apprehended as merely material in its very consumption, is totally consumable thereby, hence in need of endless replacement, substitution, repetition.

Frédéric now has money and a desire for women, pursues Mme Arnoux and cunningly contrives her seduction, fights a duel for her honor, tries his hand at law, painting, writing a novel, and finds them all equally unsatisfying. And when Mme Arnoux fails to meet him at the room he had taken (because of the illness of one of her children that she, stupidly, takes to be a sign from heaven warning her of sin), Frédéric substitutes in her place, in the same room and same bed he had reserved for Mme Arnoux, the mistress of M. Arnoux, the dissembling and opaque, and utterly sensual, Rosanette. The last scene of the last chapter of this section has Frédéric in bed with Rosanette, in a state of postcoital depression, weeping for his loss of Mme Arnoux, but telling Rosanette that he is weeping because "I am too happy . . . I have wanted you for such a long time."

The evanescent quality of Frédéric's desire for Mme Arnoux is suggested by his inability to fix her image in its specifically human incarnation. At times, his lust for her is concretized in a fascination with some part of her body, her foot, the inner side of her arm, some object that she possesses but that, magically, seems to have taken on her essence by its physical proximity to her. At times, her essence dissolves and spreads over the whole of the city of Paris in such a way that she and the city become identified in Frédéric's enfevered imagination. She remains unspecified as an individual, however, unlocatable between the universal that she represents and the particulars that characterize her as image. In this respect, the alternate sensations of lust and repulsion that Frédéric feels for her when she returns after fifteen years, in the penultimate chapter, are perfectly consistent with the relationship that he bears to her in the second section of the book. Things fall apart because their essence is indiscernible. In the end, there are only things, and the relationships they sustain with one another are nothing but their placement side by side, nearer or further, from one another in a universe of objects. Whence the seeming ease of the displacements of desire from one object to another, the slippage of desire across a series of objects, all of which turn out to be exactly the same, however the imagination, in the service of desire, construes them.

Part 3 begins with the sound of gunshots in the streets. It signals the opening phase of the Revolution of February 25, 1848, the events of which—down to the coup by Louis Bonaparte (Napoleon III), of December 1851—form alternatively the foreground and background of Frédéric's life during that time. Frédéric has much to do in these three and a half years. He must participate in the February Revolution; attempt a political career; take care of his business affairs; squander his fortune in the process; keep Rosanette as his official mistress; continue to pursue Mme Arnoux; seduce Mme Dambreuse, the wife of a wealthy banker; witness the death of the child born to Rosanette; be betrayed by his best friend, Deslauriers; reject and then seek to win Louise Rocque; and witness the death of the only true political idealist among his friends, Dussardier, shot by another of his friends, Sénécal, a socialist in principle who, in pursuit of *his* ideals, has become a policeman. Things not only fall apart, they come apart at the seams in the process, and reveal the counter-essence—the nothingness—that is the real substance behind all seemingly ideal forms.

Such, admittedly, is the moral of the story. And yet it is not the whole story. Flaubert's decision to place this grotesque series of events against the backdrop of the 1848 Revolution reflects—arguably—the despairing idealism of his vision. The absurdity of Dussardier's death is apparent enough, but so too is his goodness, decency, and humaneness. The absurdity that Flaubert finds in the events of 1848–51 does not fully hide the bitterness that he must have felt while witnessing France's last effort to construct a society on principles of social justice. To be sure, we know that he did not confuse justice with a belief in the equality of individuals, but neither did Marx. That confusion lies at the heart of social democratic sentimentalism and feeds the Utopian brand of socialism. True, he did not, like Marx, present the proletariat as the martyred heroes of the Revolution, but nor did he see them as more misguided and victimized by their own stupidity than Marx did. And he has his hero, Frédéric, participate in the events of February–March 1848 with the same enthusiasm, the same hopes, even the same bravery and idealism with which Marx credits the Parisian populace during that same period. He participates, that is, until, like the bourgeoisie itself, he becomes distracted by his own self-interest. Frédéric Moreau, it is important to recall, is not a proletarian; he is a bourgeois through and through; and his life during the period 1848–51 mirrors perfectly (in microcosm as it were) the career and betrayals, of itself and others, of the French bourgeoisie.

In part 3 of the novel, Frédéric displays a higher degree of consciousness, both social and psychological, and of conscience than he does in the rest of the book. It is as if Flaubert wished us to perceive Frédéric at this stage as one who grasps fully, even if in the end despairingly, the nature of his class, its strengths as well as its weaknesses, the disparity between its ideals and its actions, and the disillusionment that that disparity caused in that class as a result of the events of 1848–51. In this section, Frédéric's desire is—if only for a moment—generalized and idealized; it reaches out in a spirit of service and even sacrifice to the people, to the nation. He feels genuine anger when a citizen standing next to him on the barricades is shot by the soldiery, although he is as much angered by the thought that the shot might have been aimed at him as he is by the realization that it has killed a fellow citizen. He enthusiastically joins the mob in the sacking of the Tuileries and insists that "The people are sublime." Flaubert's characterization of the "carnival" mood of the days following the deposition of Louis Philippe, when "people dressed in a careless way that blurred the distinctions between classes, hatreds were concealed, and hopes blossomed," and "pride" shone in the face of the people "at having won their rights," has no irony in it at all. "Paris," he writes, was, during those days "the most delightful place."[2]

But this pride is soon smothered in the realization, by the bourgeoisie especially, that social justice threatened private property, and the tone of the account shifts perceptibly with the narrator's remark:

> Now Property was raised in men's eyes to the level of Religion and became confused with God. The attacks made on it seemed sacrilegious, almost canni-balistic. In spite of the most humane laws that had ever been enacted, the spectre of '93 reappeared, and the knife of the guillotine vibrated in every syllable of the word "Republic"—which in no way prevented the government being despised for its weakness. France, realizing that she was without a master, started crying with fright like a blind man deprived of his stick, or a child who has lost his nurse.[3]

The fragility of the alliance between the bourgeoisie and the people is symbolized by the pregnancy of Rosanette, the sickness of the child born of the union of a proletarian and a bourgeois, and, finally, by Frédéric's growing disgust for his mistress and his decision to take a new mistress, the aristocratic wife of the banker, M. Dambreuse. This decision is as cynical on Frédéric's part as it is calculated on Mme Dambreuse's part to accept him as a lover.

The narrator tells us that, as of June 1848, the time of the infamous June Days, when the proletariat was ruthlessly suppressed, "The mind of the nation was unbal-anced," a condition reflected in Frédéric's recognition that his "morality" had be-come "flabby" but also reflected in his choice of an antidote: "A mistress like Mme Dambreuse," he muses, "would establish his position."[4] We are not left with any doubts as to the nature of his attraction to her: "He coveted her because she was noble, rich, pious," and this recognition coincides with Frédéric's growing convic-tion that perhaps "progress is attainable only through an aristocracy,"[5] a conviction that is revealed to be as absurd as his earlier belief that "the people are sublime."

His deception of Rosanette now gives him infinite pleasure: "What a bastard I am!" he says; "glorying in his own perversity," the narrator adds. His political interests fade, and with them his intention to stand as a candidate for the Assembly. He now luxuriates in "a feeling of gratification, of deep satisfaction. His joy of possessing a rich woman was unspoilt by any contrast; his feelings harmonized with their setting. His whole life, nowadays, was filled with pleasures." And the greatest, "perhaps, was to watch Mme Dambreuse surrounded by a group" of admirers: "all the respect shown to her virtue delighted him as an indirect homage to himself, and he sometimes longed to cry: 'But I know her better than you do. She's mine!' "[6]

Not quite, of course. Mme Dambreuse is Frédéric's equal in venality and cunning self-servitude. The limits of his desire for her are set by his distaste for her "skinny chest": "At that moment, he admitted what he had hitherto concealed from himself; the disillusionment of his senses. This did not prevent him from feigning great ardor, but to feel it he had to evoke the image of Rosanette or Mme Arnoux. This atrophy of the heart," however, "left his head entirely free; and his ambition for a great position in society was stronger than ever."[7] The death of M. Dambreuse, the subsequent revelation of the hatred and contempt underlying the Dambreuse's marriage, and Frédéric's growing disillusionment with Mme Dambreuse foreshadow the deterioration of the political situation, a situation laconically summed up by the narrator in a two-word paragraph: "Hatred flourished." The death of Rosanette's child provides an occasion for the depiction of the total depravity of Frédéric's nature, his narcissism and emotional self-indulgence, his disinterest even in desire itself, along with a correlation of the death of realism in art (Pellerin's portrait of the dead child) and the death of idealism in politics. Frédéric's tears at the death-watch of his child are for himself. He had forgotten the child while it was gestating in Rosanette's womb. His tears are caused by the news that Mme Arnoux has left Paris forever.

His break with both Rosanette and Mme Dambreuse is followed by a decision to marry Louise, his "savage" and "peasant" girl-child; and he flees to her, but this too is frustrated when he arrives to find her marrying his best friend Deslauriers. He returns to Paris just in time to witness the coup of Napoleon III and the murder of the communist Dussardier by the former socialist, now policeman of reaction, Sénécal.

The interweaving of political events with the events in the life of Frédéric in this section of the novel is highly complex and invites a host of different interpretations. I call the mode of the whole section *synecdochic,* inasmuch as, here, it is borne in upon Frédéric's consciousness and upon that of the reader the author's conviction that in the society depicted the object of all desire is commodity possession. Desire is generalized and universalized by the equation of the value of every object with its value as commodity. This generalized and universalized form of value appears, however, in two guises: as a desire for human unity, in the first instance, reflected in the celebration of political liberation; and in the absurd form of the commodity fetishized. Mme Dambreuse is indistinguishable from her wealth and social position.

The melancholy tone of the last two chapters, the retrospective summing up of this epic of disillusionment and frustration, can only derive from the juxtaposition of the way things are in modern society and the way they ought to be. The absent ideal is present as tacit antithesis to the painful reality. The irony of the last two chapters is melancholic because, whether he knew it or not, Flaubert had succeeded in representing more vividly than Hegel himself the path of development of consciousness's encounter with reality that leads to the condition of "the unhappy consciousness"—that consciousness that is not only in and for itself, but also *by* itself, *beside* itself in its simultaneous dissemblance and awareness of this dissemblance. The melancholy of the last section is precisely similar to that that Marx depicts as a mode of bourgeois life in France under the absurd Napoleon III. And Marx's analysis of the etiology of this symptom follows the same outline as that given to us figuratively in Flaubert's novel.

You will recall that Marx opens the *Eighteenth Brumaire* with a signal that he is about to unfold a "farce." The farcical nature of the events to be depicted is manifested in their outcome: the elevation of the charlatan "Crapulinski," the roué, opportunist, and fool, Louis Bonaparte (the original Napoleon the Great's nephew), to the imperial purple by a coalition of criminals, lumpenproletariat, peasants, and high bourgeois property owners. But, Marx reminds us a number of times throughout the discourse, this grotesque or absurd outcome of events—in which the least admirable man in France is hailed as the representative and defender of the interests of all classes of French society—was already implicitly present in the first, or February, phase of the Revolution of 1848, which had swept Louis Philippe from the throne and proclaimed the Second Republic.

How had this transformation, so remarkable and unforeseen by most of the actors in the spectacle, come about? Marx's answer to this question consists of an explication of the relationship between what he calls the true content of the "modern revolution" and the forms that specific revolutions take as a result of the conflict of interests that a class-divided society engenders.

The relation between the form and the content of any social phenomenon in any specific historical situation, Marx argues here and elsewhere, is a product of a conflict between specific class interests as these are envisaged and lived by a given class, on the one side, and general or universal human interests, which derive from the system of needs, primary and secondary, that are peculiar to mankind, on the other. Ideals are always formulated in terms of putatively universal human values, but since social perceptions are limited to the range of experiences of a given social class, the universally shared common interests of living men everywhere are always interpreted in a situation in which goods and political power are unevenly distributed in terms of the immediately envisaged *material* interests of the dominant class. This is why the political program of 1848, designed to establish a republic, quickly got transformed into a program designed to undermine this republic in the interest of protecting private property. The bourgeoisie in power says "Republic," against the old regime of inherited privilege and despotism, but it means "aristocracy of wealth." It says: "Justice" when it seeks to enlist the lower classes in its struggle against the old regime; but it means "Law and Order" when the aristocracy of wealth is established. It says, "Liberty, Equality, and Fraternity" when it is at the barricades or sending the lower classes to them; but it invokes "infantry, cavalry, and artillery" when the lower classes try to claim these rights in concrete terms. It comports itself on the historical stage like a tragic hero in its early phases of development, but its avarice and fetishism of commodities soon force it to abandon in practice every ideal it continues to preach in theory, and to reveal itself as the "monster" that any human being who conceives of life as an epic of production for profit alone must become.

So much is commonplace for Marxists, but exists only as a judgment still to be demonstrated. Part of the demonstration must be historical, since the process being analyzed is construed as a historical process: Marx chooses the events in France between 1848 and 1852 as a microcosm of the plot that every bourgeoisie must ultimately play out. And his demonstration of the adequacy of this judgment to the events themselves consists of a dialectical explication of those events as products of an interplay between forms and their actual contents, on the one side, and the form of the whole and its obscured universal meaning, on the other.

On the surface of the events, Marx discerns a succession of four formal incarnations of the revolutionary impulse. Each of these incarnations is simultaneously a response to socioeconomic reality (here construed as class interests) and an attempt to deny the universal meaning of the revolution in relation to ideal human aspiration. He divides the drama into four phases, each of which is signaled by a change in the form of government established on the political level. But the form of government established is itself a projection of a form of political consciousness, itself a product of either a coalition of classes, more or less self-consciously contrived, or of a specific class.

The real protagonist of Marx's narrative is neither the proletariat (its Dussardier) nor Louis Bonaparte (its Sénécal), but rather the bourgeoisie as it lives through the longings, sufferings, and contradictions of its existence that constitute its own "sentimental education." Its *Bildung,* like that of Moreau, consists of a progressive evacuation of ideals in order to become reconciled to a reality conceived as the melancholy consumption of commodities whose real value remains indiscernible.

Like Frédéric, the bourgeoisie and the revolution in which it will achieve its "absurd" triumph pass through four stages of consciousness: February 1848 is metaphoric; political aspiration and social ideals are entertained in the euphoric spirit of unspecified desires and glimpsed in the image of "a social republic." Marx says of this period: "Nothing and nobody ventured to lay claim to the right of existence and of real action. All the elements that had prepared or determined the Revolution, the dynastic opposition, the republican bourgeoisie, the democratic-republican petty bourgeoisie and the social-democratic workers, provisionally found their place in the February *government.*"[8] "It could not be otherwise," Marx continues; "Every party construed [the republic] in its own sense." Although the proletariat proclaimed a "social republic," and thereby "indicated the general content of the modern revolution," the proclamation was both naive and premature, given the interests and powers of other social groups. And this accounts for the "confused mixture of high-flown phrases and actual uncertainty and clumsiness, of more enthusiastic striving for innovation and more deeply rooted domination of the old routine, of more apparent harmony of the whole society and more profound estrangement of its elements," which characterized this phase of the whole revolutionary process.[9]

Phase two of the Revolution, the period of the Constituent National Assembly, May 4, 1848 to May 29, 1849, represents the period of dispersion of the revolutionary impulse across a series of contending parties and groups, a period of strife and specification of contents, emblematized by the bloody street warfare of the June Days (June 23–26, 1848) and the progressive betrayal of one group by another until the bourgeois republicans accede to dictatorial power in the Legislative National Assembly, an accession that demonstrated to every observer of the event that "in Europe there are other questions involved than that of 'republic or monarchy.'" It had revealed, Marx says, "that here [in Europe] *bourgeois republic* signifies the unlimited despotism of one class over other classes." Under the sign of the motto, "property, family, religion, order," every alternative party is crushed. "Society is saved just as often as the circle of its rulers contracts, as a more exclusive interest is maintained against a wider one. Every demand of the simplest bourgeois financial reform, of the most ordinary liberalism, of the most formal republicanism, of the most insipid democracy, is simultaneously castigated as an 'attempt on society' and stigmatized as 'socialism.'"[10]

With the dictatorship of the bourgeoisie, we have passed into the third phase of the Revolution, the synecdochic phase in which the interests of a specific segment of society are identified with the interest of society as a whole. This pseudo-universalization of the interests of the bourgeoisie, this incarnation of the universal in the particular, this fetishism by a class of itself, is a preparation for the absurdity represented by Bonaparte's claims to be "the savior of society" and the irony of his use of the motto "property, family, religion, order" to justify his suppression of the *political power* of the bourgeoisie. In this, the last phase of the Revolution,

> [bourgeois] high priests of "religion and order" themselves are driven with kicks from their Pythian tripods, hauled out of their beds in the darkness of night, put in prison-vans, thrown into dungeons or sent into exile; their temple is razed to the ground, their mouths are sealed, their pens broken, their law torn to pieces in the name of religion, of property, of family, of order. Bourgeois fanatics for order are shot down on their balconies by mobs of drunken soldiers, their domestic sanctuaries profaned, their houses bombarded for amusement—in the name of property, of family, of religion, and of order. Finally the scum of bourgeois society forms *the holy phalanx of order* and the hero Crapulinsky [from Fr. *crapule*, "gluttony"] installs himself in the Tuileries as the "*savior* of society."[11]

What justification do I have for calling the modes of relationship among the elements of society represented in Marx's characterization of the phases of the Revolution by the names of the tropes of figurative language? The best reason is that Marx himself provides us with schematic representations of the modes of figuration by which to characterize the relation between the forms of value and their contents in his analysis of the "language of commodities" in chapter 1 of *Capital*. Most of this chapter consists of an adaptation of the traditional conception of the rhetorical tropes to the method of dialectical analysis. Here the problem, Marx says, is to understand the "money-form" of value, the "absurd" notion that the value of a commodity is equivalent to the amount of money it is worth in a given system of exchange. And just as the explanation of the "absurd" spectacle of Bonaparte's posing as the "savior of society"—while unleashing all of the criminal elements of society to an orgy of a consumption ungoverned by any respect for human values or the persons who produced by their labor the commodities being consumed—is contained in the understanding of the first phase of the Revolution that brought him to power, the February phase; so too the absurd form of value is explained by reference to the structure of the elementary or original form of value, the form contained in the simple metaphorical *identification* of "*x* amount of commodity *A*" with "*y* amount of commodity *B*." Once the purely figurative nature of this statement of equivalency is grasped, once it is seen that, like any metaphor, it both contains a deep truth (regarding the similarity of any two commodities by virtue of their nature as products of human labor) and at the same time masks this truth (by remaining on the superficial level of an apprehension of their manifest similarity as commodities), the secret of men's capacity to bewitch themselves into believing that the value of anything equals its exchange value, rather than its use value, is revealed for everyone to see. Just as irony is implicitly present in any original, primitive, or naive characterization of reality in a metaphor, so too the absurdity of equating the value of a product of human labor with its money value is contained implicitly in the equating of any given commodity with any other as a basis of exchange. And so too with the other two forms of value, the extended and the generalized forms, which Marx analyzes in this chapter of *Capital*. They are to *metonymy* and *synecdoche*, the relationships by contiguity and putative essential identity, respectively, as the second and third phases of the Revolution are to the same tropes.

To be sure, Marx's analysis of the forms of social phenomena, whether of commodity values or of political systems, is carried forth on the assumption that he has perceived their true contents, which the forms simultaneously figure forth and conceal from clear view. The true value-content of all commodities is for him the amount of human labor expended in their production, which is precisely equivalent to their use-value, whatever their apparent value in a given system of exchange. The true content of all political and social forms, similarly, is the universal human needs that they at once manifest and obscure. Marx's aim as a writer was to clarify this relation of content to form in a way that he thought, correctly I believe, was consistent with Hegel's dialectical method of analysis, although—in his view—Hegel had got the form-content distinction wrong way about. But he carried forward the method of Hegel's *Phenomenology* and *Logic* by divining the element of consciousness that was the basis and bane of humanity's efforts to grasp reality and turn it to its service. This element was man's capacity for what Vico called "creative error," a capacity of the figurative imagination without which reason itself would be inconceivable, just as prose without poetry would be unthinkable. Further, he divined clearly what Hegel only in passing glimpses and in his pursuit of the secret of Being-in-general too quickly passes over; namely, that the secret of human consciousness is to be found in its most original product, which is not reason, but figurative language, without which reason could never have arisen.

What does the discernment of a common pattern of tropological representations of the modes of consciousness imply with respect to the project of "realistic representation," on the one side, and the problem of style, on the other? With respect to the former, I would suggest, it permits us to identify the "allegorical" element in realistic discourse, the secondary meaning of the events depicted on the surface of the narrative that mediates between those events and the judgment rendered on them, launched from the consciously held ideological position of the writer. The progression of these structures of consciousness permits the encodation of the process through which the protagonist is passing in his/its "education," in terms that allow the writer a judgment on its end phase as a stage of cognitive awareness. This quite apart from whatever archetypal schema may be revealed in the literary encodation of the events in generic terms, that is, as comedy, tragedy, romance, satire, or farce. The discourses of Marx and Flaubert can thus be construed as correlations of events with their mythic archetypes, on the one side, and with types of cognition, on the other. And it is the twofold encodation of these events, as satires and as reductions of consciousness to a condition of "ironic" self-reflexivity, which tacitly justifies the ideological judgment rendered on them, in the narrator's voice on the diegetic level of the discourse. To be sure, the revelation of the "farcical" nature of a given set of events constitutes a judgment on their "meaning" in itself. But merely to have emplotted a given set of events as a "farce" testifies only to the literary skill of the narrator; every set of events can be emplotted in any number of ways without doing violence to their "factuality." Every specific emplotment of a set of events, then, requires at least tacit appeal to some cognitive criterion, some notion of the way things really are, in order to establish that the emplotment in question is both plausible and illuminative of the true structure of the events in question. The theory of consciousness, which construes it as a process of passage from a metaphoric, through metonymic and synecdochic phases of development, to the condition of self-consciousness represented by irony, serves this cognitive purpose in Marx's and Flaubert's discourses. Their "realism" is thus revealed to be triply allegorical, possessing levels of elaboration corresponding to the figurative, moral, and anagogical levels discriminated in the Augustinian hermeneutic tradition. The meaning of the processes depicted on the literal level of the texts is revealed by the transcoding of the processes in generic, ideological, and cognitive terms.

With respect to the problem of style, our analysis of the discourses of Marx and Flaubert suggests that we should regard style, at least in realistic discourse, as the process of this transcoding operation. When we speak of the style of a discourse, we should not feel compelled to limit ourselves to a consideration of either the linguistic-rhetorical features of a text or to its discernible ideological posture, but should seek rather to characterize the moves made, on the axes of both selection and combination, by which a form is identified with a content and the reverse.

Flaubert was certainly right when he sought to identify "style" with the "content" of the discourse, but specified that the content in question had to do with "thought" rather than with the manifest referent of the discourse, the characters, situations, and events depicted in the narrative. What he may have been pointing to here was the inexpugnable element of "construct" contained in every discourse, however "realistic," however perfectly "mimetic," it might strive to be. If the linguistic sign is to be identified with neither the signifier nor the signified but with their conjunction, then every representation of reality in language must possess, as an element of its content, the "form" of the signifier itself. Discourse turns the union of signifier and signified in the sign into the problem with which it must deal. Its aim is less to match up a group of signifiers with their signifieds, in a relationship of perfect equivalency, than to create a system of signs that are their own signifieds. To put it this way is no doubt to muddy the waters, but it at least helps to explain why every "realism" in the end fails and is supplanted by yet another "realism" that, although claiming at last to be a pure *mimesis,* is soon revealed by a vigilant criticism to be only another perspective on the ever shifting relationship between words and the things they are supposed to signify.

Finally, this approach to the problem of style, considered within the context of mid-nineteenth-century realism, as represented by Marx and Flaubert, helps us to comprehend better the seemingly substantive "modernity" of their discourses. Their embedding of the tropes of figurative language within their discourse as a model of the processes of consciousness allows them to appear to be the very types of a certain *kind* of realism, on the one side, and heralds of "modernism" in both writing and criticism, on the other. For modernism, whatever else it may be, is characterized by a hyper self-consciousness with respect to the opacity of language, by language's demonic capacity to intrude itself into discourse as a content alongside of whatever referent may be signaled on the surface of the text. Marx's and Flaubert's identification of the stages of consciousness with tropological structures, the structures of language in its prefigurative aspect, amnestied them against the perils of literalism, on the one side, and of symbolization, on the other. Their discourses are not reducible either to the manifest forms in which they appear or to the specific ideological positions they held. On the contrary, their discourses remain eternally fresh and enduringly "realistic" precisely to the degree that their "contents" were identified as the process of their own production.

CHAPTER TWELVE

The Discourse of History

{1979}

What remains to be said about the problems of historical explanation after thirty-five years of debate in this, the most recent phase of an argument which began (for our purposes) with Kant's criticism of Herder at the end of the eighteenth century? Not much, I suspect. At least, not much within the context of the Anglophone debate inaugurated by Carl Hempel in 1942, in his essay "The Function of General Laws in History."[1] Of course, there is much to be said about specific explanations offered by specific historians with respect to specific historical phenomena. And if not about explanation, then certainly about interpretation. Modern hermeneutic theory, as represented by Hans-Georg Gadamer, Paul Ricoeur, and Jürgen Habermas, among others, finds rich materials for reflection in the historian's text, traditional subject matter, and methods. And it seems safe to say that disputes between Marxists and non-Marxists over the distinction between "concrete" and "abstract" understanding, "scientific" and "ideological" arguments, and "reactionary" and "progressive" vision in historical thought will continue until one side triumphs over the other by recourse to that ultimate critical instrumentality which, as Marx said, is weapons. All of these discussions, however, have today a kind of tired quality about them, as if the disputants were writing for members of their own parties rather than for their opponents. On their periphery, a whole new problematic has been constituted that appears likely to render the older terms of discussion irrelevant and the concerns that motivated it simply uninteresting.

This new problematic has arisen in the wake of modern semiotics, which, as deployed by structuralists such as Roland Barthes and poststructuralists such as Michel Foucault and Jacques Derrida, shifts the discussion of the nature of historical explanation to a consideration of the question of *why* there are historical explanations at all. Or to put it another way, that nineteenth-century interest in founding a realistic historiography, which would present in a purely transparent discourse a "found" past, now has only a kind of ethnological interest. It is not that human beings should not have an interest in their own pasts and even the pasts of others. Consciousness of the past and awareness of a possible future seem to distinguish human beings from their animal prototypes; but why human beings should wish to know the past in the way nineteenth-century Western culture wished to know it, in such detail, with such precision, so completely, now seems to be a matter more of psychological than of epistemological moment. From a modern, poststructuralist perspective, the nineteenth-century aspiration to a historiography that would be both objective and realistic has now taken on the aspect of a symptom of that complex of myths peculiar to Western culture at a time when it was trying to deal with the social pressures caused by the impact of industrialization on institutions and beliefs peculiar to feudal social systems and agricultural economies. To inquire into why Western man has cultivated historical consciousness in a particular way now seems more interesting than to establish the proper way to cultivate it.

Roland Barthes has interpreted the nineteenth-century fascination with history as an aspect of a larger "passion for the real." This passion was manifested in a host of cultural phenomena, from the pretensions of the "realistic" novel and the absurdities of a "realistic" politics, through an interest in photography and a need to "document" everything, to the need to know the "law" governing every possible kind of phenomenon that inspired the positivistic sciences. This passion for the real was not, Michel Foucault insists, a result simply of a "disinterested" spirit of scientific inquiry and even less of the humanistic claim to a sympathy for "everything human." The very intensity of this passion for the real and its pervasive (not to say obsessional) appeal point to a profound cultural anxiety. It bespoke a deep fear that "reality," and especially social reality, had slipped from the grasp of the instruments of knowledge designed to discover and control it. As thus envisaged, the nineteenth century's interest in history, in past events and exotic cultures, its desire to determine the patterns and laws of social processes, its need to establish the "facts" of history as a means of arbitrating among contending ideologies (each with its own Utopian recommendations about the most desirable course for future action)—all these are now seen as symptoms of a cultural malaise for which they were supposed to provide the cure.

One indication of the symptomatic nature of this passion for the real and the conception of historical knowledge that manifested it is to be seen in the desire of early nineteenth-century historians and their successors down to our own time to deny the "literariness" of their discourse. From the Renaissance to the early nineteenth century, historiography had been regarded as a literary art, more precisely a branch of rhetoric; and even those eighteenth-century historians who disdained rhetoric in favor of a more properly "philosophical" approach to the subject matter of history, such as Voltaire and Gibbon, nevertheless insisted that history writing—the verbal representation of historical events, structures, and processes—was still a literary enterprise. All this changed, however, in the early nineteenth century; and this change is understandable, Lionel Gossman has persuasively argued, less as an effect of a program designed to turn history into a science (most nineteenth-century historians, like their modern counterparts, remained opposed to any attempt to scientize history) than as a consequence of a fundamental transformation in what people took to be the nature of "literature" itself.

In fact, as Foucault has suggested in *Les mots et les choses* (literally *Words and Things,* translated as *The Order of Things*), the very notion of literature as a special kind of verbal performance or writing, as a kind of writing that erases the distinction between the literal and figurative dimensions of discourse, between the poetic and prosaic aspects of speech, and problematizes its own status as a representation of reality and brings the relationship between language and its referent under question—all this is new to the nineteenth century. Literature, as against what in the eighteenth century was called "discourse," points to the mysterious or uncanny nature of language, its capacity to conceal and distort in the very act of representing and delineating a world given to perception or thought. As it came to be practiced in the nineteenth century, even in the most "realistic" of novelists, such as Flaubert, for example, literature signaled the similarities between every consciously fashioned linguistic performance and those operations of the unconscious that Freud subsequently sought to analyze as "the dreamwork" in *The Interpretation of Dreams.* Already in the work of the great literary artists of the early nineteenth century, in Wordsworth, Hölderlin, and Flaubert, in Stendhal, Baudelaire, and Jane Austen, literature displays the tendency to bring language into question, to indict its claims to transparency and univocity of meaning, which will crystallize as a self-conscious movement, now called "modernism," in Joyce, Proust, Virginia Woolf, and Stephen Mallarmé. As against discourse, which is what the eighteenth century called the verbal artwork, literature undermines the ideal of clarity, the dream of perfect correspondence between language and the world, which not only science but common sense as well had entertained as a possibility since Descartes.

Considerations such as these permit us to understand, I think, what is behind nineteenth-century historians' desire to objectify historical studies. Although many of them used the rhetoric of science, borrowed metaphors from medicine, mechanics, hydraulics, and the like to describe historical processes, and even spoke of their calling as a "discipline" (*Wissenschaft*), few academic historians of the nineteenth century wished to make history into the kind of science that physics, chemistry, and biology (after Darwin) represented. What they wished to do was disengage historiography from that literature (most often called simply "fiction") that implicitly undermined any claim to a linguistically *innocent* discourse, any possibility of establishing facts "for their own sake," as the phrase had it, and of reporting facts in plain, straightforward, unembellished prose. It was this threat of literature to these claims that probably accounts for the studied disinterest that historians showed in the most systematic analysis of the *literary* basis of historical discourse to appear in the nineteenth century, J. G. Droysen's *Historik*.

Literature, conceived as the artistic alternative to ordinary or everyday language, was an invention of the nineteenth century, an invention theoretically more fruitful for the understanding of culture, which we have recently come to understand as being grounded in language, than the putatively "objective" historiography of the same period—as the origins of modern anthropology in the literary tradition of the period plainly show. And literature, as it was developed in the nineteenth century, especially on the Continent and in the Americas (England is a notable exception to this generalization; there, for example, the novel continued to be linked to the older conception of verbal art as discourse) represented another threat to the historian. For as practiced by Flaubert and Baudelaire and their successors, literature was not only problematizing of language; it became increasingly threatening to the rhetorical mode that conventional historiography relied on to convey the authority with which it spoke: narrative. At least, it was hostile to the traditional conception of narrative, understood as a story with a beginning, middle, and end, informed by a discernible plot of a traditional sort, told by an objective (even omniscient) observer of events, and having the effect in its reader/auditor of rendering exotic events "familiar" and "understandable."

"To discover the true story," "to get the story straight" (as J. H. Hexter is constantly instructing us to do), or "to tell the story as it *really* happened"—these were the aims of most academic historians. Indeed, it was even the aim of many historians who, like Marx, pretended to have a science for explaining why the "real story" had taken the form that it had done as related in the narrative sections of their discourse (think of his *Eighteenth Brumaire of Louis Bonaparte*). But what nineteenth-century literature showed was that narration was not a simple activity. Literature (as against discourse) blurred the distinction between author, narrator, and subject of the stories it told, frustrated the expectations of the conventional reader, made the act of speaking or writing its own subject matter, and so on, thereby bringing the very notion of narrativity under question. And later on, in writers like Joyce and Proust, the notion of narrativity would be further obscured by the demonstration that any given set of events could bear the imposition upon it of a host of equally plausible but systematically confused and even contradictory plots and, most important, by the suggestion that the narrative "I" was a purely linguistic construction having no referent (as Benveniste would subsequently argue) other than "the person who utters the present instance of discourse."

We can readily understand, I think, how this turn in the history of literature should appear threatening to historians and why it was that the more "realistic" literature became, the more the historians would seek to distinguish their own discourse from it. (There is a fine irony here, for the apparent enemies of the nineteenth-century historians were the Romantic novelists, especially the novelists who, like Walter Scott, dealt in "historical novels." Yet the Romantic novelists offended only by virtue of the fact that they presented the imaginary under the aspect of the real. The realistic novelists, by contrast, can be said to have presented the real under the aspect of the imaginary. More important, however, is the fact that the realistic novelist broke with the convention of *discursive* narrativity, belief in the possibility of which was shared by the Romantic novelist and the "realistic" historian alike. It was the undermining of the authority of the narrator that made it necessary for history to dissociate itself from literature.) But if history was to be separated from literature, what course was it to follow? The answer to this question was unclear, and this accounts, I think, for the remarkable efflorescence of philosophical discussions of history, historical consciousness, and historical knowledge from Kant and Hegel on, discussions that turned on the problem of determining what, if anything, constituted the "autonomy" of history as a discipline. This latter problem, in turn, hinged upon the problem of narrativity itself, the problem of *who* was speaking in "objective" discourse, with what *authority*, to what *end* or purpose, and above all with what *means*. As for the question of the historian's *means*, the issue here was the cognitive status of storytelling itself.

The narrators' characteristic product was the story they had to tell. How did such stories explain what they related as the elements of a plot? How did the myriads of stories unearthed by historians aggregate into a comprehensible master-story of the whole of human history? If they did not so aggregate, as Hegel pointed out in the introduction to his *Lectures on the Philosophy of History*, then history could neither claim the status of a "science" nor escape the Cartesian charge of its inherent want of seriousness. Hegel recommended that the task of extracting the overall meaning of the multitude of stories told by historians be consigned to philosophy, which would translate into "reason" what otherwise had to remain merely "understandable." But this recommendation was rejected by historians who, if they were unwilling to admit to being nothing more than makers of fictions, were not about to cede their authority to endow history with meaning to the killing abstractions of philosophy.

As thus envisaged, the threat that the social sciences posed to history's cherished autonomy at the end of the nineteenth century was little more than another rehearsal of the conflict between history and philosophy fought out at the beginning of the century. Here the issues were much the same: the historians' claim to deal in "concrete" reality rather than "abstractions"; their interest in discovering the true story behind the events reported in the documents and telling that story well, in ways that would be comprehensible to the ordinary educated reader; their insistence on the desirability of time-and-space specific, rather than universal, generalizations; and their belief in the authority of narration to explain without distorting the meaning of events in the interest of making them *totally* intelligible, completely demystified, as the sciences wished to do.

It can be seen, then, that the real threat to the autonomy of history was not the sciences or even philosophy, for both of these could countenance a kind of knowledge, especially of social events, that was only proto-scientific, on the one side, and not perfectly conceptually integrated, on the other. But they could countenance such a kind of knowledge only as long as the conventional notion of a discourse that was at once literary and literal, both imaginative and cognitively responsible, remained intact; and this notion was what was being threatened within the domain of literature itself. The threat was held off by the development, in philosophical studies, of a theory of language that still envisioned the possibility of establishing, on historical grounds, absolute distinctions between the literal and figurative dimensions of speech. Once this possibility was ruled out, however, as it has been in modern linguistic and semiotic theory, the claims of historians to deal in a discourse that was realistic, transparent, concrete, and illuminative of events by virtue of the stories it told about them were fatally undermined.

It is within the context of considerations such as these that we may look once more at the most recent phase in the debate over the nature of historical explanation, that which evolved in the wake of Hempel's classic essay and occupied philosophers, historians, and social scientists in the Anglophone world for some thirty-five years. We can now see that what was at issue in the debate was less the possibility of transforming history into a genuine science or even the assessment of its cognitive validity in the light of a scientific model of valid explanation than a rearguard action intended to salvage the authority of narrative as the proper form of historical representation and of storytelling as the socially most desirable mode of historical explanation.

I believe that many of the people who took part in the debate would not accept this characterization of the issues. The philosophers—from Patrick Gardiner, W. H. Walsh, W. B. Gallie, William Dray, and Louis Mink, all deriving one way or another from Collingwood as tempered by Wittgenstein, over to Maurice Mandelbaum, Thomas Nagel, Hempel, Morton White, Arthur Danto, John Passmore, and so on, rather more Russellian in approach—saw the issues as epistemological (having more to do with the "content" of historical research, its status as a contribution to science) rather than literary and aesthetic (having to do with the style or rhetoric of historical discourse). Professor A. R. Louch was a notable exception to this generalization, although he tended to wish to assimilate historical reflection to ethical considerations rather than aesthetic ones.[2] Gallie and Mink were especially sensitive to the literary *form* in which at least *conventional* histories were presented, and they analyzed the similarities between histories and other literary genres, especially the novel, much in the manner of Frank Kermode in *The Sense of an Ending*. But this analysis proceeded within the general acceptance of the notion that the *differences* between "factual" and "fictional" discourse were more important for the understanding of historical knowledge and writing than any superficial similarities of form that might be seen between "history" and "literature." The *form* of historical discourse might be literary and it might even be said to draw upon literary techniques for providing understanding of the processes it analyzed, but its *content* distinguished it from literature in the end. This content had to do with the kind of evidence to which historians appealed as against writers of fictions—that is to say, the documentary record of events that had actually happened at specific times and places in the past, as against those imagined or invented events in which writers of fiction conventionally dealt.

And yet Hempel's classic essay, which had laid the groundwork for the earliest stages of this debate, had to do ultimately with a *formal* matter. He had maintained, let us recall, that all valid explanations of anything had to conform to or be analyzable into the model prevailing in the physical sciences, the "deductive-nomological" model. This position had been interpreted by some thinkers as amounting to the insistence that history either be transformed into a genuine science, like physics or chemistry, or be retired. And the defenders of history against the imperialist claims of scientific (or "scientistic") philosophers sought to establish that there were kinds of explanation, based on nonscientific though not antiscientific models, that generated genuine contributions to knowledge even if they did not meet the standards of verification (and falsification), conceptual integration of findings, experimental control, and predictive power prevailing in the physical sciences *in one formulation of the latter's nature* (that of Popper, as set forth in *The Logic of Scientific Discovery*).

And yet Hempel and those who followed him had not denied that history provided a *kind* of knowledge of the world and even a kind of explanation of it, even though the explanations it offered, when measured against the scientific model, had to be characterized as "porous," "sketchy," incomplete, and based on commonplaces rather than laws in their "nomological" aspect. Hempel had simply set up a hierarchy within the type of valid explanations and ranked history below the physical sciences by virtue of its failure to provide the kind of explanations that the latter produced regularly and systematically.

The opponents of Hempel wished to argue that historical explanations differed in both form and content from the kind of explanations aspired to in the physical sciences. Their content was different from that studied by physical scientists because they dealt with events that involved in some way agents endowed with consciousness, capable of envisioning intentions in the light of experience. This made social processes different from merely natural ones, *unpredictable before* they had run their specific courses even if they were *comprehensible after* the fact, or retrospectively. But even this retrospective understanding was not earned by the subsumption of events under the "laws" governing their articulation. And this not only because we did not have laws of human comportment similar to those discovered to govern nonhuman processes, but also because we asked questions about human phenomena quite different from those we asked about nonhuman phenomena and looked for a kind of answer to those questions quite different from what we might expect from nature. We wanted to know the "reasons" human beings had had for acting as they had done in situations different from or similar to our own, rather than the "causes" of their having acted that way; or we wanted to know "how" people in the past had done what they had done, rather than "why" they had done this and not something else. And the best, or at least the most legitimate, way of answering such questions, given the non- (though not anti-) scientific nature of historical investigation, was by discovering the "real" story buried in the data and telling that story in such a way as to make the reader feel that he had understood it in terms conformable to his own sensed "form of life."

The term *form of life* is taken from Wittgenstein, of course, and not everyone espousing the antinomological view of historical explanation appealed to it, but almost everyone appealed to something like it in order to account for the effect that historical *narratives* had on their readers of producing "understanding," even when scientific explanations could not be provided. And the notion of understanding was central to the effort of the antinomologists to justify belief in a mode of explanation which, though not scientific, could still lay claim to cognitive authority and a kind of veracity different from that even of realistic fiction. The reader of history read within a cultural context, a form of life, which, because it was still alive and functioning well enough to allow the activity of reading itself, attested to its adequacy to the "real" world. In *following* a storyline or series of concrete facts, in seeing *how* or seeing *that* things had happened in one way and not in another, the reader made tacit connections with modes of understanding implicit in his own cultural practice; and, insofar as he was able to see how exotic events related to those events and sets of events with which he was "familiar," of which he had tacit knowledge, it could be said that he "understood" them, even if he did not know the "laws" under which they would have to be subsumed in order to qualify as having been "explained" in scientific terms.

Different notions were advanced in the effort to characterize this kind of understanding: narrativization, serialization, colligation, reliving, or simply storytelling. But if the narrativists (if we may group them all under this name for economy of expression) wished to defend historical understanding from the criticism launched against it by the nomologists, they also wished to save this mode of understanding from a danger against which Hempel, Popper, and their followers militated as well. This danger was conceived by the scientific philosophers to be manifested in the hated "philosophy of history," the kind of holistic thinking represented by Hegel and Marx, on the one side, and the "mysticism" of certain irrationalists, such as Henri Bergson, Pierre Teilhard de Chardin, and Georges Sorel, on the other. For the narrativists, the danger to what soon came to be called "proper" history was represented by a similar twofold threat; the confusion of factual with fictional discourse, on the one side, and conceptual overdetermination of the stories to be told about historical processes, on the other. Interestingly enough, the narrativists also saw this threat as represented above all in "philosophy of history," of the sort written by Hegel, Marx, Spengler, Toynbee, and so on.

If anything, philosophy of history was more threatening to the narrativists than to the nomologists, for the latter could simply dismiss philosophy of history as myth, ideology, or pseudoscience; define what a genuinely scientific explanation was; deny such explanation to history; and counsel modesty, restraint, and measure in the historians' efforts to draw lessons or morals from the tales they told or the data they presented in their discourses. But the narrativists had denied the authority of the scientific model of explanation over history, had liberated historians to the practice of their literary or rhetorical skills, had urged them to tell their stories, construct their series, colligate their materials, and so forth. But this threw open the door to all sorts of imaginative exercises, all sorts of creative reworkings of the data, all sorts of speculative flights; and there was no telling where such liberating permissiveness might end. Supposing, for example, that some historians took this to mean that they might actually emulate the fancifulness of Michelet, the preciosity of Burckhardt, the magisterial tone of Tocqueville, or the excesses of Theodor Mommsen, who had drawn portraits of Republican Romans on models suggested by the German burghers of his own time. Supposing they followed Nietzsche's instructions, as Spengler had done, or supposing they gave themselves over to the polemical excesses of Marx. Would this not be to return historiography to the status it had had in its remote beginnings, when Herodotus had founded it but had barely succeeded in differentiating it from "myth"? At the very least, it would return it to its Romantic phase, as represented by Reinhold Niebuhr, Baron de Barante, Augustin Thierry, and Michelet; and this would not do, for everyone knew what Romanticism had led to. After all, history had been put on a respectable basis by the revolt of Ranke and his followers against Romanticism. And so it was agreed that history could be *modestly* literary and use the techniques of storytellers, and so on, as long as it was understood that the stories that historians were to tell were *simple* stories—stories modeled on such low-level art, or rather craft, forms as the detective novel, sports journalism, or the kinds of accounts an automobile mechanic gave to his customers when he sought to explain why their cars would not run. As far as I know, not one theorist of historical narrative used any example of a modernist or postmodernist novel as an analog of what went on in a historical discourse. Nor in general did any of the disputants draw upon modern literary theory, stylistics, semiotics, or rhetoric for concepts with which to analyze historical discourse. The favored analogs were either the examples of low-level art to which I alluded earlier or condensations, paraphrases, or fragments of real or invented historical accounts. It was almost as if historians were being admonished to do anything as long as they did not aspire to scientificity, on the one side, or literariness, on the other.

Why? Because everyone in the debate was opposed to philosophy of history.

And why this enmity for philosophy of history? Well, first of all, there was the well-known, or at least assumed, relationship between philosophy of history and totalitarian ideologies. This (after the general distaste for conceptual overdetermination in the handling of concrete facts) was the principal extraphilosophical objection to philosophy of history. Philosophy of history was regarded as reductionist with respect to the "variety" of human life, Manichaean or dualistic in its tendency to divide humanity into those who were on the side of future developments and those who opposed them, and extremist in the implications it drew regarding the way that those not "chosen" by history were to be treated. It privileged abstract concepts at the expense of empirical facts, forced the facts into procrustean beds of theory, manipulated data, and generated prophecies that were "self-fulfilling" when used as the basis of policy by those with power. Philosophy of history, in a word, was at best bad physics or naive theology passing for historical wisdom or at worst mere mythology or outright error. Unlike proper history, it refused to dwell upon the individual person, the unique event, the particular fact, but moved past these quickly to the abstract concept under which they were gathered in order to grasp the "world plan" (*Weltplan*); and it violated the historian's duty to illuminate the past, to dictate instead the form that the future *must* take. Did the modesty of proper history, its limitation of itself to reflection on the past, its obligation to tell simple stories about that past, its refusal to teach specific lessons for the living generations of the present, and its commitment to an "empirical" method that no one could formulate and few would defend systematically, did any of this imply that proper history was itself undergirded by a philosophy of history of its own? Narrativists and nomologists alike denied it. And this because, I suspect, they identified "philosophy" itself with the commonsensical criteria of meaning that they prescribed for historiography as its organon.

We can see in this general agreement over the impropriety of philosophy of history the manifestations of a number of ideological assumptions shared by both sides of the debate in the Anglophone world. First, there was the ideology of secularism. It was considered sufficient to identify a pattern of thought in a historian's work similar to one or another of the principal religious traditions to disqualify that work as serious historiography. Whence the commonplaces to the effect that Marx was a kind of Old Testament prophet manqué and Hegel a latter-day Saint Augustine that passed for insights among the least sophisticated of the debaters. Next, there was the ideology of civilization, which identified "civilization" with *Western* civilization and attributed to it alone a proper historical consciousness against which the mythic consciousness of all other cultures could be measured. *Myth* was what other cultures still believed in; "history" was what the West had discovered. So that anything that did not conform to the Western notion of the study of the past and historical processes was regarded as non-, anti-, or simply ahistorical on the face of it. Again, there was the ideology of modernism, which vested the authority to determine what a proper historical consciousness might be in the practice of the most recent generation of historians, and more precisely in the current generation of professional (which was to say, academic) historians (it having been forgotten that history was constituted as an academic discipline with a place in the universities only in the nineteenth century in Europe, and that this constitution was an *arbitrary* act, as much politically motivated as theoretically justified). And, finally, there was the ideology of propriety itself, the conviction, never examined openly, that truth and wisdom lay in measure, restraint, and that commonsense alone, when it was a matter of reflecting on history, lay in the *aurea mediocritas*, the golden mean, the "never too much" of a specifically bourgeois form of humanism. In fact, it is not too strong to say that these four ideologies—those of secularism, civilization, modernism, and propriety—all add up to little more than an expression of the values of a certain Western humanism in a certain phase of its development, a humanism that has shown itself incapable of addressing the issues raised by the experience of industrialization and has contented itself with defenses of the classics, recommendations of good taste and the golden mean, and ideals of individualism in the face of a social order that has rendered such ideals irrelevant when not impossible to realize.

But it must be said that the Marxist critics of this bourgeois humanism have not done much better. Although professing to have a superior insight into the true nature of historical reality, they have shown a tendency to honor a form of that principle that sustains bourgeois humanists in their defense of proper history. This is the principle, or rather the ideology, of empiricism, a residue of which remains in the Marxist insistence on the distinction between *abstract* and *concrete* historical reality. In spite of the lip service paid to a method that pretends to be genuinely "dialectical," Marxist analysts of historical processes still speak as if they believed that the historical contexts of events could be "found" or simply "pointed to" instead of "constituted"—and constituted, moreover, by the historian's discourse.

Semioticians speak of the "fallacy of referentiality," which consists of confusing the "referent" of a discourse with its *subject*. This fallacy stems from the belief that signs can stand for their referents directly, without mediation, such that a given unit of discourse can be assigned a meaning by something like ostensive definition. But the relation of a sign to its referent is always mediated by the sign's "signified" (*signifié*), the conceptual content fused with the "sound" (*signifiant*) or signifier to make up the sign. Unambiguous referentiality may be established for specific words and phrases not longer than the sentence, but discourse differs from the specific sentence and any simple list of sentences by virtue of the meaning with which it endows its referents through techniques of figuration, a process of giving the odor of literalness to metaphorical utterances—which logicians castigate as the principal source of error in imprecise thinking.

Discourse is consciously fashioned speech referring to areas of experience about which there are sufficient grounds for disagreements as to their natures and in which the aim is less to apply literal language to their description than to obscure the line between literal and figurative language in any discussion of them. Although it seems to welcome judgment on the basis of criteria of literal meaning and logical coherence, in reality prose discourse seeks to earn the appearance of literalness by the disposition of figurative techniques alone. It does this, semioticians would say, by a systematic *substitution of the signifieds* of the signs that make up its surface structure *for the referents* that the *signifiers seem to represent*. This duplicity of discourse is what Barthes criticized as "mythology" in his early work and what "scientific" students of discourse castigate as "ideology" in the works of thinkers with whom they disagree. From a consistently semiotic perspective, however, and in spite of Barthes's assertion that "myth was always of the Right," it must be admitted that all discourse is ideologically laden, that of the Left as well as that of the Right, and that the first and most important threat to any theory of discourse is the ideology of literalness, the unexamined conviction that one's own discourse has a transparency and a degree of referentiality that the discourse of others lacks. It is not too strong to say that until just recently the ideology of literalness prevailed in both Left and Right historiography as an explicit criterion for evaluating alternative styles of historical writing, with the apprehension of the figurative nature of all discourse being lost in the process. This ideology of literalness was frontally assaulted by structuralists and in historical writing by Fernand Braudel, whose great work, *The Mediterranean*, was revolutionary precisely insofar as it drew attention explicitly to its own "constructed" nature and the arbitrariness of the language in which it "constituted" its *subject*.

But if the ideology of literalness and the fallacy of referentiality prevailed in conventional historiography, so too did they prevail in the discourses about historical discourse produced by philosophers and historians in the wake of Hempel's essay. I have already noted the practice among those engaged in this debate of substituting for an analysis of a historian's discourse an analysis of a paraphrase, invented example, or fragment of such discourse. This was consistent with the practice of the dominant philosophical style in the Anglophone world at the time, which entertained no doubt that a part of a discourse could stand for the whole or that an invented example was as good as a found one for discussion of methodological problems. And yet the issue turned upon the historian's practice as a producer of discourses of a particular kind, which should have called for the kind of extensive commentary on the texts practiced by hermeneuticists rather than the reductionist tactics actually followed in the Anglophone debate over historical explanation. By and large, the historians—almost unanimously—never recognized the structures being analyzed by the philosophers as being even remotely similar to what they had

produced or what they had intended to produce. The *constructed* nature of the philosophers' examples was plain enough to the historians who even bothered to look
into the discussions carried on by philosophers. And yet something was being discussed here, something real and something important. What was it?

I would like to suggest that it was the "literariness" or, if you will, the rhetoricity
of the historian's discourse, which is to say, the inventiveness, the fictiveness of that
discourse, its status as a verbal performance that constitutes its subject in the moment that it pretends to be describing its referent. It was this literary element that
historians had had to renounce in the course of the nineteenth century in order to
permit them to pass off their work as a *kind* of science, on the one side, but a *special*
kind of science, on the other. History was to be made into a discipline by the re-
nunciation of its literary origins, its long association with rhetoric, its fictive aspect.
And this because literature itself had, with the Romantic movement, become
something other than discourse and as time went on had ceased being narrative as
well. History, considered as an autonomous discipline, was constituted by a series
of negations: it was *not* philosophy, it was *not* science, and now it was *not* literature.
But while it might renounce being both philosophy and science, it could not renounce being literature; for that in fact was what the historical discourse was, that
is, a consciously fashioned verbal performance. At best, it could decide to be bad,
banal, or low-level literature, and this is what it did, which accounts in part, I
think, for the historians' and philosophers' tendency to discuss historical work on
the analogy of that of the detective and the historian's discourse on the analogy of
the detective story.

This in spite of the fact, mind you, that most professional historians had given
up the aim of telling the kinds of stories typically analyzed by the philosophers in
this debate and in many instances had given up storytelling as a mode of explanation altogether. This makes the defense of the narrative notion of historical explanation among philosophers especially notable. Why all the energy and thought
applied to the defense of a mode of explanation that had ceased to predominate
among historians altogether? Well, first of all, it had not completely ceased to predominate. It was still very much alive as an ideal of explanation and advanced in
open contrast to a "social science" notion of explanation in England and among
historians of England in the United States who still preferred a story well told to
any "abstract" account of the past based on theory or produced by methodology.
It was also alive as a popular conception of what historians were up to, as reflected
in the selections by the more "serious" book clubs in their monthly choices of of-
ferings to their subscribers. Here biography, military history, the genre of the "one
day in the life of the president," and so on, tended to predominate. And, inciden-

tally, this preference for the well-told story was manifested even among Marxist historians who were not averse to "theory" in the way that their bourgeois counterparts were, as the examples of E. P. Thompson and Eric Hobsbawm indicate. But this preference stood in the starkest of contrasts to the virtual abandonment of narrativity, the human subject, and dramatistic methods in the historiography of the Continent. How to account for this?

Well, first of all, nineteenth-century British society did not sustain the same kinds of shocks that its Continental and American counterparts did, and British culture did not have to undergo that radical reassessment of inherited ideals in literature, philosophy, and social science in the way other, comparable cultures did. There is a direct line from the late eighteenth-century English novel to its late nineteenth-century counterpart that finds no equivalent in the French or American examples. The experimentation with the notion of literature represented by Joyce and Woolf is a late and not yet fully assimilated innovation, as compared with the examples of Flaubert and Baudelaire on the Continent and Melville and Whitman in the United States. In England, the narrative novel and the well-told story remain intact as viable instruments of social and cultural commentary precisely because the modes of social organization that had originally called them into being in their late eighteenth-century forms were still viable. The story of "society" could still be told in everyday, educated discourse; conflicts between self and society or between religious ideals and social comportment could still serve as the matter of this story because these concepts still made sense to the ordinary, educated reader. The authority of the author, considered as omniscient narrator, still prevailed, for characteristically the author spoke for common sense, mankind's generally held opinions on things, the lessons that history taught, and an ethic of good form. All of these contributed to the structuring of a relationship among authors, readers, and referents that made the telling of stories both necessary and plausible.

But by the end of the nineteenth century, this relationship (along with the social structures underlying and sustaining it) was passing. It remains alive in the historiography produced by British historians and popularizers of history, such as Kenneth Clark, Jacob Bronowski, and so on; in those novels made into television that appear on American public broadcasting channels; and among a certain kind of philosopher who nostalgically looks back on an era when storytelling was possible and seeks to find in it a mode of explaining the world that still suggests its (the world's) continuities with a more comprehensible past. This seems to be what much of that talk about "reliving," "continuous series," "colligation," and "storytelling," considered as ways of explaining history, was all about. As thus envisaged, such talk can be considered as an attempt more to save "narrativity" to "literature" than to analyze historical discourse. And this was as it should be; for if we have truly arrived, as Gérard Genette suggests, at the end of the age of narrativity, then what future does historiography have? If it is not science, as both nomologists and narrativists seem to agree, but cannot be narrative because narration itself has been shown to be *inherently* fictive, whatever its subject matter, then what is history after all?

CHAPTER THIRTEEN

Vico and Structuralist/ Poststructuralist Thought

{1983}

⁣ ‖‖‖

Is there any possible relationship—whether of influence, similarity, affinity, or opposition—between Giambattista Vico's thought and that of the current avant-garde in the human sciences: the structuralist/poststructuralist current? The question is worth asking, if for no other reason because of this avant-garde's all but uniform disinterest in Vico's work. Yet, a complete genealogy of structuralism/ poststructuralism might well include a Vichian moment. The Neapolitan thinker's affinities with Marx and Freud, with phenomenology and hermeneuticism, have been amply demonstrated in the succession of anthologies assembled by Giorgio Tagliacozzo and his colleagues at the Institute for Vico Studies in New York City over the last decade.[1] And these four strains of thought bear upon, when they do not flow directly into, the problematic that impels the structuralist/poststructuralist enterprise. In addition, Vico, in his hostility to Cartesianism, would seem at least to share a common enemy with Lévi-Strauss, Barthes, Lacan, Foucault, and Derrida, the regnant Holy Family of modernism in the human sciences. Of course, there is a fundamental difference between Vico's thought and that of this group, turning upon the place that the former accords to the concept of "history" in his "new science." History—in all its dimensions, as level of human activity, as process, as specific domain of the "social," even as a mode of thought or representation—remains the *bête noire* of both structuralism and poststructuralism. Still, Vico's conception of culture remains ample enough (or inconsistent enough) to accommodate at least a structuralist perspective and possibly even a poststructuralist one, at least on the level of analytical method.

We cannot account for the avant-garde's disinterest in Vico on the grounds of that notorious cultural ethnocentrism that marks so much of modern French thought in this century. Structuralism and poststructuralism confront and criticize, even when they do not borrow from, both German and Anglo-American thought, and French scholars have contributed as much to the revival of interest in

Vico as other national scholarly traditions have done. The reasons, therefore, for the studied disinterest of structuralism and poststructuralism in Vico must lie elsewhere.

On the face of it, the singular position that the avant-garde accords to language in the determination of the forms and processes of human culture might provide a ground for sympathetic reception of Vico's *New Science*. The structuralist/poststructuralist insistence on the figurative nature of all language and a fortiori all systems of thought might accord nicely with Vico's notions of the "poetic" origins of all cultural formations. Vico *might* be interpreted as a promoter of the kind of linguistic determinism that structuralists like Lévi-Strauss and the early Barthes, or poststructuralists such as Lacan, Foucault, and Derrida, seem to be promoting. But Vico's theory of language, whatever else it may have been, was a *philological* one, centering on the *word* as the basic unit of analysis. This "word," in Vico's thought, whatever its origination in the imagination rather than in perception or thought, was considered to bear an *indexical* relationship to its referent. Whatever its transformations, this word, Vico thought, would yield its original meaning to a process of poetic, rhetorical, and historical analysis.

Structuralism/poststructuralism, by contrast, takes its point of departure from Saussure's conception of the *sign* as the basic unit of linguistic analysis and, stressing the absolute arbitrariness of the sign's relationship to its referent, regards the philological no less than the sociological study of language as otiose. There is a fundamental cleavage here between the Vichian philological-historical study of language and the structuralist/poststructuralist conception of how, why, and to what ends *la chose linguistique* is to be studied. Far from providing the means for the de-bewitchment of human intelligence, language study for the structuralists/poststructuralists proceeds on the assumption that language is an irreducible cause of the fictiveness of all cultural constructions. If human culture has its peculiar *Unbehagen,* its unique "discontents," these are linguistic in nature; and they are not to be exorcised by any analysis, even Marxist or Freudian, that requires language as the instrument of its own hermeneutical operations. Nor are they to be exorcised by any practical activities, such as the Marxian "criticism by weapons" or a Freudian "therapy." Human beings are as condemned to language, in the structuralist/poststructuralist formulation, as they are condemned to mortality or to the play of a "power" from which there is no relief.

What, then, about the "dialectical" element in Vico's conception of human consciousness, on the one side, and human culture, on the other? Does not Vico's complex notion of the interplay of continuities and oppositions between the different phases of consciousness and culture (infantile and adult, primitive and civilized, imagination and reason, poetry and science, and so forth) at least *sound like* some of the notions broadcast by the structuralists and poststructuralists? To a certain extent it does, but only in the extent to which it posits an originary dualism solely in order to demonstrate an even more original and ultimately realizable ground of human being working itself out in history. Structuralism/poststructuralism posits a fundamental dualism—as between nature and culture (Lévi-Strauss), sign and referent (Barthes), power and resistance (Foucault), the imaginary and the symbolic (Lacan), trope and countertrope (Derrida)—and then proceeds to demonstrate that what may appear to be a progressive resolution of this dualism is only a *displacement* or at best an *inversion* of its constitutive poles, never a genuine development in nor a transcendence of them. Local changes in the configuration of any cultural structure are conceived to be functions of these displacing and inverting operations; differences between structures are attributable to different but equally arbitrary originary gestures, as in the constitution of the rules of a game. The whole congeries of possible "games" to be played out in human culture over time is unlimited, and this means, among other things, that the entire congeries cannot be a proper object of study or analysis. Even if one could study the whole system, one would not be able to represent it, since any representation would be possible only from a conceptual perspective existing solely by virtue of its *differ-ence* from that which it wished to represent. Needless to say, this conception of the limitations of the human sciences is totally at odds with the aspiration of Vico to found a "science" that would give to the study of culture what modern physics had given to the study of nature, namely, a *method* for studying the *whole* of culture as well as for investigating its parts.

This brings us to another important difference, having to do with the *values* informing the efforts to found a "new science" of consciousness, culture, and society by Vico and the structuralists/poststructuralists respectively. Ultimately, Vico suggests, the nature of any science is determined by the ends or purposes in the interest of which it is advanced. It is undeniable, I think, that the science he envisioned for the study of history, society, culture, and consciousness took these very objects of study to be *intrinsically* valuable, worthy of promotion, succor, and sustenance. Whatever the limitations or flaws in any given incarnation of them, they were all infinitely preferable to a life lived in brutal subjection to merely animal impulse and the feral conditions of their earliest instances. While fully recognizing the tyranny and repression with which civilized life burdened humankind (and it is this "realism" that differentiates Vico from the *philosophes* and links him with Marx, Nietzsche, and Freud), Vico envisioned a "science" of the human that would conduce to the refinement of human consciousness, the revitalization of society, and the ennobling of culture. His science was intended to serve the ends of the civilization that had made it possible.

This is not the case with the structuralists and poststructuralists. While it would be too strong to say that they are the enemies of "culture" in general, they are certainly hostile to "civilization" insofar as it is represented by any of its contemporary incarnations. To be sure, with the exception of Lévi-Strauss, they do not idealize primitive culture, after the manner of the Enlightenment, the Romantics, or the theorists of *Gemeinschaft* of the late nineteenth century. On the contrary, "utopianism" is for them as much of a *bête noire* as is "history." They are all "dystopian," if not eschatological, in their vision of modern civilization's immediate prospects. As suspicious of "ends" as they are of "origins," structuralists and poststructuralists are impelled "downward," to the "depths," in their search for meaning (or, more correctly, their search for the causes of a non-meaning that passes for meaning in human life), in a kind of *allegria del naufragio* (the ecstasy of the drowner), of the sort celebrated by the Italian poet Giuseppe Ungaretti. They plunge below the surface of a putatively "civil" life in order to find the dark, formless *nothing* out of which a speciously formed *something* has been *blindly* made. For Foucault, this "no-thing" is "power"; for Lacan, it is infantile "narcissism"; for Barthes, the "play of signifiers"; for, Derrida, "différance"; and for Lévi-Strauss, it is the act of parturition of "culture" from "nature" in general.

Needless to say, there is very little in this (let us call it by its name) "nihilism" that accords with the Vichian project of constituting a "science" for the redemption of human life from the cycles of "gentile" history. And having uttered the word "nihilism," we come upon the point in the development of late-nineteenth century thought that leads, via Heidegger most immediately, to the structuralists and poststructuralists—the point marked by the darker side of the thought of Nietzsche. When one seeks to characterize the giants of nineteenth-century thought who finally saw through and brought under question the vaunted "realism" of Western bourgeois culture, it is customary to group Nietzsche with Marx and Freud; or at least, it has recently become customary to so group them. And since the affinities of Vico with the thought of both Marx and Freud have seemed manifest, it seems natural to suppose that he has affinities of a special sort with Nietzsche as well. Moreover, the common origins of their thought in a tradition that was predominantly poetical, rhetorical, and philological would seem to mark them as participants in a shared enterprise. But again, the *values* on behalf of which these two thinkers undertook their respective critiques of their epochs had little in common.

However much we may wish to soften Nietzsche's celebration of the *Über-*

mensch, by attributing it to a hyperbolical manner of expression exacerbated perhaps by an incipient madness, there is no denying that what Nietzsche envisioned was nothing less than the death of that "humanity" that it was Vico's purpose to sustain. And insofar as the structuralists and poststructuralists desire to preside over the funeral of this "humanity," even if in the interests of promoting attitudes less arrogant than those that led to imperialism, racism, sexism, and the like, they share nothing of the spirit of Vico's enterprise. The differences between them are marked most strongly by the tendency among some of them (most notably Foucault, but also Barthes and such epigones as Deleuze, Guattari, Lyotard, etc.) to apotheosize the representatives of the Sadean tradition in Western thought and literature. The celebration of madness, infantilism, abnormality, and criminality by the most extreme practitioners of the structuralist/poststructuralist combine (such as Kristeva and Sollers) is only symptomatic of the "darker sublimities" that they envision. Vico's thought is certainly able to accommodate these aspects of social life as phenomena to be studied, even sympathetically; but it goes without saying that the celebration of them, as a kind of secular counterpart to saintliness, he would have taken as evidence of both a want of ethical sense, on the one side, and a failure of intelligence, on the other. The eminence of Nietzsche's place in the pantheon of precursors honored by the structuralists and poststructuralists marks the unbridgeable divide that separates Vico's thought from theirs.

CHAPTER FOURTEEN

The Interpretation of Texts

{1984}

The interpretation of texts is a matter of general concern for practitioners of those human sciences in which the understanding of the objects studied is conceived to be just as important as any explanation of how they function. The understanding of things human, social, and cultural has long been identified with that sense of having grasped the meaning of a text that follows upon a careful and sympathetic reading of it. Considered as a legitimate aim or goal of the human sciences, understanding presupposes that some things in the world are justifiably construed on the analogy of texts, that the best way to interpret them is by reading them, and that reading, therefore, provides a paradigm of what interpretation in general consists of.[1]

This connection between reading, interpretation, understanding, and texts explains the disturbing impact of the new theories of textuality that have emerged with structuralism and poststructuralism over the past twenty-five years. There is nothing particularly novel about the interpretative practices of these two movements. Even their most hostile critics will admit that structuralism and poststructuralism have produced profitable and convincing readings of texts and new and important insights into the subjects traditionally dealt with in the human sciences. What is new and disturbing about them is their agreement that texts, and especially the literary or poetic text, can no longer lay claim to the status of a paradigm of those objects in the world that *require* interpretation as the method for their comprehension.

In what follows I will consider some of the implications of current debates over "the interpretation of texts" from the perspective provided by this attempted demotion of the literary, poetic, or "creative" text from its position of paradigm of every object-to-be-interpreted. Basically, my argument will be that "textualism" represents, in the domain of interpretative theory, an attack upon a humanistic notion of creativity; that the attack is inspired ultimately by a loss of belief in the symbolic nature of language; and that the repudiation of the "work model" of the text, which follows from this loss of belief in symbolicity, indicates a loss of faith in what used to be called "the dignity of labor."

ะ๕

I do not, I am sure, have to outline the doctrine of textualism in any great detail, but it will be convenient to recall Roland Barthes's essay, "From Work to Text," published in 1971, which can be taken as the manifesto of the movement united around this doctrine.[2] In this essay, Barthes argues that

> the combined activity of Marxism, Freudianism, and structuralism requires, in the case of literature, the relativization of the scriptor's, the reader's, and the observer's (the critic's) relationships. In opposition to the notion of the work— a traditional notion that has long been and still is thought of in what might be called Newtonian fashion—there now arises a need for a new object, one obtained by the displacement or overturning of previous categories. This object is the *Text*.[3]

Barthes then proceeds to register a number of "propositions" that can be said to imply a wholly new way of conceiving the tasks of the interpreter of texts demanded by our awareness of this new object. These propositions are set forth in terms of opposed notions of "method, genre, sign, the plural, filiation, reading, and pleasure," deriving from the differences presumed to exist between "works," on the one side, and "texts," on the other.

The "work," Barthes tells us, has conventionally been thought of as a *concrete* entity, *autological* in structure, *genetically specific*, *organically* affiliated with other works, possessed of a *determinable meaning*, and properly used for "reading." By contrast, the "text" (or simply "text"—the suppression of the definite article indicating the disappearance of the text's alleged "concreteness") comprises a field of relationships, *heterological* in structure, *generically mixed*, *indeterminate* in meaning, *arbitrarily* related to other texts, and properly *used*, less is an object to be "read," than as a provocation to or occasion for "writing."

Although this set of oppositions might appear to be a basis for simply distinguishing between two kinds of verbal artifacts, rather in the manner of the classic-romantic or realist-modernist oppositions proposed by earlier critical theorists, it is in reality proposed by Barthes as a basis for the "interpretation" of verbal artifacts of whatever kind. Thus, Barthes can envision treating any "work" as if it were only so much "text" or the reverse, depending upon the ideological or more exactly, the political interests of the critic. To treat a "work" as a "text" will permit the disclosure of its particular duplicities of signification, its "mythological" function. To treat "text" as a "work" is the equivalent in criticism or interpretation to the myth-ifying operations employed by the "authors" of "works" in the domain of "creative writing."

The prophylactic or therapeutic effect of the concept of "text" on criticism con-sists, in Barthes's formulation, in its power to resist any tendency to reify and fe-tishize the notion of "literariness," considered as the essence of the creative work of art. "Text" has nothing to do with either the process (the labor) or the product (the work) of what used to be called "writing." In fact, writing itself, which used to be regarded as the kind of labor productive of works, is now detached from the con-cept of the "author" and transferred to that of the "reader."

In his discussion of the theoretical bases for his opposition of text to work, Barthes stresses the differences between the verbal artifact considered as a structure of *words* (each with a "proper" meaning, a discrete referent, and a discernible range of connotations) and as a structure of *signs* (after the manner of Saussure, who stressed the arbitrary nature of the relations of signs to their referents, on the one side, and of the signifiers of signs to their signifieds or conceptual baggage, on the other). The notion of the sign-nature of verbal artifacts permits the distinction between those that feign representation of an extra-textual meaning (which is in reality only an effect of the rhetorical focus upon signifieds) and those that direct attention to the play of signifiers alone. "Text," Barthes says, *defers* the signified indefinitely. Text resists any inclination to suggest a "deepening" of a meaning or a maturation of a thought in the process of its articulation. What "text" displays is only a play of signifiers in a "serial movement of dislocation, overlappings, and vari-ations," the apprehension of which is the occasion for whatever "pleasure" is to be accorded to the activity of writing. The "reading" of a "work" is nothing other than a subordination of the reader's consciousness to the authority of a speaker of a dis-course. "Text" lays itself open to the reader's capacity to enter into the production of signification, allowing the reader thereby to enjoy a pleasure formerly presumed to be the privileged prerogative of "authors."

Obviously, this notion of textuality does not foreclose the possibility of "in-terpretation," but rather opens it up to a kind of free play in which any notion of *responsibility* to the text goes by the board. This marks a crucial difference between both American New Criticism and Formalism, on the one side, and textualism, on the other. Whatever the disinterest of the former pair in authorial intention, his-torical context, response of readers, and problems of paraphrase and translation, they retained belief in the noumenal nature of the artistic text. The text was pre-sumed to possess a structural integrity, whether of "irony" or of various functional "devices," which it was the task of interpretation to identify, indicate, or suggest.

In its earliest stages, under the tutelage of Claude Lévi-Strauss and Roman Jakobson, structuralism, too, held out the promise of locating the noumenal ground of texts in its search for the "codes" operating therein to produce distinctive kinds of "meaning-effects."[4] But in the transition between structuralism and poststructuralism, even the notion of "code" is problematized. While many of the techniques of structuralist analysis continued to be used by interpreters of texts such as Barthes and Foucault in the 1970s, this last vestige of "meaning" disintegrated under the growing awareness of the arbitrariness that informed the constitution of codes themselves.[5] In textualism, even the notion of "structure" loses its hermeneutic authority. The effect of the denial of the relevance of both code and structure to interpretation is, finally, to de-commodify the text. The text is no longer to be thought of as an object to be exchanged (translated) or consumed. Having no essence, it can give no sustenance. On the contrary, text now indicates a place (*locus*, *topos*) for *performance*. Here, Barthes says, the writer/reader is invited to "gather up [the text] as play, task, production, and activity," in the manner of a musical artist who "plays" a score or that of an actor who "plays" a role.

It is tempting to see in textualism little more than a narcissistic fantasy, in which the "pleasures" of an idiosyncratic reading are substituted for the honest "labor" of the responsible interpreter. And so the ideology of textualism has been interpreted by those who fear the culture of narcissism on both the Left and the Right of the political spectrum. For these, textualism is a symptom of a pervasive infantilism that repudiates authority in general, but also morality, good manners, and good taste.[6] Fredric Jameson is a notable exception to this tendency.[7] He credits the Utopian impulse behind the "ideology of the text," even while regarding it as another instance of a purely "imaginary relation" to the "social realities" of advanced capitalism. The ceding of any claim to a definitive, correct, or even plausible interpretation of texts indicates a rebellion against the kind of authority enjoyed by bourgeois science—with its claims to objectivity combined with a servile attachment to the capitalist system of production, its combination of puritanical asceticism and drive for consumption as an end in itself. Viewed from this perspective, textualism is seen to have both a political and a cognitive implication: it represents in the domain of culture a rejection of authoritarian politics and bourgeois science—but in the manner of a retreat into anarchism rather than a search for an alternative on the basis of which a radical criticism could be erected. This anarchism is a function, in Jameson's view, of the fundamentally *anti-historical* bias of all textualisms, structuralist and poststructuralist alike.

The attitude toward history that structuralism and poststructuralism share is more important for the understanding of their epochal relevance than their differing attitudes toward science. Structuralism features the notion of textuality in the interest of producing a *science* of culture, poststructuralism in the interest of producing a *poetics* of interpretation. In both cases, however, the Western idea of history, conceived either as "context" of all "texts" or as the "process" that links author to reader within a distinct cultural "tradition," goes by the board. As Lévi-Strauss argues,[8] the Western conception of history is simply Western civilization's own myth, the myth that serves to justify its expansion over the globe and its destruction of all those cultures whose "primitive" status is indicated by their lack of "historical consciousness." What Western man calls "history" and appeals to as evidence of his cultural maturity, in contrast to the alleged childishness of primitive peoples, is nothing but so much textualization, which is to say a mythification, a confusion of cultural artifact with "nature."

In Barthes's essay on "The Discourse of History," the historian's putatively "realistic" text, with its naive belief in the "reality" of its "referent," is assimilated to the fictional texts of myth, legend, epic, and the novel.[9] Without "historical reality" (or its ethnographic and sociological counterparts) to serve as the baseline against which the "fictionality" of imaginative texts can be confidently measured, every representation of reality becomes merely another "text." Some of these texts may seek to pass themselves off as genuine "works" illuminative of "reality," but at best they succeed in producing only the "reality-effect." They are not to be assessed as to their realism, but treated rather as occasions for a performance by the reader-critic—in much the manner that Barthes himself treated Michelet's work in *Michelet par lui-même.* The historian's text—and indeed the very "documents" on which the historian builds his own text—will be treated as an occasion for that playfulness that the resourceful, *performing* interpreter will display in the presence of any text purporting *seriously* to represent reality as it *really* is. This is an indication of the interpreter's transcendence of a specifically *bourgeois* seriousness. Even before the seriousness of history, the interpreter will be "that uninhibited person who shows his behind to the *Political Father.*"[10] Textualism engenders naughty interpretation.

&

On the face of it, why should it matter whether one interprets texts, especially literary texts, correctly or not? Supposing that I do misread Milton or even Shakespeare. Or simply use them to display my learning or my virtuosity as a reader. So what? Milton and Shakespeare are dead; I have no obligation to them. Their texts, or versions of their texts, are here before me; they invite interpretation, even *demand* it. Why should I aspire to a *correct* interpretation? What does it matter if I get it wrong?

It would matter, I think, only if "correct" were understood to intend not only "accurate" but also "proper." Accuracy would be an issue in those situations in which the text under consideration were construed primarily as a message containing information needed for the execution of some practical task. But it is difficult to see how either fictional literature or historical accounts could serve any practical purpose—other than didactic ones. The messages contained in these kinds of texts are not in the nature of information that can be put to practical use. So whether I retrieve or decant this information accurately or not should hardly be a matter of concern to anyone.

But if "correct" is understood to imply not only "accurate" decoding of messages containing information, useful or not, but also "propriety" of response to whatever messages texts can he shown to contain, then correctness in the interpretation of texts, literary or otherwise, matters very much indeed.[11] If correctness of interpretation consists in a proper attitude of respect for (even belief in) the kinds of messages that texts convey, then one's attitude toward texts becomes indistinguishable from one's attitude toward authority in general. To give up the standard of correctness in the interpretation of texts is to give up the last vestige of respect for those traditions that texts, taken collectively and as ordered into a canon, are conceived to convey to living readers of them. To give up the standard of correctness in the interpretation of texts is to give up the possibility of determining: which texts are canonical and which are apocryphal (vis-à-vis the tradition); which are to be taken as models of propriety itself, not only in language-use but also in morals; which are to be used as paradigms of "realistic" representation of "reality" and which relegated to the status of "fiction," and so on. It is, in a word, to give up the notion of a hierarchy of texts structured on the principle of their relative dignity as to their cognitive content and, moreover, the principle of the quality of the labor expended in their production.

Of course, the obvious reason for opposition to textualism is easily stated: to make of all reading the result of a choice between "free" and "rule-bound" interpretative procedures is to make of "reality" itself an object for such a choice. In the traditionalist view (which can be dated from Friedrich Schleiermacher), interpretation is an activity whose legitimacy is defined primarily in terms of its similarities to and differences from the procedures and kind of knowledge practiced by the natural sciences. Prior to the advent of textualism, the choice in the human and social sciences was between aspiring to produce "explanations" of human phenomena (similar to those produced in the natural sciences) and remaining content with what hermeneuticists like Wilhelm Dilthey called "interpretations" that yielded "understanding." Under the textualist dispensation, both of these options are cast aside in favor of the view that the interpreter can aspire to the creation of an artifact, that is, his own interpretation, which can take its place among other *interpretanda* as a work of art in its own right.[12] The interpretation is no longer considered to be in any way dependent on or responsible to the artwork. Interpretation is no longer the explication and respectful display of the *work* of the artist, poet, or master thinker who had produced it, but the display and celebration of the interpreter's *art*. In this self-celebration, textualist interpretation violates a taboo akin to that on incest or the mixing of the kinds; it erases the difference between sovereignty and dependency within the domain of texts. It does not matter whether one holds that everything in the end, including art, is *only* interpretation, or whether one holds that interpretation is *also* art, and that therefore everything in the end is art. It is hierarchy that is undermined in either case. The erasure of the distinction between the text to be interpreted and the interpreting text replays the effort to dissolve the distinction between masters and slaves in the domain of politics, law, and society. And this is its principal sin in the eyes of those who defend interpretation as a service to cultural artifacts that enjoy the status of masterworks.

Beyond that, the notion of the text as a play of signifiers without a signified—a notion that we must credit to Jacques Lacan and Jacques Derrida,[13] who promoted the thesis that all putative signifieds are simply signifiers treated *as such*—collapses a whole series of distinctions on which interpretation has traditionally sharpened its tools since the invention of hermeneutics. I mean such distinctions as those between intentions and acts, the literal and the figurative meanings of words, the meaning and reference of propositions, the surface and the depth of discourse, the text and the context, and so on. If the text is conceived to lack these internal dimensions and external relations to things non-textual, then interpretation has no object on which to work. Interpretation loses the materials that allow it to pass for a specific kind of intellectual work, the distinguishing mark of which is the kind of commodity, that is, interpretations, it produces. If the text, like the sign, is apprehended as being nothing but surface, then interpretation can be conceived only as *labor* (endless reproduction of the same) or, alternatively, as *play* (similarly only reproductive, but at least revivifying of the interpreter, rather than draining and deadening—expensive—as labor is conceived to be).

This exteriorization of the text that textualism seeks to effect represents, as I see it, the culmination of a long process of cultural criticism centered on the attempt to retire the notion of *symbolism*—or to so revise the notion that it bears no relation to what had been referred to by that term prior to the twentieth century.[14] When the sign and by extension the text come to be conceived as *all surface*, they lose their capacity to incarnate meaning, in the manner in which the symbol was thought to do by, say, Samuel Taylor Coleridge and Goethe. Under the new dispensation, the text is permitted to function as an *index* of processes of consciousness in which "meaning-effects" are produced in discourse or as an *icon* of such processes and of their products. But under no conditions can the text be construed to *incarnate* pre-established meanings in the way that the religious symbol is presumed to do. Far from incarnating meaning by indicating the essential identity of the referents of two signs, the symbol is now viewed as nothing but a sign arbitrarily endowed with a signified (itself merely another signifier) and given the function in a specific culture of producing the specific "meaning-effect" attendant upon its "proper" use. And so, too, for all those texts called "sacred," "classical," "canonical," "poetic," or "literary" that interpreters *per vocationem* have taken as their special objects of attention since hermeneutics was constituted as a distinctive kind of intellectual work in the early nineteenth century.

ꝯ

Here we come upon the larger cultural implications of the attack upon symbolicity inherent in the modernist conception of the sign-nature of language. For it is precisely the symbol on which is erected the notion of a kind of creative activity capable of producing the kind of objects deemed worthy of being interpreted. And it is the notion of the work of art as symbol that justifies the idea that interpretation is a kind of work that is "productive" (without being "creative") rather than merely "reproductive." What I am suggesting is that the traditional notion of the symbol is linked to the notion of "action" that, in contradistinction to both "work" and "labor," forms the staple of the peculiarly Western, humanistic ideology of "creativity." So that: the dissolution of the traditional notion of the symbolic dimensions of language and textuality, of which textualism is a symptom, constitutes nothing less than the dissolution of the humanistic ideal of creativity itself.

The humanistic conception of creativity (*poiesis*) derives part of its connotative force from its oppositions to the notion of work (*techné*), on the one hand, and to that of labor (*ergon*), on the other. Work and labor in turn derive their respective positions vis-à-vis one another by the extent to which the former is conceived to be more like, the latter less like, the activity of creation itself. It is this notion of creativity, conceived as a kind of activity *qualitatively* superior to both work and labor and as being productive of a result "nobler" than anything born of either labor or work, that constitutes the myth of humanism and provides the basis for its ideology of work. From this perspective, the text, considered euphemistically as a "work," is anything but a product of the kind of work (*techné*) productive of the other kinds of commodities circulating in the system of exchange or market. Neither is it, needless to say, a result of that "labor" that is conceived to be only reproductive in kind.

The artistic work is, rather, a special kind of entity, product of the kind of activity that is called "action." And its unique property is that of a commodity that can be infinitely exchanged (read or interpreted) without any loss of value and infinitely used (if properly used) without ever being used up. This, it seems to me, is the content (or signified) of the notion of interpretability as applied to texts deemed worthy of serving as objects-to-be-interpreted in the humanist tradition.

That such is at least one of the possible contents of the notion of interpretability is suggested by the work of one of our subtlest theorists of interpretation, Paul Ricoeur. In his essay, "The Model of the Text: Meaningful Action Considered as a Text," published in 1971, the same year as Barthes's manifesto, Ricoeur offers a summary account of his theory of interpretation and textuality.[15] Interpretation, he says, is the "unmethodical method" by which "understanding" is to be achieved of those aspects of reality that resist "explanation" by the physical scientific method. What kind of aspects of reality resists such explanation? Ricoeur's answer is: human actions, which are to be distinguished from mere activity or motion not only by the intentionality informing them but also by their creativity, which is to say, their effects on the social world. These effects constitute the meanings of human actions. These meanings, in turn, are comprehensible (graspable) in the same way that the meaning of a speech act is, because they are produced by an action analogous to that productive of speech acts. Whence the paradigmatic nature of the text as the model of the interpretable object.

For Ricoeur, the theory of the speech act, as invented by J. L. Austin and developed by John Searle, provides the key to the understanding of the relation between language and action on which to erect a theory of the text as a model of the interpretable object.[16] What Austin called "illocutionary acts"—speech events in which the speaker, by the act of speaking, brings about a change in the world—are productive, Ricoeur argues, of the kinds of "texts" whose meanings are objectively accessible, because those meanings are perceivable as effects on society. When a judge sentences a criminal or a minister pronounces a "bride and groom" to be "man and wife," texts are produced whose "meanings" are their "effects" quite apart from the subjective intentions of their "authors." Here it makes sense to speak of texts as actions and even to conclude that texts can be said to "represent" actions by instantiating them.

Written texts differ from spoken ones inasmuch as they "fix" the "said" of speaking and detach the discourse from any ostensive referent and from authorial control. The fixing in writing of what is said in speaking and the detachment of the text from both any ostensive referent and authorial control are what make written texts so much more problematical as *interpretanda* than spoken discourses. It is also what makes the written text a special kind of *symbolic structure*—however much its author might have intended it to be a merely literal report or description. Like the action that creates the text, the text acquires by its "fixation" in writing a "voice" and a "will" of its own. What the written text "says" becomes more important than what its author may have intended in composing it. And this because: the written text, by being detached from its ostensible referent, becomes itself a "symbol" of the symbolic "dimensions of our being-in-the-world."[17] The similarity of the written text to a creative act undertaken by agents in domains of praxis other than those of speaking and writing resides in the text's *transcendence* of the immediate conditions of its production. The text transcends its original "situation" in the same way that the *importance* of an action in, for example, the political domain, exceeds its *relevance*.

As thus envisaged, the text can be seen to mirror its own time but also to "open up a world which it bears within itself."[18] The text's escape from the control of its author corresponds to the unforeseen and unforeseeable effects of creative actions in history. Thus, even though texts tend to be addressed to a limited group of possible readers, in fact they seek out and find (if they are "creative" texts) an "infinite range" of kinds of readers—in the same way that a creative action in politics can become an object of interest, fascination, and emulation by agents utterly different from those originally executing it.

I will not go into the ways in which this notion of the text permits Ricoeur to rewrite the classical conception of the relation between explanation and understanding. Suffice it to say that it allows him to relegate the older notion of understanding considered as a result of a "dialogue" with the text to the trash heap of Romanticism. And it allows him to salvage the referential function of the text by defining it as a referentiality in the mode of a symbol, rather than that of an icon or index. The important point for us lies in the fact that Ricoeur can recuperate the text's authority as a paradigm of all *meaningful* or, what amounts to the same thing, *creative* action only by an insistence on the symbolic nature both of texts and of the social systems in which they arise. The text becomes, in his formulation, a symbol of symbolicity itself—which is to say, a symbol of sociality; for "not only [is] the symbolic function . . . social, but . . . social reality is fundamentally symbolic."[19]

Ricoeur's defense of the text as a work that sets limits on what the interpreter is permitted to do with it while at the same time holding out the possibility of infinite reinterpretations of its meaning is purchased at the price of problematizing the author's intentions, the text's manifest referentiality, and any given audience's response to the text as determinants of meaning. This is the price he must pay to structuralism in return for the possibility of advancing a modernist conception of the distinction between a surface and depth semantics, the distinction between what the text manifestly *says* and what it is latently *talking about.* The problematization of the traditional elements of the speech event (author, audience, context) appears necessary to the construction of a theory of literary texts as symbolic systems, the referents of which are both themselves (this is the auto-referentiality thesis of modernism) and something extrinsic to themselves, in this case, social reality. But since this social reality is conceived as symbolic in nature, this means that the ultimate referent of all written discourse must be *symbol* itself.[20] It is this construal of the ultimate referent of all written discourse as the symbolic that permits Ricoeur to restore to the discourses of such putatively realistic disciplines as history, anthropology, and psychoanalysis some equivalent of the "moral" meaning that medieval textology espied beyond the interplay of the literal and figurative levels of sacred texts. This is what allows Ricoeur to suggest the possibility that even the most coldly realistic discourse of the human sciences can be said to possess *something like* that anagogic or mystical meaning that the scholastics defined as constituting the ultimate significance of religious discourse in general.

But everything hinges on the traditional notion of the symbol, which modern linguistics regards as a purely conventionalized sign, rather than as a living synecdoche (as it was viewed by the Romantics). For Ricoeur, the text is a special kind of sign that is at once an *icon* of its referent and an index thereof, insofar as it is a result or product of action. As an icon, the text can be said to *resemble* the symbolic structures to which it ultimately refers (which are always human actions and by extension human creativity conceived as the production of meaning in the world); and as an index, the text is to be regarded as itself an *effect* of a *cause* (discourse) that is the form that creative action takes in speech and writing. This is why the text lends itself to an interpretative analysis that must be conceived to be rule-governed rather than free. Validity in interpretation consists in resisting the twin dangers of allegorization, on the one side, and "gnostic" reductionism of the symbolic content of the text to a "mimic of rationality," on the other.[21] Allegorization treats the text as a play of signs without a referent; gnostic reductionism dissolves the symbol into little more than the carrier of a thought.

Responsible interpretation, however, will aspire to the reconstruction and reenactment of the process by which a given text effects a symbolization of whatever there is in human experience that cannot be spoken of directly, because that of which it speaks cannot be spoken of except in contradiction: such experiences as those of time, death, redemption, sociality, selfhood . . . Such experiences can only be spoken about in an oblique manner, which is to say, figuratively, narrativistically, or allegorically (in the literal meaning of the term: speaking otherwise), which provides a way of distinguishing between the symbolical and the literal levels of any text and between those texts demanding interpretation and those not demanding it.[22]

Thus, Ricoeur restores the distinction between canonical texts or what we might call master-texts and apocryphal or slave-texts—and therewith two kinds of textual creativity, that of writing conceived as action, on the one side, and that of writing conceived as mere work, on the other. The interpretable text is the text that demands interpretation because of the richness of its symbolic content. The uninterpretable text is the text lacking in symbolism, the "clarity" of which is purchased at the price of an impoverishment of that meaning that only action can produce. The criterion for distinguishing between these two kinds of texts is qualitative, not quantitative. It is not a matter of viewing the artistic text as a product of the play of a plurality of "codes," as the Russian textologist Jurij Lotman has suggested.[23] The symbolic text resists "explanation" because it is a manifestation in writing of that creative power that distinguishes humanity from the rest of nature.

Needless to say, it is to what Ricoeur calls a "hermeneutics of belief" (rather than to a "hermeneutics of suspicion") that he consigns the task of interpreting the symbolic text. Therewith he suggests that interpretation is not only a different and more difficult, but also a higher kind of intellectual *work* than the de-coding of a non-symbolic text for whatever message, information, argument, command, or query it might contain. And, needless to say, he also implies that the kind of interpretative freeplay authorized by textualism could hardly be called interpretation at all. For interpretative freeplay results in neither explanation nor understanding of the texts that serve as the occasion for its performances. Such interpretation does not look like action, work, *or* labor. In fact, it looks like what it openly professes itself to be, that is to say, playing or, more accurately, play-acting—or simply *acting* itself, the bane of all interpreters of a puritanical cast of mind.

※

I have used a number of theological expressions in this essay, because I wanted to suggest that what we have in modern discussions of "the interpretation of texts" is a minor reenactment of a debate that originates in the conviction that certain texts are divine in origin and that their value is therefore different in kind from the value possessed by anything of merely human or natural origin. It is a short step from the conviction that *some* texts are divine or possess a certain spirituality by virtue of their divine origin to the conviction that textuality itself is divine or spiritual in essence.[24] The step is as short as that between nomination and predication. For if even one text is sacred, then all texts can be construed as sacred insofar as they participate in that "textuality" that marks them as members of the same class. To designate one text, such as the Bible, as divine is to set up an opposition between that text and whatever else in the world can be conceived to be profane. And once such an opposition is set up, it becomes necessary to distribute across a continuum between the positively marked term (the *sacred* text) and its negative counterpart (the *profane* text) all instances of those objects that appear to have the attributes of textuality. This distribution produces a hierarchy in which the principal attribute of the paradigm, that is, divinity, becomes the standard by which to judge the worth or value of texts in general. In the case of the divine text, this attribute is, of course, creativity, since God, the source of all things sacred, is pre-eminently *creator* who marks things by fashioning them into images more or less in his own likeness. Whence the notion of textuality as the repository of creativity in general, the manifestation in the world of the principle of creation.

Even after the principle of creativity is detached from the being who is supposed to be its origin and personification —as it is progressively detached in the process of secularization that extends from the Renaissance through Romanticism—this structure of relationships that unites creativity, textuality, and value continues to function as the ground for critical theory and the interpretation of texts. This ground is sustained in modern critical theory by the notion of the symbolicity of language and the concomitant idea of the symbolicity of the artistic work. Accordingly, when modern linguistics relegates the symbol to the status of a conventionalized sign, the spirituality of the artistic work finally dissipates, the ideology of creativity is shattered, and interpretation is deprived of its raison d'être as the method of "understanding."

The principal implication of textualism, of the kind propounded by Barthes and poststructuralists in general, is the demotion of the text to the status of a commodity just like any other produced by merely human work. In their rejection of a hierarchy of texts, with the symbolic text occupying the apex and the iconic and indexical texts arranged in descending order of value, the textualists also reject that hierarchy of activities, of action, work, and labor, presumed to be productive of a hierarchy of commodities, creative, usable, and exchangeable. It is no accident that structuralism and poststructuralism alike center attention on the production and reproduction of signs, rather than on their creation. And it is understandable why Marxists might regard both of these movements as manifestations in the human sciences of that alienation of labor that is endemic to capitalist conditions of work.

But there is an ambiguity in the criticism by Marxists of this aspect of structuralism and poststructuralism, an ambiguity that derives from Marxists' fascination with the traditional humanistic notion of the kind of activity that might be called "creative." The attack upon the hierarchization of the forms of work, with which the names of Marx and Engels are associated but which is already implied in the labor theory of value developed by their despised bourgeois counterparts, John Locke and Adam Smith, was not extended to encompass the domain of artistic commodities by radicals as consistently as it was by capitalist society itself in its effective transformation of the work of art into a mere commodity and artistic production into mere labor. Marxist aesthetics continued to celebrate artistic work as a higher kind of activity than that productive of other kinds of commodities, expressive of a higher level of self-consciousness than manual labor. Georg Lukács in fact considered the artistic work as a paradigm, in the domain of human activity, of what proletarian consciousness would become once it had seized its own alienated condition in thought, that is, once it had become the commodified segment of humanity that knew itself to be such. When the proletariat attained to the level of self-consciousness possessed by all true art, work itself would be transformed into the kind of creative action of which only gods, heroes, and more recently only the very rich had formerly been thought capable. Then, when the state had withered away and society had dissolved, human life itself would be transformed into a work of art.

It is the frustration of the very hope for such a transformation that underlies and informs the recent debate over textuality, the interpretation of texts, and the nature of interpretation in general in the human sciences. Or so it seems to me. The textualists' attack upon the notion that the written text and especially the literary text can lay claim to a dignity and respect different from that of other commodities produced by human work reflects a pervasive disillusionment with the possibility of ever liberating human work from the drudgery of labor and making it into the kind of creative action formerly assigned to gods and heroes in myth. At the same time, however, this attack is mounted in the interest of dissipating the last vestige of spiritualism in our thought about culture that, in its celebration of the work of art as the noblest product of the human spirit, has served as the refuge of a sublimated religiosity since the Renaissance. To say that the work of art is *only* a commodity is quite different from lamenting the commodification of culture effected by capitalism in its reduction of everything human to its money or market value. To say that the work of art is *only* a commodity is to remind us that it too is a product of human work, to be valued for its status as an index of human beings' power to transform the material world into goods for specifically human *uses*. This move was impossible as long as the work of art retained its character as a mysterious product of an equally mysterious power of creativity that had been mysteriously given to some portions of the common humanity and denied to others. In reminding us that the work of art is *only* a commodity, just like any other produced by human work and inviting us to use art as we would anything else in the domain of human artifacts, textualism demands that we rethink the nature of work itself. In its widest implications, therefore, textualism redefines the problem of that "responsibility" to "texts" with which we have been burdened since the first interpreter decided that what lay before him demanding interpretation was an inscription of "the word of God."

CHAPTER FIFTEEN

Historical Pluralism and Pantextualism

{1986}

The age of pluralism is upon us. It does not matter any longer what you do, which is what pluralism is.

—ARTHUR C. DANTO, "The End of Art"

Become a pluralist because pluralism serves ends that are even more important than any conceivable comprehensive and coherent theory about the whole of man's discourse.

—WAYNE BOOTH, *Critical Understanding*

In the Summer 1982 issue of *Critical Inquiry*, the editor, W. J. T. Mitchell, characterized the editorial philosophy of that journal as "dialectical pluralism." As against what he called the widespread view that pluralism was "at best . . . an aimless eclecticism and at worst . . . a disguised form of repressive tolerance," Mitchell represented the kind of pluralism that *Critical Inquiry* promoted as "not liberal toleration of opposing views from a neutral ground but [rather] transformation, conversion, or, at least, the kind of communication which clarifies exactly what is at stake in any critical conflict."[1] In his view, dialectical pluralism could conduce to the revitalization of "the existing institutions of criticism by a kind of intellectual cross-pollination" and promote "the development of new institutions which answer collective needs and interests of the intellectual community."[2]

Mitchell saw the principal impediment to the realization of these goals as "the simple polarization of criticism into vanguard and old guard which passes for 'political consciousness' in so many of our current polemics."[3] This polarization he attributed to the rise of a critical ideology that he called "pantextualism," described as a strategy that "reads the entire fabric of nature and culture as a network of signs."[4] While granting that the kind of pantextualism represented by "deconstruction" was "one of the most interesting and important critical movements of the 70s,"[5] Mitchell suggested that its principal shortcoming lay in a deficient historical consciousness of what he calls "a sense of history." Thus he wrote:

> We need a sense of history, especially of our own critical history, which will get beyond the notion that we have somehow "gotten beyond" all previous paradigms. The treatment of previous criticism as a history of error which is always about to be set right in the present moment of critical breakthrough is, I would suggest, the chief error which stands in the way of our grasping our own institutional history. The ritual assertion that certain "naïve" positions—positivism, empiricism, and mimetic theories of art are the first to come to mind—have been irrevocably discredited by our recent breakthroughs strikes me as an ahistorical bit of naïveté which invariably depends on a reductive view of the supposedly discredited positions.[6] (CI 618)

I found this passage striking because of its implied linkage of pluralism with a specific "sense of history . . . which will get beyond the notion that we have somehow 'gotten beyond' all previous paradigms." I had thought that a pluralist, and especially a dialectical pluralist, would have held that our "sense of history" might be as various as the critical positions among which he wished to mediate. To be sure, any "treatment of previous criticism as a history of error" is ungenerous, but far from being "the chief error which stands in the way of our grasping our own institutional history," it is at worst merely one among many ways of defining what that "our" refers to, and in any case it is undeniably *a* way of "grasping" an institutional history, whether one likes it or not. Moreover, while "the ritual assertion that certain 'naïve' positions . . . have been irrevocably discredited by our recent breakthroughs" is not to be taken seriously, it is certainly the ritualism of such assertions that offends us rather than their "ahistorical" nature. For no amount of *historical* sophistication could possibly establish whether or not "positivism, empiricism, and mimetic theories of art" had been "irrevocably discredited." At best, historical sophistication might lead to a better understanding of what proponents of such doctrines said, argued, believed in, had in mind, intended, and so on; but whether or not these doctrines have been "irrevocably discredited" is not a matter that any historian—pluralist or not—could be expected to decide.

I presume that Mitchell did not mean to suggest that whatever pantextualists he had in mind were deficient in historical *information* about the critical enterprise. For if he had in mind Jacques Derrida, Michel Foucault, Roland Barthes, Umberto

Eco, Geoffrey Hartman, Harold Bloom, Gerard Genette, A. J. Greimas, Tzvetan Todorov, Julia Kristeva, J. Hillis Miller, Paul de Man, or Stanley Fish, what must be admitted for all of them is the astounding range of their inquiries, their inclination to deal in many cultures and periods of literary or philosophical history, their embrace of a variety of literatures and languages, and their refusal to limit themselves to the study of a discrete period of the common "institutional history." If they are guilty of anything, it is not of naïveté but sophistication. So I take it that what the pantextualists are really being accused of is having the wrong "sense of history," of viewing history and especially the history of criticism from the wrong perspective, which is to say, of viewing history from a typically modernist (or postmodernist) perspective or at least from a perspective different from that of a humanistic pluralist.

It is as if Mitchell, who in his stance as a literary theorist is willing to admit of a plurality of equally legitimate critical modes, were unwilling to extend this pluralism to the consideration of history itself. By this I do not mean that he would be unwilling to view the history of criticism as a cacophony or polyphony of contending critical positions, as a never-ending circle of critical viewpoints, with no one of them being able finally to declare itself the winner for all time, but rather that he must feel that this is the only legitimate perspective on that history. Such a perspective on history has a name, and it is *historicism*—the perspective associated with Ranke and Goethe in Friedrich Meinecke's great book on this subject,[7] the perspective which, in Erich Auerbach's *Mimesis*, is identified with the fate of literary realism in the West. Although the name given to this perspective by Meinecke suggests that it is *the* historical perspective, contemporary historical theory and practice deny it that claim. In point of fact, if we look at contemporary historical theory and practice, we must admit that there are as many perspectives on history as there are modes of critical practice in literary studies. And this for a very good reason: the referent of the term *history* is as indeterminable, is as much a matter of principled contestation, as the term *literature* (or for that matter, "philosophy" or "science") itself. So that, if one wished to "correct" certain critical positions by reminding their proponents of the necessity of a proper "sense of history," it would be just as legitimate to correct the corrector by reminding him that the history of historiography displays the same kind of confusion over the "sense of history" that the history of criticism displays over the "sense of literature." When Mitchell characterizes the current schism in criticism as another enactment of the quarrel of ancients and moderns, he is surely right; but he fails to note that this reenactment takes place within an atmosphere made murkier by the fact that there is no generally agreed upon "sense of history" to which one can appeal in order to characterize the differences between the two camps. It is not as if the ancients and the moderns agree on some body of fact from which they draw different implications regarding the attitude that one ought to assume vis-à-vis modern as against ancient literature. For what is at issue is not the interpretation of the facts but the nature of historical factuality itself.

The principal difference between the pantextualist sense of history and what I take to be the pluralist sense of it—as represented by, say, Wayne Booth and M. H. Abrams—has to do with the relationship presumed to exist between the field of past occurrences and any representation of that field. For the pantextualist, any representation of history has to be considered a *construction* of language, thought, and imagination rather than a *report* of a structure of meaning presumed to exist in historical events themselves. For Booth and Abrams, matters are quite otherwise. Not that they agree over whether it is possible to achieve a single, definitive account of what really happened in the past. For, as the exchange between them published in the Spring 1976 issue of *Critical Inquiry* makes clear, Booth wished to say that Abrams "demonstrated" the truth of the "story" he had told in his account of English Romanticism, *Natural Supernaturalism*.[8] After explicating Abrams' demonstration, Booth asks: "Has he given us *the* history of his subject as he defines it, or a history?" Then, he goes on: "If, as I am sure, he would answer the latter, how far will he go with the answer?" His aim, Booth says, is to "goad" Abrams "into discussing just how far his historical pluralism can go."[9] This on the assumption that the options are either to "go all the way," to accept even histories that visibly contradict one another, thereby revealing himself as a relativist, or "*not* go all the way," thereby proving that he is not "anything more than a monist."[10]

Abrams' response was that he could imagine a book on English Romanticism that told quite a different story from the one he had told, but which would be just as "true" insofar as each book might tell only a "*part* of the truth" but at the same time still be a "part of the *truth*."[11] "Does that make me a relativist?" Abrams asks.

The point to be noted is that for both Abrams and Booth there is a single truth to be revealed, because in history things happened as they did and not otherwise; but for Abrams the most one can hope for is a perspective that will reveal a part of this truth, while for Booth a perspective is not enough. Does this make Booth a pluralist? I must suppose that he is, for he calls himself such often enough; but on the basis of his discussion of Abrams' book, I must suppose that he is certainly not a *historical* pluralist. For historical pluralism presupposes either a number of equally plausible accounts of the historical past or, alternatively, a number of different but equally meaningful constructions of that indeterminate field of past occurrences that by convention we call "history." Booth does not accept the former kind of historical pluralism because, apparently, he believes that there is a single truth to be told about at least discrete domains of the historical past—from which it follows that all accounts of any such domains can be ranked as to their veracity. And he certainly does not accept the latter kind of historical pluralism, because here the whole problem of truth is set aside in favor of a view of historical representation that leaves it virtually indistinguishable from fiction.

Now, Mitchell's criticism of pantextualism for its want of a proper sense of history and the exchange between Booth and Abrams over the possibility of a single, truthful account of a given historical phenomenon point to a more general problem in literary studies, which makes the issues they raise difficult to resolve because it is systemic in all fields of humanistic studies. The problem has to do with the fragmenting of humanistic studies into discrete disciplines that must feign to aspire to the status of sciences without any hope of achieving the kind of procedures developed in the physical sciences for the resolution of conflicting interpretations of their specified objects of study. The result of this circumstance is that, in order to enable research in any field of humanistic studies, investigators must presuppose that at least one other field of study or discipline is effectively secured, that is to say, is effectively free of the kind of epistemological and methodological disputes that agitate their own area of inquiry.

History appears to serve this function for pluralist critics like Mitchell, Booth, and Abrams. Thus, Mitchell can chide certain of his peers for their want of a proper "sense of history" as if this were an unproblematic concept. In fact, historical studies are as divided over what constitutes a proper sense of history as literary studies are divided over what constitutes a proper notion of literary texts, criticism, or interpretation. And Booth and Abrams can debate the implications for critical pluralism of the relative truthfulness of alternative narrative accounts of English Romanticism without any indication that historical studies today are riven by disputes over whether it is truth or intelligibility for which historians should be striving and whether the narrative mode of historical representation is anything other than an impediment to the constitution of a properly scientific study of history. In other words, whatever resolution is achieved is purchased at the cost of ignoring or repressing their knowledge of contemporary historical theory and practice.

If the way one envisages the relationship between literary and historical studies is important in critical disputes, so too is the way that one envisages the relationship between literary criticism and literary history. For the way one conceives the latter relationship will determine in no small degree the way in which criticism is conceived to be free, as pantextualists are believed to view the matter, or limited in what it can say about literary phenomena, as Booth and Abrams (for different reasons) believe. Mitchell is right, I think, in linking the pantextualists' ludic conception of literary interpretation to their alleged notion that history itself is nothing but a text—and cannot, therefore, serve as a check on what can be said about "literary" texts. For Foucault, Barthes, Derrida, and so on (though not for all pantextualists), history is not a body of events lying before us in the manner of a landscape to be surveyed from a fixed standpoint and reported on in the way a geographer, naturalist, or painter might do, such that one could then compare different versions thereof and determine which is the most veracious, objective, informative, useful, and so forth. On the contrary, for the pantextualist history appears either as a text subject to many different readings (like a novel, poem, or play) or as an absent presence the nature of which is perceivable only by way of prior textualizations (documents or historical accounts) that must be read and rewritten in response to present interests, concerns, desires, aspirations, and the like. In this respect, I would argue (though I will not do so here), the present crop of pantextualists do not differ significantly from such former modernists as Lorenzo Valla and Machiavelli, Pierre Bayle and Voltaire, or Jules Michelet and Percy Shelley. Where they do differ is in their conviction that *history* cannot be appealed to as a neutral arbitrator of the conflicting claims of ancients and moderns over how the texts that comprise the canons of a tradition are to be read, interpreted, assessed, and used. Given this difference, to admonish pantextualists for a deficient or irresponsible "sense of history" is to beg the question at issue. (The situation is similar to that which recently occurred in disputes between Marxists and structuralists, in which the former criticized the latter for their ahistorical approach to the study of societies and cultures, when structuralism had been launched precisely by a decision to ignore the diachronic aspects of cultural formations in order to conceptualize them as systems rather than as processes.)[12] Therefore, if we wish to consider the implications for critical pluralism of the current fashion of pantextualism, we cannot do so by appealing to the notion of a "sense of history" that the latter seeks, as part of its critical program, to bring under question.

The exchange between Booth and Abrams over the limits of critical pluralism did not address this issue, because they shared a common notion of the "sense of history" that their common enemy, the deconstructionists, had brought under question (among other ways) by their textualization of history. This seems to me to be a critical issue, because the sense of history that Booth and Abrams share constitutes one of the mainstays in the critical pluralists' program of resisting the fall into "radical relativism," which they fear as much as the hated "monism" against which their pluralism is offered as a safeguard. This sense of history appears to consist of the notion that history is a congeries of *lived stories* that only await the historian capable of *discovering* them and then relating them in a *narrative* that figures forth (epideictically, Booth says) their *true* natures.

Thus Booth says of Abrams' account of English Romanticism: "Persuasion about any of the kinds of truths promised [in *Natural Supernaturalism*] depends on persuasion about the most obvious and perhaps the most difficult of all: Abrams purports to convince us that *all of this happened*—this *story* is *true*."[13] And in a reply to an imagined objection to Abrams' selection of evidence and his interpretation of it, Booth's rejoinder is: "Insofar as this is an objection to Abrams' view of Romanticism, the reply must be . . . show us the counter-evidence; tell us the *counter-story* in its full weight, so that we can judge."[14] As for Abrams, he writes:

> The basic mode of "proof" employed for this mixed bag of assertions is their incorporation into a story—more specifically, into a story made up of many stories, in which we can distinguish, within the overarching narrative, a number of middle-sized "novellas" and a great many "short stories"; and the book as a whole requires that the reader enter into its "narrative world" and be convinced that *"all of this happened*—this story is *true*," as a necessary condition for being persuaded of the soundness of the truth-claims and value-claims that the narrative implicates.[15]

Now, as a genuine pluralist and one who is even prepared to bear the label of radical relativist in matters having to do with *historical knowledge*, I do not wish to take issue with this *story-conception* of historical representation. I merely wish to note that it is a preconception shared by Booth and Abrams alike, on the basis of which they are able to elaborate their differing notions of the possibilities of ever telling the *definitive* story of so complex a phenomenon as "English Romanticism." I would note further, however, that there is a considerable philosophical literature on the epistemic status of narrative explanation, which is to say, explanation by storytelling, in the human and social sciences, the weight of which, if we may trust commentators as different as Arthur C. Danto and Paul Ricoeur, is to consign this representational strategy to the interpretive, rather than the explanatory, sciences. This judgment conforms to the dominant opinion among professional historians themselves nowadays, for whom narrative representations are to be accorded the status of literary, by which is meant "novelistic" or "fictional," accounts of the matters of which they treat. In other words, whatever gestures are made in the direction of an appeal to factual evidence or the reality of the events dealt with, insofar as a history purports to explain the congeries of events that serves as its putative subject matter by *telling a story about it*, the explanation provided thereby admits of no assessment as to its veracity or objectivity by criteria that might be considered "scientific." To be sure, this does not mean that a narrative (or story) account of any given phenomenon has no truth-value; but it does mean (and here I follow Ricoeur's argument as presented in his recent *Temps et récit*)[16] that historical accounts cast in the form of a narrative may be as various as the *modes of emplotment* that literary critics have identified as constituting the different principles for structuring narratives in general.

In literature, we have no difficulty thinking of a number of stories that have been emplotted in a variety of ways: the Faust and Oedipus legends are only the most obvious. It is more difficult to think that a given set of historical events might be variously but equally plausibly emplotted; yet this is exactly what we have to take account of when we encounter what appear to be mutually exclusive *narrative interpretations* of the same historical phenomenon. We are inclined to say that *certain* sets of historical events are intrinsically tragic, or comic, or epic, or farcical in nature and that, therefore, they will admit of one and only one mode of emplotment for the truthful representation of their real meaning. But real events are tragic or comic or epic or farcical only when viewed from the *perspective* of the interests of specific agents or groups involved in them. Tragic, comic, epic, and farcical are not categories *descriptive* of real events. As applied to real events, such categories are at best *interpretive*, which is to say, ways of imputing meaning to such events by emplotting them as stories of a recognizable, but culturally specific, kind. No set of real events, even those comprising an individual life, displays the kind of formal coherency met with in what we conventionally recognize as a story. We may seek to give our lives a meaning of some specific kind by telling now one and now another kind of story about them. But this is a work of construction rather than of discovery—and so it is with groups, nations, and whole classes of people who wish to regard themselves as parts of organic entities capable of living story-like lives. Neither the reality nor the meaning of history is "out there" in the form of a story awaiting only a historian to discern its outline and identify the plot that comprises its meaning.

This is *not* to say that certain events never occurred or that we have no reasons for believing in their occurrence. But a specifically *historical* inquiry is born less of the necessity to establish *that* certain events occurred than of the desire to determine what certain events might *mean* for a given group, society, or culture's conception of its present tasks and future prospects. This is why we distinguish between a specifically historical account and other kinds of inquiry that might appear to be historical in nature, such as geological, biological, journalistic, or criminal investigations. The meaning of an event like "English Romanticism," the occurrence of which is hardly to be doubted, is variously interpretable; and this means, as Abrams maintains, that we can tell equally plausible, alternative, and even contradictory stories about it without violating rules of evidence or critical standards commonly held across a wide variety of disciplines or philosophical or even ideological positions.[17]

The point is that one can imagine not only one or two but any number of alternative stories of "English Romanticism" or of any other culturally significant event, all equally plausible and equally authoritative by virtue of their conformity to generally accepted rules of historical construction. The plausibility of such stories will reside in the perceived adequacy of the plot-structures chosen by the historian to make a sense out of what would otherwise be only a chronicle of events.

This suggests two things. One is that the plausibility of any given narrative account of real events resides in the perceived adequacy of a given plot-structure to the representation of the meaning of the set of events serving as the historian's referent. The other is that the number of strategies available to the historian for endowing events with meaning will be coterminous with the number of generic story types available in the historian's own culture. For example, there will be no "tragic" interpretations of historical events in cultures lacking the notion of a tragic story. And this means, first, that "plausibility" is a function of how the audience views the account given by the historian, rather than of whether the story told "corresponds" to the events of which it is a representation; and, second, that the number of versions of any given set of events that any given audience can adjudge plausible is limited to the set of emplotting procedures known to the audience in question.

This might be conceived to give solace to a historical pluralist who could, if he accepted this view of the matter, escape the threat of radical pluralism by taking refuge in cultural determinism. In order to arbitrate among contending versions of the same set of events, one could at least exclude any account emplotted in a mode unknown to the culture for which the account was written. Moreover, such a view of the matter might appeal to a critical pluralist, because it vests the authority to determine the range of kinds of historical interpretation in the discipline best qualified to determine what is a valid mode of emplotment and what is not, namely, literary criticism.

Moreover, on this view of the possibilities of historical interpretation, one could envision a way of correlating different narrative accounts of the same historical phenomenon. One could say, for example, that Abrams' account of English Romanticism bears the same kind of relationship to some imagined counter-history that an epic plot bears to a tragic or ironic plot. This would allow us to credit Abrams' contention that "both books [might] tell a story which is true" and not be considered "contradictory." But not because, as Abrams has it, "clashing assertions" meet on different planes of discourse,[18] but rather because the plot-structures used to fashion the different stories are not in the nature of propositions that can be submitted to tests of verification or falsification in the way that "singular existential statements" can be tested.

A representation of a given sequence of events as a tragedy, comedy, farce, and so forth, belongs to the category of judgments of value rather than of fact. Or, as Ricoeur puts it with respect to historical interpretations specifically, a given emplotment of historical events is in the nature of a *performative*, rather than a *constative*, utterance. A historical interpretation cast in the form of a narrative belongs to an order of locution to which characterizing, diagnosing, grading, ranking, rating, and so on, belong—that is, the order which J. L. Austin, in *How to Do Things with Words,* calls "verdictives." At least—and here I essay a verdictive locution—so it seems to me.

Narrative accounts of real historical events, then, admit of as many equally plausible versions in their representation as there are plot-structures available in a given culture for endowing stories, whether fictional or real, with meanings. These meanings, in turn, would be as correlatable as Northrop Frye conceives the archetypes of fiction to be or as Kenneth Burke conceives the "master tropes" of figurative language to be. Far from a given narrative emplotment *ruling out* the possibility of utilizing another plot-structure as a device for generating an alternative narrative interpretation of a given set of historical events, a plausible account cast in *any* mode would authorize interpretations cast in the other narrative modes known to the culture in which the first had been produced. The demonstration that a given set of events *can be* represented as a comedy implicitly argues for the possibility of representing it with equal plausibility as a tragedy, romance, farce, epic, and so on.

But, it will be asked, is there not a further limit to be set, by the nature of the events being depicted, on the number of plot-structures that can be used to represent those events in a story type? That Booth thinks this might be the case is suggested by the question he asks of Abrams: "Has he given us *the* history of his subject as he defines it, or *a* history"?[19]

Abrams' response to this question is instructive of the problem of setting limits on the number of *kinds* of stories that one can plausibly tell about a given set of historical events, once one has opted for the narrativist notion of historical interpretation. The only kind of account of English Romanticism he rules out of play on principle is one that would be non-narrativistic. And this because, in his view, such an account could not possibly pass for a *historical* account at all. Thus, in his response to J. Hillis Miller's proposal for a deconstructionist account of English Romanticism, Abrams writes:

> If one takes seriously Miller's deconstructionist principles of interpretation, any history which relies on written texts becomes an impossibility. If a production is to be accounted a history, it must be a history of something determinate and determinable; and the elementary assumption that a cultural historian must make is that he is able to understand, in the sense that he is at least able to approximate, the core of meanings that certain writers at certain times expressed in their writings. A narrative about texts by a historian who genuinely proceeds on the belief . . . that his procedure need be nothing more than "the importation of meaning into a text which has no meaning 'in itself,' " will turn out to be a history only of what it itself expresses—a history, that is, of the historian's will to power, as manifested through that one of the many deconstructionist codes of interpretation that he has elected to press into the service of this will to power.[20]

This passage acutely positions us before the issue that must concern us in the conflict between pluralists and pantextualists insofar as what will count as "history" is concerned. Abrams suggests that the issue turns on the nature of the subject matter, content, or referent of the historian's discourse, rather than on its form or mode of representation. He takes it for granted that the form of the discourse will be a narrative and that the aim of the discourse will be to "understand" the "core of meanings that certain writers at certain times expressed in their writings."

But suppose that the historian were less interested in understanding than in characterizing the contents of a body of texts remote in time; that texts themselves were conceived to be less "expressions" of a "core of meanings" than "effects" of certain discursive practices; that the aim of the historian was to demonstrate a history of error, duplicity, illusion, and failure of meaning rather than what Booth calls a "hope . . . faith in life and joy," and so on; and that the historian was less interested in telling a story than in explaining, by the application of some principles of current philosophical or social scientific theory, how this tissue of mistakes took shape, established itself as an illusion of an epoch, and then simply fell into disuse? Would such an account pass muster as a history? Obviously, for Abrams it would not; and yet what I have described would serve, I submit, as an adequate characterization of such historical classics as Jacob Christoph Burckhardt's *Civili-*

zation of the Renaissance, Alexis de Tocqueville's *Democracy in America*, and Johan Huizinga's *Waning of the Middle Ages*, none of which could be called a narrative in the sense that Abrams understands the term in this context.

Of course, neither could any of these classics be properly called a "deconstructionist" history—or at least I am not interested in arguing that point on this occasion. The point I do wish to argue has to do with the relationship that is presumed to exist between narrative historical representation, on the one side, and the pluralists' criticism of pantextualism for its deficient "sense of history," on the other.

It seems to me that if one adopts a narrativist view of historical representation, one cannot rule out the possibility of an anti-narrativistic account of historical phenomena of the sort envisaged by Miller, that is, an account written according to deconstructionist principles. And this because there is nothing in historical events themselves to require that accounts of them be cast in a narrativist mode. The association of historical representations with narrative modes of discourse is a very old convention, but it is nonetheless only a convention. And although the debate over the desirability of a narrative representation of historical events and processes has recently heated up again, the dominant view among historians nowadays is to regard the narrative mode of representation as an impediment to history's transformation into a science, rather than as the "natural" way of representing historical phenomena.

Now, what are the implications for critical pluralism of the repudiation of narrative as the proper way to represent, if not explain, historical phenomena? The principal implication is that one cannot appeal to any specific "sense of history" as a basis for excluding any given critical practice from the list of proper critical approaches in the way that Mitchell has done in his criticism of "pantextualism." What Mitchell calls "the notion that we have somehow 'gotten beyond' all previous paradigms" is no more deficient in "sense of history" than the notion that we have *not* "'gotten beyond' all previous paradigms." It is simply *another* sense of history, and one with a long pedigree at that. And as for "the treatment of previous criticism as a history of error," it is not an "error standing in the way of grasping our own institutional history," but simply *another* way of "grasping" that history. In short, one cannot check the fall into "radical relativism" to which pluralism in general is prone by appeal to "a sense of history," as if this were an unproblematic concept not threatened by the same "relativism" that critical pluralism wishes to avoid.

A second implication for critical pluralism of the repudiation of narrative as the proper way to represent, if not explain, historical phenomena is this: there is no way of distinguishing, as Abrams wishes to do, between a history that expresses "the historian's will to power" and one that does not. Recall that for Abrams the "historian's will to power" is "manifested through that one of the many deconstructionist codes of interpretation that he has elected to press into the service of this will to power." But the same can be said of the "constructionist" historian's enterprise as well. Abrams himself notes that his "book as a whole has a structure that is deliberately iconic of the spiral form which many Romantic thinkers considered the necessary shape of all intellection."[21] In other words, he frankly admits that he has "emplotted" his story, chosen a macroform by which to connect the beginning, middle, and end of his narrative in "an exegesis that was historical (that is, retrospective and prospective as well as conspective), because I believed that the only way to understand the particulars of my humanistic investigation."[22] But was the choice of this plot-structure, because it was in Abrams' view the way "in which many Romantic writers ordered their philosophies, their histories, and their fictional writings in verse and prose,"[23] any less expressive of *his* will to power than the deconstructionist's choice of "one of the many . . . codes of interpretation that he has elected to press into the service of this will to power"? It was one of the articles of faith of classic historicism that the principles of interpretation used in the analysis of any past epoch had to be drawn from the epoch in question. And that is a perfectly legitimate way of proceeding for historians of the historicist persuasion. But the famous "crisis of historicism" of the late nineteenth and early twentieth century was caused precisely by the realization that what constituted the dominant mode of consciousness of an age was the *problem* of historical reconstruction, not a solution thereof. Abrams' choice of "the spiral form" to serve as the "structure" of the "book as a whole" is still a *choice* among a number of possible "codes of interpretation," among which those of the deconstructionists themselves must be counted. Whether it too must be regarded as an expression of Abrams' own "will to power" we can leave to others to decide.

A third implication of the repudiation of narrative as the proper way to represent, if not explain, historical phenomena has to do with Booth's notion that the choices confronting the historian are monism, on the one side, and radical relativism, on the other. In point of fact, the very notion that these are the options confronting the historian hinges upon the conviction that a story might iconically mirror a congeries of real events. We can see by Abrams' own account of what he sought to achieve in his book that he intended the story he told to conform, in some way, not to a structure of *events*, but to a plot-form, the "spiral," that he discerned in "many Romantic thinkers" as constituting an image of "the necessary shape of all intellection." Therefore, to ask of Abrams whether his story is "true" (in the sense of corresponding to the structure of the events of which it is a story) is to miss the point of Abrams' enterprise. Moreover, to ask Abrams whether his is *the* story or only *a* story, as if the answer to this question would disclose a monism or a radical relativism, is to mistake the issues involved completely.

Given the fact that Abrams had chosen to cast his account of English Romanticism in the form of a narrative, the issue of the truth or falsity of his account could hardly arise. Stories are not true or false, but rather more or less intelligible, coherent, consistent, persuasive, and so on. And this is true of historical, no less than of fictional, stories.

Booth's question to Abrams presupposes a conception of historical stories quite at odds with what he himself would hold to be the case with fictional stories. Would he ask whether a novel was true or false? Well, he might. But the point to be taken is that Booth apparently believes that one can set a limit on critical relativism by appeal to a historical reality that possesses a structure such that it can be truthfully represented in a story rather than simply be rendered intelligible by representing it as a story of a specific kind. This is a common error of historians who regard storytelling as the "natural" way of representing historical events, processes, and situations. If one adopts this point of view, then the choice between monism and radical relativism becomes unimportant. In order to tell a story about any congeries of real events, one will have to tell one story and not another, and one will have to tell it from one of many possible perspectives and not all possible ones. Which means that a narrative account of anything will be both monistic insofar as it is a single story and relativistic insofar as it is told from a single point of view.

Of course, I have not said anything about the alternatives to a narrative representation of history. But if I have not, it is because for those who deny the adequacy of narrative historiography to the representation of real events, the issue of pluralism does not arise. For contemporary non- or anti-narrativist historians, historical accounts are either true or false, intelligible or unintelligible. And this suggests that the whole question of pluralism, in both criticism and historiography, is linked in some crucial way to a narrativistic notion of historical representation. It is this linkage that I have tried to indicate in this essay. To dilate on the relationship of pluralism to a non-narrativistic "sense of history" would be another story altogether.

CHAPTER SIXTEEN

The "Nineteenth Century" as Chronotope

{1987}

I have been asked to reflect on the present state of the field of nineteenth-century studies and to consider whether the field itself might be considered a "metadiscipline" on the basis of which the various techniques and modes of analysis of the "disciplines" that comprise the human sciences of our time could be coordinated and united into a genuinely "interdisciplinary" enterprise. Obviously, this is a formidable task, and I would be foolish to suggest that it could be done in the small space available here. I thought, however, that some light might be thrown on the enterprise that interests us by reflecting on the name of our parent organization, Interdisciplinary Nineteenth-Century Studies.[1] Accordingly, I will lay out, as best I can, what I take to be "the present state of the field" and its "metadisciplinary" presuppositions, anxieties, and obsessions under the three terms comprised in that title: *interdisciplinary, nineteenth century*, and *studies*. And I shall suggest an alternate, or additional, perspective on these matters in relation to the idea of *chronotope*. I begin by noting (or rather confessing) that most of the fields that comprise the humanities are multidisciplinary inasmuch as their characteristic objects of study—works of art or literature, sacred texts, social institutions, traditions of thought, individual human beings, complex historical events—typically require more than one discipline for their analysis. But multidisciplinarity should not be confused with interdisciplinarity. It is one thing to utilize a number of different analytical techniques for the study of a complex human phenomenon and quite another to conceptualize an object of study that would require, less a combination of already established disciplines, than rather the theorization of analytical techniques hitherto unthought of by any of the received disciplinary protocols of the human sciences. As the prefix "inter" suggests, interdisciplinarity arises in the spaces between the established disciplines of a given historical moment; the interdisciplinary consists of all of those aspects of human inquiry that have had to be repressed, abandoned, or denied in the process of constituting the array of disciplines comprising the human sciences in any given moment of their historical evolution.

The point was made by Roland Barthes in his essay of 1971, "From Work to Text," when, in speaking about the condition of literary studies at that time, he remarked:

> What is new and which affects the idea of the [literary] work comes not neces-
> sarily from the internal recasting of each of [the many disciplines that may take
> it as their object of study], but rather from their encounter in relation to an object
> which traditionally is the province of none of them. It is indeed as though the
> interdisciplinarity which is today held up as a prime value in research cannot be
> accomplished by the simple confrontation of specialist branches of knowledge.
> Interdisciplinarity is not the calm of an easy security, it begins effectively . . .
> when the solidarity of the old disciplines breaks down . . . in the interests of a
> new object and a new language neither of which has a place in the field of the
> sciences that were to be brought peacefully together, this unease in classification
> being precisely the point from which it is possible to diagnose a certain
> mutation.[2]

Barthes then remarks on recent changes in our notions of the literary object of study:

> The mutation in which the idea seems to be gripped must not, however, be over-
> estimated; it is more in the nature of an epistemological slide than of a real
> break. The break, as is frequently stressed, seems to have taken place in the last
> century with the appearance of Marxism and Freudianism; since then there has
> been no further break, so that in a way it can be said that for the last hundred
> years we have been living in repetition. What History, our History, allows us
> today is merely to slide, to vary, to exceed, to repudiate. Just as Einsteinian sci-
> ence demands that the *relativity of the frames of reference* be included in the object
> to be studied, so the combined action of Marxism, Freudianism, and structural-
> ism demands, in literature, the *relativization* of writer, reader, and observer
> (critic). Over against the traditional notion of the *work*, for long—and still—
> conceived in a, so to speak, Newtonian way, there is now the requirement of a
> new object, obtained by the sliding or overturning of former categories; that
> object is the *Text*.[3]

Barthes's remarks were made in 1971, just after a number of poststructuralisms had made their appearance in cultural studies. Taken together, these poststructural-isms comprised a field that would soon be tentatively labeled "cultural criticism," an activity that cut across both disciplinary and ideological divisions in the human sciences and the "postmodernity" of which was indicated by the criticism, revision, and in certain cases, the outright repudiation of the three great systems that Barthes had named as the forgers of the *épistème* that had predominated in cultural analysis for the last one hundred years: Marxism, Freudianism, and structuralism. Between the time of Barthes's remarks and today, the antithetical aspect of these poststructuralisms has come to the fore, resulting not only in the general demand for a more *historicist* approach to the study of social and cultural phenomena but *also* in an equally strong demand for a critique of the received forms of *historical consciousness* itself.

The latter demand—for a critique of all historicisms inherited from the "nineteenth century," including its most radical mode, that of Marxism—has been most forcefully advanced by feminist and Third World theorists, who require a redefinition, not only of the "contents," the objects inhabiting the "field" we call "history," but also of the methods we shall use to study this "field" and the discursive techniques we use to represent and describe historical structures and processes.

In "nineteenth-century studies" the effect of these demands for a radical *reconceptualization* of what shall pass for a specifically "historical" approach to the study of the "nineteenth century" has been profound, amounting, I would say, to nothing less than the kind of mutation that Barthes signaled for literary studies in general in his announcement of the supplanting of the notion of the "work" by that of "text." But here it is a matter of problematizing not simply one aspect of culture, such as "literature" or "politics" or "academic institutions," but rather bringing under question the very notion of that "history" of which all of these, along with the modes and means of production and the social relations determined by these in specific periods of history, are component parts. In a word, considered as a distinct historical configuration, as a general object of study located in "a past" but bearing a distinct relationship to our "present" as one of its conditions of possibility, the "nineteenth century" is being *re-invented*. One way of characterizing what is going on in this process of reinvention would be to say that the "nineteenth century" is being transformed from a "period" into a "chronotope."

༃

The notion of the *chronotope* I of course borrow from the work of Mikhail Bakhtin and especially from his great essay: "Forms of Time and of the Chronotope in the Novel: Notes toward a Historical Poetics." Suffice it to recall that Bakhtin devised the idea for the designation of "a formally constitutive category of literature," but suggested ways in which it could profitably be extended to serve as a possible subject of general cultural-historical analysis. "In the literary artistic chronotope," he wrote, "spatial and temporal indicators are fused into one carefully thought-out concrete whole. Time, as it were, *thickens*, takes on flesh, becomes artistically visible; likewise space becomes charged and responsive to the movements of time, plot, and history. This intersection of axes and fusion of indicators characterizes the artistic chronotope."[4]

That, however, chronotopes are anything but figments of the writer's imagination, that they function as well as effective organizing structures of individual and of general social consciousness, beyond the confines of "literature," within the domain of reality we designate by the term "history"—all this is signaled by what Bakhtin says regarding the relation between chronotopes, genres, and the categories of all cultural self-representations. "The chronotope in literature has an intrinsic generic significance. It can even be said that it is precisely the chronotope that defines *genre* and *genetic distinctions*. The chronotope as a formally constitutive category *determines* to a significant degree the image of [the human] in literature as well. The image of [the human] is *always* intrinsically chronotopic," and this because the literary chronotope "assimilates *real historical time and space* to discourse."[5]

Bakhtin's examples of chronotopes suggest that, far from being only inventions of a writer's imagination, they are more importantly instances of socially determining structurations of practices that set limits not only on what can possibly *happen* within their effective confines but also what can be *perceived* and even *imagined* by agents acting within their constraints. Unlike the notion of the "worldview," conceived as a fact of consciousness, the chronotope directs attention to the effective conditions of possibility of both *thought* and *action*, *consciousness* and *praxis* within discrete milieus, structured as fields of institutional and productive arrangements. The mini-worlds of "the castle," "the highway," "the boulevard of the capital," "the slums of the industrial city," "the colonial outpost," "the salon," are not only socially structured, but also, and above all, imaginary spaces, each with a different *possible* experience of time, within which the *bodies* and *psyches* of human agents and the relations they can bear with others, whether indigenous to that space-time or only visitors to it from elsewhere, are rigidly delimited. The experience of a chronotope is at once more concrete and more real than the experience of a "period" could ever be, because whereas the notion of a period directs attention to the interplay of process and change, continuities and discontinuities, that of the chronotope directs attention to social systems of constraints, required repressions, permissible sublimations, strategies of subordination and domination, and tactics of exclusion, suppression, and destruction effected by a local system of social encodations.

In *The Political Unconscious*, Fredric Jameson has shown the usefulness of the notion of the chronotope for mapping out what are presumed to be the "conditions of possibility" for the occurrence of the kinds of events conceived to be imaginable in the literary works, or, indeed, the whole "style" of a literary period. In his analysis of *Lord Jim* as a proto- or semi-modernist novel, he identifies as the chronotope within which the characters, events, themes, and plots of the work will appear to having "happened naturally," as being the kinds of things, happening in the order and rhythms in which they happen—however melodramatic, fantastic, or metaphysical they may be—that could be expected to happen when, where, and how they did, given the nature of the chronotope identified by Conrad as their symbolic "container." The "sea," Jameson argues, is "the privileged place of [Conrad's] strategy of containment." The sea furnishes the images, themes, motifs, and symbols of the conventional adventure story that comprises one half of the novel's manifest "content." But this "sea" is not just any bit of ocean on which just any kind of adventure may happen; in *Lord Jim* the sea serves as chronotope, a nature organized as "a place of work and [as] the very element by which an imperial capitalism draws its scattered beachheads and outposts together, through which it slowly realizes its sometimes violent, sometimes silent and corrosive, penetration of the outlying precapitalist zones of the globe."[6] The sea, then, in Conrad, is

> both a strategy of containment and a place of real business; it is a border and a decorative limit, but it is also a highway, out of the world and in it at once, the repression of work—on the order of the classic English novel of the countryhouse weekend, in which human relations can be presented in all their formal purity precisely because concrete content is relegated to the rest of the week—as well as the absent workplace itself.[7]

The chronotope is nature, more or less dominated by human agents and specific social institutions that determine the kinds of work, the forms of violence, the very possibilities of human community held open to both dominant and subordinant groups, and even the forms of alienation to which the casualties of the system may legitimately aspire. Much more "active" than what used to be called "the background" or "scene" of the action by an older criticism or what narrative historians call "the context" of the acts, agents, and events whose story they wish to tell, the chronotope lies halfway between an environment or *milieu*, on the one side, and the fantastic "Zeitgeist" of Hegelian historical metaphysics, on the other. For the chronotope belongs neither to nature nor to culture, but is the form that the mediation between these two orders of existence takes in discrete historical places and time periods. The chronotope must, therefore, be doubly invented: first, as a product of human labor, domination, repression, and sublimation; second, as a fact of consciousness, in the minds both of those who produce it and of those who reproduce it—either as a recognizable condition of possibility for their own labors or as an object of study by historians of the events that take place within its confines and are recognizable as events "belonging" to the age or period in which they occur by their concomitance with the conditions of possibility dictated by the chronotope itself.

For historical studies, the idea of the chronotope has advantages over the notion of the period in a number of ways. As a combination of temporal, spatial, and sociocultural categories, the chronotope demands a greater degree of specificity and of referential concreteness than does the notion of the "period." Secondly, considered as a product of a mediation among nature, specific kinds of modes of production, and the social relations determined by these modes, the chronotope is directly accessible to analysis by study of both the documentary records of a society and the testimony of individual writers, novelists, poets, journalists, letter-writers, autobiographers, scientists, philosophers, and so on—whose work permits the drawing of a set of the "mental maps" of a given time, place, and cultural condition and the construction of the "legend" that they all took for granted as the common code they shared both for making and reading the terrain of consciousness that they *effectively* occupied. The construction of something like an "atlas" of such "mental maps" would give us a good idea both of what was conceived to inhabit the terrain of possible action for agents, individual and collective, at given times and places (as well as what this terrain itself consisted of) and what, having been systematically and generally forgotten, repressed, or simply excluded or marginalized, constituted the latent "content" of the Unconscious—political or otherwise—of an age, epoch, or era. For, as Jameson suggests, chronotopes are not only symbolic "strategies of containment" and "modes of exclusion," but "they can also take the form of repression in some stricter Hegelian sense of the persistence of the older repressed content beneath [a] later formalized surface"[8] of "the spirit of the age" or "the dominant structures of hegemony" or "mode of production." The idea of the chronotope provides us with a medium-range, molar unit for conceptualizing regional variations of a cultural epoch somewhere between the atomic event and the galactic expanses of "periods" as broadly envisaged as the "nineteenth century." It is only at this level of conceptualization that we shall be able to perceive the interrelations, continuities, ruptures, gaps, antitheses, and so on, between what we call high culture—art, literature, philosophy, science, religion, and law—on the one side; and the social realities, the practices, experiences, and urgencies of everyday life, on the other.

Considered as a designator of the fundamental unit of historical inquiry, the notion of the "period" has the effect of flattening out, linearizing and dispersing the events presumed to mark its development across a temporality apprehended as made up of befores and afters, beginnings and ends, anticipation and realizations, and so on—in other words, of reinforcing our tendency to think of historical relationships on the analogy of biological ones, which is to say, to think of them as *genetic* in nature. Analyses of social and cultural phenomena carried out under the aegis of the period concept incline us to view the phenomena of change under the aspect of a dialectic between what appears to be *explicit* in the practices of an age and its own representations of itself to itself and what is *implicit* in these; where the implicit is seen as consisting of sets of unacknowledged or unapprehended assumptions and presuppositions on the basis of which the characteristic thought, actions, and representational practices of the age are permitted to proceed—to the point at which certain "contradictions" inherent in the set finally come to the fore in the eruption of a "crisis" requiring that agents finally confront directly what they had formerly taken for granted.

Here *historical* knowledge is built on the presumed advantages enjoyed by a later era in the form of historical hindsight. We know more about the prior age because we can see what it could only imagine, that is, how things *really* came out—where "came out" means the eruption of some crisis caused by the "working out" of contradictions implicit in the prior age's basic assumptions about the nature of "reality." We know how things "came out" in the nineteenth century, because our own society is conceived to be—under the terms given by this approach to history—a product in large part of the *contradictions* underlying and informing that prior age.

To conceive a prior age as a chronotope, however, has a distinctively different effect upon the way we approach the study of a segment of history and the *attitudes* with which we approach it. This is so because the chronotope will be apprehended as having a dimension of *depth* quite different from that of the period. Here depth is apprehended, not so much as what is *implicit* in the thought and practice of an age, as rather what is *latent*—in the sense of being dynamically repressed—in the form of the valorizations, obsessions, fantasies, and anxieties that inform and provide the systemic "secrets" of the age's actual and *manifest* practices. Unlike the notion of a "content" that is only *implicit*, and that will inevitably insist itself into the consciousness of succeeding generations as they wrestle with the "contradictions" contained therein, the "content" of an age conceived as a chronotope is identifiable with the sleights of hand by which a society and its cultural endowment seek to suppress a tacit awareness of the contradictions between what it regards as its ideals and what it knows to be its dominant practices.

Here is not a matter of analyzing sets of propositions to see whether they are *logically consistent* with one another (whether the "logic" used is Aristotelian or dialectical), but rather of determining the *modalities* of the peculiar forms of *illogic* by which a society, an age, or a whole culture negotiates the distance between its *manifest practices* and *self-representations* and its systematically *hidden*, because psycho-dynamically *repressed*, thoughts, perceptions, and affects. The difference between the two approaches to historical analysis is like that between a grammatical and logical "analysis" of a sentence or a discourse and a rhetorical and figurative "reading" of it. Better: the differences are similar to those in a situation in which a friend, beset by existential suffering, is met with a logical analysis of the contradictions he or she is trying to live in and through and a psychoanalytically informed effort to "understand" that condition as a consequence of ambivalent feelings or the perfectly normal condition of desiring to have one's cake and eat it too. It is the difference between approaching the study of a cultural configuration as a set of contradictions and approaching it as a set of paradoxes, between seeing it as a situation equally describable as a condition of logical contradiction and one of psychological or moral ambivalence.

The notion of chronotope directs attention to the psychological, social, moral and aesthetic, political, economic, and epistemological *ambivalences* of an age. As a consequence, we may revise our perspective on what had been formerly apprehended as a merely *cognitive* problem, a flaw in the "knowledge" of an age. Privileging our position on the temporal downstream side of the problem, feeling ourselves both smarter and more "historically" experienced, we assumed that we could "now" see clearly that the problem was a failure to *think through* what was *implicit* in the age's *explicit* cultural wagers. Considering the age as chronotope, however, we come to understand the problem as a particular enactment of a generally *social condition* in which we are as much involved as were the objects of our inquiry "back there" in the nineteenth century.

The result of all this is to change our attitudes with respect, not only to our object of study—the nineteenth century—and to the methods of historical analysis and representation that we have inherited from that age (Marx, Freud, and Durkheim now appear to be as much parts of the problems we have inherited from the nineteenth century as contributors to the solution thereof), but also to the whole question of the theories, methods, and modes of representation we should use in an inquest that is just as much into ourselves and our age as it is into the nineteenth century. This adds up to the difference between approaching any given past *genetically* and an approach to it more specifically *genealogical* in nature. We bear a relationship to the nineteenth century utterly different from that which we bear to any other epoch of our past because the nineteenth century, while undeniably belonging to history, does not yet—for us—belong to "the past." In fact, a sense of the difference between the genetic and genealogical in our unique relationship to the nineteenth century informs recent studies that display an emergent critical spirit especially suited to the current need to come to *political* terms with our nineteenth-century heritage.

It is the substitution of a genuinely *political*, for the ethical and aestheticist conventions that have predominated in social and cultural criticism in our traditions—from the nineteenth century down to about 1950—that constitutes the possibility for us, in the last decades of the twentieth century, of finally getting out of the nineteenth century itself. Such a critical practice must be "historically self-conscious," to be sure, if we are ever to be able to come to terms with those aspects of nineteenth-century social and cultural praxis that have continued to serve as models for our own institutions and systems of belief long after they have lost their capacities to respond creatively to problems unique to our own historical moment and cultural condition—if we are ever to be able to put them away, consign them to "the past," and cease trying to live out our lives in thrall to *their* superannuated imperatives and structures of repression. We at least deserve our *own* structures of repression.

But the summons to return—after a long period of formalist and structuralist critical practices—to a criticism informed by "historical self-consciousness" and charged with "historicizing" its apprehensions, not only of past periods and preconceptions, but its own present ones as well—this summons is as ambiguous as the notion of "history" itself; and this is where the formalist/structuralist heritage can be seen to have a distinctive payoff in our efforts to rethink the kind of *history* we will wish to live in. To the question: "What is history?" history answers: "history is mystery"—the mystery of change in continuity and continuity in change, the mystery of a cause that is its own effect, the mystery of a child that is its own parent, a sphinx, a medusa, a wife, a mistress (*historia magistra vitae*), an adulteress (as fickle fortune), a whore (as chance and opportunity), and a mother of which we are all children, a father of which we are all fearful, and, above all, a fate, the graveyard, for which we are all destined. History not only explains the unexplainable, it explains why whatever *seems* to have been explained has never been *adequately* explained.

One advantage to be derived from formalist and structuralist critiques of the "historical consciousness" of our culture is the realization that "historical reality," far from serving as a bedrock of "facts," is as much a construction of human consciousness as any ideologized version of that putative "social reality" in the present whose delusory opaqueness and phantasmatic illocatability provide our reasons for studying periods we conceive to have immediately preceded our own in the first place. Prior historical periods, such as "the Renaissance" or "the Age of Reason"—which we know never really existed as *things* graspable, even in principle, by perception—have the appeal, as possible objects of study, of appearing as *completed* series or cycles of events, which, because they have been effectively *closed*, can yield up their meaning, rather in the manner of the classical novel when the last events contained in its "story" permit us, finally, to grasp its "plot." Even if *that* could legitimately be said of the ages, periods, and sociocultural foundations that any given society considers to be effectively remote in time from itself, it would still be the case for the closure of the age immediately preceding our own, that is, for the nineteenth century, the point at which it can be apprehended, less as a process still continuing than as suddenly taking on the aspect of a story that is finally over and the plot of which can at last be grasped—all of this would remain for us to decide.

All of us recognize the extent to which the "nineteenth century" is still alive in our own age, in the form of residues of institutional practices and dogmas that are causes of as well as impediments to the resolution of problems unique to our age, the very possibility of which was unimaginable to the framers of the great analytical systems (ideologies and master narratives) on which we still depend for the conceptualization of them. Our problem is not so much to destroy or disintegrate these residues as to simply provide, by our criticism, of both their nineteenth-century original and their twentieth-century copies, the distancing in the historical consciousness of our culture that must precede the practical work of finally releasing them to "our" *past*. Such is the political task of the kind of criticism we should seek to promote in Interdisciplinary Nineteenth-Century Studies and in *Nineteenth-Century Contexts*.

CHAPTER SEVENTEEN

Ideology and Counterideology in Northrop Frye's Anatomy of Criticism

{1991}

The principal charge of ideological contamination leveled against Northrop Frye's *Anatomy of Criticism* by such critics as Terry Eagleton, Frank Lentricchia, and Fredric Jameson turns upon the question of its formalist—structuralist or proto-structuralist, by which is meant its intrinsically ahistorical—orientation. Here "ideology" consists of a certain blindness to the true nature of the relation between "literature" and "history," a tendency to repress the awareness of "history" conceived as "social reality" and to displace this awareness onto some level or dimension of human consciousness—such as religion, spirit, or consciousness itself—that will be treated as the "substance" of "literature," such that "literature's" meaning will be conceived to reside therein rather than in its relation to "history," conceived as the ultimate determining instance of what every aspect of "culture" must finally be about.

But, of course, Frye's *Anatomy* contains what amounts to a philosophy of history. It directly confronts the question of what a distinctively "historical criticism" might or should consist of. It explicitly distinguishes "historical criticism" from "ethical," "archetypal," and "rhetorical" criticism. And it directly addresses the question of the kind of theory that must inform a specifically "historical" criticism or, to put it in somewhat different terms, what a "historically self-conscious" criticism might or should consist of.

By way of considering the "ideology" of Frye's *Anatomy*—and what I conceive to be its implicit or inherently counterideological element—I want to reflect on the "First Essay" in the *Anatomy*, the section of the work entitled "Historical Criticism: Theory of Modes." The question that interests me is this: If, among other things, the ideology of any given notion of criticism can be said to reside in its denial, repression, or sublimation of a consciousness of "history," wherein does such denial, repression, or sublimation consist in the *Anatomy*? The "First Essay" suggests that

"Historical Criticism" is a necessary element of criticism in general; indeed, by the very placement of this topic as the "first" essay, the *Anatomy* suggests that "historical criticism" is primary, perhaps even foundational to the whole literary-critical enterprise; that, indeed, the distinctive natures of the other kinds of criticism— ethical, archetypal, and rhetorical—can be comprehended in terms of the differences between them and a criticism distinctively historical in nature. So that it might be thought: what the *Anatomy* projects in the "modes" of ethical, archetypal, and rhetorical criticism can be comprehended in terms of their differences from the *historical* mode.

As thus envisaged, and insofar as ideology would be understood as a specifically ahistorical mode of criticism, it would seem that the *Anatomy* provides some insight into the specifically ideological aspects (insofar as they are contrasted more or less explicitly with the historical mode of criticism) of ethical, archetypal, and rhetorical criticism. These latter would be ideological precisely insofar as they represent a different modality, a specifically ahistorical modality, of critical address. For which limitation, which ideological and ideologizing limitation, the historical mode would serve as a corrective, a specifically "counterideological" corrective—given the fact that, from a certain perspective, e.g., that represented by critical theorists such as Eagleton, Jameson, and Lentricchia, the principal corrective to an ideological perspective on literary history is provided only by a distinctively "historical" perspective on "history" itself. But if "history" is the corrective of ideology, what is meant by "history"? And more pertinently, what is meant by historical consciousness or—more commonsensically—a historical perspective on literature?

Here we must confront directly the implications of the strangely reticent, certainly ambiguous, title of the "First Essay," namely, "Historical Criticism: Theory of Modes." The title of this essay suggests some crucial relation between a specifically "historical" mode of criticism, a critical practice launched from within a specifically "historical" perspective (as against those of "ethical," "archetypal," and "rhetorical" criticisms), and a (or some) "theory of modes." Just as ethical criticism presupposes a theory of symbols, archetypal criticism a theory of myths, and rhetorical criticism a theory of genres, so "historical criticism" presupposes a (or some) "theory of modes."

On the face of it, the relation indicated by the colon (that at once joins and disjoins "Historical Criticism" and "Theory of Modes") is more striking than the other couples designating the relation of a critical practice (ethical, archetypal, rhetorical) to a general *kind* of theory (of symbols, of myths, and of genres respectively). The coupling of the practice of historical criticism with a (or some) theory of modes is striking (puzzling, provocative), because we do not normally think of a distinctively historical consciousness as being characterized by (informed by, governed by, determined by) a theory of *modes*. Historical inquiry, analysis, and reflection is usually thought to be informed either by no "theory" at all (the empiricist illusion), or by some general notion (a loose theoretical perspective) of the nature of the relation of events to their social contexts, the point of view indicated by the term "contexualism." Historians conventionally deal with events (small-scale or large-scale) and the relations of events to their social contexts (small-scale or large-scale). Historical criticism deals with such "events" as texts, corpora, canons, traditions, genres, authors, audiences, and so on, and seeks to relate them to their contexts (more or less extensive in space and time). What Frye suggests in the *Anatomy* is that the categories relevant to the characterization and analysis of such relationships are those that derive from our notions of "modality" rather than those of either "quantity" (unity, plurality, totality), "quality" (reality, negation, limitation), or "relation" (inherence and subsistence, causality and dependence, activity and passivity)—to use Kant's proposed classification of the species of categories set forth in his first *Critique*. Recall Kant's definition of the fourfold nature of the "judgments of taste" in the third *Critique*: as to quality: the judgment of the beautiful is "disinterested"; as to quantity: it pleases universally without requiring a concept; as to relationship: it apprehends a non-purposive purposiveness; as to modality (of satisfaction): the beautiful is that which, without any concept is cognized as the object of a *necessary* satisfaction. The categories proper to our apprehension of "modal" relationships are, in Kant's view, those of "possibility-impossibility," "existence-nonexistence," and "necessity-contingency."

Now, these categories are, I submit, precisely those that predominate in any specifically *historical* apprehension of reality—whether historians, individually or as a group are aware of this or not. Historical consciousness, considered as a mode of consciousness different from though continuous with scientific, philosophical, poetic, religious, and mythic consciousness (to use Ernst Cassirer's classification of the modes of consciousness), is characterized by the predominance of the categories of modality for the representation and analysis of reality apprehended as being "historical" in its nature. It is the degree of awareness of the predominance of the categories of modality—and the prominence given to the elaboration of this awareness in reflections on history—that distinguishes "normal historians" from their openly theoretical (always *too* theoretical) enemies, "philosophers of history," as they are called (always disparagingly). Normal historiography is based on the dream of a theory-less knowledge—which would mean a "blind" knowledge insofar as by the term "theory" we might mean something like what the Greek term meant, that is, "sight," "prospectus," and so on.

That philosophy of history—a historical consciousness conscious of the necessity of a theory of its own practice—is continuous with, rather than antithetical to normal history is confirmed by the extent to which the former characteristically features the categories of modality in its practice. Witness: Hegel's notion of history as a spectacle of the development of the *modes* of human consciousness; Marx's notion of history as the development of "the modes of production"; Vico's notion of history as the development of *modes* of (poetic) figuration; and Spengler's notion of history as a cycle of *modal transformations* analogous to those met with in mathematics and music alike—the modes of something like Nietzsche's "spirit of music."

It is not that a historical perspective excludes consideration of reality under the categories of quantity, quality, and relation. It is only that the *historicity* of this reality is comprehensible primarily in terms of the categories of *modality* (possibility-impossibility, existence-nonexistence, necessity-contingency). Whatever "history" *may* be—in contrast to "nature," "spirit," or whatever else we may conceive the ahistorical dimensions of reality to be—it is graspable *as history* only insofar as it appears as a system in process of change, to which the notion of *modality* alone is capable of doing justice in a manner that is cognitively responsible to the data of history, on the one side, and our awareness of the *limits* of our understanding of these data, on the other. Whence the rectitude of the intuition that an *ideological* representation of history is characterized always by some assertion about the real, true, or ultimate meaning of history, that it claims to have explained the whole historical process or even some part of it exhaustively and in full detail, and to be able, not only to explain everything worth explaining in the past, but also to be able to explain the present fully and to predict the course that human development *must* follow in any imaginable future. In the realm of historical knowledge, ideology is marked by a fall from (or suppression of) consciousness into quantitative, qualitative, or relational thinking (as in positivism, idealism, and structuralism, respectively). On this view, the counterideological force of Marx's idea of history would consist not so much of its materialism or its discovery that the ultimate determining instance of historical causation resides in the modes of production and their relationship to the social relations of production, and so on, but on its insistence on *modality* as the ultimate determining instance of a specifically historical comprehension of history. This is what, as I would see it, the term "dialectical" in the phrase "dialectical materialism" is all about. Counterideological criticism, then, a criticism capable of guarding against and providing an *autocritique* of the inherent and ineluctably "ideological" elements in its own constitution, would be a criticism that founds the historical (or historicist) moment in its practice, not on a specific philosophy or theory of the true nature of historical events, a theory of historical causation, or some notion of history as an epiphenomenon of some other order of being (such as nature or spirit), but rather on a "view" of history as a system undergoing constant changes in both its forms and its contents, on the one side, and in the *modes* in which the forms and the contents are related to one another, on the other.

This is why a "theory of modes" is a necessary (though not a sufficient) precondition of a distinctively historical perspective on reality. And this is why a specifically "historical criticism," a critical practice informed by a specifically historical consciousness of its object of study's "historicity," must presuppose or entail a "theory of modes" as a necessary precondition of its practice. And it is for reasons such as these that we might be able to account for Frye's placement of the topic of "historical criticism" as the first of the four kinds of critical practices he chose to examine in his *Anatomy*. This placement signals the intention to produce a metatheory of literary criticism that will be scientific, which is to say, counterideological; and counterideological precisely in the degree to which it takes historical consciousness as the *proteros* or first note, the note that sets the tone, for the consideration of the other *modes* of criticism identified by him as requiring individual characterization and analysis. Considered as a reflection on various *modes* of critical practice, each of which bears a *modal* relationship to all the others, the "First Essay," on "Historical Criticism: Theory of Modes," provides the basis for a specifically *historical* reflection on relations among these critical practices, including that of a distinctively "historical criticism." And this privileging of historical reflection negates the charges of formalism, mere structuralism, and ahistoricism often leveled by Left theorists of criticism against the *Anatomy*. The *Anatomy* is not *formalist* in its primary orientation but rather *modalist*, and as such is more historicist, less ideological, than the perspective provided by those theorists who claim to be able to see through the "forms" of history and to have grasped its true "contents" without ever having reflected at all on the problem of the "form-content" distinction itself.

What gets *repeated* in (literary) history is "mode" (not myth, not symbol, not even genre). An age or period will appear to repeat an earlier one because it shares a common *mode* (e.g., the repetition of "classical" forms and contents in the fifteenth- and sixteenth-century Renaissance).

Frye's critics have seized upon his theory of myths as the substance of his theory of history or, in the case of Jameson, his theory of symbols. But every new period of cultural (no less than of social) history is marked by a modal transformation that, because mode has to do with ratios of relationships (rather than with forms or contents), cannot but resemble in some way the mode of some period preceding it. Thus, if there is such a thing as postmodernism, it will resemble *in mode* some period other than that of modernism itself—even though its informing myths, privileged symbols, and dominant generic conventions may very well be those associated with the modernism to which it bears the historical (modal) relationship signified by the prefix "post" (*meta* or "coming after"). Thus, for example, the putative referentiality, narrativity, pastiche aspect, spatialization, and so on, of postmodernism *resembles* the "realism" against which modernism reacted, but more in *mode* than in "myth," "symbol," or "genre."

What about the kinds of modes adumbrated by Frye in the "First Essay": the two genera (fictional and thematic) and the species thereof: mythic, romantic, high-mimetic, low-mimetic, and ironic, indicated as common to both genera of modes; the registers ("naive" and "sentimental"); and the ratios of relationship ascribed to them (their status as "phases" in a recurring but constantly evolving cycle of occurrences)? It is obvious that the modes identified as characterizing the fictional (forms) and thematic (contents) of literary works direct attention to the categories that permit reflection on socio-spatial relationships: superior-equal-inferior (relationships figured by the relations of the protagonist to his milieu in the modalities of fiction), and centered, marginalized, and excluded (relationships figured by the relations of the poet to his audience in the modalities of theme). Here "scale" would correspond to measures of *degree*, and "tone" would correspond to measures of *kind* that mark the distinctive modes by which similarity and difference are apprehended in a given instance of *stylized* (or fashioned) utterance. The notion of mode functions, exactly as it does in the thought of Hegel, Marx, Vico, Spengler, and so on, namely, as marking the specific structures of subordination and domination within any given disposition of the "means" of historical production and reproduction. Interestingly enough, the categories used by Frye for characterizing the fictional and thematic modes of literary production (and of cultural production in general) are explicitly *social* and *economic* (in the extended meaning of the latter term, that is, "house management" or "management of expenditure") in nature. The relationships presumed to exist between a protagonist and his milieu, on the one side, and between the poet and his audience, on the other, presuppose distinctive modalities for construing the relationships obtaining among the "means" of literary (and, by extension, cultural and social) production and reproduction. The dialectical relationship between the processes of production *and* reproduction Frye grasps in the figure of "repetition," conceived in the manner of Kierkegaard, but in a way conformable to the thought of Hegel, Marx, Vico, and Spengler, that is, as *modal* transformation. Change the means and you change the mode; change the mode and you affect the relationships obtaining among the means. In either case, what you end up with is a distinctively *historical* kind of change: that is to say, a difference in similarity or the reverse, a changing continuum or a continuity in change.

It is because Frye has grasped that historical process (unlike natural process grasped at the gross or supra-atomic level of organic organization) is characterized preeminently by modal relationships and their transformations, rather than by discontinuous or catastrophic changes in either the forms or the contents of social and cultural phenomena, that his work seems so formalist to critics still indentured to a nineteenth-century "realist" view of history and its processes. The fundamental or modal presupposition of this "realist" view is that of "viewing" itself. Realistic history favors the illusion that history—whether conceived as "the past" or as a process of change by which past, present, and future are linked together in a unitary temporal continuum—can be comprehended in the manner of a "seeing," as if it were accessible to "visual" perception. But neither the past, nor for that matter, the present, much less the future, nor the process of which these are considered to be phases or periods, can be "seen." If they could be so apprehended, it would be possible to represent them adequately in pictures or other kinds of visual images. That we might wish to believe that history could be apprehended as though "seen" is perfectly understandable, given the fact that, in our culture, "sight" is the sense we privilege as the principal arbiter between truth and falsity, the real and the illusory. History—the past or the process—would yield its secret could we but "see" it: seeing is believing.

But the problematic of historical inquiry (that *historia* inaugurated by Herodotus) is laid down by the realization that the past is inhabited by all those things that were once "seeable" but *are no longer so*. Or if we take history to be a process rather than a (temporal) place, "the past," the problematic motivating our inquiry is laid down by the circumstance that it is a process that can only be apprehended by its effects on a system and grasped as a concept that can be posited by thought or imagination but never directly perceived.

The dynamics of historical inquiry, representation, and analysis arise from the disparity between our desire for some equivalent of a visual perception of objects and processes that are apprehendable only by traces of the "sounds" they once emitted (cf. "Ozymandias"), only in the extent to which they "speak" to us or can be made to respond to our verbal interrogations of them. As Jameson says: "History is not a text, but we have access to it only by way of its prior textualizations." Material remains of "the past," which, by their "ruination" (and resistance to it), *show* the effects of history as process, can be made into distinctively historical evidence only in the extent to which these remains can be made to speak, transformed into or endowed with "texts" that can be "read" as if "heard." Jameson again: "History can be apprehended only through its effects, and never directly as some reified force."[1] This is why a distinctively historical knowledge of history is a knowledge based primarily on the assessment of evidence that is more *aural* than visual in nature. The peculiar problematic of historical knowledge is laid down by the circumstance that we know "the past" only by its "words" and the "historical process" only by its effects. This means that we "hear" and "feel" history rather than see it.

Jacques Barzun recently remarked that history can never be "taught," it can only be "read." Frye remarks relevantly:

> The world of social action and event, the world of time and process, has a particularly close association with the ear. The ear listens, and the ear translates what it hears into practical conduct. The world of individual thought and idea has a correspondingly close association with the eye, and nearly all our expressions for thought, from the Greek *theoria* down, are connected with visual metaphors.[2]

What might a comment such as this tell us of "Historical Criticism: Theory of Modes"?

Well, for one thing, it tells us that "theory" of modes is a product of an effort to translate what is essentially an "aural" apprehension into something like a "visual" equivalent. Second, it suggests that "historical" criticism must begin with the effort to "hear" as much "how" the evidence "sounds" as "what" it "says." Third, it suggests that a historical knowledge of literature will consist of the comprehension of the relation between the "how" of "saying" and the "what" of saying: that is, the *modal* relations obtaining between the fictional and the thematic modes of literary artifacts. In the translation of this "hearing" into a "seeing," there will be some slippage, some loss of meaning. But if hearing and seeing are themselves viewed, less as either forms or contents of perception, than, rather, as *modes*, this translation will be at once more "certain" and more "true" than any translation based upon a simplistic notion of the history of literature considered as either a succession of forms or a succession of contents could ever be.

CHAPTER EIGHTEEN

Writing in the Middle Voice

{1992}

In an essay published in 1970 entitled "To Write: An Intransitive Verb?" Roland Barthes raised the question of whether the verb "to write" (*écrire*) could be properly used in the passive as well as in the active voice. Barthes raised the question because, in his view, modern writing appeared to differ from that of earlier epochs by virtue of its seeming *intransitivity*. The modern writer, Barthes observed, is "no longer one who writes *something*, but one who writes absolutely," which is to say, one who is engaged in writing *as such*, without any aim or purpose beyond that of "writing." Barthes goes on to remark that, "it would be interesting to know at what point the verb *to write* began to be used in an apparently intransitive manner," because "the passage from the verb *to write*, transitive, to the verb *to write*, intransitive, is certainly the sign of an important change in mentality."[1]

Actually, the question both of when and why writing became "intransitive" had been dealt with a few years earlier by Michel Foucault in *Les mots et les choses*.[2] In this work, Foucault dates the origin of "intransitive" writing from the early nineteenth century when, on his account, language was "demoted" from the status of the *medium* by which "the things of the world could be known," to that of simply one among the many things that science might take as an object of inquiry. Instead of being regarded as "the first sketch of an order of representations of the world . . . the initial, inevitable way of representing representations," as once had been the case, "starting with the nineteenth century, language . . . became one object of knowledge among others, on the same level as living beings, wealth, and value, and the history of events and men."[3]

However, Foucault argues, this demotion of language was "compensated" by the appearance, sometime in the early nineteenth century, of a new mode of language-use, the kind we have come to call "literature." To be sure, Foucault concedes, the form of language that we today call "literature" had existed at least since Homer; but, he insists, just as the word "literature" dates only from the late eighteenth century, so too does the notion of a "particular language whose peculiar mode of being is 'literary.'" The form of ancient poetic speech may be similar to that of modern(ist) literature, but their substances, Foucault maintains, are totally different. For, Foucault says, in the modern acceptation of the term, "literature" refers to a kind of language that is not only opaque, indirect, figurative, but one that "folds back upon the enigma of its own origin" and exists "wholly in reference to the pure act of writing" (repliée sur l'énigme de sa naissance et tout entière ré-férée à l'acte pur d'écrire). In sum, in the modern age, literary language becomes detached from the earlier "discourse," "poetry," "belles lettres," even "fiction." It takes up a position (s'enferme) within a "radical intransitivity . . . addressing itself to itself as a writing subjectivity (subjectivité écrivante)." As "literature," language assumes the aspect of simply an effect of "a silent cautious deposition of the word upon the whiteness of a piece of paper, where it can possess neither sound nor in-terlocutor, where it has nothing to say but itself, nothing to do but shine in the brightness of its being." Modern(ist) writing has its end within itself, is its own means of expression, and possesses as its "content" nothing other than its own "form" (elle n'a plus alors qu'à se recourber dans un perpétuel retour sur soi, comme si son discours ne pouvait avoir pour contenu que de dire sa propre forme).[4] This is what is meant by the "radical intransitivity" of modern writing.

But at the end of his essay of four years later, almost as if in response to Foucault, Barthes asks: "Is it really a question of intransitivity?" Might it not be that "the modern verb *to write*" indicates, not so much passivity as, rather, the kind of meta-transitive relationship between an agent, an act, and an effect as that expressed in what grammarians call the "middle voice" of the verb? For, Barthes points out: "In the case of the middle voice . . . the subject affects himself in acting; he always remains inside the action, even if an object is involved. The middle voice does not, therefore, exclude transitivity."[5] Invoking what he calls a "classic example" from Sanskrit grammar, Barthes notes that (in Sanskrit) "the verb to sacrifice (ritually) is active if the priest sacrifices the victim in my place for me, and it is middle voice if, taking the knife from the priest's hands, I make the sacrifice for myself." If the verb is cast in the active voice, the action of sacrificing will be presumed to have been accomplished "outside the subject, because, although the priest makes the sacrifice, he is not affected by it," whereas in the middle voice of the same verb, the subject is presumed to have acted both *on* the victim and also *upon himself* and, moreover, to have remained "inside the action" of sacrificing. A similar kind of metatransitivity, a similar kind of dual action on an object and on oneself, a similar kind of enclosure within the action are presumed by Barthes to characterize modern(ist) writing. Thus, he concludes:

Today to write is to make oneself the center of the action of speech (*parole*); it is to affect writing in being affected oneself; it is to leave the writer (*scripteur*) inside the writing, not as a psychological subject (the Indo-European priest could very well overflow with subjectivity in actively sacrificing for his client), but as the agent of the action.[6]

There is, then, Barthes argues, nothing at all "passive" about writing in the middle voice. The middle voice is, if anything, doubly active, at once productive of an effect on an object (for example, on language) and constitutive of a particular kind of agent (namely, the writer) by means of an action (specifically, writing). Indeed, Barthes even goes so far as to say that, in order to express the past tense of the verb *écrire*, "we should no longer say '*j'ai écrit*' [I wrote], but, rather, '*je suis écrit*' [I am written], just as we say '*je suis né*,' '*il est mort*,' '*elle est éclose*.'" For, Barthes says, although the verb "to be" appears in these expressions, it has none of the force of a passive construction: "it is impossible to transform '*je suis écrit*' (without forcing things, and supposing that I dare to use the expression at all) into '*on m'a écrit*' ['I have been written' or 'somebody wrote (to) me']."[7]

Barthes invoked the grammatical category of the middle voice in order to characterize a kind of "writing" quite different from that associated with both the Classical and the Romantic "author." The modernist writer both acts and is acted upon in the act of writing, but not in the way suggested by the reflexive form of an active verb ("I write myself"). The writer does not "write herself" in such a way that her "written self" could be separated from her "writing self." It is only in writing and by writing that the writer can be said to exist at all. The "writer" is what exists in the interior of the activity of "writing."

Now, all of this is quite mystifying and appears to express little more than Barthes's enthusiasm for modernist literature, the originality of which he had sought to characterize in terms of what he called the "fundamental categories of language, such as person, tense, and voice."[8] But aside from providing a grammatical equivalent of "style indirect libre" (*erlebte Rede*, free indirect discourse or interior monologue), the notion of the middle voice provides little aid in defining the specific features of modernist writing. And indeed critics of Barthes took him to task for the ambiguity of his formulations, both of the middle voice and of modernist writing. In the discussion that followed upon Barthes's first presentation of this view of modernist writing, Jean-Pierre Vernant questioned whether Barthes was making a historical argument regarding the actual reappearance or rediscovery of the grammatical category of the middle voice in modernist literature or whether he was using the idea only as a metaphor for certain aspects of modernist writing. Paul de

Man, in turn, argued that the peculiar relationship of the writer to writing that Barthes attributed only to modernism was already present as early as the eighteenth century. In addition, de Man maintained, Barthes's category of middle-voicedness could add nothing in the way of better readings of modernist texts than those already provided by Russian and American formalism.

These were crippling observations, pointing up the pervasive ambiguity of Barthes's formulations—an ambiguity to which Barthes himself freely admitted. And yet both observations, the one raising the question of historical fact and the other that of heuristic utility, missed what Jean Hyppolite pointed out was the crucial concern of Barthes's discourse, namely, the progressive isolation of modernist writers from their interlocutors. Commenting on Barthes' remark that, "we are all trying, with different methods, styles, even prejudices, to get to the core of [the] linguistic pact [*pacte de la parole*] which unites the writer with the other." Hyppolite observed that writing appears to differ from speech precisely by virtue of its status as a "phantasm of interlocution." "What transformation," he asked, "does the *pacte de la parole* undergo in a creation like writing which, paradoxically, is capable of uniting with a sort of monologue, curiously cut off from real interlocution?" To which Barthes responded: "I think you have pointed to . . . a very important problem: the relation between the story, or phantasm, and interlocution."[9]

In fact, or so it seems to me, Barthes had been concerned primarily less with the question of style or modernism than with the psychological topic of the phantasmatic scene of writing. In what sense, he had asked, could one say that "writing" was a kind of communication that was neither a communication with a real other nor with oneself? And the answer was indicated in Hyppolite's suggestion that Proust had been able to "succeed in writing" only "by addressing the phantasm of his mother in an interlocution which profoundly challenges the *pacte de la parole*, transforming it into a sort of mimicry of the *pacte de la parole* in writing."[10] In other words, the notion of the middle voice had provided Barthes with a way of characterizing, in grammatical terms, a kind of writing that denies the possibility of real interlocution by parodying it. This kind of writing, which Barthes himself had claimed to be perfectly exemplified in Proust, is the equivalent of the kind of nonpathological masochism that Freud, in his essay on "The Instincts and Their Vicissitudes," finds in cases of obsessional neurosis.

Freud himself invokes the Greek middle voice in his discussion of the "instincts" (or "drives") of love and hate and their "vicissitudes" (or possible "scenarios"), which he regards as "modes of defense against the instincts." The modes of defense are four in number: Repression, Sublimation, "reversal of an instinct into its opposite," and "turning round upon the subject's own self."[11] Since he will have dealt with Repression and Sublimation elsewhere, Freud concentrates in this essay on the operation of the two last-named modes of defense in cases of sadism and masochism, in which love can become transformed into hate and at the same time the subject can be changed into an object. In the case of "a reversal of an instinct into its opposite," we can observe, Freud says, a twofold transformation: first, in *aim*, from activity (the desire to torture) to passivity (the desire to be tortured), and, secondly, in content (from love into hate).[12] In the case of "the turning round of an instinct upon the subject's own self," we witness a change of the *object* of the drive, from one that is external to one that is internal to the subject. In the case of both sadism and masochism (as well as in scopophilia and exhibitionism), the two processes (turning around upon the subject's self and transformation from activity to passivity) "converge or coincide." The double process of change passes from (1) a primary sadism (in which a subject actively exercises "violence or power upon some other person as object") to (2) a masochism, in which an extraneous person is sought to exercise violence or power upon the subject, who now passes from an active to a passive attitude.

It is all quite symmetrical. But Freud is forced, on the basis of observation of cases of obsessional neurosis, to posit a third position in this process, in which the "object [of violence or power] is given up and replaced by the subject's self" and "a change from an active to a passive instinctual aim is also effected," but without the gratification that either the sadist or the masochist would feel in the situation. In this situation, Freud writes, "the desire to torture has turned into self-torture and self-punishment, not into masochism. The active voice is changed, not into the passive, but into the *reflexive, middle voice.*"[13]

Freud thus invokes the notion of the middle voice to characterize the specific psychological state or condition of "obsessional neurosis" and to distinguish it from both sadism and masochism. Obsessional neurosis is characterized by a "turning round upon the subject's self but "without an attitude of passivity" (the subject's attitude remains active) and without fixation upon another person (the person's own self is taken as the object of "the desire to torture"). The result is "self-torture and self-punishment," but "not masochism."[14] So, in the case of obsessional neurosis, neither the aim nor the content of a drive undergoes change. The *content* of the drive (hate) undergoes no change; the *aim* (to torture) remains active. The *object* of the drive is changed from something external to the subject to the subject's own ego, but without any payoff in pleasure of the kind that might be felt by either the masochist or the sadist.

In this passage, Freud speaks of the "reflexive middle voice," but the qualification "reflexive" is inconsequential. In Greek, the reflexive pronoun was combined with the middle form of the verb only to produce emphasis in contrast. The important point for our understanding of what Barthes might have intended by his likening of modernist writing to the middle voice is Freud's invocation of the middle voice to characterize the structure of obsessional neurosis.

Barthes had based his intuition on an essay by Emile Benveniste, "Active and Middle Voice in the Verb."[15] Benveniste had argued that the Greek middle voice (*mesotes*) was neither a form used to express a special interest on the part of the subject in the action represented by the verb nor some mixture of the active (*enargeia*) and passive (*pathos*) voices. Indeed, Benveniste held that, in ancient Indo-European languages, the passive voice had been a late development. Originally, the crucial diathetical distinction had been between (what only much later became called) the "middle," expressing the condition of the subject's being "interior" to the action indicated by the verb, and the "active," which expressed exteriority to the action, whether as agent (subject) or as patient (object). The middle voice expressed a relationship that later became sublimated into the reflexive and deponent forms, while the passive voice became progressively differentiated from the active, not in terms of inferiority-exteriority, but in terms of whether the subject of the verb was presumed to be the patient (object) or the agent (subject) of the action. In the case of both the active and the passive constructions ("I hit" / "I am hit"), the subject ("I") is *exterior* to the action that is completed, in the first instance, in the effect this "I" has had on some object, and, in the second, in the effect that another subject may have had on a "me." So, too, in both the active and the passive, the tenses of the verb express a relation of diremption or separation between the time of the inauguration of the action and the time of its completion. In the middle voice, it is quite otherwise; here actions and their effects are conceived to be simultaneous; past and present are integrated rather than dirempted, and the subject and object of the action are in some way conflated. All this is connoted in Barthes's use of the notion of the "middle voice" to suggest the relation obtaining between the modernist "writer" and the activity of "writing."

But does all this add up to a notion of modernist writing as obsessional neurosis? And if so, so what? In my view, Barthes was amplifying a notion of "writing" that he had set forth in 1953, in *Le degré zéro de l'écriture*.[16] Here he had sought to establish significant distinctions among language (*la langue*), style (*le style*), and writing (*l'écriture*). He had argued that whereas language is a public and style a personal matter, "writing" was neither public nor personal but rather the "choice of a human attitude" (le choix d'un comportement humain). Language and style were "objects," writing a "function" of "the relationship between creation and society." In writing, the "literary language" is "transformed by its social aim" (sa destination sociale) . . . into a form grasped in its human intention." And because it is all these things, writing is thus nothing other than "the morality of form" (la morale de la forme).[17]

This phrase ("la morale de la forme") gives us a clue to the function of the idea of the middle voice in Barthes's characterization of modernist writing. Although in Greek the middle voice of the verb is employed to designate the subject's "interiority" to a wide variety of actions (*louomai* "I wash myself"; *apodidomai ten oikian* "I sell my house"), it is used especially to indicate those actions informed by a heightened moral consciousness on the part of the subject performing them. Thus, for example, the active form of the verb *airein* means simply "to take," but the middle form of the same verb (*aireisthai*) means "to choose." So, too, the phrase *logou poiein* (in the active voice) means "to compose a speech," but the same phrase rendered in the middle voice (*logou poiesthai*) means "to deliver a speech." Similarly, the verb *gamein* in the active means "to marry" (but only of a man), whereas the same verb in the middle voice (*gamesthai*) means "to wed" (but only of a woman). The differences here indicated between the active and the middle forms of the same verb have to do with the kind of consciousness on the part of the subject involved in the action indicated and the force of involvement of the subject in the action. Thus, for example, the difference between *gamein* (active) and *gamesthai* (middle) indicates the difference between the ways a man and a woman are respectively involved in "marriage." It is not a matter of doing something, on the one side, and having something done to one, on the other. It is a matter of distinguishing between two kinds of transitivity, one in which either the subject or the object remains outside the action and one in which the distinction between subject and object is obliterated. For Barthes, writing in the middle voice is creative and liberatory insofar as it places the writer-agent *within* the writing process and reveals the constitution of the subject-of-writing as the latent principle, aim, and purpose of all writing. Indeed, for Barthes, writing in the middle voice is a perfect example of the kind of "speech act" that J. L. Austin called "performative."[18] For just as such acts as "promising" or "swearing an oath" or "judging" have the force both of the active and of the middle voice, inasmuch as in doing them one not only acts on the world but also changes one's own relationship to it, so too modernist writing both acts on something (language, above all) and transforms the writing subject's relationship to the world. This is why Barthes can conclude in his essay "To Write: An Intransitive Verb?" thus:

> It is my opinion that in the middle verb *to write* the distance between the writer and language diminishes asymptotically. We could even say that it is

subjective writings, like romantic writing, which are active, because in them the agent is not interior but *anterior* to the process of writing. The one who writes here does not write for himself, but, as if by proxy, for a person who is exterior and antecedent (even if they both have the same name). In the modern verb of middle voice *to write*, however, the subject is immediately contemporary with the writing. . . . The case of the Proustian narrator is exemplary: he exists only in writing.[19]

Much the same could be said of the subject who "promises," "swears an oath," or "judges." The promiser exists only in the act of promising, the oath-taker only in the act of taking an oath, and the judge only in the act of judging. So, too, unlike the author, the writer exists only in the act of writing. But the act of writing is impossible without the writer to perform it. And it only remains to ask whether such speech-acts as "promising," "oath-taking," and "judging" are as obsessionally neurotic as modernist writing must, on the basis of Barthes's and Freud's analyses, be considered to be.

CHAPTER NINETEEN

Northrop Frye's Place in Contemporary Cultural Studies

{1994}

On wild trees the flowers are fragrant; on cultivated trees, the fruit.

—SØREN KIERKEGAARD

In this essay I want to reflect on what I take to be Northrop Frye's enduring contribution to cultural studies. I once characterized him in print as the greatest natural cultural historian of our time; and I want to expand on that generalization in order to pay tribute to Professor Frye's brilliance as a theorist of culture and renovator of humanistic studies in the second half of our century.

I cannot pretend to any special intimacy of acquaintance with Professor Frye. We met and talked a few times, first at Cornell University in the spring of 1970, at the Society for the Humanities, where we occupied contiguous offices for a few weeks. He would stop by from time to time and lean on the door-frame to chat. I attended some seminars he gave on Blake, Stevens, Joyce, and Yeats. We met a few times afterward, when I was a visiting lecturer at the University of Toronto, at the MLA celebration of his seventy-fifth birthday, and finally, during the summer before his death, for a moment at the entrance of Massey College. I recall that, on the last two occasions we met, we talked about "mode" and the relation between the musical and the literary or poetic notions of modality. He was unfailingly courteous although always slightly reserved; I had the feeling that he was always in that shop in the back of the mind of which Montaigne spoke, working on some intellectual issue.

The name Frye has always been, since the moment I first opened *Anatomy of Criticism* in 1960 or thereabouts, a metonymy for serious, systematic but flexible and always developing reflection on the nature of culture, the conditions of cultural creativity, and the fate of our civilization. Frye remarks somewhere that "the great synthesis of Marx and Spengler has yet to be written." Whether Frye thought such a synthesis could be written or should even be attempted is difficult to say, but only a scholar with Frye's range of interests and desire to make sense of history could even have envisioned such a project. It might be instructive to reflect on some of the implications of his envisioned coupling of Marx and Spengler, the radical and the reactionary, the would-be scientist of history and the Nietzschean aesthete. Presumably, a synthesis of these two "metahistorians"[1] would have resulted, not in a monstrous mixture of species, but in something quite new and radically different from earlier philosophies of history. It would be a comprehensive theory of history that refused either to reduce culture to a function of material determinations, on the one side, or to inflate, spiritualize, and fetishize it, on the other—the kind of theory of culture that is implicit in Frye's *Anatomy of Criticism*.

Contemporary practitioners of what has come to be called "cultural studies" have not on the whole found much of use for Frye's work. In part, this is because cultural studies is a neo-Marxist activity, inspired by the example of such figures as Antonio Gramsci, Raymond Williams, Stuart Hall, Jürgen Habermas, and Louis Althusser, adamantly historicist therefore and paranoically hostile to anything smacking of formalism, structuralism, idealism, or organicism. Insofar, then, as Frye's work is noted at all by practitioners of cultural studies, it is as an example of these fallacious or misguided (insofar as they are ahistorical) ideologies. He is put down as one who believed that literature was paradigmatic of culture, that culture itself was autonomous vis-à-vis society and the modes of material production that determine dominant social formations, and that, accordingly, both culture and society can be studied only in an ahistorical, which is to say, a synchronic, structuralist, or formal manner. The panorama of historical occurrence that Frye is thus supposed to have confronted consists of a finite set of forms of cultural expression of which literature is a paradigm. These interact significantly only with one another and not at all with the more mundane world of economic, political, and social praxis, and they develop only insofar as they succeed one another in positions of dominance and subordination cyclically (rather than progressively or developmentally or dialectically). For Frye, it would seem, everything happens in cycles. So goes the negative account of Frye's system.

It seems incredible that anyone who has taken the least trouble to read any of Frye's work would credit him with such a banal conception of culture, literature, and history. It would take someone profoundly ignorant of history to think that history develops in either a cyclical or a linear (or for that matter a spiral) form. And I have never understood why historians of historical thinking attribute such models to sophisticated thinkers like Spengler or Nietzsche or John Stuart Mill or Hegel. It will not do, however, simply to dismiss this hostile characterization of Frye's position as a product of prejudice or ignorance alone. First, because the cultural studies Marxists who criticize Frye for his formalism, structuralism, idealism, and so on, are not equally prejudiced against Frye's critical practice, his theory of criticism, and his idea of the relation of criticism, literature, and culture. Some of them have read Frye closely; a number are sympathetic to his larger project of systematizing literary studies; and a few even consider him to have provided a viable model for a Marxist theory of culture. (In this last category I place Fredric Jameson in particular.)[2] Then, too, it must be said that a good number of conservative critics and students of culture concur with Frye's Marxist critics in their suspicion of his systematicity, the formalist-taxonomic bent of his work, his demystification of tradition, and what appears to be the determinism of those patterns he purports to find not only in literary criticism but in the historical development of literary styles as well.

It is this agreement across what would otherwise be radically opposed ideological positions on the seemingly ahistorical nature of Frye's system that must give us pause in our effort to identify Frye's enduring contribution to contemporary cultural studies. For, on the face of it, there is some truth to the charge that Frye's system is ahistorical, in the way, for example, that Spengler's system, so subtly analyzed by Frye in an essay of 1974,[3] was, and indeed still is, thought to be ahistorical. The alleged ahistoricity stems from what appears to be a cyclical model of literary, critical, and cultural change. In this model progress is measured, if at all, only by an originary displacement of mythic structures of consciousness into a variety of kinds of fiction, of which literature or poetry is one, and then a recurrence within fiction of a discrete set of kinds of modes, symbols, story forms or myths, and genres, the natures of which are defined primarily in terms of their relationships with one another, rather than with some extra-literary, social, or material-causal principle that would allow us to explain their transformations in other than autotelic terms. Progress in this system, if such there be, consists only in the recombination of a finite (though unbounded) set of discrete elements and a rearrangement of hierarchies of relationships among them in ways that appear to render useless any effort to identify the intentions of individual human agents or authors, the expectations of patients or readers, or the constraints imposed by social and cultural institutions that might be appealed to as causal forces in order to explain why any given change in the field of literature—and by extension in culture in general—occurred when, where, and in the way that it did. Changes in modes (from romance through high and low mimetic to ironic), in symbols (from sign through image and archetype to monad), in archetypes (from romance through tragedy and comedy to satire), and in genres (from epic through lyric and dramatic to encyclopedic) appear to replicate the sequence of the main kinds of critical practice (from historical through ethical and archetypal to rhetorical), never breaking the cycle but only going back to the first in order to permit the pattern to be repeated again and again. Whence the opinion, often expressed, regarding Frye's similarity not only to Spengler but also, and above all, to Jung.

While this understanding of the nature of Frye's system can be justified by a reading of his work that focuses on his exploitation of the technique of synchronicity for characterizing the structure of literature, culture, and civilization, it yields insight into only one aspect of his system and neither the whole nor the essential element of it. Frye was nothing if not a philosopher of human freedom, of artistic creativity, and beyond that of a generally human power of species self-creation. This is the Vichian component in his thought, and it is absolutely essential for an understanding of both his project and his articulation of it across a very long and very consistent career of intellectual work. Frye often cites Vico's famous formula *verum factum est*. This is usually translated as "the true is the made" and cited as a tag for Vico's idea that one can truly know only that which one has oneself made or is capable of making. Vico used the idea to distinguish between the kind of knowledge that human beings can have of culture and that which they can have of nature. This theory is called "maker's knowledge," and it holds that, since nature was made by God, human beings can never hope to have the kind of knowledge of it that only God could possess. However, the theory also says, since culture is a distinctively human creation, human beings can aspire to a knowledge of culture of a kind and degree utterly different from that which they can have of the rest of nature. And since history is the record of this process of cultural creation, human beings can legitimately aspire to a knowledge both of history and of themselves as the agents of a specifically historical mode of existence that is both truer and more certain than any knowledge they can ever hope to have of nature. Historical knowledge, in short, is human self-knowledge and specifically knowledge of how human beings make themselves through knowing themselves and come to know themselves in the process of making themselves.

Vico's theory of "maker's knowledge" provides an epistemological basis for an ethics and pedagogy of humanism radically different from that of Enlightenment rationalism.[4] "Maker's knowledge" is not only a way of characterizing the kind of activity we might wish to call "poetic"; it is also a way of characterizing the kind of knowledge we get from reflecting on human creativity. Recall that it was Vico who, against the emergent rationalist dogmas of the Enlightenment, purported to find the secret of human creativity, of culture, and therefore of human history, not in reason or even in the will but rather in the imagination, specifically in the human capacity to think in images as well as in concepts, to coin metaphors and then use them as a basis for action in, against, and with the rest of nature, and thereby to humanize nature and make of it a dwelling place adequate to the satisfaction of distinctively human, as against generally animal, needs and desires.[5] Whereas Kant and the Enlightenment in general viewed metaphor as the source of all error, Vico viewed metaphor as the basis of a uniquely human kind of intellection, an intellection that was projective as well as reflective, capable not only of registering and combining experiences but of shaping them as well—in precisely the same way that the poet shapes language and, in shaping it, revivifies it, remakes it, makes it new, at once revealing hitherto unapprehended potentialities for expression in it and permitting the world to appear in a new and unexpected light at the same time. For Vico, metaphor and image were not presumed to stand over against concept and perception as madness to reason or error to truth. On the contrary, Vico envisioned a continuity between metaphoric thinking (what he called "poetic logic")[6] and rational or scientific thinking, the former being related to the latter not as an inferior or childish kind of thinking to a superior or adult kind of thought but rather as an opening stanza of a poem might be related to its final stanza or, more pertinently, as a poetic prefiguration is related to its fulfilled form.

This relationship of the beginning of a poem to its conclusion, or of a prefiguration to its fulfilled form, served Vico as a model of the relationship between primitive and civilized consciousness, of that between the earliest age or originary period of a civilization and its latest or decadent period, between the imagination and reason, between popular culture and high or elite culture, and between the human body and the human mind. He did not view the relations thus posited as being either causal or teleological in kind. Those aspects of human nature and culture conventionally regarded as higher or more advanced were not to be regarded as effects of causes more basic nor were they to be seen as aims, ends, or purposes inherent in things by virtue of genetic endowment, in the manner of an Aristotelian oak-in-acorn. They are, rather, more in the nature of modal transformations of the kind encountered in music or mathematics, with the difference that they exist in things human and historical rather than only in concepts or in algorithms.

Like Vico, and, it might be added, like Hegel, Marx, Nietzsche, Freud, and Max Weber—thinkers who have learned to see dialectically[7]—Frye apprehends continuities and inter-animations, rather than oppositions, between those phenomena conventionally called truth and error, sanity and madness, good and evil, objectivity and subjectivity, the letter and the spirit, the literal and the figurative, and even between art and life or, within literary art, between poetry and prose, and within each of these, between great, noble, or high forms, on the one side, and their humble, popular, or low counterparts, on the other. As thus envisaged, the world of cultural forms is a stable plenum that, rather than undergoing the kind of change we would call historical, would seem to resemble more a field of electromagnetic force or a mathematical matrix marked less by evolution than by changing intensities, displacements, and modalities. Certainly, this is the kind of thing suggested by those numerous schemata and descriptions of modular relationships (as between mythic archetypes, genres, modes, symbols, and the like) encountered in works like *Anatomy*, *Words with Power*, or the essays collected in *Fables of Identity*.

But such schemata apply only to those moments in which Frye—drawing back from the panorama of Western cultural history or the history of Western literature from the Greeks and the ancient Hebrews to the present—seeks to view it whole and synchronically and to capture its most prominent structural features as if in a kind of still photograph or holographic reproduction. That this system has undergone change and continues to undergo change goes without saying. The crucial role of the concept of "displacement" in Frye's work from first to last indicates as much. But displacement is a concept used to characterize the translation of the structures and imagery of myth into literature; it is a concept that makes it possible to conceive of literature as having a history.[8] And while displacement continues within literature—for example, "displacement in the direction of the moral,"[9] when desire is subjected to "ethical refinement," as with the Victorians[10]—it can hardly be conceived as a principle of qualitative change of the kind we associate with real historical development. The displacement of a genre, mode, myth, symbol, or whatever, from one place to another in the system of literature would be an example of what Spengler called "pseudo-morphosis." Like another fundamental concept in Frye's system, condensation (the equivalent of Freud's *Dichtungsarbeit*, in *The Interpretation of Dreams*), displacement indicates a quantitative rather than a qualitative change.[11] The field of literature or criticism or culture undergoes change, but only of either local intensities (condensations) or pseudo-morphosis (displacement).

But this is as it should be for any builder of a system. A systematization is a spatialization of a process that must, in the nature of its operations, suppress awareness of temporality and change and fix attention solely upon what remains constant. But when it comes to historical phenomena, which is to say, phenomena that have as their fundamental mode of being in the world their responsiveness to time and its effects, it is necessary to switch, as it were, from the synchronic to the diachronic mode in order to theorize a model, not of structure but of sequentiation, for which the notions of condensation and displacement, with their suggestions of intensification, on the one hand, and of movement, on the other, must be inadequate.

I think it is fair to say that Frye had trouble with history, and he had trouble with it because, first of all, he believed in it, which is to say, he believed that culture and society did change and changed in qualitative as well as quantitative ways; but, secondly, he believed that the ways in which culture and society changed were quite different from the ways in which nature or different aspects of nature changed. And I think it fair to say that historical change was a problem for Frye, because unlike, say Freud, he did not believe that things had to be viewed from the perspective of the final entropic "blah." Nor did he believe, at least as a principle of professional, as against personal, faith, that everything was going to come out all right in the end. What Frye needed was some kind of equivalent to Kant's idea of the purposiveness of the art object, which is to say, an idea of non-purposive purposiveness, in order to be able to say that both literature and criticism and, finally, culture itself displayed evidence of the kind of progressive closure with reality as that promised in the Book of Revelations. In my view, this is the idea that reappears, again and again, in Frye's work, at least since *Anatomy*, but especially in both *The Great Code* and *Words with Power*.

Frye explicitly rejected a conception of historical inquiry directed at a perfect recovery or even minimally adequate reconstitution of the past. In *Anatomy*, he cited a fascinating little book called *Repetition* by Søren Kierkegaard, and proposed using "repetition" as an alternative to the "Platonic" notion of anamnesis or "recollection." By "repetition" Frye tells us, Kierkegaard apparently meant, "not the simple repeating of an experience, but the recreating of it which redeems or awakens it to life, the end of the process . . . being the apocalyptic promise: 'Behold, I make all things new,'"[12] Without this sense of "repetition" Frye concludes, "historical criticism tends to remove the products of culture from our own sphere of interest. It must be counterpoised, as it is in all genuine historical critics, by a sense of the contemporary relevance of past art."[13] In his "fascinating little book," Kierkegaard used the notion of repetition to characterize those aspects of life in which what otherwise would seem to be mere "transition" is grasped as a "becoming." And he writes: "Repetition and recollection are the same movement, only in opposite directions; for what is recollected has been, is repeated backwards, whereas repetition properly so-called is recollected forwards."[14]

"Repetition" or "recollecting forwards" constitutes the basis of Frye's conception of an "ethical criticism," a criticism that "relates culture . . . to the future, to the ideal society which may eventually come" just as "the imaginative element in works of art . . . lifts them clear of the bondage of history."[15] It is the Utopian impulse that provides Frye with his unique conception of historical change and historical understanding.

It is interesting to note that Frye returns to the idea of repetition again and again over the course of his career, especially in the two late works, *The Great Code* and *Words with Power*. For example, in the former work, he cites the notion as marking a difference between "a past-directed causality and a future-directed typology. The mere attempt to repeat a past experience" he observes, "will lead only to disillusionment, but there is another kind of repetition which is the Christian antithesis (or complement) of Platonic recollection, and which finds its focus in the Biblical promise: 'Behold, I make all things new' (Revelation 21:5)." Frye goes on, then, to identify Kierkegaard's "repetition" with "the forward moving typological thinking of the Bible."[16] And he argues that typology is "essentially a revolutionary form of thought and rhetoric," the "metaphorical kernel" of which it is the "experience of waking up from a dream, as when Joyce's Stephen Dedalus speaks of history as a nightmare from which he is trying to awake." The kind of transition indicated here is like that of waking from sleep: "one world is simply abolished and replaced by another." We have revolutionary thought, he says, whenever "the feeling 'life is a dream' becomes geared to an impulse to awaken from it." It is the "typological structure and shape of the Bible" that makes "its mythology diachronic, in contrast to the synchronic mythology characteristic of most of the religions outside it."[17] Thus Frye concludes:

> What typology really is as a mode of thought, what it both assumes and leads to, is a theory of history, or more accurately of historical process: an assumption that there is some meaning and point to history, and that sooner or later some event or events will occur which will indicate what that meaning or point is, and so become an antitype of what has happened previously.[18]

Here we get to the crux of Frye's theory of historical change, or what amounts to the same thing, his theory of cultural/literary change. Repetition—"not the simple repeating of an experience, but the recreating of it which redeems or awakens it to life"—names the process productive of the type/antitype relationship by which a later event, text, period, culture, thought, or action can be said to have "fulfilled" an earlier one—in the same way that a figure of speech such as metalepsis or irony can be said to have "fulfilled" another figure—such as prolepsis or metonymy—that may have preceded it in a verbal sequence. "Fulfillment" here is to be understood as the product or effect of a kind of reverse causation—a kind of causation peculiar to historical reality, culture, and human consciousness, by which a thing of the past is at once grasped by consciousness, brought into the present by recollection, and redeemed, made new, by being put to a use theretofore unforeseeable by human beings responding to the press of what Frye calls "secondary concerns" and having been diverted from their "primary concerns": food and drink, sex, property, and "liberty of movement."[19] Fulfillment (or "antitypicality") is less like the kind of thing that happens as a result of a process of mechanistic causation than the kind of thing that happens when a person fulfills a promise, honors a vow, remembers an oath, or performs a duty. It is a peculiarly human kind of "construal" of a relationship between a past and a present.

The archetype or paradigm of this process of change Frye found, of course, in the Christian appropriation of the Hebrew Bible (or the whole of ancient Judaic culture in general) treated as a prefiguration (or type) of which the New Testament (or Christianity in general) was held to be the fulfillment (or antitype). Needless to say, his seeming valorization of this process of cultural appropriation by virtue of his treatment of it as the very paradigm of cultural creativity did not endear him to critical theorists—both Jewish, like Harold Bloom, and not Jewish, like Barbara Johnson—for whom a notion of creativity based on a concept of what they regarded as "expropriation," however benign or merely "symbolic" it was presumed to be, was repugnant. Thus, for example, Bloom feels "moved to reject . . . idealized modes of interpretation . . . stimulated [by the historical triumph of Christianity], from the early typology on to the revival of *figura* by Erich Auerbach and the Blakean *Great Code* of Frye." "No text," Bloom informs us, "fulfills another text, and all who insist otherwise merely homogenize literature."[20]

Bloom's criticism of Frye's typological or figural model of historical change (which was explicitly embraced by Frye in 1957 as that which led him to the conceptualization of *Anatomy*)[21] seems unduly harsh inasmuch as Bloom's own theories of the "anxiety of influence," or "misprision" and the necessarily "agonistic" nature of all writing can legitimately be viewed—or so it seems to me—as another version of the prefiguration-fulfillment model. And far from leading to an "idealized mode of interpretation" that promotes the notion of a "homogenized literature" (or history, for that matter), the prefiguration-fulfillment model provides a way of construing the processes of cultural production that we alone wish to call "historical." For this notion of the relation obtaining between the earlier aspects or periods of a culture's history and later ones allows us to take into account the fact that—in history at least—there is no such thing as creation *ex nihilo*. It dispels thereby the myth of a creativity without violence. Moreover, it allows us to conceptualize the problem of the relationship between tradition (that body of cultural artifacts inherited from the past) and the kinds of cultural innovation that, though manifestly different from what had come before, still appear to be linked in some essential, but non-genetically, determined way to the past. The prefiguration-fulfillment model, indeed, provides a notion of genealogical affiliation as a historically responsible alternative to the physical and biological conception of a genetic relationship. Finally, and this strikes me as the most importantly realistic aspect of Frye's idea of cultural history (as against its alleged "idealism"), the prefiguration-fulfillment model of cultural change, with its notion of retrospective expropriation of the products of past creative efforts, reminds us of the "fallen" nature of any exercise of merely human creativity, namely, that it is always an exercise of power, that it is violent, and that it redeems itself only in the extent to which it "makes new" the cultural artifacts it used as the material cause of its own operation.

CHAPTER TWENTY

Storytelling

Historical and Ideological

{1996}

The question currently being posed by theorists of historical discourse is whether storytelling—or what we can call, more technically, the narrative mode of discourse—is not in some way ideological in its very nature. This question has important implications for historical theory, inasmuch as historical discourse has traditionally featured narration or storytelling as a preferred mode of representation and even of explanation. To be sure, our representations of history do not have to be cast in a story form; they can also be cast in non-narrative discursive modes: descriptive, analytical, even lyrical, as the case may be. And indeed, in modern, "scientific" historiography, the tendency has been to suppress storytelling in favor of synchronic representations of historical phenomena, structural-functional analyses of long-term and for the most part "impersonal" historical processes, and model building as a means of explicating complex forces and long-term trends discernible in the historical record. Storytelling or narration has been reduced to the function of providing specific examples, instances, or illustrations of classes of events, structures, and processes derived by non-narrative representational and analytical procedures. In other words, storytelling in historiography has for quite a while been deprived of its traditional function of explaining historical events and consigned to the more modest roles of explication and illustration.

It is because of the subordinant function of narrativity in contemporary historiography that the recent call for a "return to narrative" in historical writing invites attention from theorists of the social and human sciences. To be sure, the proponents of a "return to narrative" in historical writing explicitly grant to "storytelling" only a rhetorical function. They recommend it only as a means of reviving an interest in history among a laity disaffected by the abstractive methods of structuralist and social scientific historiography and the dryness or impersonality of scientific prose. The suggestion is that it is merely a matter of dressing up their findings—produced by the application of social scientific methods to their objects of interest—in the garb of a story, in order to make the results of their research more palatable to their lay audience.

However, such a recommendation presumes that narration is a neutral discursive form, an ornamental device that carries no message in its own right and does not therefore affect in any important way the representation either of the events spoken about or the historian's thought about the events produced by the application of scientific principles of analysis. It would appear that narrative is a *form* of discourse that can be adapted to the presentation of a wide variety of cognitive *contents*, whether commonsensical in nature or produced by the application of "scientific" procedures—such as econometrics, statistical demography, dialectics, ethnography, psychoanalysis, and so on. It is as if one could simply present the *results* of a structural-functionalist, synchronic, or algorithmic analysis of historical phenomena in a *narrative form* without thereby adding any significant conceptual or cognitive content to the account.

But this notion of narration is at odds with the results of some four decades of research into the nature of rhetoric in general and of narrative discourse or storytelling in particular. This research suggests that far from being a neutral medium in which events, whether imaginary or real, can be represented with perfect transparency, narrative is an expression in discourse of a distinct mode of experiencing and thinking about the world, its structures, and its processes. Indeed, the millennial association of the narrative mode of discourse with mythic and religious thought, on the one side, and with literary fiction, on the other, was what led to the condemnation of narrative history as a manifestation of mythical thinking in historical reflection in the first place.

Braudel and Barthes on Narrative in Historiography

Thus, for example, as early as 1950, Fernand Braudel, the leader of the *Annales* group of structuralist historians and social scientists, attacked the use of narration in historical representation, not so much as a *container* of one or another ideological messages, as rather the very ideological *content* of any historical account cast in this form. In an essay on the then current situation in historical studies, Braudel wrote:

> The narrative history so dear to the heart of Ranke offer[s] . . . a gleam but no illumination; facts but no humanity. Note that this narrative history . . . always claims to relate "things just as they really happened." In fact, though, in its own *covert* way, narrative history consists of an interpretation, an authentic *philosophy of history*. To the narrative historians, the life of men is dominated by *dramatic*

accidents, by the actions of those *exceptional beings* who occasionally emerge, and who often are the masters of their own *fate* and even more of ours. And when they speak of "general history," what they are really speaking of is the intercrossing of such exceptional *destinies*, for obviously each *hero* must be matched against another. A delusive fallacy, as we all know. (My emphases)[1]

Note here that Braudel calls narrative *as such* a "philosophy of history" and goes on to characterize it as informed by a specifically *dramatistic* perspective on historical events. The "ideological" effect of this perspective consists in its transformation of history into a spectacle, unfolding before the mind's eye of the reader with all of the color, intensity, and fascination of a theatrical production. The events of a narrative representation must be charged with all the mythic resonances attending the notions of "fate" and "destiny": the characters must be larger than life ("heroic") and more complex, more noble and more interesting ("exceptional") than ordinary people. Everything has to be focused on those grand "conflicts" and "climaxes" of which only "heroes" can be agents.

A similar attack on the use of narrative for the representation of history was mounted from the quarter of literary theory a few years later by Roland Barthes. He put the matter this way:

As we can see, simply from looking at its structure and without having to invoke the substance of its content, [narrative] *historical discourse is in its essence a form of ideological elaboration* [my emphasis], or to put it more precisely, an *imaginary* elaboration, if we can take the imaginary to be the language through which the utterer of a discourse (a purely linguistic entity) "fills out" the place of the subject of the utterance (a psychological or ideological entity).[2]

On the basis of his own structural analysis of narratives, Barthes concluded that "claims concerning the 'realism' of narrative" must be "discounted" and that "the function of narrative is not to 'represent,' it is to constitute a spectacle."[3] We do not, Barthes argued, "experience" reality more vividly and immediately in narrative than in descriptive discourse; what we experience is the effect of being disengaged and effectively mesmerized "observers" of "spectacular" events.

The indictments of narrative by Braudel and Barthes reflected a general, structuralist suspicion of a kind of historiography that, because it took the form of storytelling, retained too many formal similarities to mythic thought and fictional discourse. "Does the narration of past events," Barthes asked, "really differ, in some specific trait, in some indubitably distinctive feature, from imaginary narration, as we find it in the epic, the novel, and the drama?"[4] The question was rhetorical, of course, because Barthes supposed that the *form* of a narrative discourse marked it as "imaginary" rather than as "realistic," quite apart from whatever political position or class interest it could be shown on analysis to be implicitly promoting. And this was because narrative discourse inevitably cultivated such mythological notions as the transcendental observer of historical processes, the sovereign subject (whether an individual or a collectivity) as the principal agent of historical events, the episodic event as the basic unit of historical reality, dependence on the anecdote to explain what in reality it only posited, and *post hoc ergo propter hoc* reasoning as the principal means of linking events in chains of causes and effects.

Barthes's analysis of narrative discourse was part of a wider inquiry into the history and potential fate of the ideology of realism inherited from the period of bourgeois hegemony in the nineteenth century. In Barthes's view, nineteenth-century "realism," in historical no less than fictional writing, was intimately linked to the narrative mode of discourse. Since, for him, "realistic representation" itself was nothing but an effect produced by nineteenth-century bourgeois discursive practices, it followed that as long as narrative remained a dominant mode of historical representation, historical inquiry must remain a merely pseudoscientific and therefore ideological enterprise. A structuralist approach to historical analysis, Barthes maintained, would gain in scientificity precisely in the degree to which it abandoned the idea that "reality" could be "realistically" represented in the form of a story and substituted, not only non- but explicitly anti-narrative representational and explanatory procedures. Historical reality could be rendered more "intelligible" by being detheatricalized, its "drama" played down, and the impersonality of its processes highlighted. History could be made into an object for analysis rather than an object of "specular" fascination only by being "defamiliarized"—in the manner proposed by Brecht for the reformation of the classical theater.

According to Braudel and Barthes, then, historical storytelling was ideological in the extent to which it transformed historical events into the stuff of "theater." This transformation conditioned readers to occupy the imaginary position of "spectators" of a scene on which superhuman "actors" played out "roles" as representatives of "forces" more mythical than natural, in kind. Ordinary mortals could only marvel at what transpired on this scene; they could never hope to inhabit it effectively themselves or change the "forces" appearing thereon by their own actions. The general ideological effect of such theatricalization of history by storytelling was to produce "subjects" who were content to be the "patients" of historical "forces" because they had been deprived of any hope of becoming "agents" in their own right, whether as individuals or as members of social collectivities. As thus envisaged, the task of progressive criticism and theory was to destroy the authority of narration, not only in historical writing but also and perhaps preeminently in fictional writing as well.

Lukács on Narrative in Realistic Representation

The Braudel-Barthes critique of storytelling *as* ideology differs from the view of the function of narration in "realistic" writing that Georg Lukács had developed in his work of the interwar years. The problem of the relation between ideology and narrative was raised by Lukács, in terms relevant to our interests, in his studies on literary realism in the 1930s, and it may be helpful to review one of his considerations of it before proceeding to our own.

According to Lukács, narration is linked to ideology in a complex means-end relationship. On the one hand, ideology alone makes effective narration possible. "Without an ideology," he wrote in 1936, "a writer can neither narrate nor construct a comprehensive, well-organized and multifaceted epic composition." The alternatives to narration, "observation and description," were at best "mere substitutes for a conception of order in life."[5] They were not so much a manifestation of another ideology as rather indices of the effort to repress ideologically inflected consciousness altogether.

On the one hand, then, for Lukács, narration is a manifestation of "ideology" in discourse; narrative discourse is a *means* of ideological production. This view was consonant with that later developed by Braudel and Barthes. But Lukács differed from them in the generally positive value that he assigned to ideology itself in the representation of historical reality. Indeed, Lukács held that it is only by a narrativistic apprehension of reality that the "infinite variety," depth, and epic sweep of human life in history can be grasped in consciousness.[6] Thus, it would seem, narrative is not only a *means* of ideological production but also a *mode* of consciousness, a way of viewing the world that conduces to the construction of an ideology. Consequently, narrative discourse does not serve ideology. It produces ideology, and it is ideology that serves a narrativistic apprehension of reality.

Unlike Braudel and Barthes, Lukács did not regard the use of a narrativistic mode of discourse in "realistic" representation, whether in historical or in fictional writing, as an expression of a specific political or even general class perspective. The choice of the narrative mode for the representation of reality indicated, rather, the impulse to engage reality in ideological rather than in non-ideological terms. Thus for example, in the case of such conservative writers as Walter Scott, Balzac, and Tolstoy, the predominance of a narrative over a descriptive mode of representation stemmed from the immediacy with which narrative, as against description, would represent historical events: "In Scott, Balzac, or Tolstoy we experience events which are inherently significant because of the direct involvement of the characters in the events and because of the general social significance emerging in the unfolding of the characters' lives. We are the audience to events in which the characters take active part. We ourselves experience these events."[7] By contrast, such seemingly progressive writers as Flaubert and Zola undermined their own consciously held ideological convictions in the degree to which they featured "descriptive" over "narrative" representations of events, characters, and situations: "In Flaubert and Zola the characters are merely spectators, more or less interested in the events. As a result, the events themselves become only a tableau for the reader, or, at best, a series of tableaux. We are merely observers."[8] The distinction indicated here, between narration and description, hinges upon the difference between the effect of "experiencing" the events represented in the discourse and that of merely "observing" them. In narrative representation, both the characters in and the readers of the story experience the events from the "inside," whereas in descriptive representation, the events are not "experienced" at all. They are simply "observed" from the "outside" of their occurrence.

It should be noted that in this case, Lukács was not analyzing the difference between "realistic" and "imaginary" (or "historical" and "mythical") discourse, but rather the differences between two kinds of "realistic" fiction. Flaubert and Zola, no less than Scott, Balzac, and Tolstoy, claimed to be representing the world "realistically," though by "fictional" means. The principal difference between the two styles of realism hinged upon the absence of "ideology" in the one and the presence of it in the other. The presence of ideology in the novels of Scott, Balzac, and Tolstoy was signaled by their use of a narrative mode for the representation of reality, while the absence of ideology in Flaubert and Zola was indicated by their tendency to allow "description" to triumph over "narration" in their work.

Now, this view of the matter has interesting implications for any consideration of the relation between storytelling and ideology in historical discourse. In our own cultural moment, the term "ideology" does not carry the same, generally positive, connotation that it did for Lukács. For him, it was better to have a "bad" or reactionary ideology than to have no ideology at all. It was not a matter of feigning to have no ideology, since every putatively "objective" or "scientific" worldview feigned the capacity to rise above ideology and to represent reality as it truly was. The principal danger to creative social and political action lay in the impulse to de-ideologize one's experience of the world, which was to say, to adopt the attitude of a purely neutral observer and describer of reality rather than that of an active participant in it. Indeed, this is what "modernism" in general consisted of, in Lukács's view.

Nor was it a matter of "seeing" reality right side up and in true perspective. In literary (and, by extension, historical) representation, Lukács said,

> the opposition between experiencing and observing is not accidental. It arises out of divergent *basic positions about life and about the major problems of society* and not just out of divergent artistic methods of handling content or one specific aspect of content . . . There are no writers who renounce description absolutely. Nor, on the other hand, can one claim that the outstanding representatives of realism after 1848, Flaubert and Zola, renounced narration absolutely. What is important here are *philosophies of composition*, not any illusory "pure" phenomenon of narration or description.[9]

But what does it mean to experience life from the "inside" of "events," and how does a narrative representation of reality produce the effect of experiencing events in a way that is more "realistic" ("truthful," "genuine," "authentic," "verisimilar"—the reader can provide the adjective) than other modes of representation? Evidently, what Lukács meant by narrative representation in literary fiction was nothing other than the representation of the "dramatic" nature of historical reality, the very feature of narration taken by Braudel and Barthes as an index of its ideological (in the bad sense) nature. Thus, for example, Lukács took issue with Flaubert's own critique of his "historical novel," *L'Education sentimentale* for being so "true" to life that it could have neither a "perspective" nor a "climax."[10] "Do 'climaxes' exist in art alone?" Lukács asked. "Of course not," he answered; Flaubert's "belief that 'climaxes' exist only in art and that they are therefore created by artists at will is simply subjective prejudice."[11]

Here Lukács raised, only to sweep aside, the crucial question for any consideration of the problem of the relation between historical and ideological storytelling: does life, reality, or history display the same kind of formal attributes as those met with in stories? Do historical agents behave like characters in novels? Do historical processes describe the kinds of trajectories met with in tragedies and comedies? Do historical events or at least some of them have "climactic" significance, turning the general course of history, in the way that certain events function in novels to reveal the "plot" or the "point" of what has happened prior to their occurrence? Or has Lukács fallen victim to a kind of Bovaryism, confusing historical reality with the world represented in a certain kind of literary genre, for example, the epic and possibly even the romance? To raise these questions is to inquire into the kind of coherence that stories in general possess. More specifically, it is to direct attention to the relation between stories and the plots that inform them and give them generic coherence.

Story and Plot in Historical Narrative

What kind of coherence do stories and especially historical stories typically present? This is a question having to do more with *representation* than with *explanation*. For it is obvious that narrative accounts of real events, whether of individual lives or of complex social processes, do provide a kind of explanation of such events. They explain the events of which they treat by endowing them with the kind of coherence—the structures, tonalities, auras, and meanings—typically met with in "stories." But to put the matter this way is tautologous: it is to suggest that historical storytelling produces a general "story effect" that is grasped by readers as a general "story meaning" as against some other kind of meaning. But I would suggest that there is no such thing as narration-in-general, that there are only different kinds of stories or story-types, and that the explanation effect of historical storytelling derives from the kind of coherence with which it endows events by its imposition upon them of a specific plot-structure. This is to say that narrative accounts can be said to explain real events by representing them as possessing the coherence of generic plot-types—epic, comic, tragic, farcical, and so on. But is this kind of coherence found in reality, or is it imposed upon reality by what we have come to call the technique of *emplotment*?

That the endowment of real events with the kind of coherence that we associate with plots or plot-structures is creditable was suggested by Lukács himself when he identified the narrative point of view with that informing the specific literary genre of the epic. While the emplotment of a sequence of real events as an epic, tragedy, or farce is hardly to be considered a scientific explanation thereof, it is nonetheless a kind of explanation. A narrative explanation implicitly invokes principles of classification, characterization, causation, and meaning that are at least analogous to those used in the physical sciences to explain natural events and processes. That such principles are culturally determinate does not deprive them of their authority as explanations.

The problem—as Barthes later insisted—is that the same can be said of both manifestly "fictional" and identifiably "mythical" narrativizations of real events. These too provide explanations of a kind of the events whereof they treat. But this means that one is forced to consider the possibility that any narrative account of historical events remains contaminated by representational practices of a distinctively fictionalizing and mythicalizing kind. And it follows that if accounts of

historical reality are to become truly scientific, then such accounts must be purged
of any impulse to represent this reality in a generally narrative form. But this conclusion can be said to follow necessarily only if the kind of coherence provided by
the imposition of a plot-structure—of the sort met with in mythical and fictional
discourse—on a given set of historical events has no counterpart in reality.

To pose this last problem is to raise the question of the cognitive status of literary or fictional and, by extension, mythic discourse. If we presume that literature
is a purely *imaginary* mode of expression and representation, then of course the
issue of the "realism" and veracity of any historical account cast in an identifiably
literary form is resolved in advance. Thus, for example, the "epic" plot-type, which
Lukács took to be the structuring principle (the "philosophy of composition") of
all genuinely realistic narration, would have to be taken as an index of the fictionality of any historical account in which it was used, to endow historical events with
this kind of "generic" coherence. But can we be certain that the apprehension of
historical events as possessing the form and manifesting the structures of meaning
typically conveyed in such literary genres as the epic, romance, tragedy, comedy,
and farce, is mistaken or, as Braudel called it, "a delusive fallacy"? Is it possible, as
Lukács might have asked, that not only "climaxes," but also the kinds of plots that
utilize the "climax" in different ways, *occur* in "reality" or at least in "historical reality," as well as in "fiction" and "myth"?

Emplotment as Figuration

The plausibility or lifelikeness of fictional representations of imaginary events,
their resemblance to the kinds of experiences met with in "real life," is not limited
to their depiction of recognizable character types and "possible" situations. It
extends as well to their depiction of events as possessing generic plot-structures.
David Carr has recently argued that narrative representations of historical reality
can be considered realistic and veracious to the extent that human agents inhabit
a sociocultural world that is structured narrativistically and intend their actions in
such a way as effectively to make of them the kinds of actions about which "true"
stories can be told. In Carr's view, it is not a matter of historians' *imposing* a narrative form on specific sets of historical events as, rather, of *discovering* the real, lived
story of which these events are component elements. In line with Paul Ricoeur's
recent work on narrative, Carr argues that human agents *prefigure* their actions as
narrative trajectories, such that the outcome of a given action is at least *intended* to
be linked to its inauguration in the way that the ending of a story is linked to its
beginning.[12] Thus, one meaning of a given sequence of specifically "historical" (as

against, say, a sequence of "natural") events, can be said to derive from the "configurative" relations obtaining between the intention motivating an action and its outcome, effects, or consequences. In this view, historical reality differs from natural reality by virtue of the kind of narrative meaning with which the former is endowed by human agents' capacity to structure their actions narrativistically.

A historical-narrative representation of a set of such actions is not, then, to be considered as a product of an arbitrary imposition by the historian of a narrative *form* on what would otherwise be a non-narrative *content*. Carr accepts Ricoeur's view that every historical representation cast in the mode of a narrative discourse constitutes a "refiguration" of action sequences. But he concludes that historiographical "refigurations" should not be accounted as "fictional" insofar as the narrative forms they ascribe to sequences of events are inherent in the structures of the events themselves. In other words, historical narratives should not be considered as "allegorizations" of the events of which they speak—as Braudel and Barthes (and others, including myself) have suggested—but rather should be viewed as *literal* accounts thereof. As thus envisaged, historical narrative is a peculiar kind of discourse, the product of a process of verbal *figuration* that, insofar as the story told conforms to the outline of the story lived in real life, is to be taken as *literally* true.

If we accepted this line of analysis, we could then conclude that historical storytelling is neither inherently ideological nor exactly scientific in nature, nor even a mixture of the two, but rather some third kind of discourse especially suited to the representation of that one animal that not only *tells* stories but *lives* them as well. If that were the case, the task of the historian would be what it has always been thought to be, namely, to discover the "real" story or stories that lie embedded within the welter of "facts" and to retell them as truthfully and completely as the documentary record permits.

I am inclined to credit Carr's account of the cognitive authority of narrative representations of historical reality and even the view, which Carr shares with Lukács (and also with Louis Mink, Arthur Danto, Ricoeur, Fredric Jameson, and others), that narrative is a distinct cognitive mode rather than *only* a form of discourse. But the notion that narrative explains events by "configuring" them as stories is still too general to aid us in our effort to distinguish between historical and ideological storytelling. One can think and speak "narratologically" while telling many different kinds of "stories" about the same set of events. And this suggests that we might profitably distinguish between a narratological *mode* of thought and speech, on the one side, and the various *techniques* of narration, such as characterization, thematization, and emplotment, on the other.

Generic Plot-Types in Historical Narration

Narrators typically (though not always) *emplot* the events of which they speak. This means that they do not tell a story-in-general, but always a story of a specific kind (or a mixture of different kinds of stories). In other words, historical narrators often claim to find in the events of which they speak the forms of one or another of the *plot-structures* typically met with in the different genres of artistic fiction, myth, fable, and legend. In historiography, this activity of emplotment can generate alternative and even mutually exclusive interpretations of the same set of phenomena— as when, for example, what one historian has emplotted as an epic or tragedy is emplotted by another as a farce. And it is here, in what appears to be the projection of a given generic plot-type onto a given set of historical events, rather than in the choice of a narrative as against a non-narrative discursive mode, that the question of the ideological nature of historical storytelling can be said to arise. In sum, the question of the ideological content of narrative representations of reality hinges on the cognitive authority of the various generic story-types available within a given cultural endowment for the provision of real events with a distinctive kind of story meaning, not on the cognitive authority of the narrative mode of speaking about the world.

Thus we might conclude that the ideological content of a specific historical account can be said to consist not so much in the discursive mode in which it is cast as in the dominant plot-structure chosen to endow the events spoken of with the form of a recognizable story-type. Theorists of historiography have long recognized the ideological nature of certain "master narratives" (what Jean-François Lyotard calls *grands récits*), which purport to disclose the *Weltplan* or overarching "meaning of history." The classical concept of Fate, the Christian doctrine of Providence, the bourgeois notion of Progress, and the Marxist vision of the world-historical destiny of the Proletariat are cases in point. But within the main line of historical thought in the West, there has always been a tradition of "critical" historical writing, both narrative and analytical, that has laid claim to a certain scientificity or at least to a certain kind of realism in virtue of its resistance to such totalizing conceptions of historical reality. Indeed, critical historiography purports to gain its status as a kind of science precisely by its repudiation of the neat schemata of such "philosophies of history" at the level of concrete historical detail. Traditionally, evidence of professional historians' capacity to resist the seduction of all "master narratives" is provided by their reluctance to deal with "history-in-general" and to confine themselves to the production of "small narratives" of local and, as it were, regional domains of the historical totality.

However, whether the historian limits herself to the investigation of a finite domain of historical occurrence and to the production of a "small" rather than of a "grand" account thereof, if she decides to cast her account in the form of a story, she must still tell a story of a specific kind (or mixture of specific kinds of stories). This means that she must emplot the events according to the principles informing the structures of distinctive story-types or genres. Otherwise the account will not be recognizable as a story and will not provide the kind of understanding or explanation of the events that storytelling, among the various narrational techniques available to the culture of which she is a member, can alone provide. What are we to do with two or more narrative accounts of what, *grosso modo*, appear to be the same set or sequence of historical events, when the stories told about them are manifestly different, contradictory, or even mutually exclusive?

This formulation of the question concerning the nature of narrative explanations of historical phenomena permits us to address the problem of the relation between historical and ideological storytelling in terms of the relative adequacy of different generic plot-types to the representation of real events. Thus, for example, instead of locating the problem of the ideological content of historical accounts at the level of their factual accuracy, we are now licensed to ask such questions as the following: Is the employment of a set of historical events as an epic inherently more "realistic" and "truthful" (as Lukács thought) than an emplotment of the same set of events as a romance or comedy? Are comic representations of historical events ethically more responsible than tragic representations (as Hegel thought)? Or is it a matter of the common "fictional" nature of all such modes of emplotment? Does the use in a historical narrative of techniques of emplotment, typically met with in myth, fiction, fable, and legend for the representation of "imaginary" events, indicate that the account is more "ideological" than "historical" in nature? Or is it a matter of choosing a specific plot-type for the representation of a discrete set of historical events because those events display the form and therefore can be said to possess a meaning of the sort that this particular plot-type and no other can adequately represent? Questions such as these permit us to locate the question of the ideological content of historical storytelling at the level of the figurative meaning of the discourse, rather than at the level of its literal factuality.

Ideology and Plot-Type in Historical Narrative

The relevance of this notion of the ideological content of historical storytelling to current discussions of the relation between historical narration and ideology can be suggested by cursory reference to a recent review by C. Vann Woodward of Eli N. Evans's life of Judah P. Benjamin, a Jewish member of Jefferson Davis's Confederate cabinet during the American Civil War. After summarizing the gripping story of Benjamin's life as told by Evans, Woodward suddenly interrupts his paraphrase of the story told, in order to register the following, seemingly cautionary remarks regarding the appeal of the tale:

> But this is an outrageously romantic and improbable tale that few properly scientific and up-to-date historians would likely deem worthy of serious attention. It is very largely concerned with doings of the elite and advances no good cause being currently promoted. Moreover, it is a story told by means of old-fashioned traditional narrative, tests no hypotheses, and employs no approved analytical techniques.[13]

Note that Woodward's characterization of the reasons for which Evans's story might not appeal to "scientific and up-to-date historians" has to do, first, with what it contains ("it is concerned with the doings of the elite") and what it does not contain (it "advances no good cause being currently promoted . . . tests no hypotheses . . . employs no approved analytical techniques"). This suggests that the book's contents consist of "facts" ("doings of the elite") rather than of facts plus a certain kind of scientific demonstration or argument and/or ideology (it "advances no good cause being currently promoted"). Yet Woodward astutely discriminates between these two orders of possible content (facts and arguments) and two orders of the form of Evans's account: generic ("an outrageously romantic . . . tale") and modal ("it is a story told by old-fashioned traditional narrative"). Unless we attended to these distinctions, we might find it difficult to credit Woodward's judgment on the truthfulness of Evans's representation of Benjamin's life. For he at once grants it the status of a literary fiction ("an outrageously romantic tale") and absolves it from the kind of distortion we normally associate with ideological special pleading seeking to pass for a simple relating of events "as they really happened." Thus Woodward writes: "Granting all this, I am persuaded that what is told us actually happened and that it happened pretty much, as far as I can see, as the author tells it."[14]

Woodward seems to be suggesting that certain kinds of events, in this case "the doings of the elite" recounted in Evans's history, are appropriately emplotted as a romantic tale—that, in a word, the structure of the romance plot-type can be used to represent truthfully and to explain adequately "what really happened" for at least certain domains of historical reality. Thus the events are conceived to be narratable because they comprise a story actually lived, and the story is justifiably emplotted as a romance because the story actually lived was a romantic kind of story. Indeed, Woodward suggests that, had Evans used another plot-type, he might very well have been unable to tell a story fully adequate to the specific set of events he wished to represent. To be sure, Woodward does not go this far; he merely indicates that the romance plot-type was a suitable vehicle for a veracious representation of the life of Judah Benjamin and of the "doings of the elite" whose story he wished to tell. But in so indicating, Woodward directs our attention to the problem of the veracity of generic plot-types in general and to the question of the status of figurations of historical events as instantiations of generic plot-structures effected by the technique of emplotment in historical representation.

Arguably, the ideological element in historical storytelling could be viewed as the misrepresentation of the plot-type a given set of historical events *actually* possessed. Thus, for example, in a late preface to his *Eighteenth Brumaire of Louis Bonaparte*, Marx criticizes Victor Hugo and Pierre-Joseph Proudhon for their misrepresentation of the plot informing the cycle of events that comprised the Revolution(s) of 1848–51 in France. In his view, they erred by making Louis Napoleon, the protagonist of the events, in the one case "great" and in the other "heroic." The error was a product of a certain kind of historical "objectivity" that takes events at their face value as facts. Thus Marx writes that Proudhon "falls into the error of our so-called *objective* historians," whereas "I, on the contrary, demonstrate how . . . circumstances and relationships . . . make it possible for a grotesque mediocrity to play a hero's part."[15] It is not Bonaparte's triumph, but its absurdity that has to be accounted for. And it is accounted for in at least two ways: a demonstration of how "the *class struggle*" produced these "circumstances and relationships" and the emplotment of the concatenation of events as a farce. This emplotment of the events as a *farce* should not be viewed as merely a rhetorical ornament of the argument, but as a figurative representation of the events in such a way that poses the problem of historical analysis for which the formal argument will provide a solution.

Were the events leading up to the coup d'état of 1851 truthfully characterized as a "farce"? Is the characterization of these events as a farce to be taken literally or is it only a matter of a figure of speech? Does the emplotment of these events as a farce add to our understanding of "what really happened" in France between February 1948 and December 1851? Is it only a matter of Marx's genius as a rhetorician and polemicist, a question of his "literary" style? Or is it, rather, that Marx has himself "ideologically" distorted the events in the way that he accused Hugo and Proudhon of doing, though in a different, more "ironic" manner?

Literal and Figurative Meanings in Historical Narrative

Consideration of these kinds of questions returns us to the problem of the relation between the literal and the figurative dimensions of historical discourse in general and of historical narrative in particular. If storytelling can be said to endow historical events with a figurative meaning by emplotting them in terms of a generic story-type, does this mean that historical stories cannot be held to criteria of truthfulness and consistency that we would use for assessing their factual and explanatory contents? If such were the case, we might be able to conclude that the ideological element in historical representations consists, first, in the substitution of figurative for literalist representations of events and, second, in the specific figurations used to endow events with meanings that they do not *in fact* possess.

As we have noted above, such indeed was the argument advanced by semiotic-structuralist analysts of historical ideologization such as Barthes. Ideology or, as Barthes preferred to call it, "mythical thought," worked in historical representation by surreptitiously substituting a Signified (a specific conceptual content treated as an essence, such as "Frenchness" or "Woman" or "Italianicity") for the Referent (such as "the citizens of France," "a specific group of women," "Italian cuisines or clothing styles," etc.) it pretended merely to describe. This covert substitution of a putative "essence" for a concrete historical reality was ideology, in this semiotic view of the nature of ideological production. Thus it would follow that the ideological element in Marx's representation of Louis Bonaparte consists in his attribution to Louis Bonaparte's coup d'état of a kind of essential "farcicality." And the same would go for Evans's life of Judah Benjamin: it would have to be considered an ideological representation insofar as it endowed the "doings of the elite" with a kind of essential "romanticality."

But it seems evident that Marx at least intended his "farce" to be taken both figuratively and literally. In other words, the characterization of these events as a farce was intended to be taken as "substantially" true. It is a matter less of metaphysical "essences" than of what the Danish linguist Louis Hjelmslev has called "the Substance of the Content" of all discourses more extensive than the single predicative sentence.[16]

Levels of Analysis of the Historical Story

The significance of Hjelmslev's work for the problem of distinguishing between historical and ideological storytelling consists of his multiplanar theory of discourse. In place of the simple opposition between the literal and the figurative levels of a discourse, Hjelmslev constructs a dual-binary model. First, he distinguishes between the "Expression" level and the "Content" level of a discourse. Then he proceeds to distinguish further between the "Form" and the "Substance" of both. This model has the advantage, for any analysis of the cognitive content of "historical stories," of allowing us to specify the differences between the *two kinds of referentiality*, literal and figurative, that will be present within such stories. Put most briefly, Hjelmslev's model allows us to say that the "story" told about a given set of historical events unfolds at the level of the "Form of Content" of the discourse, whereas what we have called emplotment can be seen to operate at the level of its "Substance of Expression."

On this view, a historical story can be adjudged literally true in the extent to which the "Form of [its] Content" (the story told) "corresponds" to the form of the historical referent (the *facts* of the matter diachronically organized). At the same time, however, the story told can be said to endow historical events with a figurative meaning by endowing them with the structure of a generic plot-type, such as farce, romance, tragedy, and so on, at the level of its "Substance of Expression." At the latter level, the criterion to be employed in assessing the truth-value of the historical story is not so much that of literal correspondence as, rather, that of verisimilitude or plausibility. At the level of the "Substance of Expression," historical events are endowed with plot meaning by complex operations of figuration. We can say that at this level historical events are endowed with figurative meaning by being encoded as elements of a generic story-type. At this level of narrativization, it is not a question of the outline of a generic plot-type *corresponding* to the form of the events that constitute the referent of the discourse. It is a question, rather, of the *plausibility* of the plot-type chosen to endow events with a specific kind of figurative meaning (epic, tragic, comic, farcical, romantic, as the case might be).

This may appear to be a needlessly complicated way of speaking about such a seemingly "natural" activity as "storytelling." But there is nothing natural about storytelling; it is a highly complex art—or craft, depending on how you look at it. And its use is especially complex when it is a matter of representing real, rather than imaginary, events. This is because, whereas the writer of fictions can "invent" events to conform to the exigencies of storytelling, the writer of a history enjoys no such inventive freedom. Since the events of a historical story are given by research into the historical record, the inventive freedom of the writer of a narrative history consists of the choices that can be made among culturally provided plot-types by which to endow the events with different kinds of figurative meaning. In fact, historians can tell many different kinds of stories about the same set of real events without in anyway violating criteria of truthfulness at the level of the representation of the facts of the matter.

Hjelmslev's complex multiplanar model of discursivity thus permits us to identify the relationship between the "factual" content of a historical story, on one hand, and what is usually called its "interpretive" (and more derogatorily, its "ideological") content, on the other. The "factual" content is encountered at the level of the "Form of the Content" (in the "facts" registered), whereas the latter appears at the level of the "Substance of Expression" (in the plot-type used to endow the events of the story with a specific symbolic meaning). The story told is appropriately assessed according to its "factuality," while the plot-type used to generate an interpretation of the events can only be properly assessed in terms of its plausibility.

Consider, for example, what happened in the 1988 primary elections for the Democratic Party's nominee for president of the United States. Senator Joseph Biden was forced to withdraw from the contest when it was shown that he (or his aides) had stolen the "story" of British Labour leader Neal Kennock's life and passed it off as Biden's own life story. It would have been quite another matter had Biden merely adopted the "plot" of Kennock's life and used it to endow his own life story with a general symbolic significance. American politicians regularly use the "plot" of Abraham Lincoln's life (simple man of the people rises from obscurity by hard work and self-education to attain the highest office in the land and to lead the country in a time of crisis) for the representation of the "meaning" of their own lives. It would be quite improper for them to use Lincoln's "story" to tell their own life history. Biden's media advisers failed to distinguish between the Form of the Content of the senator's life and the Substance of Expression that they wished to use in its representation.

It might be objected that Hjelmslev's terminology does little more than translate what we are accustomed to call "story" and "plot" into the jargon of linguistics. But that is not the case at all. I have said nothing about the two levels of discursivity Hjelmslev designated as "Form of Expression" and "Substance of Content." By the term "Form of Expression" Hjelmslev designates the specifically linguistic features of a verbal discourse such as the historical narrative: lexical, grammatical, and syntactical. At the level of analysis thus indicated, we would have to ask whether "historical" and "ideological" discourse are discriminable by their linguistic features alone. And of course they are not thus discriminable. It is because the two kinds of discourse have the same or similar linguistic features that we are forced to confront the problem of the relationship between "ideological" and "historical" stories in the first place. Ideological storytelling *looks like* historical storytelling in its manifest form. Ideological discourse refers to historical events, *tells stories* about these events, purports to tell the true story of these events, tries to *explain* why they happened as they did, and, finally, claims to reveal the *real historical significance* of these events. In a word, at the level of formal exposition, the Form of Expression, an ideological story is *exactly like* the historical story.

And so too at the level of Substance of Expression. Here the ideological story works exactly like the historical story, which is to say, it transforms "facts" into the elements of a specific story-type by complex operations of figuration, poetic and rhetorical in nature. Historical events, agents, and agencies are "characterized" in dramatistic terms and presented as if they were the kinds of things met with in manifestly "fictional" genres: fables, legends, myths, novels, plays, and the like. At this level of analysis, the *identity* of historical with ideological stories, argued for by Braudel and Barthes, can be affirmed. And it is possible to argue that there is no difference at all between the two kinds of discourse.

For example, at this level, that of Substance of Expression, it is impossible to distinguish between Proudhon's and Marx's representations of Louis Bonaparte's coup d'état and, at the same time, specify the ideological elements in both accounts. Both Marx and Proudhon have emplotted the event as a story of a specific *kind*. The difference consists only in the kind of plot-structure, epical and farcical respectively, chosen by each to represent the event. In both cases, we witness the deposition of a meaning at the level of the Form of Content, which consists of the plot-structure used to represent events as figurations of a story of a specific kind. What one sees as an epic, the other sees as farce. Both interpretations are plausible, given the difference of political perspective informing them. We cannot, then, conclude that the story told by Marx is more historical than ideological, whereas the story told by Proudhon is more ideological than historical. If there is a difference between the degrees of historicality informing the two accounts of the same event, this must be said to arise at the fourth level of analysis stipulated by Hjelmslev's model: that of the Substance of Content.

Substance of Content and Ideology

It is only at the level of the Substance of the Content of the discourse that the difference between historical and ideological storytelling can be established. At this level, the representation of real events, emplotted as a story of a specific kind (as epic, romance, tragedy, comedy, or farce) can be identified as a special case of a general notion of the nature of historical reality. It is on this level of his narrative that Marx, for example, invokes the "class struggle" as the historical reality that at once justifies his emplotment of the *Eighteenth Brumaire of Louis Bonaparte* as a *farce* and explains why this farce could have taken place when, where, and how it did. On Marx's view, the farcical nature of the event derived from the failure of *all* parties in the conflict to discern that they were engaged in a *class* conflict and their resultant incapacity to act in a manner consistent with their respective class interests. Proudhon's failure to apprehend that class struggle was the key to the understanding of this event is what drove him, in Marx's estimation, to fall back upon the mythical notion of the "hero" to explain Louis Bonaparte's triumph. For Marx, the notion of "heroic" action could "explain" nothing, and the invocation of this notion by Proudhon to explain Louis Bonaparte's triumph is what marks Proudhon's "story" as "ideological" rather than "historical."

In what sense might we confidently affirm that the notion of the "hero" or that of "heroic action" is more "ideological" (and therefore less "historical") than the notion of "class struggle"? The usual response to this question, especially by Marxists, is that the notion of "class struggle" is more realistic, less "imaginary" (less "mythical") than the notion of "heroism." But wherein does the "realism" of the notion of "class struggle" consist? It is not as if the notion of "heroism" is alien to Marx's notion of history. Indeed, it must be said that Marx's characterization of the role of the proletariat in world history effectively endows this social class with all of the attributes of a "hero" (albeit a collective one).

But, and this is crucial to the distinction between a historical and an ideological account of historical events, Marx indicates that a class can be "heroic" in one phase of its development, become, as it were, "villainous" in another, and simply be swept from the scene in yet another. Whence the acuity of his observation that the bourgeoisie played a heroic role in the "tragic" events of 1789 only to become the protagonist of a "farce" in its attempt to replay the events of 1789 under the changed conditions of 1848. Unlike the notion of "heroism" used by Proudhon to explain the triumph of Louis Bonaparte, Marx's notion of "class struggle" is susceptible to being endowed with different specific contents at different times and places in history. This is one reason for considering the former as a mythical and the latter a historical concept.

Thus, although Marx's "farce" is not less "ideological" than Proudhon's "epic"—or for that matter, Marx's own suggestion that the events of 1789 were "tragic" in nature—the Substance of the Content of Marx's account is more historical than that of Proudhon's account. This is not because the historical record contains no accounts of heroic actions by individuals and groups. It is, rather, because a view of history centered upon actions, individuals, and groups considered to be more or less heroic provides no basis for discriminating between heroes and those individuals and groups that, as Marx put it with respect to Louis Bonaparte and his followers, only played the "parts" of heroes.

Considered as the Substance of the Content of Marx's conception of history, the notion of "class struggle" is of an entirely different order from Proudhon's notion of "heroism." Whatever the merits of this notion when considered as an explanatory principle of a determinate set of historical events, there is nothing ideological about it at all. This is indicated by the fact that the reality of class struggle is presumed by all historians of every conceivable kind of political persuasion or ideological orientation. Beyond that, this notion provides for the stipulation of a principle by which to admit the reality of heroic actions on the part of individuals and groups and at the same tune to discriminate between genuinely heroic achievements and those that only appear to be so. For unlike a notion of heroism that identifies it with a kind of spiritual superiority of one person over all others, the notion of class struggle links heroism, not with an ideal of individual success in a particular line of endeavor, but rather with the global effort of humanity to achieve the conditions of freedom from both natural necessity and social division.

CHAPTER TWENTY-ONE

The Suppression of Rhetoric
in the Nineteenth Century
{1997}

||||||||||||||||||||||||||||||||||||||||||||||||||||||||||||||||||||||||||||||||||||||||||||||||||||||||||||||||||||||||||||||||||||||||||

The concept of literature—as against stylized speech or writing in general—is a relatively recent invention. Moreover, the notion that literary writing is virtually unteachable is also a relatively recent idea. It was not always so. Prior to the early nineteenth century, what we call literature was called *belles-lettres*. It was regarded as a branch of rhetoric, which was itself considered to be the science of speech and writing in all their aspects, and the principles of which could be taught because they were regarded as inherent in the general human capacity to speak. One important practical difference between the kind of rhetorical theory that developed between the Renaissance and the late eighteenth century and the various theories of composition that supplanted it in the nineteenth century turned on differences between the notions of the nature of language itself that informed them. Put most simply, pre-nineteenth-century rhetorics recognized the figurative and tropical nature of all linguistic conventions and made of this recognition the basis of a general theory of speech as discourse, of which the various kinds of speech and writing (prosaic and poetic; narrative and dissertative; factual, fictive, and mixed; communicative, expressive, and performative) were treated as instances, the relations among which were presumed to be identifiable and the different possible uses of which in different situations could be specified.

This notion that all speech should be treated as discourse and that all discourse should be viewed as a function of the figurative and tropical nature of all linguistic conventions was what got lost sight of in the process of cultural reorganization that attended the transition from feudal to capitalist society in the early nineteenth century. It is this loss that explains both the mystification of "literature" and the peculiar idea of what basic "literacy" should consist of that inform the general ideology of writing and of which the presumed qualitative difference between them is the constituent element.

❧

The term *literature* inhabits the semantic field constituted by the nineteenth-century ideology of aestheticism, one effect of which has been to so mystify art in general and literary art in particular as to render the idea of teaching students how to produce them virtually inconceivable. The process of literary production has been rendered so mysterious by the ideology of aestheticism that the idea that we might presume to teach its principles, in much the same way that we teach basic literacy skills, is often regarded—especially in the departments of literary studies that are the principal beneficiaries of this ideology—as little short of heresy, as the ghettoized status of most programs in "creative writing" amply attests.

Yet, prior to its sublimation by the ideology of aestheticism, the kind of writing that came to be called literary only in the nineteenth century was not regarded as particularly mysterious at all, its principles were not viewed as unfathomable, and the teaching of those principles was not unthinkable. For before the invention of "literature" in the nineteenth century, rhetoric effectively served as a science of speaking, writing, and reading, on the basis of which instruction in their processes of production could be—and was—provided. This is why the suppression of rhetoric was a necessary precondition for the separation of literary from other kinds of writing, the constitution of "literature" as the virtual antithesis of mere literacy, and the establishment of the myth of the unteachability of the latter as against the teachability of the former. But any effort to lead students "from literacy to literature" presupposes the necessity of dissolving the presumed opposition between a writing that is merely literate and another that is distinctively literary. This project will entail the dissolution of the ideology of aestheticism that underwrites this opposition, the reconceptualization of literate and literary writing as simply different kinds of what is substantially the same activity, and the restoration of some version of rhetoric as the science of speaking, writing, and reading on the basis of which the teaching of both basic literacy and literary writing once again may be theorized and practiced.

It is no accident that the terms *literacy* and *literature* were coined and entered into general usage at about the same time, in the early nineteenth century, because they belong to the same process of a general reorganization of culture as that which attended the establishment and integration of the nation-state, the transition from an "estate" to a "class" organization of society, the advent of corporate capitalism, and the transformation of the masses from subjects into citizens capable of taking their place as functionaries in a system of production and exchange for profit rather than use. The separation of what had formerly been called belles-lettres from the general domain of "discourse," of which it once had been considered to be a branch or department, and its elevation to a new status for the designation of which the term *literature* was coined, were effects of this process of cultural reorganization. From that point on, literature would be regarded as a kind of writing, the value of which lay in part precisely in its differentness not only from speech but also from the kind of writing that would henceforth be considered to be merely literate.

The ideology of aestheticism from now on will teach that the difference between literary and merely literate writing is only a special case of the more fundamental difference, amounting to a strict opposition, between beauty (or the beautiful) and utility (or the useful). Literature is beautiful writing—writing that appeals, even fascinates, by virtue of its form alone, irrespective of its content or subject matter. The value of a writing that is merely literate, by contrast, will be held to reside less in its form than in its function, specifically its communicative function, its usefulness in serving as a medium for the transmission of information, thought, and—perhaps more crucially—commands, within every department of social life organized for the realization of purely practical ends or purposes. The ideology of aestheticism has it, as a matter of pride, that society does not need literature in the way that it needs literacy. Literature is a luxury, as anything that is merely beautiful is a luxury, which is to say as a supplement or ornament. But literature, as thus envisaged, becomes disposable in any situation in which the interests of work and struggle are conceived to take precedence over play or the restful contemplation of things merely beautiful. Or so the ideology of aestheticism would have it.

In these convictions, of course, the ideology of aestheticism reveals its complicity with the ideology of utilitarianism that comes to serve as the dominant theoretical basis for the ascription of value to the various practices of our society and, by extension, of our pedagogical institutions. These two ideologies, aestheticism and utilitarianism, conspire to deprive art in general of any claim to a distinctively cognitive authority and therefore of any practical utility. They conspire especially in the relegation of literary art to the status of a luxury, the social value of which varies in direct proportion to its scarcity, on the one hand, and, on the other, its uselessness as measured against the presumed need that every member of society is supposed to have of basic literacy. This is one of the reasons training in basic literacy skills comes to consist not so much of an introduction to a general writing practice that will culminate in the achievement of a capacity to produce a distinctively literary kind of writing as well, as rather of a training in a kind of writing in which every evidence of literariness is suppressed in the interest of making it useful.

On this formulation, the relationship of literacy to literature directs our attention to a problem that is as much theoretical as practical. The theoretical problem has to do with the difference, apprehended as an opposition, between literacy and literature—where literacy is considered as consisting of basic writing skills to be used primarily for the efficient communication of practical information, a certain kind of thought, and commands; and literature is considered as the product of a writing practice, the creativity of which is thought to consist of its capacity to permit the expression of intuitions, feelings, and thoughts of a certain impractical nature by virtue of their individuality, subjectivity, or idiosyncrasy, on the one side, and their status as products of a rare, inborn talent, even genius, on the other.

It is a commonplace of our pedagogical ideology that "creative" writing cannot be taught in the ways used—and used effectively, I might add—in programs designed to teach basic writing skills to the general run-of-the-mill undergraduate student. Literary writing, it is held by many, cannot be taught because, the ideology has it, only a small number of the mass of students come provided with the talent requisite for the cultivation of a specifically literary language, just as only a small minority are supposed to come equipped with the kind of sensibility permitting the cultivation of a capacity to appreciate the classics of literature.

I forbear discussing at length the extent to which this notion of the inherently literary type of student participates in the nineteenth-century myth of a genius distinctly "poetical" in nature and of a sensibility effectively identified with the passivity ascribed to women in the psychological economy of Victorian society. The feminization of artistic work in general and of literary work in particular goes hand in hand with the masculinization of other kinds of practical work in Victorian society and has had the same pacifying effect on male writers that the domestication of women has had on females in our society. This process of pacification works through the seemingly benign, twofold operation of simultaneously idealizing and marginalizing the social roles assigned to both groups. For literary writers, the idealizing process consisted of the ascription to them of a genius limited to the expression of a sensibility wholly imaginative (neither rational nor practical) in nature, a sensibility that distinguished them from those "real men" to whom the well-being, protection, and provision of the necessities of life to their families had been consigned as a right both genetic and generic in nature. Needless to say, this literary sensibility was tacitly conceived to be of the same nature as that which women were supposed to possess by virtue of their lack of a fully rational soul and their endowment with a practical capacity limited to the bearing and care of children, the maintenance of the home, and the provision of love and support for their husbands, and as having nothing of value to contribute to the management of public affairs consigned, by a right more divine than natural, to men whose practical talents were manifested in their capacities to repress both their feelings and their imaginations—which was to say, any impulse identifiably poetic in nature. It was this twofold process—the domestication of women and the feminization of literature—that underwrote and determined the masculinist ideology of the literacy movement throughout the nineteenth century in Western Europe and America.

This masculinist ideology explains why middle- and even upper-class women were for a long time denied access to literacy training while being allowed and even encouraged to cultivate their literary talents. The sexism of this ideology explains why training in grammar and logic would become established as the principal bases for literacy training, while poetic training in the techniques of literary writing would be excluded therefrom. Safely consigned to the preserve of literary writing, itself domesticated by its effective feminization, *poetic*, the art of linguistic figuration, could be left to the cultivation of those sensitive souls—male, female, and androgynous—who had no part to play in the real world of manufacture, business, politics, and war.

But this interpretation of the sociopolitical bases of what I have called the literacy system does not explain another exclusion required for its establishment in its nineteenth-century form. I refer to the progressive derogation of rhetoric in favor of the elevation of poetic to the status of the very principle of literarity, on the one side, and its effective repression, in favor of promoting grammar and logic as the twin components of training in basic literacy, on the other. What explains this subjugation or at least neutralization of the kind of knowledge that rhetoric provides for the understanding of principles of discourse production, exchange, and consumption, in a culture increasingly devoted to the promotion of both sciences and arts whose principal authority was thought to reside in their practical utility alone?

We know the reasons given in justification of this exclusion from the standpoint of the ideology of aestheticism: discourse composed on the basis of rhetorical principles of composition could be neither sincere (the touchstone of all genuinely poetic expression, according to Romanticist aestheticism), authentic (the ideal of post-Romanticist literary art down through Modernism), nor truthful (the principle of every Realism from Balzac's historicist version down to Georg Lukács's socialist variant). Rhetoric, whether considered to be the art of eloquence, the theory of representation and the composition of discourses, or the craft of persuasive speech and writing (a craft that specializes in the promotion of what Jakobson calls the "conative function" of language use), was officially condemned on ethical grounds by scientists, philosophers, theologians, and, above all, literary artists alike as the very principle of immoral speech.

Kant himself, in his *Critique of Judgment*, the founding text of the ideology of aestheticism, provided the ethico-economic justification for this condemnation. In comparison to scientific, philosophical, religious, and poetic discourse, Kant maintained, rhetoric (by which he meant oratory) produced nothing but fraudulent discourse. Rhetoric taught the art of appearing to be "serious" while actually engaging in a wordplay purely frivolous in nature. Unlike the poet, who pretended to be playing with words but was actually engaged in examining the most serious of matters and who therefore always delivered much more than he had promised, the orator always delivered less than he promised. This was because the orator traded in form alone, while pretending to deal in pure content, real value. The orator's seriousness, Kant maintained, is always feigned, because he is never concerned with truth, goodness, or beauty as ends in themselves but only as means to the end of producing an immediate emotional effect on his audience or, failing that, of bludgeoning them into submission to his point of view—against all reason, logic, or truth—by verbal means alone.

Given this notion of rhetoric, the truth of which is presumed in the vehement rhetoric that Kant uses to condemn it, one might have expected that the ideologists of utilitarianism would have embraced it as the keystone of a training designed to endow students with a literacy intended to be primarily practical in its uses, especially within the context of a triumphant capitalism in which making a profit by whatever means was rapidly becoming the rule rather than the exception.

But no such luck for rhetoric. No less an authority than Jeremy Bentham, the founding father of utilitarianism, joined Kant in condemning rhetoric as the very antithesis of rational discourse, as the pseudo-art of substituting "sound" for "sense," and as the enemy of that morally neutral speech alone capable of reflecting reality as it truly was, on the one hand, and of representing a purely rational, by which he meant a purely logical, thought, on the other.

What Bentham called "neutral speech"—characterized by a diction concrete, definite, and specific, a grammar that had been "orthologized" (which is to say standardized) and presided over by a logic that bore no relation to that of living conversation or dialogue, a speech that could be produced only by the process of written composition or, if spoken, could only sound like writing being read, which is to say, a grammatico-logical speech—became the Utopia of the literacy system set up in the nineteenth century in the United States to train a nation of rude farmers and foreigners in a comportment that would be proper in a political no less than a cultural sense. As Noah Webster put it, with his characteristic bluntness and "neutral" forcefulness: "our political *harmony* is concerned with a *uniformity* of language."[1] It is the ideal of the uniform that inspired the program for standardizing American English in the nineteenth century. This program entailed not only the elimination of dialectal variants and languages other than English but also the creation of a sociolect for that part of the citizenry whose social destiny was to serve as functionaries in the emerging manufacturing and business complex, whose political role was to be that of passively approving the policies decided on by the holders of power and wealth, and whose role in the cultural system was to be that of consumers only, never producers.

The poetic aspect of language was left to the cultivation of what would become a class faction of "literary writers," while the rhetorical aspect was domesticated into the principles of clear, concise, and sincere expository prose or those of forceful elocution appropriate for the kinds of mock debates carried out by lawyers, politicians, journalists, and what later became majors in departments of speech and communication. Though there remained a rhetorical dimension to the kind of literacy that was to be provided for every child entering the public school system, it was the rhetoric of anti-rhetoric, which, while masking itself as plain speech and practical prose, was in reality the rhetoric required of subjectivities whose principal function was to collect and communicate information, limit themselves to the practice of commonsensical thought, and save the expression of their feelings for their diaries and private correspondence, both regarded primarily as feminine genres.

What was really behind the condemnation of rhetoric in general as an inherently immoral or at least duplicitous discursive practice? What prompted the suppression of training in rhetoric during the period of formation of mass democracies, the nation-state, capitalism, and imperialism, and its progressive exclusion from programs designed for training students in basic literacy in the public schools of the country?

Anyone who knows the history of rhetoric or is willing to look at it from beyond the perspective provided by Plato's misrepresentations of it in the *Gorgias* and the *Phaedrus* will be able to answer this question easily enough.

First, rhetoric was born not so much as the art as rather the science (*technê*) of speech, language, and representation in general. It comes after the invention of artistic speech and writing and takes both these and their nonartistic counterparts as its object of study and analysis. As a general science of discourse, then, rhetoric purports to explain not only the principles of literary-artistic discourse but also those of all nonartistic, practical discourses, such as those of politics and the law, not to mention philosophy and history, and, more importantly, the relation of these to power—political, social, and economic. Rhetoric thus represents a kind of knowledge with a distinct social value insofar as it yields insights into the relation between political power and the control of language, speech, and discourse, which political elites always have recognized as a necessary basis for effective rule. If rhetoric always has been "the possession of the most highly literate" members of society, as Keith Hoskins remarks, this is because the most highly literate members of society always have belonged to the most powerful classes.[2] If the relationship among rhetoric, literacy, and social class power is as intimate as the history of that relationship suggests, then the democratization of society in the nineteenth century should have been attended by the extension of training in rhetoric to all classes of society as a necessary component in their political empowerment to which their training in basic literacy was meant to contribute. The exclusion of rhetoric from such training can thus be seen as an aspect of a more general program of political domestication of the mass of the citizenry by the powerful classes, who never ceased, incidentally, to provide training of a kind in rhetoric for their own children in elite schools and universities.

Second, rhetoric—especially as cultivated by the Sophists, its first practitioners—was conceived as the study and practice of speech, not only in politics but also and above all as politics, as the politics of language use, for purposes both defensive (against the power of the state) and offensive (in the exercise of that power). Rhetoric studies speech and language in its active rather than passive aspects alone; traditionally, it has been treated as the study of speech and language as used in those practical situations in which there is not only no agreement on first principles or on the facts of the matter at hand but not even any agreement on what shall constitute the facts themselves, situations in which first principles have to be hammered out in an operation more dialectical than demonstrative—as Aristotle himself insisted. This is why—from the fifth century BC in Sicily, where, according to legend, rhetoric was born, to the end of the eighteenth century, rhetoric was regarded as a sine qua non for the training of politically active citizens in democracies and of elites in aristocracies. Neither poetic, grammar, nor logic directly addresses the question of the politics of language use, and therefore any training that takes these—to the exclusion of rhetorical training—as providing the fundamentals of a basic literacy effectively deprives students of access to a kind of practical knowledge without which they can never develop their political-critical capacities fully.

Third, and most pertinently to our purposes, rhetoric served or intermittently aspired to be the science of figuration, a science not only of the figurative dimensions of discourse but of language understood as being figurative in its very nature, as being what speech-act theorists call performative or illocutionary, constitutive of every form of meaning—and, as such, a science taking precedence over and laying claim to being able to mediate among all the various kinds of representational practices resembling speech and language and at all levels of articulation, from simple nomination to the most sophisticated and formalized representations of pure logic.

The claim of rhetoric to be a general science of verbal and visual representation hinges upon the perception of the inevitably tropical nature of all discourses at every level of their articulation, from the phonemic-morphemic level up to that most elusive of gross structures of discursivity, the paragraph. Rhetoric claims to know the secret of the mode of expression called *poetic*, and this is why, from the standpoint of the modern ideology of aestheticism, it had to be suppressed. It claims also to know the secret of practical speech, speech in its active, conative, and political uses, speech as an instrument of power and rule. And this is why, from the standpoint of political elites who want a citizenry literate enough to receive messages but not so savvy as to be able to read them, it was desirable to suppress the teaching of rhetoric to the masses while continuing to cultivate its principles, in an appropriately masked form, which is to say, as "the humanities," in the education of their own children.

But here it will be objected that the very principle of poetic or literary writing is figurative language, the cultivation of which distinguishes it from mere literacy, as it has become identified with the cultivation of "literalist" discourse and productive of a sensibility that seldom rises above "literal-mindedness." Indeed, it might well be asked, is not literary writing above all the kind of writing that rises above and becomes qualitatively superior to mere literacy by virtue of its expression of a figurative mode of thinking and a specifically metaphorical manner of expression?

This was the position taken by I. A. Richards some fifty years ago in his still influential call for a new rhetoric, centered on a reconsideration of metaphor as the very soul of creative thought in general and culminating in a celebration of Coleridge's theory of the symbol as a "translucent instance, which, 'while it enunciates the whole, abides itself as the living part of that unity of which it is the representative.'"[3] Richards went on to desiderate the study of metaphor—considered the basis of that "skill in thought" that it alone made possible—into "discussable science."[4]

But while suggesting that metaphor should become the object of a science of our skill in thought, Richards concluded that "our reflective awareness of that skill" must inevitably be "very incomplete, distorted, fallacious, oversimplifying." Thus, the discussable science envisioned had as its business "not to replace practice, or to tell us how to do what we cannot do already; but to protect our natural skill from interferences of unnecessarily crude views about it." To be sure, he added that such a science should "above all . . . assist the imparting of that skill from mind to mind"; but he qualified this recommendation by noting that "progress here, in translating our skill from observation and theory, comes chiefly from profiting from our mistakes."[5]

Richards anticipated modernist—semiotic, structuralist, and poststructuralist—

rhetorical theory, which begins with the presumption of the figurative nature of all discourse, factual or realistic, historical or scientific, logical or poetic, narrative or analytical. But the notion of figuration that informs modernist rhetoric is utterly different from that proposed by Richards. Whereas he had regarded figuration as a mode of thought based on comparison, similitude, analogical thinking, the capacity of language to say one thing and mean another, and so on, modernist rhetorical theory, while presuming the figurativeness of all discursive practices, takes its rise in an apprehension of the utter arbitrariness of all figuration. Metaphor ceases to be the basis of figurative language and becomes once again, as it was in the seventeenth century, only one figure among many and by no means the essence of literary speech, as against merely literate or, for that matter, illiterate speech. If anything, it is the figure of *catachresis*, *"abusio"* or "misuse," that is considered to be the secret, not only of both figurative speech and its literalist counterpart but also of the relation between them. Merely literate speech or writing becomes only a special case of the abusive relationship that obtains between words and those other things in the world they are called upon to signify, but neither is less nor more abusive than its supposedly qualitatively superior counterpart, literary speech.

The application of this fundamental rhetorical hypothesis—that all language use is figurative in nature—to the study and teaching of discursive practices would prescribe an approach to teaching basic literacy in which the differences between a merely literate and a distinctively literary writing were considered to be simply a matter of different uses of the strategies of figuration common to both. It would not exclude the teaching of grammar and logic as elements of composition, but it would introduce them as tropical strategies neither more nor less conventional than those informing the production of literary works. It would distinguish between literate expository prose and a literary work on the basis of the extent to which the latter kind, unlike the former, makes of figuration and troping an element of its explicit content and in so doing demands that we confront the problem of the relation between the form and the content of discourses in terms of a general theory of figuration. In terms of such a theory, grammar, logic, and what we conventionally think of as poetic would be represented as components of every discourse, the enabling feature of which is nothing other than language's capacity to figurate.

This capacity, in turn, would be presented as being in everyone possessing the capacity to speak, not as some arcane gift of a talented few, those poets supposedly possessed of genius or of a sensibility different from that possessed by everyone else. Literary writing would be presented as what it manifestly appears to be, merely a species of writing in which the act of figurating is presented as an element of its manifest content as well as the dominant characteristic of its form. A merely literate writing, by contrast, would be presented as only another species of writing, as a mode of writing in which figuration is no less present but is systematically masked, hidden, repressed, in the interest of producing a discourse seemingly governed by standardized rules of diction, grammar, and logic that produce their distinctive meaning-producing effects by the employment of strategies of selection and combination just as figurative, however formalized, as any poetic discourse.

This argues of course for the utility of introducing students to basic writing by way of the study and imitation of the kinds of texts we conventionally call literary, not because such texts contain the moral and aesthetical wisdom of the ages (although some of them may do so) or because they incarnate a beauty or sublimity accessible only to poets endowed with a sensibility adequate to the apprehension thereof, but rather because such texts take language's power to posit and trope as a part of their manifest content. A literary text, in short, is any in which figuration itself is an *aspect of its content no less than of its form.*

It is in the consideration of such texts from a specifically rhetorical perspective, which includes but is not exhausted by grammatical, logical, and poetical analyses of them, that our students can be introduced to, taught the principles of, and perhaps even encouraged to imitate the practices of figuration in general. On this basis, they might be able to comprehend what is really going on, both on and beneath the surfaces, not only in literary discourse but in the peculiar kind of exercise in repression and sublimation that we call merely literate writing.

Every verbal artifact that we might wish to call *literary* always can be shown to feature the problem of figuration as an element of its manifest content. The difference between literary and merely literate writing would not be presented as residing in the presence of figurative language and tropical strategies of combination in the one and their absence in the other. As Paul de Man put it, in a seminal article entitled "The Epistemology of Metaphor":

> Contrary to common belief, literature is not the place where the unstable epistemology of metaphor is suspended by aesthetic pleasure, although this attempt is a constitutive moment of its system. It is rather the place where the possible convergence of rigor [in thought] and pleasure is shown to be a delusion.[6]

And this is because with the suppression of rhetoric, the modern conception of literary writing, based on the ideology of aestheticism, which identifies literature with poetry and poetry itself with the expression of genius, has effectively denied that the processes of linguistic figuration can ever be the object of scientific study— one aim of rhetorical studies.

CHAPTER TWENTY-TWO

Postmodernism and Textual Anxieties

{1999}

⁞⁞⁞

Of what possible use could postmodernism be to Eastern Europe? For that matter, what use is it to the West? The suggestion that postmodernism is something to be lived through or "survived" rather than cultivated and embraced (see Meštrović's essay)[1] seems to foreclose any serious consideration of these questions. But Eastern Europe[2] shares with its Western counterpart one problem that postmodernism addresses more seriously than its critics: this is the problem of history. For postmodernism is nothing if not a worldview based upon a distinctive conception of history: its nature, its meaning, and the different ways it can be studied and used.[3] And the reconstitution of history as a ground for the endowment of modernist social life with a meaning that transcends the interests and needs of a single generation is the problem that East and West have shared, possibly since 1956, but certainly since the collapse of the Berlin Wall, the dissolution of the Soviet Union, and the (putative) end of the Cold War. But postmodernism undercuts the foundationalist nature of the Western idea of historical knowledge. It insists that when it is a matter of studying the past, the historian must accept responsibility for the construction of what previously he or she had pretended only to discover.

The nations of Central and Eastern Europe face the problem of integrating the Stalinist past—indeed the whole of the twentieth century—into a coherent historical narrative that would at once justify their rejection of certain aspects of that past and affirm their continuity with it. So, too, in Germany, Italy, Spain, and to a certain extent even France, there exists the same kind of problem vis-à-vis the fascist, Nazi, and collaborationist past, and especially with respect to the genocide of the

[This essay was originally presented at a conference held near Lund, Sweden, in September 1996. The contributions to this conference were later published in a volume entitled *The Postmodern Challenge: Perspectives East and West*, edited by Bo Stråth and Nina Witozek (Amsterdam: Rodopi, 1999).]

Jews, not only a German but a generally Western crime as well. But in addition, Western European communities are searching for ways of integrating the past of the nation with what appears to be new, global forces that effectively dismiss the nation itself as a superannuated and inefficient relic of an earlier and now transcended system of political economy. Eastern European communities, on the other hand, attempt simultaneously to enter this global world and reconstitute the nation as a viable unit of social organization. These developments explain the pressures felt by historians both East and West to conceive new ways of integrating the immediate pasts of their national communities with a present that is experienced as being not only trans- but even anti-national in its dominant tendencies.

Historians always have problems with transitional moments in the histories of their subjects. This is not only because, properly speaking, every historical moment is a transition at some level of being between one phase or aspect of the historical process and another. It is also because a "transition" is precisely what *cannot* be represented in any medium (even cinema) because it is what happens "between" two states considered to be (relatively) stable: it is the moment of the "switch," the moment of the "trans-substantiation" in which the "wine" of one historical reality suddenly "becomes" the "blood" of another. And this moment cannot be represented because it has the same status as the blank space that divides two frames of a movie film. The moment in which something becomes something else or something other than what it had earlier been cannot be represented in verbal or visual images because this moment is precisely a moment of the absence of presence, the moment at which one presence is drained of its substance and filled with another. And on any scientific account of this phenomenon, it must be said that such a moment is over-determined—*too* full of causal forces, too fraught with "miracle" to be the subject of an *explanation*.

Take the problem of the transition between the "Middle Ages" and the "Modern Age." Dare we ask what "caused" this transformation? How could we, without inquiring first into whether the gap presumed to exist between the two periods in question (the "Middle Ages" and "Modernity") really existed or not? We must admit that the problem of the transition between the Middle Ages and Modernity can be said to exist only on the strength of our faith that something called "the Middle Ages" and something called "Modernity" actually existed and are not mere figments of our capacity to assign names to different parts of a continuum and create difference-within-continuity thereby.

In fact, the problem of the transition from—and therefore that of the distinction between—Modernity and Postmodernity is of the same aporetic order. Modernity can be defined as what came after the Middle Ages or as what came before

Postmodernity. But in that case, the substance of the concept of modernity still remains indeterminable.

It is this indeterminability of history that postmodernism knows—whether it knows that it knows it or not. Postmodernism knows that it comes after modernism even without knowing what modernism consisted of and without knowing what its own "posterity" consists of. This is because postmodernism extends the modernist project of demystifying the past to include the very "historical knowledge" on which the demystification was based. In the nineteenth century, a newly disciplined and professionally produced "historical knowledge" had been used to demystify the older feudal world of priestliness, aristocracy, and monarchy. It was historical knowledge that revealed the extent to which the Old Regime had been based on magic, delusion, fantasy, and fiction—in fact, a "made up" world. Over against this fictional or fantastical world, history set the truth of reality—the past about which one could have certain knowledge because, being "over and done with," it could change no further, and could therefore be an object of a purely "factual" determination. Postmodernism treats this idea of historical knowledge as being itself "made up."

This is not of course the whole story. Indeed, postmodernism is born in part as a response to what I wish to call the distinctively "modernist" events of the twentieth century.[4] One does not have to rehearse every event that makes our century different from any time preceding to make the case, but a few indications might be useful. First, it is only in our century that the full implications of industrialization (massive population expansion, urbanization, and international economics) and its effects (mass famine, boom and bust economic cycles, pollution of the ecosphere, world wars and mass death by techno-weapons such as the hydrogen bomb) have been realized. The scale, intensity, and reach of these events render them impervious to the traditional categories of historical representation and explanation. By this I mean that what we have been used to calling "historical consciousness" contains neither the categories nor the representational techniques required for the effective historicizing of these events. For example, these events do not lend themselves to the kind of "dramatistic" treatment that served historians for two millennia as the basis for the representation of specifically "historical" events. This means, among other things, that they do not lend themselves to interpretation by narrativization.

Second, the speed with which news of events in the technological age spreads over the globe and the rapidity with which they are archived and disseminated to worldwide publics, served by satellite television systems and computerized networks, have destroyed the traditional rhythms of pre-industrial transmission practices, which allowed for the gradual and selective absorption of events to what used to be called "the historical record." Sometime during the last fifty years, this "historical record" reached a condition of overload, much like those massive warehouses used to store the documents produced by modern states and corporations, glutted beyond capacity and incapable in any case of holding anything more than a fraction of the total documentary output. The closer one comes to the present, the more events are hidden behind the massive amounts of documents that attest to their occurrence.

Third, this condition of masking by means of over-documentation is itself a product of radically new, electronic instruments of recording and presentation— such as cinema, video, and digitalized photography—that possess such an awesome power to transform, metamorphosize, or otherwise manipulate images as to bring under question the traditional and traditionally simple idea of perception itself.[5] The image is no longer a recording or index of what might otherwise have simply been perceived by the five senses. Now, rather, the image is regarded as something produced or invented rather than found, as something that, because it was produced by the instruments of recording in the first place, can be infinitely re-produced and re-made such that the differences presumed to exist between the phenomenon and its nominal occasion, between the phenomenon and the image, between the original image and its reproduction or simulacrum, are gone by the board.

This is not to suggest that a postmodernist suspicion of documentation extends only to modernist events, for if modernist events appear infinitely complex and at the same time insubstantial due to the ways in which the media can be used to manipulate images and indices of them, one has only to look for a moment at past events—such as battles and revolutions or famines or the fall of empires—to realize that they are similarly complex and insubstantial and that their seeming substantiality and openness to perception were primarily functions of the paucity of the documents we have for them and the crudity with which they were recorded by their witnesses. With the multiplication of images of "historical" reality, we now appear to be further from rather than closer to the past itself.

It appears to me, then, that our century is justified in feeling detached from rather than continuous with the centuries that preceded it. We are separated from "the past" by some kind of quantum leap or radical change that has inaugurated a new order of historical existence.

There has been a qualitative transformation of what we used to think of as a "historical" event, a transformation that requires new categories for thinking about it and new techniques of representation to grasp its form and aspect. This sense of discontinuity between our modernity and the various modernities that have pre-ceded our own is what leads to the devaluation of every previous past. If the differ-ence between our immediate past and the more remote pasts of the old history appears greater than any similarities between them, then this more remote past—everything that is supposed to have happened before our century—can be appre-hended as simply a reserve of curiosities and "collectibles."[6] These can be wrenched from their historical contexts and inserted into any of various presentations of the past—less as documents, relics, monuments, or indices thereof than as merely *virtual* past objects or objects of a *virtual past.*[7]

Now, I would like to suggest that when it is a matter of representing past reality, postmodernism could teach us that a virtual past is the best we can hope for. Al-though we all know that the past—or certain persons, institutions, events, and so on—once existed or happened or lived, we also know that this past *no longer* exists, happens, or lives. Although there is indubitable evidence—in the form of monu-ments, relics, remains, and documents—that the past once existed, these traces of the past can be said to be effects whose original causes have ceased to exist. These remains live on into the present as indices of the past but they no longer function as effects of the (past) causal forces that originally produced them. They are now sets of effects belonging to one order of being sustained by causal forces belonging to another. Thus, for example, the Cathedral at Vezelay, France—a supreme "mon-ument" of late Romanesque and Early Gothic ecclesiastical art—is much more an effect of the nineteenth-century efforts of Viollet-le-Duc, its original restorer, and the French office of historical monuments, which maintains it, than it is of the efforts of its original builders or the culture to which they belonged.[8] And the same can be said for most of the institutions that make up the substance of our societies in the modern world.

Also, apropos of our attitude towards those "old things" that comprise our "his-torical heritage" and on the basis of which we are enjoined—by conservatives and liberals alike—to build our future, it seems to me that postmodernism offers us an eminently healthy attitude. It invites us to assess the past from the standpoint of its utility for the present—which is not to suggest that this "present" is something known in its essence or something to which we should commit ourselves without reservation. On the contrary, the "present" is as much a construction as the "past" or the "future." So, from a postmodernist perspective, when it comes to the aporias of history—the past, the present, and the future—we find ourselves caught be-tween or among three constructions. "Everything solid melts into air" indeed! But whose fault is this? It is not the fault of postmodernism. On the contrary, postmod-ernism is a response to this condition, itself a product of capitalist modernity.

It may be helpful as this point to specify some of the implications of a postmodernist idea of history and to index some of the fears and anxieties that postmodernism arouses in the devotees of old-fashioned or as it is called "professional" historical research. A well-known defender of traditional values (specifically, those of Victorian middle-class life), Professor Gertrude Himmelfarb, has spelled out the objections of professional historians to postmodernism in historical thought in the following terms:

> Postmodernism amounts to a denial of the fixity of any "text," of the authority
> of the author over the interpreter, of any "canon" that "privileges" great books
> over comic strips . . . of any correspondence between language and reality, in-
> deed of any "essential" reality . . . In history, it is a denial of the fixity of the past,
> of the reality of the past apart from what the historian chooses to make of it, and
> thus of any objective truth about the past.[9]

Professor Himmelfarb proceeds to draw out the moral (or rather the immoral) implications of this string of denials of "fixity": "Postmodernist history, one might say, recognizes no reality principle, only the pleasure principle—history at the pleasure of the historian."[10] This amounts to what she calls "the 'aestheticization'" of history, the conceptual opposite, in her view, of the cognitively and morally responsible "critical" history of the modern age. Indeed, Himmelfarb's view of truth, like that of her nineteenth-century prototypes, entails a moral commitment not to the truth in general—of which there may be many different species[11]—but to the specific kind of truth produced by historical research and writing. This kind of truth stands surely, not only against "anarchy," but also against every form of interested historical research that would revise the received historical "doxa" in either its form or its content. Thus, Himmelfarb ends her polemic in defense of "the reality principle" in historical scholarship with a diatribe against unredeemed Marxists, feminists, blacks and other ethnic groups, multiculturalists, and New Historicists for their "radicalist" efforts to revise what she finally calls "traditional history."[12] "In the common cause of radicalism," she concludes:

> structuralists and post-structuralists, new historicists and deconstructionists,
> have been able to overlook whatever logical incompatibilities there may be in
> their theories. Like the communists and socialists of an earlier generation, they
> have formed a "popular front" marching separately to a common goal.[13]

In the process, they have jettisoned not only the "discipline, moral as well as professional," required for historical "methodology," but also "the very idea of historical reasoning, of coherence, consistency, factuality." Consequently, she concludes, although "postmodernism entices us with the siren call of liberation and creativity . . . it may be an invitation to intellectual and moral suicide." For not only is postmodernism "radically anti-humanistic," it is also "profoundly anti-historical." While pretending to free men from the "burden of history," it actually only frees them from the "burden of humanity." In this, its "liberationist" impulse, postmodernist history reveals itself to be "not a new and higher form of the discipline" but discipline's very "negation."[14]

I do not wish to dispute Professor Himmelfarb's characterization of some of the implications of postmodernist historical thinking for traditional ways of doing history. But I would like to point out that she shows a distinct lack of interest in accounting for the appeal of postmodernist history.[15] And she certainly does not historicize her own position and ask whether there might not be good reasons for the appeal of postmodernism to scholars and intellectuals less satisfied than she is with present social realities and desirous of conceiving of ways of thinking beyond them.

It might be illuminating, however, to speculate on the import of her shrewd insight on the relation between what Fredric Jameson calls "the ideology of the text" and postmodernism. Postmodernism, she says, is based on the denial of the "fixity of any text." A bit later, she equates this to the denial of any "fixity of the past." And she is fully justified in this equation, for it follows from her identification of the heart of postmodernism, its "textualist" bias.

"Textualism" is not, of course the only feature of postmodernism, but it is crucial for the understanding of postmodernist conceptions of history and the anxieties postmodernism arouses in anyone who might still be devoted to "traditional" history. For it is indeed the case that traditional history—like tradition itself—is based upon a fundamentalist belief in the "fixity of texts." Textualism does indeed deny the fixity of texts and therewith any possibility of definitively fixing the meaning of any "history" based on texts themselves. But it is necessary to spell out a bit more in detail than Professor Himmelfarb has done the specific kind of textualism on which postmodernism is based.

By textualism, I mean the idea that the written text constitutes a paradigm of culture, that cultural production can best be understood on the model of textual production, and that the interpretation of culture is best carried out by practices of reading exactly analogous to those used in the reading of texts.[16] On the face of it, there is not much in his position to give offense to the most traditional of humanists, who, insofar as they are philologists or old-fashioned historians, might be expected to carry a conception of the "world as text" into their analysis of any cultural artifact. But the "text" being invoked by postmodernists as a paradigm of both culture and selfhood is not the text of the humanists. It is a text that is always at odds with itself, a text that knows neither its archetype nor its genealogy, a perverse text that may be said to write its reader quite as much as its writer can be said only to read it. For the postmodernist textualist, the text is a tissue of tropes and figures, a "self-consuming artifact" that always obscures what it seems to wish to reveal, undoes at the figurative level of enunciation what it seems to be saying at the literal level and the reverse, and ends up displaying itself as a kind of endless "free play" that recognizes neither logic nor rationalism as its master. A denial of the "fixity of texts" indeed.[17] But if the fixity of texts were denied, so too must be denied the fixity of the line supposed to exist between ideological and objective versions of historical reality. For postmodernists, this line is always shifting, depending upon the way in which objectivity is being defined in the social sciences, but it is always shifting in such a way as to absorb objectivity to ideology—in order to expose objectivism in the social sciences as itself an ideology. And the idea that objectivism is itself an ideology has important implications for the conceptualization of the social sciences at the present moment.

It is a commonplace of contemporary post–Cold War talk that we have at last become post-ideological, as if the breakup of the Soviet Union confirmed the claim of the United States that its own foreign policy had been based on "reality" while that of its Russian enemy was based on "ideology." Whence the well-known "end of ideology" argument on which Francis Fukuyama based his seemingly "postmodernist" book on the end of history itself.[18] From a postmodernist perspective, of course, it is not "ideology" that has ended with the putative defeat of "communism," as rather that ideology of objectivism that purported to be able to distinguish between "ideology" and "reality" on the basis of an appeal to the "facts" of "history." From a postmodernist perspective, the alleged "end of ideology" is nothing more than an aftereffect of the triumph of the ideology of objectivism itself. From a postmodernist perspective, our view of history is and can only be ideological through and through, with objectivism being the ideology that happens to enjoy a precarious position of hegemony at the moment. The important distinction from a postmodernist point of view is not between ideology and objectivity but between ideological constructions of history that are more or less open about the "constructed" nature of their versions of history and more or less willing to make of their own modes of production elements of their contents. Postmodernist versions of history are like those movies about movie making or those novels about novel-writing or those (Brechtian) spectacles that insist on drawing attention to their own "fictionality." Of course, such versions of history are seldom produced by professional historians—since what it means to *be* a professional historian is to have become committed to the "ideology of objectivity"—but who (other than the profession itself) authorized professional historians to determine what is "proper" and what is not in the representation of history? Does one have to believe in "the fixity of the past," the "fixity of texts," "moral as well professional" discipline, and "the reality principle" as defined by Professor Himmelfarb in order to have the right to construct a truthful version of the past that is at the same time implicitly or even explicitly critical of the present? If postmodernist notions of history are informed by a critique of the ideology of objectivism, this does not necessarily mean that they are opposed to the truth and committed to lie, delusion, fantasy, or fiction. It means rather that postmodernism is more interested in reality than it is in truth as an end in itself. But postmodernism recognizes that "reality" is always as much constructed in discourse as it is discovered in the historical record. Which means that postmodernist "objectivity" is aware of *its* own constructed nature and makes this work of construction the subject of its discourse.

It is in their commitment to determining the limits of reality that postmodernist ideas of history find the grounds for an alliance with "literature," by which I mean "literary writing" in its distinctively twentieth-century or "modernist" form.[19] For it is or was modernist literary writing that, in its effort to probe the limits of "the real," transcended so many of those distinctions that, having become dogmas, underwrote the illusions of objectivism in the modern social and human sciences. Among the distinctions that have been so transcended are:

1) That between events and their representation in discourse. Postmodernists believe that events exist and have existed in the real world but that in our efforts to represent them, we inevitably obscure them or distort what might have been perceptions of them.

2) That between documents and (literary) texts. Postmodernists believe that all (written) documents (what an older scholarly tradition called "monumenta") are texts and that this means that they must be submitted to the same explicative techniques as those used on literary texts. This belief opens up the document to criticism of the fictional nature of its "literalness" and the revelation of its systematic distortion of its referents, even while it pretends to be nothing but an innocent index of some process or institution of its context.

3) That between (literary) texts and their social contexts. Postmodernists do think that the social context is itself a text or is apprehensible only by way of texts. This idea challenges the objectivist contention that while the text can be read only by way of the most arcane hermeneutic and diplomatist prac-

tices, the context is immediately accessible to commonsensical procedures of reading and interpretation.

4) That between literal and figurative speech. Postmodernists think that any attempt to describe or represent reality in language must run up against the fact that there is no literal language, that all language is in its "essence" figurative. Therefore, textualists think, the text is always saying something more or other than it seems to be saying; so its "truthfulness" can be determined only after interpretation. The truth or the facts cannot be used to interpret the text because any version of the truth is itself another text.

5) That between the referent of a discourse and the subject of a discourse. Postmodernists believe that the subject of a discourse is always being substituted for its apparent referent. Objectivism confuses this constructed subject for the referent. It is not the events that are constructed, but rather, first, the facts and, second, the subject of the discourse. In historical representation, this process of double construction leads the historian further and further away from the referent rather than closer and closer to it. Postmodernist objectivism takes this process of alienation of the referent into account and features it as an element of its own discourse.

6) That between fact and fiction. Since facts are themselves linguistic constructions, "events under a description," *facts* have no reality outside of language. So while events may have happened, the representation of them as *facts* endows them with all the attributes of literary and even mythic subjects.

And, finally,

7) That between history and literature. Postmodernism presumes that since historical writing is a kind of discourse, and especially a narrative discourse, there is no substantial difference between *representations* of historical reality and *representations* of imagined events and processes. But it goes further than this and maintains that modernist literary writing is more "objective" than historical writing based on facts insofar as it features its own modes of production as elements of its "contents." It is this auto-referentiality of the modernist literary text that liberates it from its status as "fiction" and permits us to see the ways in which, simply by the absence of such self-reference, the traditional historical text inevitably falls into "ideology." This does not mean that self-referentiality guarantees an avoidance of ideology, only that it guards against the ideology of objectivism, the ideology that does not know itself as such.

It is easy to see why the custodians of culture and society in Western Europe and the United States—self-proclaimed "victors" over their former "communist" opponents in the Cold War—should fear the spread of textualist ideas among the human and social sciences. Texualism undermines the claim to moral authority of those "truths" (yes, in quotation marks) about politics, society, and culture produced by the human and social sciences on both sides of the Cold War since 1945. Textualism refuses the distinction between "objectivity" and "ideological" distortion on which the human and social sciences in Western Europe were founded in the late nineteenth century. And this refusal is, indeed, something worthy of support—in the West to be sure, but in the East especially—and especially insofar as the West is concerned about (and wishes to control?) the future of the East.[20] If this is the case, then obviously the East and the West both need postmodernism—but for different reasons.

I have seen evidence that many Russian scholars and very many Western ones seem to think that the "victory" of the West (capitalism) over the Soviet Union (communism) confirms the validity not only of Western free market economic practices and American democracy but also bourgeois historical consciousness and Western social sciences. In the face of a need to reconceptualize the pasts of Eastern European communities, historians of these countries are being advised to jettison dialectical materialism and take up Western, bourgeois "social scientific" methods of historical reconstruction and explanation. In my view, this is the last thing that Russian—or any other—society needs.

First, because no one "needs" any specific social scientific methodology or conception of history. Secondly, because both the social sciences and conceptions of history are more or less useful depending upon the situations in which communities find themselves. If "utility" is substituted for "needs" in any assessment of what is desirable for any given community at any given moment in its development, it is obvious that a postmodernist conception of history could be of better service to Eastern European countries today than any version of Western objectivism. Indeed, Western nations would profit as well from a good dose of postmodernist historical consciousness insofar as it might help dispel the illusion of their historians that the triumph of capitalism in the Cold War confirms the objectivity and the realism of the social sciences developed in the West for the prosecution of that conflict. But the most important contribution that postmodernism might make to Eastern European historians today would be to permit them to face the question of how national communities can *begin again*. Insofar as historical inquiry can contribute to the answering of such a question, it can do so, not by looking for the single truth about the origins of the nation or the one true account of its formation over time, but by multiplying *possible* accounts of both origins and evolutionary patterns. This would be consistent with the postmodernist conception of historical inquiry articulated by Michel Foucault in his later work. It is perfectly legitimate to write the history of the past, Foucault wrote, but much more interesting and ultimately more productive to imagine the history of the present.

There are many ways to characterize the disciplines of knowledge production—by the genera of objects they have chosen as their own, by their methods of analysis, or by their function in the societies they serve. But the disciplines of the human and social sciences can be defined as well by the anxieties and fears that motivated their establishment as special fields of study in the first place. Modern sociology and psychology are cases in point. The former is an obvious response to the fears and anxieties caused by the socially disruptive effects of industrialization and urbanization in the West; the latter a response to the fears and anxieties caused by the destabilization of the notion of the self that served as the subject of post-Renaissance ethics, politics, and law. The establishment of the field of anthropology was a product of a response to the fears and anxieties aroused by the experience of empire in the late nineteenth century.

The study of history is another matter. Until the early nineteenth century, historical studies were the domain of amateurs, dilettantes, pedagogues, antiquarians, genealogists, and devotees of various religious and political confessions. Except for the necessary languages and perhaps a certain legalistic interest in public documents, no particular expertise was needed to study the past. It helped to have had practical experience in the field one was studying: the history of war was regarded as a proper subject for former soldiers, the history of public institutions for retired legists, histories of families by members, and so on. While since the Renaissance there had been scholars who named themselves historians, the study of the past for use by teachers, moralists, and other custodians of the public good had not required any particular license or introduction to a special methodology for people interested in the study of the past. Only in the nineteenth century was the profession of historian disciplinized, moved into the universities and academies, endowed with the status of *Wissenschaft,* and subsidized by the newly forming nation-states as providers of services those states could not do without.

On the face of it, it seems strange that a government would pay a group of men to study the past of the nation that it had been charged to manage and supervise. One can understand well enough that states would pay administrators, teachers, police and military establishments, and even natural scientists and physicians to serve the citizenry. But what earthly reason would impel states to pay a group of scholars to study the past, not as an aid to the fulfillment of their duties as teachers and moralists, but as an end in itself, as a contribution to knowledge—as if a knowledge of the past, not only the national past but of any past whatsoever, were a good in itself? The answer is obvious, of course. In the nineteenth century, historical studies were disciplinized (institutionalized, moved into the universities, constituted as a kind of science) in order to provide legitimization for those nations whose origins were as obscure as their ethnic composition was uncertain. What the newly disciplinized cadres of historians were supposed to allay were the fears aroused by the uncertainty of origins and the anxieties inspired by the specter of hybridity or mongrelization. By providing for the nation an equivalent of what the genealogist provided for the family, professional historians of the nineteenth century not only established the purity of the group's bloodlines but also confirmed the claim of the dominant ethnic group within the nation to the land it ruled.

So much is obvious—and commonplace. Historians studied periods and places other than those of the nations to which they belonged; and they made contributions to the knowledge of pasts that manifestly bore no genetic or genealogical relation to their own nations. They also debated among themselves and with members of other disciplines questions about the nature of history, how best to study it, what social uses it might properly serve, and so on, in ways that had not been thought of previously. Not thought of because previously historical studies had not laid claim to the status of a science, with standards of objectivity for the assessment of evidence, and legitimator of the nation's origin and substance.

But not thought of also because the newly disciplinicized "history" had radically changed the content of that "history" of which "historians" were supposed to write a "history." They had removed the "future" from consideration as an aspect of "history." Earlier forms of historical reflection had often been openly undertaken as basis for an effort to predict the future or divine its general drift or at least to assess the possibilities for acting in the present. No more. From the mid-nineteenth century on, historical studies would have the task of studying only what had already happened, what was over and done with and could not be undone, what lay in comforting fixity beyond the horizon of living perception in the past, and what could be known with certainty because it could no longer not be what it was. All this was undertaken in order to allay the fears and anxieties of an uncertain origin and fears of corruptive mixtures of blood, genes, and essences.

But if history was disciplinized in order to allay the fears and anxieties of new social constituencies obsessed by a desire for purity of blood and soil, these were not necessarily the fears and anxieties of the discipline that promised to allay them. Historians' anxieties were of another order, having to do with the nature and status—cognitive and moral—of the knowledge they were producing. For historical studies had been disciplinized without having gone through anything like the "Copernican Revolution" that had laid the foundation for the modern scientific study of the natural world. History was supposed to study the human past, humanity insofar as it differed from the rest of nature and transcended the constraints of merely natural determination. Since the agent of history was man, and since man transcended the limits of merely natural determination, this meant that historical causation differed radically from natural causation. But if this was the case, of what did a specifically historical (as against a naturalistic) explanation consist? Moreover, if, as the doxa had it, historical events differed from natural events in virtue of their individuality—their uniqueness and unrepeatability—how were they to be comprehended, grasped in their individuality, and subjected to considerations of a minimally objective kind?

These two issues—the nature of the agent of history and the method by which to grasp the effects of this agent's acts—were resolved by the incorporation into history's procedures of the one technique that attested to its status as a mythological activity and its linkages to literary art. This technique was narration. By the narrativization of facts, presumed to have been established by scientific or at least "objective" procedures, historical studies positioned itself at the confines between theology and metaphysics, on the one side, and the emergent "therapeutic" social and human sciences of psychology, sociology, political economy, and anthropology, on the other. At this position within the circle of the sciences, history could serve as a paradigm of a zero-degree of social and political factuality. It could content itself with the activity of establishing the truth and reality of social facts, which could be drawn on by the other social and human sciences whose "realism" could be confirmed in the extent to which its "facts" were of a "historical" nature.

CHAPTER TWENTY-THREE

Guilty of History?

The *longue durée* of Paul Ricoeur

{2 0 0 7}

⁜⁜

In his book *Memory, History, Forgetting* (*La mémoire, l'histoire et l'oublie*, 2000),[1] Paul Ricoeur reiterates that he had conceived the work as a supplement to his great trilogy, *Time and Narrative* (*Temps et récit*, 1983–85), and his autobiography, *Oneself as Another* (*Soi-même comme un autre*, 1990), because he had, as it were, forgotten forgetting.[2] This forgetting of forgetting was important for Ricoeur because his reflections on history and historical writing, undertaken to provide a basis for the reconstruction of the modern (Western) humanistic *trivium* of history, literature, and philosophy, had not, in his own opinion, done justice to memory and its relation to historical consciousness. *Time and Narrative* had been a magnificent, really Herculean effort to redeem historical consciousness as a crucial component of the modern Western mind and to establish historical knowledge as both mediator between contemporary and traditional (classical and Christian) metaphysics under threat by modernity itself in the guise of relativism, skepticism, and Heideggerian existentialism. His aim had been to show, after the manner of Kant, how history—demeaned by positivists, existentialists, analytical philosophers, and skeptics in general—was not only possible but was also necessary to a properly human conception of our humanity, our identities as both individuals and members of communities, and our roles as good citizens of the polities to which we belonged. Put in somewhat different terms, it might be said that in his great trilogy, Ricoeur wanted to show how the past bore upon the present, how the past could responsibly be remembered in the present, and how this remembrance could be used to justify belief in a better future in spite of the realization that, in any strictly "objective" account of history, there was little reason to feel sanguine about humanity's future or proud of its past. To be sure, Hegel had provided his own version of a theodicy

[This piece was written as a review article of Paul Ricoeur's *Memory, History, Forgetting* and was published in the journal *History and Theory*.]

or justification of the ways of God to humans in the form of a philosophy of history. But Ricoeur could not abide Hegel's notion of the "plot" of this history and especially the way the Hegelian story ends, that is to say, Hegel's idea of the modern age. Hegel's modernity could not be ours. We have had too much history and, moreover, since Hegel's time, history of a different kind. This is modernity-history, as much a product of "the great crimes" of the twentieth century as it is of Western humans' astonishing "progress" in the mastery and destruction of their world. In a way, it can be said that if we are suffering from anything, it is from too much history. The guilt producing that sickness unto death from which we suffer is guilt by history.[3]

Recently, I heard it said that Ricoeur's "problem" was that he never "got over" Heidegger—it might have been added, just as Heidegger never succeeded, despite all his efforts, in "getting over" metaphysics. This meant that Ricoeur's deeply conservative instincts led him to resist—in the name of Plato, Aristotle, and Saint Augustine, the "constellation" of his conscious philosophical commitments—the kind of radical break with tradition that Heidegger wished to effect in Western thinking. It is my conviction that, like Heidegger, Ricoeur genuinely wanted to think "the new," but not in the modernist sense in which the "new" is identified with "the modern" itself. He was prevented from doing so because to embrace the "new" in the sense of "the modern" would be to grant a presupposition of contemporary modernism that demands a complete break with "the past," with tradition, heritage, ancestry, the origin, the archaic, and everything else that presumes the relevance of "the past" to the understanding and valorization of "present life." But it was not to save the past either that Ricoeur spent fifty years thinking about history.

I begin with a characterization of the theoretical background against which Ricoeur's work in philosophy of history has been elaborated over the last five decades.[4] This is necessary to account for the amount of labor he has expended in trying to transform "history" into a master discipline that, properly understood, could provide answers to the great existential questions raised by the advent of what he calls "'our' modernity." Our modernity Ricoeur viewed as both a problem and an opportunity for the West: a problem because in its "modernity," the West had consummated the great programs of demystification that had deprived us of the consolations of religion and the certainties of metaphysics; an opportunity because the demystification had forced Western humanity to face the fact of its own responsibility to and for "history."

Ricoeur's *philosophical* interest in modern professional historians' inquiry into the past and its relation to fiction was wrapped up in the first two volumes of *Time and Narrative*, which was more about narrative explanation in history, fiction, and philosophy than about historical method.[5] In volume 3 of this work, he did reflect on the metaphysics of history, but without, he said later, taking into account the relation of memory to history. It is memory, after all, that compels us to confront the enigma of how what is past can perdure into the present and, no matter how we might wish it, that refuses to go away on command but remains present to consciousness, even getting in the way of perception and pressing for attention however distracted we may be by current affairs. Memory, or a sense of absent presence, is the basis of a specifically historical consciousness, even if history has conventionally been presented as a corrective to memory and a more reliable approach to the study of the past than "memorization."

And yet, why the invention of history, a scholarly if not scientific discipline for the study of the past? After all, all cultures have an interest in memory and customs or institutions designed to discipline memory or turn it to the uses of the group, but not every culture has developed historical consciousness in the same way as the West. Ricoeur regards memory as more fundamental for the understanding of the human condition than historical inquiry, for memory is still in a certain sense "wild," belonging more to (human) nature than to culture. History seeks to discipline memory by setting up standards regarding what should be remembered and in what manner and what form. Thus, history is memory cultivated in the interest of producing a "collective" past on the basis of which a collective identity can be forged. In many respects, therefore, historical knowledge is disciplined memory, based on some extra-historical criterion of what can be legitimately remembered and, indeed, what ought to be remembered and what ought to be forgotten by members of the community.

The examination of the history-memory connection provides Ricoeur with a whole new departure for the consideration of the social and political, which is to say, the ideological function of historiography in the modern era. In an earlier work, *Lectures on Ideology and Utopia* (*L'idéologie et l'utopie,* 1997), Ricoeur had reversed the conventional assessment about the relation among history, ideology, and Utopian thinking. Whereas the received opinion was that ideology "distorted" history and Utopian thinking simply avoided it, Ricoeur tried to salvage Utopian thinking as a way of integrating the future into history. As for the idea that ideology "distorted" history, he argued that the only "distortion" of "historical reality" was that which purported to be completely and unequivocally "true." Historiography was not a science precisely insofar as it tried to ignore the present and the future as aspects of the historical process. He thought that professional historians were too narrowly fixated on "the past" to comprehend fully the contribution to the understanding of the present that a fully realized historical consciousness could make. He was interested, vitally interested, in the relation between historical consciousness (of which professional historical inquiry was but one manifestation) and what he called "the historical condition" (which he regarded as a product of the West's discovery that history was the story of humankind's own self-creation). Indeed, Ricoeur envisioned nothing less than the transformation of historical consciousness into a comprehensive worldview, a philosophy of life, and a kind of therapy for a West deprived of its sense of selfhood and its pride of place in world culture by the disastrous wars and "the great crimes" of the twentieth century. After the death of God and the end of metaphysics, history seemed to be the only thing "we" had left on which to build an ethics of care (*Sorge*) and a politics of responsibility.

So grandiose a calling for history, the humblest, the least scientific, the least presentist, the most contemplative of the human sciences seems at first glance outlandish. After all, historical studies is the last of the "sciences" known to Aristotle (unless of course one considers philosophy a science) surviving into the modern world. It has retained its respectability in large part by its insistence that it is *only* a commonsensical practice of inquiry into the past, needing neither philosophical justification nor a sophisticated theoretical apparatus to do its work.

To be sure, certain great historians have risen to sublime heights, producing works that serve as paradigms for successive generations of professional historians to admire but not necessarily to emulate. What is called the "ordinary" historian, the "working" historian, the "bread-and-butter" historian, the "nuts-and-bolts" historian, the foot soldier of the profession working "in the trenches," in order to add to the information we have about the past however minimally—this is the ideal held up by the masters of the profession to its tyros, apprentices, and journeymen practitioners. Modesty, deferral of judgment, caution, prudence, patience, attention to detail—these are the virtues of the historian: hardly the basis of a "worldview," much less of a "philosophy of life." Rather more a tactic for getting through a scholar's day in an ordinary way.

Yet over the course of his long career as a philosopher, Paul Ricoeur came to believe that what he called "the historian" implicitly harbored an attitude toward the world, a certain manner of approaching the world's enigmas and paradoxes, and a certain awareness of the relation between time and humanity that, if adequately expanded and refined, could close the gap, ethical as well as epistemological, between professional historical research, on the one hand, and the philosophy of history, on the other, to create a mode of consciousness adequate to the imperatives of "our" modernity. To be sure, what he called "the historian" was less a professional specialist in the study of a given era of the past than a combination of student of the past, philosopher of time, and poet of representation. He thought that this particular combination of intellectual roles had become possible only in the modern epoch, which is to say, in "our" time, because every philosophy of history is a distillation of the experience of temporality peculiar to a given place and epoch in world history. Our time and our place is the *chronotope* (Bakhtin's helpful term)[6] of globalization on the cultural plane, internationalization on the political plane, and universalization on the moral plane.[7] This is our modernity, the moment when we must choose between remaining isolated parts of the common humanity (each of us frantically defending the truth of his or her own little "history") and leading the rest of the world into the promised land of a single, unified, and genuinely universal "history."

Memory, History, Forgetting is in many respects Ricoeur's *summa;* it brings together and distills all the main ideas developed since his first two books, the first on Karl Jaspers (1947),[8] the next on Gabriel Marcel and Jaspers (1948). The title of the latter book—*Gabriel Marcel el Karl Jaspers: Philosophie du mystère et philosophie du paradox*—is instructive.[9] The younger Ricoeur (he was thirty-four when the book on Jaspers was published—five of those years spent in a German prisoner of war camp) existentialistically believed that human being was a mystery, human existence a paradox. But he did not believe that humanity was (as Sartre had it) a "useless passion"; nor did he believe that humans are only what humans do or happen to have done. He thought that there was something intrinsically "human" in humankind, not so much an "essence" or a "substance," as, rather, a *Tendenz, Streben,* or *Stimmung,* which, following Heidegger, he will later come to call "care" (*le souci, die Sorge*). On the contrary, the younger Ricoeur was or wished to be the antithesis of a Sartrean existentialist—the good existentialist, the responsible citizen, the bourgeois philosopher, the optimist who thought not only that human life was meaningful but that meaning was a human creation, a product of actions taken, as Socrates taught, by humans always seeking the good.[10]

I am not going to try to summarize *Memory, History, Forgetting,* because it is too finely textured, too rich in allusion and citation, too "dialectical," and really too long to be adequately summarized. Ricoeur knew this and tried out what he called "a new form of presentation" that breaks down the text into levels of generality and provides "guidelines to the reader at the main strategic points of the work that will tell the reader at what point I am in the investigation."[11] There are three main parts ("On Memory and Recollection"; "History, Epistemology"; and "The Historical Condition") and an "Epilogue" entitled "Difficult Forgiveness" (*le pardon difficile*). The titles of the parts do not quite line up with the three topics indicated in the title of the work as a whole (*Memory, History, Forgetting*), because the "forgetting" alluded to in the title seems to be assimilated to the topic of "The Historical Condition." At first blush, this seems strange because, on the face of it, it suggests that "the historical condition" must have more to do with "forgetting" than with remembering or recollecting, which is what "history" is usually thought to be about. But it will turn out, once we make our way to the end of this long and difficult book, that history is indeed as much about forgetting as it is about remembering and that, indeed again, a great deal of history has been written in order to cover over or hide or deflect attention from "what really happened" in the past, by creating an "official version" that substitutes a part of the past for the whole.

We can immediately see, however, that "the historical condition" indicates an existential situation in which human beings are caught in a complex interplay of the three modes (called *extases* in Ricoeur's earlier work) of temporality: present, future, and past, in which conventional historical knowledge (the history of the historians) has the function of obscuring and repressing recognition of that "being towards death" that is the ultimate cause of human anxiety, melancholy, and despair, and the principal impediment to the achievement of the kind of love that would make a creative "forgiveness" (of oneself as well as of others) possible. Historians show us that we can adequately "recollect" that past that is present to us in the form of memories and tokens, documents or monuments, as the case may be. And they can, in the process, create for us a public (or "collective") memory. But being based on documents and proofs of a quasi-juridical nature, the professional historians' accounts of the past do not, because they cannot, deal with those aspects of the past experienced in memory as absent presences demanding remembrance—if not justice and compensation—for offenses given by their own communities to their humanity.

Historians purport to correct memory by asking what of it can be documented and proven as true. But memory, whatever else it may be, has to do more with emotions than with facts: the memory traces that matter are those that come in the form of an image charged with an emotional valence. For us, in "our" time, in "our" modernity, the emotion in question, the emotion that has to be dealt with in a way that is more important than that appertaining to physical violence, is humiliation. Our age, our modernity stands condemned not only for having visited more physical violence on more people than any other age, but primarily for having developed the institutions and instruments for the systematic humiliation of entire populations.

I am referring, of course, not only to the Holocaust but also to a number of other political programs designed, so it seems, to abject that very humanity that the rest of "history" seemed to have been striving to create. It is the Holocaust, however, that constitutes the moral center of Ricoeur's effort to save history as a way of justifying the ways of man to God—an anthropodicy, a vindication of a merely human justice in the face of the existence of a humanly created evil in the world.[12] This is why historical consciousness needs, in addition to an adequate theory of memory, a theory of forgetting as well. But not an indiscriminate forgetting as a way of forgiving. Rather, a way of forgetting that will distinguish between what can be legitimately forgiven and what cannot. This distinction is the burden of the tortured and torturing "Epilogue" to Ricoeur's *summa*: "Difficult Forgiveness."

Ricoeur offers the epilogue on forgiveness as a supplement to the three main parts of the book proper. Earlier he had said that he had written this book because, in his massive *Temps et récit* (*Time and Narrative*), which wished to straighten out the relation between history and fiction in the light of their shared form of narrative, he had neglected to deal adequately with "memory" and "worse yet" with "forgetting, the median levels between time and narrative."[13] But now, having wrapped up the memory problem to his own satisfaction in Part 1, he finds himself faced with a problem that had inspired him to conceptualize "the historical condition" from the beginning: the problem of unbinding an individual or a group from its past, of being able to forget events of the past "that won't go away," but live on obsessively in the consciousness of later generations and impede the capacity of living generations to get on with their lives, make new beginnings, and enter their futures with confidence and hope.

Not that Ricoeur preaches the possibility of a "happy consciousness" set up against the slings and arrows of an "unhappy history."[14] The point is that memory and history are not after the same thing in "the past" upon which they commonly fix. History is about the "truth" of the past, memory about "faithfulness" to what *ought* to be remembered, what *can* legitimately be forgotten, and what *might* be forgiven (of oneself and of others). Professional historians, looking into the facts of a given matter, have no authority as *historians* to forgive or to condemn anyone; the most they are required to do is to try to tell the truth and understand. It is quite otherwise with what Ricoeur calls "the citizen-historian."

In an interesting excursus on Carlo Ginzburg's little book[15] on the historian and the judge, Ricoeur criticizes the commonplace that affirms the similarity of their respective social functions. The judge (in the Continental European court system) must at the end of the presentations by prosecutors and defenders render a verdict: guilty, innocent, mistrial, not proven, and so on—a verdict that effectively exonerates the accused or leads to sentencing and punishment for the crime. Ginzburg, after a careful "historical" examination of the evidence in a case that had resulted in the imprisonment of a friend, claims that the historians' methods are better suited to the imperatives of a fair and just trial than are those of advocates or judges or juries. Ricoeur points out that the similarities between the operations of the historian and of the judge pertain only to the deliberative phase of the juridical process, in which evidence is being sifted, tested, vetted, and verified in the interest of determining whether a trial is even called for. And then immediately the differences between the two operations spring to the fore. After the presentation of the evidence, the judge (or the jury) *must* reach a decision. Not so the historian. Indeed, the historian is always encouraged to defer judgments of the kind judges must make whether they have sufficient evidence or not. In the face of epistemic imperatives appertaining to the nature of the evidence, the incompleteness of the facts of the matter, the absence of witnesses for direct interrogation, and the difficulty of establishing motive and responsibility for actions and the consequences of actions taken long since, historians must always come to conclusions that can only be provisional and subject in principle to infinite revision.

Indeed, Ricoeur suggests that the proper social function of the historian in dealing with criminal deeds is *dissensus*, the raising of questions and problems regarding both the facts and the evidence available for judgment of actions taken in the *past*. For, however confident a historian may be that he or she has surveyed all the evidence pertaining to a given matter, and however morally certain one may be that one has been fair, in the end, every historian's book or article must remain open to revision and supplementation—either in the light of the discovery of new evidence, or of changing notions of how evidence is to be assessed, or of changing ideas regarding the idea of "responsibility" for one's actions, especially when they are undertaken as a member of a group or a community "under orders" from duly constituted authorities.

Does this suggest a kind of historical relativism? Not to Ricoeur. In his discussion of the "great trials" following World War II for a new kind of crime—crimes against humanity—the question of "historical singularity," the exceptional nature of the crimes that the Nazis committed against just about everybody, arose in terms of whether the Nazi crime was "commensurable" with any other historical event. And whether, if it were commensurable, this circumstance might somehow exonerate the Germans from their crimes, because it was not they but the Russians who had invented this kind of crime in the first place. In the course of the *Historikerstreit* (Historian's Debate) in the late 1980s in Germany, Ernst Nolte argued that Nazism and Stalinism were not only "comparable" but that the former could be understood as a plausible or understandable—if not forgivable—reaction to the latter. Did Nolte give solace to the "revisionists" who had argued not only that the destruction of the Jews, Gypsies, homosexuals, and so on had been misunderstood, but that nothing like what historians had come to call the "Holocaust" had ever happened? Or was Nolte, in suggesting the comparability of Nazism and Stalinism, merely doing what any historian, in trying to characterize the species to which a given individual belongs, has to do?

Ricoeur suggested that the argument about comparability was a red herring, since on principle every historical event was by definition unique and unrepeatable. The point about the "great crimes" of the totalitarian regimes of the twentieth century was not that they were or were not "historically" singular but that they were *morally so*. Supposing, Ricoeur writes, "that the thesis of incomparability applied to the Holocaust is plausible on the historiographical plane, the mistake would be to confuse the absolute exceptionally on the moral plane with incomparability relative to the historical plane."[16]

The confusion, he continues, often stems from the thesis that Bolshevism and Hitlerism "belong to the same genus, namely, here, the totalitarian" and that, therefore, crimes committed in one system exonerate perpetrators of crimes committed in the other system. The proper use of the concept of singularity is that which identities it less with incomparability than with "nonrepeatability." This has to do with the choice that communities and individuals must make in the face of the possibility of a repetition of what had been—up until its occurrence—a whole genus of specific and hence comparable crimes against humanity. The Holocaust was not the first crime against humanity even if it is, due to the nature of the perpetrators, morally the most execrable.

Nolte was justified in raising the question of comparability and, indeed, it seems, was only performing one of the functions of the historian in studying juridical proceedings that have consoled the public by seeming to have wrapped them up and archived them, never to have to be examined again. In such a situation, it is the duty of the historian to suggest in what ways certain crucial events such as the Holocaust can never be fully and finally dealt with, because their shadows are cast down the ages for the communities that have them in their pasts. So that, in this case, the task of the historian is to keep memory of them alive, rather than to try to wrap them up, classify them, and return them to the archive.

Here—for Ricoeur—is the historiological significance of the European and Jewish debates over the *Historikerstreit* of the late 1980s: they showed how, in its critical dimension, the historiological reexamination of any morally charged event in a community's past would produce a healthy *dissensus* against the tendency of a community to forget the maxim of *summum ius summum iniuria* (the extreme justice is extreme injustice).[17] Historical specificity countered a comforting consensus to the effect that even the most horrible crime could be wiped from the books by punishing a few perpetrators and allowing the ordinary guy, who was only following orders, or the bystander who did nothing, not even bear witness, to go free.

What historical dissensus achieved, in the case of the *Historikerstreit*, was to remind the Western public that the Holocaust was and should remain unfinished business in the sense of being an event in "our" history that not only we should never forget, but that compels us to "pledge to prevent its recurrence."[18] It is here that we can see the relevance of Ricoeur's expanded notion of "the historical condition" to encompass the moral and political dilemmas of "our modernity." With the pledge of "never again," the historically self-conscious community turns its gaze from the past of "the having once lived" to the future of the "yet to be born" and finds in its own present the task, not so much of doing the good, as rather foreclosing the evil that history, all too pertinently, shows us *humans* can do.

So much for Ricoeur's epilogue—which is surely the point of the book. What about the book itself, those 592 pages (in the French edition; 577 in the English) that lead up to this sixty-four-page peroration? Forgiveness turns out to be the point as well as the *telos* and *eschaton* of this book.[19] We can now begin to understand, I hope, the reasons (apart from Ricoeur's dialectical inclinations) for the ternary organization of *Memory, History, Forgetting*. (I would prefer "oblivion" rather than "forgetting" for *l'oubli*, because, recall, the section dealing with "forgetting" lines up with "the historical condition," and the historical condition requires us to mediate between remembering and forgetting over against the impulse simply to "obliviate.") Recall that Ricoeur's "personal" reason for writing this book was his awareness that "our modernity" was characterized by incessant demands to "remember," which is to say, build monuments and memorials, set up museums of remembrance, and hold ceremonies and rituals, but also an equally insistent pressure to "forget," to "get over it" and get on with the job of whatever it is that we are supposed to be doing. Obliviation would clear the boards of both moral imperatives and permit the calm consideration of what is worth being forgiven. Here no historian, nor indeed any social scientist, can help us. Here we must revert to a historical consciousness that is both chastened and expanded, chastened by its knowledge of its limitations and expanded to encompass the present and the future as well as the past.

The section of this book that I would commend most urgently to professional historians is Part 3, which has to do with the question: what is the proper object of a specifically historical mode of inquiry? This is a question seldom raised—at least consciously—by what are called "working" historians. To be sure, anything "in history" stands open to a historical treatment. Some things have been taken to be historical from the start: politics, for example, war and conquest, trade, and so on. But what about women? Or slaves? Or primitive peoples, barbarians, savages, and the like? Hegel thought that history began only with the appearance of the State, which, in his view, made history possible by both "making history" (undertaking enterprises that significantly moved forward the march of Reason in the world) and, in its necessity to keep written records, laying the foundation the possibility of "making histories," telling the story of how the State especially went about doing its world-historical work. History, in Hegel's account, can begin to occur only with the appearance of peoples capable of thinking and acting historically, which is to say, thinking about themselves as having an identity that is continuous across time and about which a documentable "story" can be told. Thus Hegel was quite clear about what was in history and what was outside it. He knew or purported to know when real history began (with the Chinese), where it was going (from East to West), and what it meant or signified (the progress of Reason in the world and consciousness reconciled to itself, for and by itself). Ricoeur enjoys no such certitudes. He only knows that history is all we are left with after the death of God and the end of metaphysics, that we are ineluctably "in" history, and that our principal obligation as human beings burdened by existential "care" is to live our lives "historically."

Part 3 of *Memory, History, Forgetting* is especially interesting, to me at least, because it tries to approach the problem of historicity by way of a negative dialectics: we cannot begin by simply positing history even though we know we are in it, but because we know ourselves to be in it (we know it because we sense it as a "burden"), we can begin by asking what, in human and natural life, appears to be decidedly and unexceptionally *not* historical?[20] As we have seen, in the later sections of his book, Ricoeur will pick up the idea of the "nonhistorical" as a kind of "*pharmakon*" (the poison that can serve as a remedy if properly administered) distilled in the alembic of our modernity, capable of serving as an antidote to "too much history," on the one side, and "too little history," on the other, from which "we moderns" suffer. This linkage of the idea of the nonhistorical with the notion of modernity is one of the most interesting moves in Ricoeur's thinking, and places him smack in the middle of the current debate over "postmodernism."

Modernism is one of those terms that W. B. Gallie called "essentially contestable," which means that it can be used in both a positive and a negative sense, as designating a good thing or a bad thing equally well, as praising or damning depending upon the way one shares modernism's own predilections. On the one hand, there is "modernization," generally identified with the Enlightenment program of rationalizing the world and pushing it toward a future free of all tradition, superstition, and magical thinking. Here "modernism" indicates a belief in the desirability of this program and a commitment to critique of everything old and worn out and promotion of everything new, youthful, and optimistic about the future. This kind of modernism we will have to call "modernist modernism," in order to distinguish it from the many modernisms that have appeared in the history of Western culture since the coining of the term *modernus* in Christian circles sometime during the fourth century A D.[21] For the original sense of *modernus* suggested the difference between Christian times and the pagan and Hebrew times that had come before. The late-Latin term *modernus* meant "now" or "just now" or "right now" (as against classical Latin *hodie* and *nunc*). It was thought that Christ had ushered in a new time, differing from the old time of the pagans in that the Christian could escape from time itself, escape death, and enter into an eternal "now" in which there was neither past nor present, and none of the "care" that came with them. Christian time is continually new, continually ecstatic, continually fruitful, superior qualitatively and quantitatively to the old time of the pagans and Jews.

It is this emphasis on the now and the new and the superiority of the present to the past that has become attached to the idea of modernism across the ages. This accounts for what is often seen as the inherent antipathy of modernism to history, understood as either the past or as an approach to the study of the present that requires study of the past for the present's full comprehension. But this is to confuse "modernity" and the program of "modernization" of the world with the ideology of modern*ism*, which, in its twentieth-century form, is born of a reaction to modernization, which is regarded as sterile, mechanistic, and nihilistic, and the fear that the roots of culture and art have been forever lost and can never be redeemed. This is the view of the first generation of cultural modernism, the generation of James Joyce, Virginia Woolf, Ezra Pound, T. S. Eliot, Franz Kafka, Gertrude Stein, William Faulkner, and so on, who felt the newness of "the present age" as an oppressive burden but who regarded this burden as bequeathed by "history." Modernism is "presentist" and anti-historical, as a number of its critics allege, but it is at the same time nostalgic for a time when the past provided a legacy to be inherited and when history was more than "information" about the past and produced a kind of knowledge that could endow the present with meaning and the future with hope.

For Ricoeur, all this—both the negative and the positive—is included in the problematics of modernism. But he sees this problematics as evidence less of a disbelief in history than as, rather, an obsession with time, epochality, and destiny. Modernism is sick, sick *of* (fed up with) history, to be sure, but also sick *from* (made ill by) history as well, and this because the "sickness unto death" from which the West especially has come to suffer is nothing but "the historical condition" of "modernity." This modernity in turn is nothing other than a product of the discovery that we are responsible for our humanity and can look to no one other than ourselves to heal us of the memories of "the great crimes" committed during the twentieth century.

❧

Ricoeur's notion of the modern implies a revision of our notion of the history of history. Although he thinks that our modern sense of history is implicit in earlier conceptions of history's theory and practice, from the Greeks on, he also thinks that we moderns have an experience of history radically different from anything that could have been experienced before. Whereas earlier epochs had thought of themselves as having a history, they did not think of themselves as "making history." They tended to think, rather, that the cosmos was governed by forces and processes—God, Fate, Chance, Fortune, Providence, and so on—the aims of which were unknowable and the operations of which were fortuitous. Following Reinhart Koselleck's lead in *Futures Past*,[22] however, Ricoeur accepts the thesis that "history," considered as a medium of human action and subject to control and domination by human beings, arises in the early nineteenth century and takes the place of various ideas of the "cosmos" as the place where humanity finds its identity and essence and aim. Instead of being a congeries of the various "stories" that different groups tell about their various pasts, "history" now is thought of as a "collective singular" (phenomenon). History is now both a causal force in its own right ("history happens" and "history" now "causes" things to happen as they do) and a something that can be "made" by humans and groups. The idea that history is a *cause* of change rather than a consequence of it and that, moreover, this cause of change can itself be changed by the right action at the right time, all this provides the basis for an "experience of history" peculiar to "our modernity."[23] It was these changes in historical change that rendered arguments about historical determinism moot and promoted belief in the possibility of a kind of human freedom unknown to the rest of nature. Such is the nature of "our modernity," such is the nature of "the historical condition." Our modernity consists of the coming to consciousness of our existence in the "condition" of "historicality."

But what does it mean to be "in history"? Does history have limits or barriers or borders such that some parts of our humanity fall within them and others remain outside? Petrarch is supposed to have said that all history is the history of Rome, thus nailing the historical to a place, a time, and a people but also to a system of laws and a destiny. Other peoples might not be less human than were the Romans, but they were certainly, in Petrarch's mind, less historical. For Petrarch, history was the story of Rome's expansion in space, its duration in time, and its gradual assimilation of a panoply of other peoples to the rule of her law and her language. And so it was for Machiavelli: Rome held the secret of a life lived in history without any aid from God or favor by ontology. To live in history was to live as a community for a long time and to expand in space as far as possible. It also meant to learn how to live with, by, for, and under the rule of law. Thus peoples become historical. To be historical is to live under the law. When the law is subverted and turned against the people to whom it is supposed to provide justice, history is cancelled. This is what "the great crimes" of the twentieth century teach us.

This, too, is the secret of "our modernity." It was only "advanced" communities, communities that had prided themselves on their "modernity," their newness, and their enlightenment that possessed the means by which to subvert the very idea of legality. The Nazi crimes against humanity are the paradigm of immorality because they subverted the very idea of law itself as the principle of community. Moreover, the Nazis committed these crimes in full consciousness of what they were doing, employing the most advanced means, technologies, and knowledges, to carry out their destructive aims—carrying them out against their own people as well as against others, carrying them out calculatedly, rationally, scientifically, and all the while proclaiming their superiority to life itself; carrying them out with the aid and support of their philosophers, scientists, clergy, jurists, artists, musicians, and (not that it mattered so much) historians. The Nazis and their cohorts do represent a new phenomenon in history, though not a new historical phenomenon: they are an *immoral* singularity.

This is what I get from reflection on Ricoeur's idea of historicity. The death camps are not prominently featured as a subject of Ricoeur's discourse, but they loom over it as the place of the nonhistorical *par excellence*. Here people deprived of their names, their citizenship, their civil and above all their human rights, deprived of their histories, were subjected to treatment intended to deprive them of their humanity before they were to be cast—abjected—like garbage into mass graves or "disappeared"—another of modernity's contributions to the political lexicon of our time—into the crematoria. If this was not a revolt against historicity in the name of modernity it is difficult to think of what might be.

Thus, for "us," to be in history is to be in "modernity," so that, in "our" time, to experience history is to experience modernity. None of this would be the kind of thing that ordinary, everyday, nuts-and-bolts, bread-and-butter historians could be expected to conclude or even recognize as true on the basis of their application of professional standards of scholarship to their chosen areas of expertise in the remote past. It is not even a point of view that could be expected to arise in the consciousness of a professional student of modern German history, the Nazi phenomenon, or the death camps. Which is why, it seems to me, that in spite of his respect for the kind of scholarship produced by professional historians in their study of the past, Ricoeur wished to expand the concept of historicity to include not only a philosophically responsible idea of its relation to temporality, on the one side, but also, and even more importantly, its relation to ethics, morality, and political life, on the other.

Unlike conventional notions of historiography as the study and representation of "the past," Ricoeur insists that both the present and the future must be brought within the compass of a specifically historical way of thinking, acting, and feeling. In the absence of religion and metaphysics, history itself becomes the ground, the occasion, and even the aim of human existence. What our modernity teaches us is that this history has ceased to be a panorama of difference and variation and has begun to manifest its unity and sameness. The very extent and extremity of the human capacity for destruction manifested in the twentieth century's wars of extermination and depredations of nature indicate—ironically—how far mankind has come on the road to unification. All that is needed for the actualization of human unity is the realization that love can fulfill the law as well as cancel it. Such is the Pauline dimension of Ricoeur's philosophy of history.

According to Ricoeur, historical thinking is implicitly universalist; the idea of world or cosmopolitan history is implicit in the idea that "humanity" is both the subject and the object of historical reflection—an idea that we have only recently but inevitably come to. The nineteenth century at once discovered and disavowed the idea that the word "history" was a "collective singular" in which the three tenses of temporality (present, future, past) were inseparable moments of what Ricoeur calls "the historical condition." Only in the nineteenth century did it become possible to think that the various peoples and nations and communities who had their own little histories could be sublated into a single grand story in which each could be legitimately and not just Utopianistically seen as contributing to the constitution of the whole. It is this possibility of a universal history that constituted for Ricoeur the key to the understanding of "our modernity." "What is held to be modern [*ce qui est déclaré modern*] par excellence," he writes, "is this omnitemporal character of history. At the same time . . . history is the history of humanity, and in this worldwide sense, the history of peoples. Humanity becomes both the total object and the unique subject of history, at the same time as history becomes a collective singular."[24] It is this history—history understood as the story of a single humanity—that constitutes the basis of what Ricoeur, following Koselleck, calls "the experience *of* history."

The "experience of history" is quite a different thing from the so-called "experience of the past" or the experience of feeling that the past has somehow returned in the present, in the manner of a revenant or a ghost. To experience history is to experience the *process* that informs or results from "the historical condition" of mankind, a process not unlike that posited by Saint Augustine in *The City of God* or by Hegel in his *Lectures on the Philosophy of History*. But with this difference: whereas Saint Augustine thought that the process informing history was Divine Providence and Hegel thought it was Reason, Ricoeur thinks that the historical process is a story of humanity making itself whole out of all the parts of the historical process previously known. Thus, Ricoeur suggests that we can legitimately speak of "the experience of history," after the manner of Koselleck, to "the extent that the concept of history can claim to fill the space previously occupied by religion."[25]

This is a startling claim, especially for a philosopher who has in general criticized the great material philosophies of history such as those of Hegel, Marx, and so on.[26] But it provides Ricoeur with grounds for criticizing the fetishism of the particular, the celebration of a local reason, and the fad of multiculturalism, all of which, in his opinion, undermine the idea of history as a collective singular and the story of humanity in time. The idea of a world history is irresistible on both theoretical and practical grounds, Ricoeur argues, so that the "resistance of human plurality" to this idea "constitutes a paradox and, ultimately, a scandal." Then, in a thought that is so much a part of his *forma mentis* that it appears as only an afterthought, Ricoeur writes:

> The concept of collective singular would truly be honored only if one managed to renew the Leibnizian principle of sufficient reason, for which the diversity, variety, and complexity of phenomena constitute welcome components of the idea of the whole. This interpretation [of history as a collective singular] midway between regulative and constitutive ideas does not seem to me to be beyond the reach of a properly dialectical conception of history.[27]

"A properly dialectical conception of history..." It has been Ricoeur's purpose over the last three decades, since his "conversion" from existentialist phenomenology to ontological hermeneutics, to provide such a conception of history. But for whom? Is it for proper historians? These have shown a remarkable capacity to resist the allure of such "Hegelian" possibilities since the time of Ranke. Most historians feel that such macro-historical visions of "the origins and goals of history" provide no help either in identifying or executing realistic research projects. It is not, as I used to think, that historians are conditioned to avoid theory. Modern historians typically go to the social sciences for models and methods of research that might help them to characterize certain phenomena in the past in terms that permit one to see analogical similarities with current counterparts in modern societies. But they have no use for theories *about* history. As Paul de Man used to say, historians presuppose the referent. They only have to find it and identify it; they do not, as in other sciences, have to constitute it "theoretically," in the way that a subatomic physicist does or, for that matter, any student of "society" has to do. Since historians study the individual event and work their way "down" to the particular—to the micro-historical detail—rather than "up" to general and (Heaven forbid!) universal, they have no sense of constructing anything. By the same token, proper historians simply presume or presuppose "the present" as the relatively stable platform from which to launch their investigations of an equally stable (because it is over and done with, a dead and fixed) past. This present is treated as if it were not only stable but also epistemically neutral or at least could be neutralized in such a way as to be inconsequential as a distorting factor in the historian's perceptual apparatus. Historians do not deny that the past has a significant relationship to the present; a genealogical connection with the past of a *given* present is presupposed. But no genealogical connection is presumed to exist among all the current presents of the various communities and groups and above all "races" (ethnic groups) that make up the wondrous variety of world-historical "families." For most historians, the present is not and cannot be (any more than the future) an object of a specifically "historical" investigation. Indeed, being interested in the past "for its own sake" and being interested in the past for what it can tell us about our present "situation" constitutes the principal difference between conservative and radical historiological reflection. It is the difference between, say, Ranke and Marx or, to take modern examples, J. H. Hexter and Michel Foucault.

No doubt Ricoeur was interested in appealing to historians to turn their expertise to the study of the relation between the past and the present, and, in the case of the current generation of historians, to a consideration of the *recent* past defined as a period by "the great crimes" that marked it as distinctive of "our modernity." But actually Ricoeur was more interested in the cultivation of a kind of historical culture that would function pedagogically to create a citizen capable of acting responsibly in a "postmodern" world.

At the conclusion of his discussion of "the historian and the judge," in the context of the "great crimes" of our era, Ricoeur says that, in order to arbitrate the differences between the two, we need an "impartial but not infallible third party." This third party is "the citizen."

Obviously, Ricoeur is not suggesting that either the historian's specialized research findings or the judge's juridically informed judgments are to be overridden by the ordinary man in the street or average citizen. What he means, it seems to me, is something like this: Neither juridical knowledge nor historical knowledge is scientific in the strict sense of the term. Both kinds of knowledge and the judgments based on them must always be in principle provisional, subject to judicial appeal in the case of the judge, subject to revision in the light of new evidence or different perspectives in the case of the historian. Consequently, the actions taken on the basis of such judgments always have to be assessed on the basis of their adequacy to the ideals informing the goals and aims of the community. This is especially the case with judgments rendered on "the great crimes" of "our" time that have continued to cast their shadows over three generations of "our" civilization. Ricoeur would not be asking either historians or judges to reconsider the nature of their social functions if these great crimes had not been committed, because among other things they have proven to be impossible to deal with adequately both by historians, who have brought to their consideration outmoded notions of their obligations to their profession, and by judges, who have been unable adequately to deal with a new kind of criminal and a new kind of crime. It is this fact that raises the issue of the relation between politics and knowledge in our time. Here the will of the citizenry must ultimately prevail, but not the kind of citizenry that was so badly educated that it could not distinguish between what was or had been made legal and what was moral, or between crimes *against* the state and crimes committed *by* the state and with the compliance of a citizenry betrayed by both its leaders and its teachers. Insofar, then, as historical knowledge and juridical knowledge are produced within and for the benefit of the community, it is the citizen who must finally bear responsibility for affirming or denying not the truth or falsity, but the *relevance* of these knowledges to the lives they would wish for their children. Thus, Ricoeur writes:

> Having set out to find an impartial yet not infallible third party, we end by adding a third partner to the pair formed by the historian and the judge: the citizen. The citizen emerges as a third party in the order of time: with a gaze that is structured on the basis of personal experience, variously instructed by penal judgment and by published historical inquiry. On the other hand, the intervention of citizens is never completed, placing more on the side of the historian. But the citizen is in search of an assured judgment, intended to be as definitive as

that of the judge. In every respect, the citizen remains the ultimate arbiter. It is the citizen who militantly carries the "liberal" values of constitutional democracy. In the final analysis, the conviction of the citizen alone justifies the fairness of the penal procedure in the courts and the intellectual honesty of the historian in the archives. And it is this same conviction that, ultimately, allows us to name the inhuman, retrospectively, as the absolute contrary of "liberal" values.[28]

Ricoeur's great book—and it is a great book—challenges all of the commonplaces of those discourses in which we simultaneously praise ourselves for being so enlightened, so "modern," and wring our hands over the current generation's lack of "values" and flight from history. It is written with great and fine moral passion, with intellectual generosity, and exquisite historical sensibility to the singularity of "our modernity." It is a long, demanding book, but attuned to every ideological zephyr of the time: from the debates over political correctness and multiculturalism to the discourses of postmodernism. I once commended *Time and Narrative* to Norman O. Brown who, having looked it over in his way, said to me, "What's wrong with Paul Ricoeur? Paul Ricoeur never goes *too far!*" Brown would have probably thought the same about *Memory, History, Forgetting*: not *messianic* enough.

That is true. Teleology and eschatology turn up in this text, but they are always dealt with cautiously and played down, muted. There is a decidedly religious aura in the presentation, but it is the aura of the sage rather than that of the prophet. In the reviews of the book that I have read thus far, I perceive a disinclination to take issue with it, in fact, a reluctance to engage it head on. Much of this reluctance is no doubt justified: phenomenological hermeneutics defies summary, condensation, and paraphrase.

But the main task of the book, which is to break down the distinction between what Michael Oakeshott called "the historical past," on the one hand, and "the practical past," on the other, is well worth taking up and completing by scholars in many fields and by citizens of all persuasions. Let me explain.

Oakeshott was fond of distinguishing between two kinds of past: the first he called the practical past, by which he meant the *mélange* of memories, information, snippets of knowledge about our own and our community's past that we all carry around with us and refer to or draw upon for aid in solving everyday problems in all sorts of domains of practical life. The other past Oakeshott called "the historical past," by which he meant the picture of the past constructed by professional investigators thereof and which, he insisted, was a purely theoretical construction, a past inferred from the various kinds of evidence available to a given group of investigators in a given time and place.[29] The historical past, Oakeshott said, was a past that no one had ever experienced while it was in the process of taking shape, that no one had ever observed, that existed only in the minds of and books written by historians, and that, therefore, had no practical use whatsoever. This past was an object of study by investigators whose principal, indeed only, interest was in its construction. Nor could this past be profitably subjected to philosophical scrutiny for the purpose of identifying its substance, essence, or meaning, after the manner of Hegel or Marx; because, properly speaking, the historical past, being a construction of historians, has no substance at all. The historical past is and will be whatever historians decide to make it. This radically constructivist idea of history does not throw history open to the kind of willful manipulation and ideological uses that totalitarian regimes practiced, because history does not teach anything at all, consisting as it does of a body of statements about what might have happened in the past, could never happen again, and even if it did, could not happen in precisely the same way as before.

To be sure, ordinary people and even historians tend to mix up the two pasts, using the practical past as a basis for historical speculation and using the historical past to flesh out and give the odor of science, wisdom, or common sense to the practical past. This is the origin of the so-called "speculative philosophy of history," which, in the modern period especially, has traded in various versions of "meaning in history" or has sought to use "history" as a basis for a science of human nature, to predict the future, or simply to discern a pattern in history justificatory of a particular group's sense of its destiny, identity, or election. Oakeshott came to believe that the study of history was a purely intellectual enterprise, yielding extensive information about the past but very little that could pass for scientific knowledge, and certainly nothing relevant to the solution of the great philosophical problems of ontology, epistemology, and ethics.

Now, Oakeshott's idea of historical knowledge can be understood as a part of his more general attempt to guard Western thought and science from ideological deformation. It is a reprise of the Humean principle that one cannot legitimately (that is, with any kind of logical consistency) derive "ought" statements from "is" statements, or, to put it another way, you cannot derive ethical imperatives from scientifically established facts. But Oakeshott succeeded in quarantining historical knowledge from ideology by concluding that historical knowledge had absolutely no practical use and that, as far as historical science was concerned, history could not be said to possess any "meaning" at all. In a word, history teaches nothing and means nothing. It is just another "mode of experiencing" the world, and a peculiarly contemplative or passive one at that.

We will never know what Ricoeur's response to this position would be. I find no allusion to Oakeshott in any of my books by Ricoeur. And Oakeshott did not, as far as I know, ever refer to Ricoeur. But the two positions could not be more different. Were they, in spite of their shared interests, including a shared interest in Heidegger, inhabiting different intellectual and ideological universes? Is the difference that between an Englishman and a Frenchman? Is it a matter of experiencing "history" differently? Or is it a matter of experiencing different "histories"?

Envoi

Paul Ricoeur, who died in May of 2005, was a longtime member of the personalist-humanist "L'Esprit" group, which included Emmanuel Mounier and Emmanuel Lévinas. He received much of his philosophical education in a German prisoner of war camp. His early moral and political "formation" was Protestant, conservative, *Action française,* and, during the early years of the War, *Petainiste.* I am not sure whether it is significant for his philosophical development that he was orphaned as a child, was technically considered a ward of the French state, and was raised by grandparents. Nor am I sure of the importance of his disillusionment with the students of May '68, in which he had an experience not unlike that endured (badly) by Theodor Adorno in Frankfurt at the same time. It is interesting to observe, though, that Ricoeur had a heightened sense of his role as a citizen, of one's obligations to one's community, and of the nefarious effects of ideology on modern life. He speaks of a kind of "orphaned" knowledge peculiar to history, in which historical testimony appears as a manifestation of an "absent past" in the present, a kind of "ghostly" presence that requires aid and succor in order to come back to life as a living presence.

Ricoeur began contributing to the philosophical refoundation of the human sciences during the post–World War II period in a French intellectual scene dominated by such imposing figures as Jean-Paul Sartre, Gabriel Marcel, Jacques Maritain, Raymond Aaron, Albert Camus, Maurice Merleau-Ponty, Louis Althusser, A. J. Greimas, Lévinas, Fernand Braudel, Claude Lévi-Strauss, Jacques Lacan, Roland Barthes, Michel Foucault, Jacques Derrida, etc., etc. He engaged all of them; and, with the exception of Lévi-Strauss, he outlived them all. There were also a number of prominent women intellectuals on this scene: Simone de Beauvoir, Nathalie Sarraute, Michelle Le Boeuf, Hélène Cixous, Julia Kristeva, Sarah Kofman, Luce Irigaray, but as far as I can find out, Ricoeur did not engage them at all. An indefatigable thinker and writer, a witty and engaging lecturer, a generous mentor, and a critic, Ricoeur brought his erudite and cosmopolitan intelligence to all the major issues in the human sciences—from religion, myth, and language to social theory and ideology, literature, historiography, and psychoanalysis—and always in the interest of community and humaneness. Yet, or so it seems to me, one could not say that Ricoeur's vast output of philosophical, literary, and theoretical work adds up to anything like "Ricoeurism," a doctrine or "position" that one might be tempted to argue against or attempt to justify by commentary on it that was intended to clarify it or explain away apparent contradictions or infelicities of expression. In part, this is because of the extent of his compass, but it is also a result of the kind of synthesizing drive that led him to read virtually everything in every language he knew that bore upon his topics of interest. Had he not been so graceful and measured, one would have been tempted to call his interests Gargantuan, so long, was his reach, so vast his appetite for thinking.

Editor's Introduction

1. Hayden White, *Metahistory: The Historical Imagination in Nineteenth-Century Europe* (Baltimore: Johns Hopkins University Press, 1973).

2. I could mention in particular the recently published collection of essays devoted to White's work, which features an interdisciplinary group of scholars: *Re-Figuring Hayden White*, ed. Frank Ankersmit, Ewa Domanska, and Hans Kellner (Stanford, CA: Stanford University Press, 2009).

3. Hayden White, *Tropics of Discourse: Essays in Cultural Criticism* (Baltimore: Johns Hopkins University Press, 1978); Hayden White, *The Content of the Form: Narrative Discourse and Historical Representation* (Baltimore: Johns Hopkins University Press, 1987); Hayden White, *Figural Realism: Studies in the Mimesis Effect* (Baltimore: Johns Hopkins University Press, 1999).

4. White is more prolific than many realize, since the commentary on his work tends to focus on his four major critical books (all of which have remained continuously in print since their initial publication). Less well known are his more than sixty uncollected articles and book chapters, in addition to numerous—and often quite substantial—review essays, interviews, commentaries, and responses, which would fill several thick volumes. The selection of the essays for this anthology was thus a difficult task; unfortunately, some worthy essays had to be excluded because of space constraints.

5. Richard Vann, "The Reception of Hayden White," *History and Theory* 37, no. 2 (1998): 144.

6. Dominick LaCapra, review of *The Content of the Form*, *The American Historical Review* 93, no. 4 (Oct. 1988), 1007.

7. Arthur Danto declared that Bossenbrook's lectures would have led him to become a historian instead of a philosopher "were it not for the discovery that they were unique" (preface to *The Uses of History: Essays in Intellectual and Social History Presented to William J. Bossenbrook*, ed. Hayden White [Detroit: Wayne State University Press, 1968], 10). Among Bossenbrook's publications are: *Development of Contemporary Civilization* (1940), *The German Mind* (1961), and *Mid Twentieth-Century Nationalism* (ed. 1965). In the preface to *The German Mind*, Bossenbrook thanks White for his comments on the manuscript.

8. The volume included contributions by Danto and Harootunian, in addition to

White's essay "Romanticism, Realism, and Historicism: Toward a Period Concept for Early Nineteenth-Century Intellectual History" (chap. 4 in this volume).

9. From 1953 to 1955 White studied in Rome, sparking a lifelong interest in Italian letters and culture. One of White's first publications was an English translation of Italian historian Carlo Antoni: *From History to Sociology* (Detroit: Wayne State University Press, 1959). Though White did not publish his doctoral dissertation, he did put out two articles derived from it: "Pontius of Cluny and the Curia Romana," *Church History* 27, no. 3 (Sept. 1958): 195–219; and "The Gregorian Ideal and St. Bernard of Clairvaux," *Journal of the History of Ideas* 21, no. 3 (July–Sept. 1960): 321–38. Herman Paul has discussed these texts in his essay "A Weberian Medievalist: Hayden White in the 1950s," *Rethinking History* 12, no. 1 (2008): 75–102.

10. See Ewa Domanska's interview with White in her *Encounters: Philosophy of History after Postmodernism* (Charlottesville: University of Virginia Press, 1998), 18. Among Mandelbaum's publications are: *Purpose and Necessity in Social Theory* (1987); *Philosophy, History, and the Sciences* (1984); and *The Anatomy of Historical Knowledge* (1977), all published by the Johns Hopkins University Press. Mandelbaum also contributed to a special issue of *History and Theory* devoted to *Metahistory*, though he offered a rather scathing assessment of White's magnum opus. See Maurice Mandelbaum, "The Presuppositions of *Metahistory*," *History and Theory* 19, no. 4 (1980): 39–54.

11. White relates that as a young professor he taught medieval and cultural history (Domanska, *Encounters*, 13).

12. In 1983, White was named Presidential Professor of Historical Studies at the University of California, Santa Cruz, and, in 1990, University Professor. White was elected to the American Academy of Arts and Sciences in 1991.

13. One could trace a similar trajectory for Richard Rorty, White's late colleague at Stanford. Finding himself unwelcome in his home discipline of philosophy, Rorty left the philosophy department at Princeton (where he had spent twenty-one years) to join the University of Virginia as a professor of humanities, finally ending up, like White, in a department of comparative literature (at Stanford).

14. Exceptions would be historians such as Frank Ankersmit, Dominick LaCapra, Gabrielle Spiegel, and Hans Kellner (who teaches in a literature department). Though Jacques Derrida, Jacques Lacan, and Claude Lévi-Strauss had been discussed since the famous 1966 conference at the Johns Hopkins University (The Languages of Criticism and Sciences of Man: The Structuralist Controversy), the watershed event in the reception of "French Theory" in the United States was the translation of Derrida's *Of Grammatology*, published by Johns Hopkins in 1976.

15. White published four essays in *Critical Inquiry* between 1980 and 1986: "Historical Pluralism" (included in the present volume as chap. 15); "The Narrativization of Real Events" (a reply); "The Politics of Historical Interpretation: Discipline and De-sublimation"; and "The Value of Narrativity in the Representation of Reality." The last two essays were collected in *The Content of the Form*. The current reputation of the journal as the vanguard of "critical theory" dates from 1978, when W. J. T. Mitchell took over as editor-in-chief. Mitchell remains the editor to this day.

16. Paraphrasing Roland Barthes, White describes textualism thus: "By textualism, I mean the idea that the written text constitutes a paradigm of culture, that cultural produc-

tion can best be understood on the model of textual production, and that the interpretation of culture is best carried out by practices of reading exactly analogous to those used in the reading of texts" ("Postmodernism and Textual Anxieties," chap. 22 of this volume).

17. The other six volumes in the series are: Dean Arthur Miller, *The Byzantine Tradition* (1966); J. H. Hexter, *The Judeo-Christian Tradition* (1966); Milton Convensky, *The Ancient Near-Eastern Tradition* (1966); Robert Anchor, *The Enlightenment Tradition* (1967); John Weiss, *The Fascist Tradition: Radical Right-Wing Extremism in Modern Europe* (1967); and John B. Christopher, *The Islamic Tradition* (1972).

18. One important exception in this regard is Hans Kellner, whose essay "A Bedrock of Order: Hayden White's Linguistic Humanism" (*History and Theory* 19, no. 4 [1980]: 1–29) is a model of subtle exegesis.

19. In the last chapter of *La pensée sauvage* (*The Savage Mind*), Lévi-Strauss attacks the notion of history advanced by Jean-Paul Sartre in his *La critique de la raison dialectique* (*Critique of Dialectical Reason*). See Claude Lévi-Strauss, *The Savage Mind* (Chicago: University of Chicago Press, 1966), 245–69.

20. Kellner, "A Bedrock of Order." However, White is not intent on promoting just any concept of humanism. In "The Discourse of History" (chap. 12 of this volume) he speaks of "the values of a certain Western humanism in a certain phase of its development, a humanism which has shown itself incapable of addressing the issues raised by the experience of industrialization and has contented itself with defenses of the classics, recommendations of good taste and the golden mean, and ideals of individualism in the face of a social order which has rendered such ideals irrelevant when not impossible to realize."

21. White, *Metahistory*, xii.

22. White also published an essay on Ricoeur's *Time and Narrative* (though only the first two volumes had appeared at the time), entitled "The Metaphysics of Narrativity: Time and Symbol in Ricoeur's Philosophy of History," which was collected in *The Content of the Form*, 169–84.

23. Semiology, as the science of sign systems, was designed to replace the humanistic discipline of philology, which was derived from rhetoric. Thus White's somewhat ambivalent attitude toward structural linguistics reveals a desire to continue the philological tradition while at the same time making common cause with the exponents of semiology.

24. White co-edited a volume with Giorgio Tagliacozzo entitled *Giambattista Vico: An International Symposium* (Baltimore: Johns Hopkins Press, 1969), and wrote several essays on Vico, including: "What Is Living and What Is Dead in Croce's Criticism of Vico" (included in the aforementioned collection, and republished in *Tropics of Discourse*, 218–29); "The Tropics of History: The Deep Structure of the *New Science*," in *Giambattista Vico's Science of Humanity*, ed. G. Tagliacozzo and D. Verene (Baltimore: Johns Hopkins University Press, 1976, reprinted in *Tropics of Discourse*, 65–85); "Vico and the Radical Wing of Structuralist/Poststructuralist Thought Today," *New Vico Studies* 1 (1983): 63–68 (included in the present volume as chap. 13); and an encyclopedia entry: "Vico, Giovanni Battista," in *International Encyclopedia of the Social Sciences*, vol. 16, ed. David L. Sills (New York: Macmillan/Free Press, 1968), 313–16.

25. In Vico's theory, this cycle repeats itself in ascending and descending movements he calls *corso* and *ricorso*, though the overall movement of the cycles is upward.

26. In the introduction to *Tropics of Discourse*, White observes that "the moral implications of the human sciences will never be perceived until the faculty of the will is reinstated in theory" (23).

27. I use the term *historical writing* instead of *historical work*, which is the term White uses in *Metahistory*. While the use of "work" appeared to be unproblematic at the time of *Metahistory*, White would later have occasion to oppose "work" to "text." See White's article "The Interpretation of Texts" (chap. 14 of this volume). I thus use "writing" as a more inclusive and general term, which also better expresses White's notion that the very act of writing involves *invention*, in the twofold sense of imagination and discovery.

28. See the special issue of *History and Theory* 19, no. 4 (Dec. 1980): "Metahistory: Six Critiques," which contained the following articles: Hans Kellner, "A Bedrock of Order: Hayden White's Linguistic Humanism"; Philip Pomper, "Typologies and Cycles in Intellectual History"; Maurice Mandelbaum, "The Presuppositions of *Metahistory*"; Eugene O. Golob, "The Irony of Nihilism"; Nancy Struever, "Topics in History"; and John S. Nelson, "History and the Social Sciences." See also Adrian Kuzminski, "A New Science?" *Comparative Studies in Society and History* 18, no. 1 (Jan. 1976): 129–43; Fredric Jameson, "Figural Relativism, or the Poetics of Historiography," *Diacritics* (Spring 1976): 2–9; Georg G. Iggers, "Style in History: History as an Art and as a Science," *Reviews in European History* 2, no. 2 (June 1976): 171–81; and David Carroll, "On Tropology: The Forms of History," *Diacritics* (Fall 1976), 58–64.

29. White was not the first to use the term *metahistory*. R. G. Collingwood is credited with having coined the term, which he used to refer to the philosophy of history as practiced by Hegel and Marx. But the term also appeared in an important 1951 essay by Christopher Dawson, entitled "The Problem of Metahistory" (reprinted in *Dynamics of World History*, ed. John Mulloy [LaSalle, IL: Sherwood Sugden & Co., 1978]: 287–93). White's 1958 essay on Dawson, "Religion, Culture, and Western Civilization in Christopher Dawson's Idea of History," is included in the present volume as chap. 2.

30. Immanuel Kant, *Kritik der reinen Vernunft* (*Critique of Pure Reason*), A308/B364. White freely acknowledges the Kantian aspect of his thought. See Hans Kellner, "Hayden White and the Kantian Discourse: Freedom, Narrative, History," in *The Philosophy of Discourse*, ed. C. Sills and G. Jensen (Portsmouth, NH: Boynton/Cook, 1992): 246–67.

31. In *Figural Realism* (11), White defines the tropological functions thus: similitude (metaphor), contiguity (metonymy), identification (synecdoche), and opposition (irony).

32. In the conclusion to *Metahistory*, White writes: "I have suggested that a given historian will be inclined to choose one or another of the different modes of explanation, on the level of argument, emplotment, or ideological implication, in response to the imperatives of the trope which informs the linguistic protocol he has used to prefigure the field of historical occurrence singled out by him for investigation. I have suggested, in short, an elective affinity between the act of prefiguration of the historical field and the explanatory strategies used by the historian in a given work" (427).

33. Fredric Jameson speculates on the possibility of the tropes forming a fourth set of variables in his essay "Figural Relativism: or, the Poetics of Historiography" (*The Ideologies of Theory, 1971–1986*, vol. 1: *Situations of Theory* [Minneapolis: University of Minnesota Press, 1988]: 159).

34. In *Figural Realism*, White writes: "The tropological structures of metaphor, metonymy, synecdoche, and irony (and what I take—following Northrop Frye—to be their corresponding plot-types: romance, tragedy, comedy and satire), provide us with a much more refined classification of the kinds of historical discourse than that based on the conventional distinction between linear and cyclical representations of historical processes" (11). This dyadic structure will also allow White to later drop the reference to the tropes when discussing modes of emplotment, since they are, in effect, inextricable from them (though without thereby reducing tropes to plot-types).

35. While there is some resonance here with Thomas Kuhn's notion of paradigm shifts and Michel Foucault's concept of *épistème*, White's conception is strictly tropological; epistemological implications are secondary. There is, however, a seeming disconnect between interpretive freedom and the constraining relationship White posits between the tropological tendency of a given society (its state of consciousness) and the one adopted by the historian. According to White, only those historians who are in tune with the dominant trope of their age will be seen as relevant: "A historian such as Burckhardt, who was precritically committed to a prefiguration of the historical field in the Ironic mode, has no authority in a public which is precritically committed to the prefiguration of the historical field in the Metonymical mode" (*Metahistory*, 430). However, on the last page of *Metahistory*, we learn that, with the help of the tropological reduction, "historians and philosophers will then be freed to conceptualize history, to perceive its contents, and to construct narrative accounts of its processes in whatever modality of consciousness is most consistent with their own moral and aesthetic aspirations" (434). The tension between the interpretive freedom of the individual historian and the tropological influence of the community is not easy to reconcile.

36. White, *Metahistory*, 428.

37. Original emphasis, White, *Metahistory*, 434.

38. In addition to the special issue of *History and Theory* mentioned above, readers should also note the more recent work of the Dutch historical theorist Frank Ankersmit and his student Herman Paul. See Ankersmit's *History and Tropology: The Rise and Fall of Metaphor* (Berkeley and Los Angeles: University of California Press, 1994), and *Historical Representation* (Stanford, CA: Stanford University Press, 2001). See also Herman Paul, "Metahistorical Prefigurations: Toward a Re-interpretation of Tropology in Hayden White," *Journal of Interdisciplinary Studies in History and Archaeology* 1, no. 2 (Winter 2004): 1–19; and Paul's doctoral thesis *Masks of Meaning: Existentialist Humanism in Hayden White's Philosophy of History* (University of Groningen, 2006).

39. Many if not most commentators on White's work see a great deal of "evolution" in White's thought, i.e., changes in position or inconsistencies. I, however, see only changes in emphasis; for, as I argue in the final section of this introduction, the crux of White's thought is his synthesis between Frye and Auerbach, and this synthesis is present virtually from the very beginning and runs throughout his entire career.

40. Emphasis added. "Man hat der Historie das Amt, die Vergangenheit zu richten, die Mitwelt zum Nutzen zukünftiger Jahre zu belehren, beigemessen: so hoher Ämter unterwindet sich gegenwärtiger Versuch nicht: er will blos zeigen, wie es eigentlich gewesen" (Leopold von Ranke, Preface to *Geschichten der romanischen und germanischen Völker* [Duncker & Humblot, 1885; original publication date, 1824], vii).

41. White is also critical of the way in which literary scholars or philosophers are inclined to use history as the unproblematic ground on which their own work can be based. See White's essay "Historical Pluralism and Pantextualism" (chap. 15 of this volume).

42. In 1942, Carl Hempel published a famous essay entitled "The Function of General Laws in History," which had an enormous impact at the time. White discusses Hempel's essay in "The Discourse of History" and "The Politics of Contemporary Philosophy of History," chaps. 12 and 9 of this volume.

43. Hayden White, "Historical Discourse and Literary Writing," in *Tropes for the Past*, ed. Kuisma Korhonen (Amsterdam: Rodopi, 2006), 30.

44. Some commentators, such as Fredric Jameson in "Figural Relativism: or, the Poetics of Historiography," see White's idea of the "content of the form" as *separating* form from content: "the content of the text is maintained at a certain determinate distance from its form" (Jameson, "The Ideologies of Theory," 155). I do not see how this could be the case; for the meaning of the content is *shaped* by the meaning of the form; there is no disjunction between them. The meaning of the form is *merely* conventional prior to its marriage to a particular content. As White writes in *Figural Realism*, "the content of the historiographical discourse is indistinguishable from its discursive form" (5).

45. Some commentators resist what they consider to be the tropological or narratological straitjacket that White appears to be advocating. But this reduction does not prohibit diversity within archetypes, e.g., different kinds of tragedy, the mixture of genres and styles. In fact, the very idea of "emplotment" presupposes it.

46. The category of "literature" is anachronistic, coming into widespread use only at the beginning of the nineteenth century, largely as a result of Madame de Staël's *De la littérature* (1800). See White's essay "The Suppression of Rhetoric in the Nineteenth Century" (chap. 21 of this volume), in which he discusses the birth of "literature" as concomitant with the "suppression of rhetoric."

47. White has been criticized for his use of the term *event*, which can refer to simple occurrences like the fall of the guillotine's blade as well as complex realities such as the French Revolution. For a discussion of this question, see Richard Vann, "The Reception of Hayden White," in which he notes that "the most under-analyzed term White uses is 'event'" (154).

48. White, *Figural Realism*, 9.

49. White, *The Content of the Form*, 45.

50. In this debate, German philosopher Jürgen Habermas criticized certain German historians for attempting to minimize the exceptional nature of the Holocaust by comparing it to other historical massacres and genocides.

51. For a discussion of some of the controversy surrounding White's work, particularly in relation to the question of historical representation of the Holocaust, see *Probing the Limits of Representation: Nazism and the "Final Solution,"* ed. Saul Friedlander (Cambridge, MA: Harvard University Press, 1992), especially the essays by Carlo Ginzburg and Martin Jay, as well as Friedlander's introduction. White's essay "Historical Emplotment and the Question of Truth" appears in the collection (and was later republished, with minor revisions, in *Figural Realism*, 26–42).

52. This is not to say that the selection and arrangement of facts is not part of what

"interpretation" entails. But ignoring a fact and asserting that something does not exist are two different things.

53. Thus White does not believe that the Holocaust is "unrepresentable." See also White's essay "The Modernist Event" (in *Figural Realism*, 66–86).

54. And to the extent that they can be so judged indicates that they are a linguistic entity or, as Arthur Danto says, "events under a description" (an expression that White often cites approvingly).

55. White, *Figural Realism*, 70.

56. Here the term "false" (as opposed to true) is distinguished from "fictional" (as a conventional, meaning-giving discursive structure).

57. White, "Historical Discourse and Literary Writing," which was later revised and published as "Figural Realism in Witness Literature," *Parallax* 10, no. 1 (Jan.–Mar. 2004): 113–24. This essay was not included in the present volume because it will be part of White's next book.

58. White, "Historical Discourse and Literary Writing," 26.

59. Auerbach's "Figura" essay has been translated and collected in Erich Auerbach, *Scenes from the Drama of European Literature* (Minneapolis: University of Minnesota Press, 1984), 11–78.

60. Hence the first definition of "type" in Webster's Dictionary: "a person, thing, or event that represents or symbolizes another, especially another that it is thought will appear later" (*Webster's New World College Dictionary*, 4th ed. [Cleveland, OH: Wiley Publishing, 2002], 1548).

61. Quoted in "Typology," in *Augustine through the Ages*, ed. Allan Fitzgerald and John C. Cavadini (Grand Rapids, MI: Eerdman, 1999), 856. The quote is from Augustine, Ser. 300.3.

62. See Robert Doran, "Literary History and the Sublime in Erich Auerbach's *Mimesis*" *New Literary History* 38, no. 2 (2007): 353–69.

63. White, *Figural Realism*, 98. The title of the essay is "Auerbach's Literary History: Figural Causation and Modernist Historicism."

64. Connecting his 1972 essay "What Is a Historical System?" (chap. 8 of this volume) with his 1994 essay on Northrop Frye, White writes: "the prefiguration-fulfillment model, indeed, provides a notion of genealogical affiliation as a historically responsible alternative to the physical and biological conception of a genetic relationship" ("Northrop Frye's Place in Contemporary Cultural Studies," chap. 19 of this volume).

65. White, "Northrop Frye's Place" (my emphasis).

66. Invoking Nietzsche, White also describes figural-fulfillment relations as "genea-logical" in his essay on Auerbach, mentioned above.

67. One can also argue that the modern media operate in the same way, which explains their fascination for patterns and repetitions. The most important thing for the media to determine is if something is an "isolated event" or an event that can be connected to other similar events, for it is in this way that *meaning* (in the strong sense) is generated. As White related to me in personal conversation: something that happens only once is meaningless; something that happens twice, a coincidence; something that happens three times: a narrative.

68. Hayden White, *The Greco-Roman Tradition* (New York: Harper & Row, 1973), 5.

69. Jameson, "Criticism in History," *The Ideologies of Theory*, 120.

Chapter 1 · Collingwood and Toynbee

1. A. J. P. Taylor, *Rumors of Wars* (London: Hamilton, 1952), 1. For a general survey of English historiography see Eduardo Fueter, *Storia della storiografia moderna* (Naples: Riccardo Ricciardi, 1944), vol. 2, 212ff. The best survey of the origins of the English historicist tradition is by Friedrich Meinecke, *Le origini dello storicismo* (Florence: Sansoni, 1954), 155–246. See also the appraisal of Robertson and the modification of Meinecke's views in Manfred Schlenke, "Aus der Frühzeit des englischen Historismus. William Robertsons Beitrag zur methodischen Grundlegung der Geschichtswissenschaft im 18. Jahrhundert," *Saeculum* 7 (1956): 107–25. For an examination of English historiography in the past fifty years, see F. M. Powicke, *Modern Historians and the Study of History* (London: Odhams Press, 1955), 159ff. Other evaluations of the English historical tradition may be had in R. G. Collingwood, *The Idea of History* (Oxford: Oxford University Press, 1946), 134–56; Herbert Butterfield, *The Englishman and His History* (Cambridge: Cambridge University Press, 1945), *History and Human Relations* (London: Collins, 1951), *The Whig Interpretation of History* (London: G. Bell and Sons, 1931); and Geoffrey Barraclough, *History in a Changing World* (Oxford: Blackwell, 1955), 1–54, 135ff.

2. See Butterfield, *The Whig Interpretation of History*, 8ff. Cf. Arnold Toynbee's critique of English historiography and its relation to the empirical tradition in his *Civilization on Trial* (Oxford: Oxford University Press, 1948), 16ff.

3. See the discussion between Toynbee and his Dutch critic Pieter Geyl in Pieter Geyl, Arnold J. Toynbee, Pitirim A. Sorokin, *The Pattern of the Past: Can We Determine It?* (Boston: Beacon Press, 1949), 73ff. Cf. Toynbee *Civilization on Trial*, 23ff., and R. G. Collingwood, *Autobiography* (Middlesex: Penguin Books, 1944), 62ff. All of the significant criticisms of Toynbee can be found in Ashley Montague, ed., *Toynbee and History: Critical Essays and Reviews* (Boston: Porter Sargent, 1956).

4. W. Windelband, *A History of Philosophy* (New York: Harper, 1958), 476.

5. Schlenke, "Aus der Fruhzeit," 112, note 32. Cf. Meinecke, *Le origini dello storicismo*, 191–96.

6. Schlenke, "Aus der Fruhzeit," 117, note 63.

7. The most perceptive essay on German historicism is, in the opinion of the present writer, that of Carlo Antoni, *Dallo storicismo alla sociologia* (Florence: Sansoni, 1951). [Hayden White translated this book under the title *From History to Sociology: The Transition in German Historical Thinking* (Detroit: Wayne State University Press, 1959).] Currently the term *historicism* has assumed many connotations not all of which are admissible. For Karl Popper, it means any social philosophy based upon monistic principles. See Popper's article "The Poverty of Historicism," *Economica* 11 (1944): 86–103. [See also Popper's book of the same title, which was published in the same year as White's essay: *The Poverty of Historicism* (New York: Basic Books, 1957).] For both German and Italian historicists, one must escape the urge to explain all phenomena in terms of one concept or even many and seek to intuitively grasp the individuality and uniqueness of every historical event. See Antoni, *Dallo*

storicismo alla sociologia, 87ff; Walter Hofer, *Geschichtschreibung und Weltanschauung* (Munich: Oldenbourg, 1950), 319ff.; Ernst Troeltsch, *Der Historismus und seine Probleme* (Tübingen: C. B. Mohr, 1922).

8. Collingwood, *The Idea of History*, 249.

9. Quoted in G. J. Renier, *History: Its Purpose and Method* (London: Allen & Unwin, 1950), 49.

10. Patrick Gardiner, *The Nature of Historical Explanation* (Oxford: Oxford University Press, 1952), 60–64.

11. See Popper, "The Poverty of Historicism," 86ff.; Isaiah Berlin, *Historical Inevitability* (Oxford: Oxford University Press, 1955), 40–44; and A. L. Rowse, *The Use of History* (New York: Macmillan, 1948), 123ff.

12. Collingwood, *Autobiography*, 60ff.

13. Morton G. White, *The Age of Analysis: Twentieth Century Philosophers* (New York: Mentor Books, 1955), 14ff.

14. Quoted in A. J. Ayer, *The Revolution in Philosophy* (London: Macmillan, 1956), 45ff. See Bertrand Russell, *Our Knowledge of the External World as a Field for Scientific Method in Philosophy* (Chicago: Open Court, 1929), 3–63.

15. Errol E. Harris, *Nature, Mind, and Modern Science* (London: Allen & Unwin, 1954), 319.

16. Russell, *Our Knowledge*, 19ff; Ayer, *The Revolution in Philosophy*, 5ff.

17. G. E. Moore, *Principia Ethica* (Cambridge: Cambridge University Press, 1951), 6ff.

18. Quoted in Ayer, *The Revolution in Philosophy*, 60.

19. E. W. F. Tomlin, *R. G. Collingwood* (New York: Longmans, Green, and Co., 1953).

20. Collingwood, *Autobiography*, 66.

21. Ibid., 36.

22. James Collins, *The Existentialists: A Critical Study* (Chicago: H. Regnery, 1952), 193.

23. Collingwood, *Autobiography*, 70.

24. Ibid., 64.

25. See Harris, *Nature, Mind, and Modern Science*, 445–46.

26. Collingwood, *Autobiography*, 64ff.

27. Collingwood, *Idea of History*, 302.

28. Ibid., 308; *Autobiography*, 302.

29. *Autobiography*, 20ff.

30. Benedetto Croce, *La storia come pensiero e come azione* (Bari: G. Laterza, 1943), 287–93.

31. Collingwood, *Idea of History*, 199.

32. Benedetto Croce, *Teoria e storia della storiografia* (Bari: G. Laterza, 1917), 119; Collingwood, *Idea of History*, 199.

33. Collingwood, *Idea of History*, 200.

34. Harris, *Nature, Mind, and Modern Science*, 445–46.

35. Collingwood, *Idea of History*, 449ff., 282–302.

36. Ibid., 315–19, 324ff.

37. R. G. Collingwood, *Speculum Mentis, or the Map of Knowledge* (Oxford: Clarendon

Press, 1924), 399ff. The best discussion of Collingwood's epistemology is to be found in H. A. Hodges, *The Philosophy of Wilhelm Dilthey* (London: Routledge & Paul, 1952), 341ff. Collingwood's concept of culture is not unlike that of Dutch historian Jan Huizinga, who writes, "History is the spiritual form in which a civilization gives itself an account of the past" (quoted in Renier, *History*, 35, note 1). Cf. the view of Croce: "la cultura storica ha il fine di serbare viva la coscienza che la società umana ha del proprio passato, cioè del suo presente, cioè di se stessa, di fornirle quel che le occorre sempre per le vie da scegliere, di tener pronto quanto per questa parte potrà giovarle in avvenire. In questo alto suo pregio morale e politico si fonda lo zelo di promuoverla e di accrescerla, la gelosa cura di preservarla incontaminata, e insieme con ciò, il biasimo severo che infligge a chi la deprime, la distorce e la corrompe." (Historical culture has for its object the keeping alive of the consciousness which human society has of its own past, that is, of its present, that is, of itself, and to furnish it with what is always required in the choice of the paths it is to follow, and to keep in readiness for it whatever may be useful in this way, in the future. This high moral and political value of historical culture is the basis of the zealous endeavor to promote and to increase it, of the jealous care used to preserve its security, and also of that heavy censure which falls upon him who abuses or distorts or corrupts historical culture [Croce, *La storia come pensiero e come azione*; English version, *History as the Story of Liberty*, trans. Sylvia Sprigge (London: Allen & Unwin, 1941), 199]).

38. Hodges, *The Philosophy of Wilhelm Dilthey*, 341–43.

39. Collingwood, *Speculum Mentis*, 58ff.

40. Ibid., 111.

41. Ibid., 157.

42. Ibid., 194.

43. Ibid., 311.

44. See Bronislaw Malinowski, *The Foundations of Faith and Morals* (Oxford: Oxford University Press, 1936), 32ff. Cf. Ernst Cassier's analysis in *The Myth of the State* (New Haven, CT: Yale University Press, 1946), 278; and Robert Redfield, *The Primitive World and Its Transformation* (Ithaca, NY: Cornell University Press, 1953), 23ff.

45. Collingwood, *Speculum Mentis*, 199.

46. Hodges, *The Philosophy of Wilhelm Dilthey*, 342.

47. Collingwood, *Idea of History*, 332.

48. Karl Jaspers, *The Origin and Goal of History* [*Vom Ursprung und Ziel der Geschichte*], trans. Michael Bullock (London: Routledge & Paul, 1953), 234ff.

49. I can find no better way of illuminating this statement than by quoting the words of Professor Errol Harris: "It is all one continuous process of development in and through which the basal activity which is the 'substance' of the real—the activity of thought—comes to consciousness of itself in and as mind, makes its own history and reflects upon itself and the process of its own development, and by so doing makes still further progress towards the completion of the development in the infinite spiritual consummation which is God" (*Nature, Mind, and Modern Science*, 446).

50. Collingwood, *Speculum Mentis*, 299.

51. Collingwood, *Idea of History*, 257–61.

52. Collingwood, *Autobiography*, 78–79. Cf. Collingwood, *Idea of History*, 10.

53. Collingwood, *Autobiography*, 75.

54. Ibid., 73.

55. Collingwood, *Idea of History*, 246.

56. Cf. Morris Cohen, *The Meaning of Human History* (LaSalle, IL: Open Court, 1947), 38–39; and Maurice Mandelbaum, *The Problem of Historical Knowledge: An Answer to Relativism* (New York: Liveright, 1938), 295ff.

57. [Giovanni Gentile (1875–1944) wrote *A Doctrine of Fascism*, which was published under Mussolini's name in 1932.]

58. See C. G. Jung, *Modern Man in Search of a Soul* (New York: Harcourt, Brace, 1934), 95ff. It is important to note that Collingwood's concept of the relation between mind and body is essentially that of Jung and the Gestalt psychologists, because criticism of him is based upon a misunderstanding of his psychology. It has usually been termed "idealist" and ignored—as though idealism was a self-defeating philosophical position. For example, Gardiner seeks to show that in fact most disputes between philosophers of history are really disputes between "idealists," on the one hand, and "materialists," on the other. Thus Gardiner quotes Marx as an advocate of "materialism" and Collingwood as a defender of "idealism." After having formulated a dichotomy that exists only in his own mind, Gardiner then seeks to resolve the argument with an appeal to "common sense." He writes: "Human beings are not 'really matter' or 'really mind': they are human beings. Different ways of talking about them dictated by different interests have been hypostatized into different ingredients" (Gardiner, *The Nature of Historical Explanation*, 137–38). It is strange to hear a trained philosopher speak thus. Few serious philosophers have ever argued that man was "really mind" or "really matter" (Gardiner does not indicate why he has used quote marks), neither Plato nor Marx—and certainly not Collingwood. One need only quote Collingwood to expose the fallacy in Gardiner's criticism of him: "So far as man's conduct is determined by what may be called his animal nature, his impulses and appetites, it is non-historical; the process of those activities is a natural process. Thus the historian is not interested in the fact that men eat and sleep and make love and satisfy their natural appetites; but he is interested in the social customs which they create by their thought as a framework within which those appetites find satisfaction in ways sanctioned by convention and morality" (*Idea of History*, 216).

It is hardly necessary to point out that in arguing that the natural functions of the human organism are not the material of historical investigation, Collingwood is not asserting that man is "really mind." To mistake Collingwood's position for such an assertion and then to "refute" the assertion by holding, as Gardiner does, that Collingwood posits a "world of mental agencies, *mysteriously* lying *behind* the world of historical bodies and actions, *separate from* it and yet controlling it" is sheer nonsense (the italics are mine—Hayden White). Cf. Gardiner's exposition in *The Nature of Historical Explanation*, 51ff., and Harris, *Nature, Mind, and Modern Science*, 29–42.

59. Richard Hertz, *Chance and Symbol: A Study in Aesthetic and Ethical Consistency* (Chicago: University of Chicago Press, 1948), 9ff.

60. Toynbee, *Civilization on Trial*, 16–28.

61. Arnold J. Toynbee, *A Study of History* (Oxford: Oxford University Press, 1954–), vol. 1, 179.

62. Collingwood, *Idea of History*, 162.

63. Ibid.

64. Ibid., 163.

65. Ibid.

66. Toynbee, *A Study of History*, vol. 9, 732.

67. Ibid., 732. For a further exposition of this theme, see Toynbee's more recent book, *An Historian's Approach to Religion* (Oxford: Oxford University Press, 1956), 56–73.

68. Toynbee, *A Study of History*, vol. 9, 737. See the review of Toynbee's last four volumes by F. H. Underhill, "The Toynbee of the 1930s," *Canadian Historical Review* 36 (Sept. 1955), 225. Here is given a list of reviews of Toynbee's work that supplements that of Montague cited above, note 3. Further bibliography will be found in Karl D. Erlmann, "Toynbee: Eine Zwischenbilanz," *Archiv für Kulturgeschichte* 33 (1951): 174–256, and Aloys Wenzl "Die philosophischen Grundlagen von Toynbees Geschichtsbild" *Speculum* 4 (1953), 201–6.

69. Toynbee, *A Study of History*, vol. 9, 128–77.

70. On Schelling, see Windelband, *A History of Philosophy*, 616–20, and Heinrich Knitermeyer, *Schelling und die Romantische Schule* (Munich: Reinhardt, 1929), 415ff. Cf. Toynbee's personal religions credo in his *A Study of History*, vol. 7, 420–21, note 6. For a further examination of Toynbee's journey from empiricism toward a modified Germanic idealism, see Othman Anderle, *Das Universalhistorische System Arnold Joseph Toynbees* (Frankfurt am Main: Humboldt-Verlag, 1955), 441–49; and Oskar Kohler, "Toynbees Bild der Menscheitsgeschichte" *Saeculum* 1 (1950), 165ff.

71. Toynbee, *A Study of History*, vol. 10, 1.

72. Ibid., vol. 10, 2.

73. Ibid., vol. 7, 500–501.

74. Ibid., vol. 7, 445.

75. Ibid., vol. 7, 449.

76. Ibid., vol. 7, 442–49. [Verses are from a poem by Saint Francis of Assisi: "Cantico delle creature."]

77. Toynbee, *A Study of History*, vol. 10, 141; Barraclough, *History in a Changing World*, 1–31, 135ff.; Barraclough, Cobban, et al., "Historical Writing," *Times Literary Supplement*, Jan. 6, 1956.

78. H. W. Walsh, *An Introduction to Philosophy of History* (New York: Hutchinson University Library, 1951), 168. Is it possible that a generation that responded to the intellectual development of T. S. Eliot from "The Waste Land" to "The Rock" would be totally insensitive to Toynbee's attempt to correlate the immanent with the transcendent? Nor is Toynbee unaware that his task is similar to that of Eliot. He writes on the title page of *An Historian's Approach to Religion* a phrase from Eliot's "Four Quartets": "Only through time time is conquered." Furthermore, Toynbee's work must be likened to that of Christian existentialists such as Paul Tillich, who approaches Toynbee—at least in mood—in his "Existential Philosophy," *Journal of the History of Ideas* 5 (1944): 44–70.

79. Taylor, *Rumors of Wars*, 18.

80. Jaspers, *Origin and Goal of History*, 211.

81. Ibid., 269.

*Chapter 2 · Religion, Culture, and Western Civilization
in Christopher Dawson's Idea of History*

1. See my article "Collingwood and Toynbee: Transitions in English Historical Thought" (*English Miscellany* 7, 1956), especially 148–52. [This essay is chap. 1 of the present volume.]

2. C. V. Wedgewood recently wrote: "Very few historians today would take a stand unequivocally for history as art or for history as science. It has by now come to be generally agreed that history is a compound of the two" ("History as Literature," *The Times Literary Supplement*, Jan. 6, 1956, xi). See also in the same issue the article by Geoffrey Barroclough, "The Larger View of History," ii; and the same author's *History in a Changing World* (Oxford: Blackwell, 1955), 1–53, 154ff.

3. White, "Collingwood and Toynbee," 152ff.

4. See Christopher Dawson, "The Problem of Metahistory," *History Today* 1 (June, 1951), republished in Christopher Dawson, *Dynamics of World History*, ed. J. J. Mulloy (New York: Sheed & Ward, 1957), 293. For his evaluation of the contribution and limitations of Saint Augustine's conception of history, see Dawson's article "St. Augustine and His Age," in M. C. d'Arcy and others, *Saint Augustine* (New York: Meridian, 1957), 44.

5. See Carlo Antoni, *Dallo storicismo alla sociologia* (Florence: Sansoni, 1940), 39–86, 121–88. [English translation by Hayden White: *From History to Sociology: The Transition in German Historical Thinking* (Detroit: Wayne State University Press, 1959).]

6. Of Saint Augustine, Dawson wrote: "It is true that St. Augustine did not consider the problem of secular progress, but then secular history, in Augustine's view, was essentially unprogressive. It was the spectacle of humanity perpetually engaged in chasing its own tail. The true history of the human race is to be found in the process of enlightenment and salvation by which human nature is liberated and restored to spiritual freedoms" (d'Arcy, *Saint Augustine*, 71). On Dawson's attempt to integrate a theological conception of history and modern sociology and anthropology, see J. J. Mulloy's essay, "Continuity and Development in Christopher Dawson's Thought," in Dawson, *Dynamics of World History*, 419–47.

7. Christopher Dawson, *The Age of the Gods: A Study in the Origins of Culture in Prehistoric Europe and the Ancient East* (London: Sheed & Ward, 1928), xiii.

8. Christopher Dawson, *Progress and Religion* (London: Sheed & Ward, 1929), 55.

9. Ibid., 55.

10. See R. G. Collingwood, *The Idea of History* (Oxford: Oxford University Press, 1946), 88–93; Carlo Antoni, *Lo storicismo* (Turin: Edizioni Radio italiana, 1957), 95ff.

11. See Mulloy, "Continuity and Development in Christopher Dawson's Thought," 435; and Christopher Dawson, *Understanding Europe* (New York: Sheed & Ward, 1952), chaps. 1 and 10. On his conceptions of natural law, see Christopher Dawson, *Religion and Culture* (London: Sheed & Ward, 1948), 42–44.

12. *Age of the Gods*, xiv.

13. *Dynamics of World History*, 287ff.; *Progress and Religion*, 24ff.

14. Ibid., 45.

15. *Religion and Culture*, 48–49.

16. *Progress and Religion,* 65–66.

17. *Age of the Gods,* xviiff., 87–107, 235–57.

18. Ibid., xix.

19. *Progress and Religion,* 46.

20. Collingwood first presented his concept of culture in his *Speculum Mentis, or the Map of Knowledge* (Oxford: Clarendon Press, 1924). This book constitutes the best statement of his basic position. For an examination of its modifications, see H. A. Hodges, *The Philosophy of Wilhelm Dilthey* (London: Routledge & Paul, 1952), 341ff., where much space is devoted to a comparison of Collingwood, Croce, and Dilthey; and Errol Harris, *Nature, Mind, and Modern Science* (London: Allen & Unwin, 1954), 445ff.

21. Collingwood, *Speculum Mentis,* 288ff.

22. Ibid., 291.

23. [See chap. 1 of this volume.]

24. Ibid., 80–91, 117–58.

25. Ibid., 138–46.

26. Dawson, *Dynamics of World History,* 293. In all fairness to Dawson, it must be pointed out that he feels it is impossible to write great history without "intuitive understanding, creative imagination, and finally a universal vision transcending the relative limitations of the particular field of historical understanding." But, as we shall see, all of these are, in Dawson's thought, subsumed under his general religious conception.

27. *Age of the Gods,* 22.

28. Jacques Maritain, Peter Wust, and Christopher Dawson, *Essays in Order* (New York: Sheed & Ward, 1940), 179.

29. *Religion and Culture,* 49–50.

30. Ibid., 58.

31. *Essays in Order,* 176; *Religion and Culture,* 66ff.

32. *Religion and Culture,* 50.

33. Christopher Dawson, "Civilization and Morals," *The Sociological Review* 13 (Apr. 1921), republished in *Dynamics of World History.*

34. *Age of the Gods,* xx.

35. This is not to say that Dawson does not recognize the importance of the city in the progress of civilization. He sees it as the point of concentration of the cultural heritage of a people and gives it the central place in the process of fusion that occurs after the conflict of cultures. See *Dynamics of World History,* 434. But in the tradition of Amos and Hosea, Dawson also sees it as the place where the traditional morality breaks down. It tends to sever its relation with the countryside, which supplies the vital material without which the culture cannot survive. Thus, he argues that Hellenic civilization collapses not from a failure of nerve but from a failure of life. Its strength rested on a "regional and agrarian foundation." When it shifted and became a nation of town dwellers, it destroyed its own source of power (*Progress and Religion,* 65).

36. Ibid., 104; *Religion and Culture,* 69.

37. *Progress and Religion,* 111–12.

38. Ibid., 120; cf. also *Age of the Gods,* 235–37.

39. *Progress and Religion,* 119ff.; *Essays in Order,* 186ff.

40. *Religion and Culture*, 207ff.

41. *Progress and Religion*, 149ff.

42. Ibid., 155–56.

43. Ibid., 162. See also Christopher Dawson, *The Making of Europe* (New York: Sheed & Ward, 1945, first published 1932), 141ff., 159, 166.

44. Ibid, 105ff., 113–22.

45. Dawson conceives of a "classical age" as that period in the history of a civilization that reemerges after a culture sustained an invasion by an alien people and fused with it. The resultant cultural forms "thus acquire a classical character that endures, as long as the particular culture survives" (*Religion and Culture*, 200).

46. *Progress and Religion*, 166. See *Making of Europe*, 189ff., and Christopher Dawson, *Religion and the Rise of Western Culture* (New York: Sheed & Ward, 1950), chaps. 4 and 7.

47. *Making of Europe*, 214–33; *Religion and the Rise of Western Culture*, 193–239.

48. *Religion and Culture*, 201; *Making of Europe*, 286–90.

49. *Progress and Religion*, 167.

50. Ibid., 171.

51. Ibid., 170.

52. Ibid., 171.

53. Ibid., 173–74.

54. *Making of Europe*, 288ff.; *Progress and Religion*, 177ff.

55. Ibid., 178.

56. Ibid., 180.

57. Ibid., 185; *Essays in Order*, 161.

58. *Religion and Culture*, 106.

59. *Progress and Religion*, 210–11. See also 212–19 passim.

60. *Dynamics of World History*, 412.

61. *The Idea of History*, 77.

62. Naturally, Dawson finds that he has much in common with T. S. Eliot. See his essay, "T. S. Eliot on the Meaning of Culture," *The Month* 1 (Mar. 1949), republished in *Dynamics of World History*, 103–10.

63. Bronislaw Malinowski, *The Foundations of Faith and Morals* (Oxford: Oxford University Press, 1936), 32ff., and *Magic, Science, and Religion and Other Essays* (Garden City, NY: Doubleday, 1954), 25ff.

64. Robert Redfield, *The Primitive World and Its Transformations* (Ithaca, NY: Cornell University Press, 1953), 15–23.

65. See V. Gordon Childe, *Man Makes Himself* (New York: New American Library, 1951), especially chap. 5 and following.

66. Redfield, *The Primitive World*, 22ff.

67. Sir Sarvepalli Radhakrishnan, *The Hindu View of Life; Upton Lectures Delivered at Manchester College, Oxford, 1926* (London: Allen & Unwin, 1927).

68. This is the inevitable consequence of any philosophy of history conceived on a religious (or monist) base. As Croce pointed out long ago, such a view of history can only be regarded as a form of myth the distinguishing characteristic of which is the confusion of concept and imagination. See Benedetto Croce, *La storia come pensiero e come azione*

(Bari: G. Laterza, 1943), 138. Dawson must be adjudged guilty of the same error that marked the work of Hegel; and of his work it may be said what Croce said of all "philosophy of history":

> Since the philosophy of history does its work or plays its game, if you like, upon the divisions and subdivisions which are the usual groupings of historiography, it is not concerned with the original thought or construction of history, but deals with it ready made, thought out, recounted, and provided with headings, summaries which are then used as a foundation. By refining or rather contorting these it is said the "inside" history, the true, underlying the apparent, history is produced; and this is simply the mythology already referred to. In this way, we get a duality: on the one hand, historical accounts constructed by way of criticism; on the other, interpretations which lie beyond criticism being the result of revelation or of ulterior vision, or a faculty which cannot be described or find any relationship or harmony with the other faculties of the human spirit. This duality takes the practical shape in the dualism known as "allegorism": which [is not] either induction or deduction, but a poor mixture of the two. (Ibid., 139–40; English trans. Sylvia Sprigge, *History as the Story of Liberty* [New York: Meridian Books, 1955], 135–36)

It may be said that instead of succeeding in enclosing within a single system the faith of Saint Augustine and the reason of the modern age, Dawson has merely restated the traditional subservience of the latter to the former that must always result from any attempt at synthesis of this sort. He ends by denying secular culture a positive position, his assertions to the contrary notwithstanding. He agrees with Newman, for example, in holding that the State is founded in sin. See "St. Augustine and his Age," 63. In this aspect of his thought, Dawson errs as far in this direction as the eighteenth century *philosophe*, with his unequivocal hatred for religion, erred in his. The result of the radically rationalist attitude of the Enlightenment was a basically anti-historical position (Collingwood, *The Idea of History*, 77). Dawson's anti-historical view results in his asserting that there are insights into the historical picture that require special forms of understanding. For example, of the Middle Ages and its spiritual life he states: "It is very difficult for anyone who is not a Catholic to understand the *full meaning* of this great tradition" (*Making of Europe*, xviii; the italics are mine). Here "full meaning" must be taken to imply that there is a truth available in the historical documents which requires not human understanding, historical ability, but a special epistemological dispensation.

Chapter 3 · *The Abiding Relevance of Croce's Idea of History*

1. Erich Auerbach, *Mimesis: The Representation of Reality in Western Literature*, trans. W. Trask (Princeton, NJ: Princeton University Press, 1953), 17.

2. See Gilbert Murray, "Croce as a European," in *Benedetto Croce: A Commemoration*, ed. Gilbert Murray (London: Publications of the Italian Cultural Institute, 1953).

3. For a review of the debate over Croce's political activities and his political philosophy before, during, and after fascism, see Giovanni Mastroianni, "La polemica sul Croce negli studi contemporanei," *Società* 14 (July 1958): 711–37.

4. Guido De Ruggiero, *Il ritorno alla ragione* (Bari: G. Laterza, 1946), 12.

5. On the place of Croce in contemporary Italian intellectual life, see: Norberto Bobbio, *Politica e cultura* (Turin: Einaudi, 1955), 100–120, 211–68; and Pietro Rossi, *Storia e storicismo nella filosofia contemporanea* (Milan: Lerici, 1960), 287ff.

6. See the remarks of A. L. Rowse, *The Use of History* (London: Hodder & Stoughton, 1946), 149; G. J. Renier, *History, Its Purpose and Method* (Boston: Beacon Press, 1950), 41; Patrick Gardiner, ed., *Theories of History* (Glencoe, IL: The Free Press, 1959), 249, 268.

7. H. Stuart Hughes, *Consciousness and Society* (London: MacGibbon and Kee, 1959), 229.

8. See, however, Antonio Gramsci, *Il materialismo storico e la filosofia di Benedetto Croce* (Turin: Einaudi, 1955), 174–77, 210ff. Gramsci was the respected leader of the Italian Communist party who ended his life in a Fascist prison. But he was not alone in pointing to Croce's class and regional royalties as determinants of his philosophical position. In 1954, Gaetano Salvemini, a liberal, could still write "born into a family he inherited and preserved, in political and social questions, the interests and mental attitudes peculiar to the great southern landowners" (letter to *Il Ponte* 10 [Nov. 1954], 1741).

9. Benedetto Croce, *History of Europe in the Nineteenth Century,* trans. H. Furst (New York: Harcourt Brace, 1933), 317.

10. Benedetto Croce, "Les études relatives à la théorie de l'histoire en Italie durant les quinze dernières années," *Revue de synthèse historique* (1902), now republished together with other early essays on historiographical theory in *Primi saggi* (Bari: G. Laterza, 1951), 171–99.

11. See the essays collected under the title *Saggio sullo Hegel seguito da altri scritti di storia della filosofia* (Bari: G. Laterza, 1927), especially the important "Ciò che è vivo e ciò che è morto della filosofia di Hegel" (What Is Living and What Is Dead in Hegel's Philosophy), 78, 96ff.

12. Benedetto Croce, "Contributo alla critica di me stesso," first published in 1918 and supplemented in 1945, and now republished in *Etica e politica aggiuntovi il contributo alla critica di me stesso* (Bari: G. Laterza, 1956), 441.

13. See Croce's review of the Italian translation of Friedrich Nietzsche's *Birth of Tragedy* (1907), republished in *Saggio sullo Hegel,* 411ff.

14. *Primi saggi,* 190.

15. Benedetto Croce, *La storia come pensiero e come azione,* translated into English by Sylvia Sprigge as *History as the Story of Liberty* (New York: Meridian Books, 1955), 273.

16. Benedetto Croce, *Teoria e storia della storiografia* (Bari: G. Laterza, 1954), 85.

17. Cf. Carlo Antoni, *Commento a Croce* (Venice: Pozza, 1955), 131ff.

18. See Catherine Gilbert's superb essay on Croce, "The Vital Disequilibrium in Croce's Historicism," in *Essays in Political Theory Presented to George H. Sabine,* ed. M. Konvitz and A. Murphy (Ithaca, NY: Cornell University Press, 1948), 216ff.

19. Croce, *History of Europe in the Nineteenth Century,* 319–20.

20. Croce, *History as the Story of Liberty,* 274.

21. Ibid., 153.

22. Ibid., 286.

23. Croce, *Storiografia e idealità morale* (Bari: G. Laterza, 1950), 112.

24. Federico Chabod, "Croce storico," *Rivista storica italiana* 14 (1952): 484–85, 497.

25. Croce, *History of Europe,* 33.

26. Erich Heller, *The Disinherited Mind* (New York: Meridian Books 1959), 83.

27. The best study in English of Croce's historical work is A. Robert Caponigri, *History and Liberty: The Historical Writings of Benedetto Croce* (London: Routledge & Paul, 1955).

28. Croce, *History of Europe,* 13.

29. Georg Lukács, *La distruzione della ragione* (Turin: Einaudi, 1959), 19ff. (Italian translation of *Die Zerstörung der Vernunft*).

30. Croce, *History of Europe,* 362.

Chapter 4 · *Romanticism, Historicism, and Realism*

1. Ludwig Wittgenstein, *Philosophical Investigations,* trans. G. E. M. Anscombe (Oxford: Blackwell, 1953), §67.

Chapter 5 · *The Tasks of Intellectual History*

1. Lucien Goldmann, "The Genetic Structuralist Method in the History of Literature," *Towards a Sociology of the Novel,* trans. Alan Sheridan. (London: Tavistock, 1975), 159.

Chapter 6 · *The Culture of Criticism*

1. Since writing this, I have been convinced by discussion with my colleagues at Wesleyan—and especially by Frank Kermode, Norman Rudich, and Victor Gourevitch— that my grouping of Auerbach with Popper and Gombrich obscures the differences in affective predisposition with which each of these three thinkers views the advent of the revolt against realism in the modern imagination. I am prepared to concede that Auerbach is much more inclined to view the apocalyptic aspects of this revolt with somewhat more sympathy than either Popper or Gombrich is inclined to do. And this because he has a somewhat more ample (specifically Hegelian) awareness of the creative possibilities of any revolution in consciousness, whether in the direction of formal consistency or in the direction of a "paratactical" resistance to such consistency. For the purposes of this paper, however, which is to characterize the cultural preconceptions of the centrist tradition in humanistic criticisms, the three thinkers can be conveniently grouped together. Auerbach would simply have to be conceived as a representative of the left wing of that tradition by virtue of the sympathy he is inclined to extend to attempted revolutions of the sort envisaged by the avant-garde of this century. The categories of his *analysis* of the situation appear to me to be substantially the same as those used by both Popper and Gombrich.

Chapter 7 · *The Structure of Historical Narrative*

1. [Jacob Burckhardt, *The Civilization of the Renaissance in Italy,* trans. S. G. C. Middlemore (Charleston, SC: BiblioBazaar, 2007), 428.]

2. [One can find extensive discussions of each of these three historians in Hayden White, *Metahistory: The Historical Imagination in Nineteenth-Century Europe* (Baltimore: Johns Hopkins University Press, 1973), chaps. 4, 5, and 6, devoted to Ranke, Tocqueville, and Burckhardt respectively.]

3. [See the Introduction to White's *Metahistory* (1973).]

4. Louis Mink, "The Autonomy of Historical Understanding," *History and Theory* 5 (1965): 24–47.

5. This paper was written before I came upon Haskell Fain's *Between Philosophy and History: The Resurrection of Speculative Philosophy of History within the Analytic Tradition* (1970), which deals with many of the same issues. After I read it, I felt compelled to rephrase some of my original remarks but not in such a way as to change the argument. I merely want to note, however, that whereas I stress the utility of the story-plot distinction for the analysis of historical narratives, he does not think this distinction very helpful. Also, while I agree with him that E. M. Forster's analysis of the story-plot relationship in the novel, in his *Aspects of the Novel*, is wrong, it is not for the reasons that Professor Fain gives. In the background of this paper are two articles by Louis Mink (in addition to the 1965 article mentioned above) that bear directly on the subject. These are: "Philosophical Analysis and Historical Understanding," *Review of Metaphysics* 31 (June 1968): 667–98; and "History and Fiction as Modes of Comprehension," *New Literary History* 1 (Spring 1970): 541–58. All three are illuminating of the problem I am dealing with, and much of what I say is an amplification of some of the points raised by Mink in these articles.

My own conception of the story-plot relationship derives in large part from the study of the work of Northrop Frye, whose *Anatomy of Criticism* (Princeton, NJ: Princeton University Press, 1957) no student of narrative should neglect to study. Brief expositions of his views are to be found in two articles: "Myth, Fiction, and Displacement," and "New Directions from Old," both in Frye, *Fables of Identity: Studies in Poetic Mythology* (New York: Harcourt, Brace & World, 1963). In addition, see Frank Kermode, *The Sense of an Ending* (Oxford: Oxford University Press, 1967), chaps. 1 and 2, where the problem of the "consonance" between beginnings and endings in literary fictions is dealt with.

Naturally, in my discussion of "story" concepts of explanation, I have in mind Dray and Gallie, especially the article by the former which appears as a commentary on Mandelbaum's notion of historical explanation in *History and Theory* 8 (1969): 287–94; and the book of the latter, *Philosophy and the Historical Understanding* (New York: Schocken Books, 1964), especially chaps. 2, 3, and 5. I did not find Arthur Danto's otherwise excellent book much help in my reflection on this subject because he takes such an uncharacteristically conservative view on the problem of the nature of narrative and even on narrative sentences. Compare Danto's remarks in *Analytical Philosophy of History* (Cambridge: Cambridge University Press, 1968), chaps. 7, 8, and 11, with Mink's remarks in the article in the *Review of Metaphysics* cited above, 689–97. Also compare the discussions of the relation between story and plot in Boris Tomashevsky's classic essay, "Thematics," in *Russian Formalist Criticism: Four Essays*, trans. Lee T. Lemon and Marion J. Reis (Lincoln: University of Nebraska Press, 1965), 61–95, and also, in the same work, Boris Eichenbaum, "The Theory of the 'Formal Method,'" 99–139.

Finally, the notion of the "relational cryptogram" is a central concept of E. H. Gombrich's study of realistic representation in the visual arts: *Art and Illusion: A Study in the Psychology of Pictorial Representation* (New York: Pantheon Books, 1960), chaps. 5 and 6, recently amplified in his essay, "The Evidence of Images," in Charles Singleton, ed., *Interpretation: Theory and Practice* (Baltimore: Johns Hopkins Press, 1969), esp. 35–68.

Chapter 9 · *The Politics of Contemporary Philosophy of History*

1. This essay was originally written for presentation as the opening address at a conference on philosophy of history held at York University in spring 1969. It was consciously polemical and meant to raise issues for subsequent discussion at the conference. If I were rewriting it today, I would probably cast it in a different tone, but the point of view would remain the same. It could also stand some amplification in the light of Professor Dray's acute criticism.

2. G. R. Elton, *The Practice of History* (New York: Crowell, 1967), v.

3. Ibid., 39.

4. Karl R. Popper, *The Poverty of Historicism* (London: Routledge & Kegan Paul, 1961), 143.

5. Ibid., 144.

6. [Jean-Paul Sartre, *Critique of Dialectical Reason* (New York: Verso, 1991).]

7. William H. Dray, *Philosophy of History* (Englewood Cliffs, NJ: Prentice-Hall, 1964), 65.

8. Leonard Bloomfield, *Language* (New York: H. Holt and Company, 1938), 48.

9. Maurice Merleau-Ponty, *Phenomenology of Perception*, trans. Colin Smith (New York: Humanities Press, 1962), 346.

10. Claude Lévi-Strauss, *The Savage Mind* (Chicago: University of Chicago Press, 1966), 262.

11. H. I. Marrou, "From the Logic of History to an Ethic for the Historian," *Cross Currents* (Winter 1961): 68.

12. Iris Murdoch, *Sartre, Romantic Rationalist* (New Haven, CT: Yale University Press, 1953), 42.

Chapter 10 · *The Problem of Change in Literary History*

1. M. H. Abrams, *The Mirror and the Lamp: Romantic Theory and the Critical Tradition* (Oxford: Oxford University Press, 1953), 3–29.

2. For a discussion of the relation between *explanans* and *explanandum* in the logic of explanations, see C. G. Hempel, "Explanation in Science and History," in *Philosophical Analysis and History*, ed. W. H. Dray (New York: Harper & Row, 1966), 95–126.

3. Claude Lévi-Strauss, *The Savage Mind* (Chicago: University of Chicago Press, 1966), 260.

4. Lucien Goldmann, "Structure: Human Reality and Methodological Concept," in *The Languages of Criticism and the Sciences of Man: The Structuralist Controversy*, ed. Richard Macksey and Eugenio Donato (Baltimore: Johns Hopkins Press, 1970), 98–109. [A new edition of this seminal anthology has been published under the title *The Structuralist Contro-

versy: The Languages of Criticism and the Sciences of Man, 40th anniversary edition, ed. Richard Macksey and Eugenio Donato (Baltimore: Johns Hopkins University Press, 2007)].

5. [This essay originally appeared in *New Literary History.*]

6. *Style in Language,* ed. Thomas A. Sebeok (Cambridge, MA: MIT Press, 1960), 356, 358.

7. Ibid., 375.

8. Roman Jakobson and Morris Halle, *Fundamentals of Language* (The Hague: Mouton, 1956), 77–78.

Chapter 11 · *The Problem of Style in Realistic Representation*

1. [Jonathan Culler, *Flaubert: The Uses of Uncertainty* (Ithaca, NY: Cornell University Press, 1984, rev. ed.), 151–55.]

2. Gustave Flaubert, *The Sentimental Education,* trans. Perdita Burlingame (New York: New American Library, 1972), 287–88.

3. Ibid., 290.

4. Ibid., 357.

5. Ibid., 362.

6. Ibid., 366.

7. Ibid., 367.

8. Karl Marx, *The Eighteenth Brumaire of Louis Bonaparte,* in *Marx-Engels Reader,* ed. Robert C. Ticker (New York: W. W. Norton, 1972), 441.

9. Ibid., 442.

10. Ibid., 444.

11. Ibid., 444–45.

Chapter 12 · *The Discourse of History*

1. C. G. Hempel, "The Function of General Laws in History," *Journal of Philosophy* 39 (1942): 35–48.

2. But see A. R. Louch, *Explanation and Human Action* (Berkeley and Los Angeles: University of California Press, 1966), 235.

Chapter 13 · *Vico and Structuralist/Poststructuralist Thought*

1. [The Institute for Vico Studies has since moved to Emory University (in Atlanta, Georgia), and is now directed by Donald Phillip Verene. See their Web site at www.vico institute.org. Tagliacozzo and Verene co-founded the journal *New Vico Studies*; White's essay appears in the inaugural issue of this journal.]

Chapter 14 · *The Interpretation of Texts*

1. My assignment for this essay, originally delivered as a conference paper, was to provide some "general perspectives" on the current debate over "the interpretation of texts." I

trust that the remarks are general enough; I hope that the perspectives are possible ones. The topic is huge, and I have tried to condense it to the limits of an essay by using Barthes and Ricoeur as representatives of the two principal conceptions of the "text" that occupy center stage in the current debate. I have also presumed that the audience to which my lecture was addressed was informed concerning the general history of hermeneutics and the argument over explanation and understanding in the theory of the human sciences. The essay is not meant to be a survey of a topic, but a provocation to a reconsideration of the cultural significance of "textualism," an ideology that is understandable only in reference to the humanistic notion of the text-as-work that it seeks to displace.

2. Roland Barthes, "From Work to Text," in *Image, Music, Text*, trans. S. Heath (New York: Hill and Wang, 1977), 155–64. See also Barthes' article "Texte (Théorie du)" in *Encyclopedia Universalis* (Paris, 1974), vol. 15, 1013–17; and the articles entitled "Text" in *Encyclopedic Dictionary of the Sciences of Language*, ed. Oswald Ducrot and Tzvetan Todorov and trans. Catherine Porter (Baltimore: Johns Hopkins University Press, 1979), 294–99, 356–61. The most comprehensive statement of the new textualism, at the point of its transformation from a structuralist to a poststructuralist theory, is to be found in "Tel Quel," *Théorie d'ensemble* (Paris: Seuil, 1968). See also Josué V. Harari, ed. *Textual Strategies: Perspectives in Post-Structuralist Criticism* (Ithaca, NY: Cornell University Press, 1974), especially the editor's introduction, "Critical Factions/Critical Fictions," 17–72.

3. Barthes, "From Work to Text," in *Textual Strategies*, ed. Harari, 74.

4. Roman Jakobson, "Closing Statement: Linguistics and Poetics," in *Style in Language*, ed. Thomas A. Sebeok (Cambridge, MA: MIT Press, 1960).

5. See J. Sturrock, ed., *Structuralism and Since: From Lévi-Strauss to Derrida* (Oxford: Oxford University Press, 1979); and Jonathan Culler, *On Deconstruction: Theory and Criticism after Structuralism* (Ithaca, NY: Cornell University Press, 1982), introduction and chap. 3.

6. See René Wellek, "Destroying Literary Studies," *The New Criterion* (Dec. 1983), 1–8; L. A. Jackson, "The Freedom of the Critic and the History of the Text," in *The Politics of Theory*, ed. Francis Barker et al. (Colchester: University of Essex, 1983), 100.

7. Fredric Jameson, "The Ideology of the Text," *Salmagundi* 31–32 (Fall 1975–Winter 1976): 204–46. [Republished in Fredric Jameson, *The Ideologies of Theory: Essays 1971–1986*, vol. 1, *Situations of Theory* (Minneapolis: University of Minnesota Press, 1988): 17–75.]

8. This is the famous thesis of the "Conclusion" of Lévi-Strauss's *The Savage Mind* (Chicago: Chicago University Press, 1966).

9. Roland Barthes, "Le discours de l'histoire," *Social Science Information* 6, no. 4:63–75. (1967).

10. Roland Barthes, *The Pleasure of the Text*, trans. Richard Miller (New York: Hill and Wang, 1975), 59.

11. If there is any one theme that informs Derrida's work, it is the deconstruction of the "proper." See especially "White Mythology," *New Literary History* 6, no. 1 (Autumn 1974): 5–74. [Reprinted in Jacques Derrida, *Margins of Philosophy*, trans. Alan Bass (Chicago: University of Chicago Press, 1982), 207–72.]

12. See Geoffrey H. Hartman, *Saving the Text: Literature/Derrida/Philosophy* (Baltimore: Johns Hopkins University Press, 1981), introduction.

13. Culler, *On Deconstruction*, 26–30, 97–100.

14. On the fate of symbolism and the symbolist notion of the text, see Tzvetan Todorov, *Theories du Symbole* (Paris: Seuil, 1977), 10ff. [*Theories of the Symbol*, trans. Cathrine Porter (Ithaca, NY: Cornell University Press, 1982).] See also Roland Barthes, *Elements of Semiology* (New York: Hill and Wang, 1968).

15. Paul Ricoeur, "The Model of the Text: Meaningful Action Considered as a Text," in Paul Rabinow and William M. Sullivan, ed., *Interpretive Social Science* (Berkeley and Los Angeles: University of California Press, 1979), 73–101.

16. Ibid., 77.

17. Ibid., 79.

18. Ibid., 86.

19. Ibid., 99.

20. Paul Ricoeur, "The Hermeneutics of Symbols and Philosophical Reflection," in *The Philosophy of Paul Ricoeur: An Anthology of his Work*, ed. Charles K. Reagan and David Stewart (Boston: Beacon Press, 1978), 36–58.

21. Ibid., 47–48.

22. Such is the argument offered in Ricoeur's latest book, *Time and Narrative*, vol. 1 (Chicago: University of Chicago Press, 1984), chaps. 1 and 2.

23. Jurij Lotman, *The Structure of the Artistic Text*, trans. Ronald Vroon (Ann Arbor: University of Michigan Press, 1977), chap. 4, "Text and System."

24. Any future discussion of "text" must take account of the recent book by Brian Stock, as learned as it is original in its insights, *The Implications of Literacy* (Princeton, NJ: Princeton University Press, 1983), which investigates the formation of "textual communities" and the assimilation of the notion of the text to the notion of the sacrament in the Middle Ages.

Chapter 15 · *Historical Pluralism and Pantextualism*

1. W. J. T. Mitchell, "Critical Inquiry and the Ideology of Pluralism," *Critical Inquiry* 8 (Summer 1982): 612, 614.

2. Ibid., 616.

3. Ibid., 618.

4. Ibid., 617.

5. Ibid., 618.

6. Ibid.

7. [Friedrich Meinecke, *Historicism: The Rise of a New Historical Outlook*, trans. J. E. Anderson (London: Routledge & Kegan Paul, 1972), originally published in German as *Die Entstehung des Historismus* (Munich: R. Oldenburg, 1936).]

8. Wayne C. Booth, "M. H. Abrams: Historian as Critic, Critic as Pluralist," *Critical Inquiry* 2 (Spring 1976): 416, 434.

9. Ibid., 434.

10. Ibid., 434–35.

11. M. H. Abrams, "Rationality and Imagination in Cultural History: A Reply to Wayne Booth," *Critical Inquiry* 2 (Spring 1976): 460.

12. See Ferdinand de Saussure's criticism of the philological approach to the study of language in *Cours de linguistique générale,* Henri Lefebvre's criticism of Claude Lévi-Strauss in *Le langage et la société* (Paris: Gallimard, 1966), and Lévi-Strauss's criticism of Sartre's conception of history in *The Savage Mind* (Chicago: University of Chicago Press, 1966) [*La pensée sauvage* (Paris: Plon, 1962)]. Within Marxism, the same kind of dispute can be seen in E. P. Thompson's *"The Poverty of Theory" and Other Essays* (New York: Monthly Review Press, 1978.), which is an attack on the structuralist Marxism of Louis Althusser.

13. Booth, "M. H. Abrams," 421.

14. Ibid., 444; my emphasis.

15. Abrams, "Rationality and Imagination in Cultural History," 449.

16. [Paul Ricoeur, *Time and Narrative*, 3 vols. (Chicago: University of Chicago Press, 1984–88).]

17. But see Booth, "M. H. Abrams," 433, note 18, where Booth appeals to John Searle's conception of speech-act theory for arguing otherwise.

18. Abrams, "Rationality and Imagination," 459.

19. Booth, "M. H. Abrams," 434.

20. Abrams, "Rationality and Imagination," 458.

21. Ibid., 450.

22. Ibid., 461.

23. Ibid., 450.

Chapter 16 · The "Nineteenth Century" as Chronotope

1. [This essay originally appeared in the journal *Nineteenth-Century Contexts*, which is affiliated with Interdisciplinary Nineteenth-Century Studies, a scholarly association.]

2. Roland Barthes, *Image, Music, Text,* ed. and trans. Stephen Heath (New York: Hill & Wang, 1977), 155.

3. Ibid., 155–56.

4. Mikhail Bakhtin, *The Dialogic Imagination*, ed. Michael Holquist and trans. Caryl Emerson (Austin: University of Texas Press, 1981), 84.

5. Ibid., 85.

6. Fredric Jameson, *The Political Unconscious: Narrative as a Socially Symbolic Act* (Ithaca, NY: Cornell University Press, 1981), 213.

7. Ibid., 210.

8. Ibid., 213.

Chapter 17 · Ideology and Counterideology
in Northrop Frye's Anatomy of Criticism

1. Fredric Jameson, *The Political Unconscious: Narrative as a Socially Symbolic Act* (Ithaca, NY: Cornell University Press, 1981), 102.

2. Northrop Frye, *Anatomy of Criticism: Four Essays* (Princeton, NJ: Princeton University Press, 1957), 243.

Chapter 18 · *Writing in the Middle Voice*

1. Roland Barthes, "To Write: An Intransitive Verb?" in *The Languages of Criticism and the Sciences of Man: The Structuralist Controversy*, ed. Richard Macksey and Eugenio Donato (Baltimore: Johns Hopkins Press, 1970), 142. [A new edition of this seminal anthology has been published under the title *The Structuralist Controversy: The Languages of Criticism and the Sciences of Man,* 40th anniversary edition, ed. Richard Macksey and Eugenio Donato (Baltimore: Johns Hopkins University Press, 2007)].

2. Michel Foucault, *Les mots et les choses: Une archéologie des sciences humaines* (Paris: Gallimard, 1966). [Translated as *The Order of Things: An Archeology of the Human Sciences* (New York: Pantheon Books, 1970).]

3. Ibid., 309.

4. Ibid., 313.

5. Barthes, "To Write," 142.

6. Ibid.

7. Ibid., 143.

8. Ibid., 144.

9. Ibid., 146.

10. Ibid., 146, 147.

11. Sigmund Freud, "Instincts and Their Vicissitudes" [1915], in *On Metapsychology*, The Pelican Freud Library 11, ed. Angela Richards (New York: Penguin Books, 1984) 123.

12. Ibid., 124.

13. Ibid., 125; my italics.

14. Ibid.

15. Emile Benveniste, "Active and Middle Voice in the Verb," *Problems in General Linguistics*, trans. Mary Elizabeth Meek (Coral Gables, FL: University of Miami Press, 1971; originally published, 1950).

16. Roland Barthes, *Le degré zéro de l'écriture* (Paris: Seuil, 1953). [Translated by Annette Lavers and Colin Smith as *Writing Degree Zero* (New York: Hill and Wang, 1953).]

17. Ibid., 17–18.

18. J. L. Austin, *How to Do Things with Words* (Oxford: Oxford University Press, 1973).

19. Barthes, "To Write," 143.

Chapter 19 · *Northrop Frye's Place in Contemporary Cultural Studies*

Epigraph. Søren Kierkegaard, *Repetition: An Essay in Experimental Psychology* trans. Walter Lowrie (Princeton, NJ: Princeton University Press, 1946), 2. Kierkegaard published this essay in 1843 under the pseudonym Constantine Constantius. He claims to have found the saying in *On Heroes* by Philostratus the Elder.

1. This was a term that Frye used in the essay "New Directions from Old" many years ago and from which I took the title of one of my books. I first encountered the term, used in a derogatory sense, somewhere in the work of Collingwood. Frye's use of the term was

not derogatory, although in later life he sometimes grouped it with a number of other *meta* words that he used to connote an overly ambitious kind of system-building. Yet Frye's own enterprise, from his book on Blake (*Fearful Symmetry*) on through *Anatomy of Criticism* to *Words with Power*, is nothing if not "metacritical."

2. See especially Fredric Jameson, *The Political Unconscious: Narrative as a Socially Symbolic Act* (Ithaca, NY: Cornell University Press, 1981), 68–74.

3. Frye's "Spengler Revisited," in Northrop Frye, *Spiritus Mundi: Essays on Literature, Myth, and Society* (Bloomington: Indiana University Press, 1976), 179–98. The essay originally appeared in *Daedalus* 103, no. 1 (Winter 1974): 1–13.

4. Cf. Isaiah Berlin, "Vico's Theory of Knowledge and Its Sources," in Isaiah Berlin, *Vico and Herder: Two Studies in the History of Ideas* (New York: Viking Press, 1976), 99ff.

5. Lest this be considered as little more than a namby-pamby Enlightenment progressive thought, I should stress that Vico recognized that humanity contained within itself the capacity for its own and nature's (or at least the world's) destruction as well as a capacity for transforming "nature" into "culture." Had humanity not had the capacity to destroy as well as to create, it could not be considered free.

6. See Giambattista Vico, *The New Science of Giambattista Vico*, trans. Thomas G. Bergin and Max H. Fisch (Ithaca, NY: Cornell University Press, 1970), book 3.

7. By "dialectically" I mean, literally, "reading across," not what is supposed to be the Hegelian trinitarian concept of "thesis, antithesis, synthesis." Frye's system is not trinitarian but what biblical scholarship called "diatessaronic," consisting of the "fourfold" rather than the "trinitarian" web of relationships. I invite readers curious about this notion of the fourfold—which has nothing to do with number mysticism but, rather, everything to do with the theory of taxonomy that requires at least a "dual binary" in order to be what mathematicians might call interesting—to look at the *Oxford English Dictionary* entry under "diatessaron." [The OED entry for diatessaron contains three definitions: "(1) In Greek and medieval music: the interval of a fourth; (2) In old *Pharmacy*, a medicine composed of four ingredients; (3) A harmony of the four Gospels." Accessed on September 4, 2009, at http://dictionary.oed.com.]

8. "The presence of a mythical structure in realistic fiction . . . poses certain technical problems for making it plausible, and the devices used in solving these problems may be given the general name of displacement" (Frye, *Anatomy*, 136).

9. Ibid., 155.

10. Ibid., 156.

11. Frye's "displacement" resembles, of course, Freud's notion of "*Verschiebungsarbeit*" (usually translated as "displacement"). It is an aspect of "primary process" thinking that, in the "dreamwork" transfers an affect from one ideation to some other one in the service of denial or negation. [See White's essay "Freud's Tropology of Dreaming" in his *Figural Realism: Studies in the Mimesis Effect* (Baltimore: Johns Hopkins University Press, 1999), chap. 6.]

12. Frye, *Anatomy*, 345.

13. Ibid., 346.

14. Kierkegaard, *Repetition*, 4.

15. Frye, *Anatomy*, 346–47.

16. Northrop Frye, *The Great Code: The Bible and Literature* (New York: Harcourt Brace Jovanovich, 1982), 82. Frye writes: "Kierkegaard's 'repetition' is certainly derived from, and to my mind is identifiable with the forward moving typological thinking of the Bible" (ibid.).

17. Ibid., 82–83.

18. Ibid., 80–81.

19. Frye, *Words with Power*, 42–46.

20. Harold Bloom, " 'Before Moses Was, I Am': The Original and Belated Testaments," in *Notebooks in Cultural Analysis: An Annual Review*, ed. Norman F. Cantor and Nathalia King (Durham, NC: Duke University Press, 1984, vol. 1), 13. It was mentioned to me after the lecture at which this text was originally presented that the Christian and specifically the Pauline notion of "fulfillment" implies or presumes or connotes, in addition to the sense of "realization" or "consummation," the idea as well of "abolition." This secondary (or primary) connotation would thus account for the resentment that Jewish scholars might feel for typological thinking in general and the version of it that takes as unproblematical the idea that Christianity might be a "fulfillment" of Judaism. The notion that the Christian Testament might be a "fulfillment" of the Hebrew Testament would imply that Christianity not only "realizes" or "consummates" ancient Judaism but also "abolishes" it. It should be said, however, that the idea of "fulfillment" found in the Christian Testament (in Romans, 2 Corinthians, and Galatians) is expressed in *pleroo* and *pleroma*, neither of which, as far as I can tell, connotes "abolish" or "abolition" (rendered in the Christian Testament as *katargeo*). There can be no doubt that later Christian theology treated the idea of fulfillment as entailing the abolition (in the Hegelian sense of *Aufhebung* or "sublimation") of Hebrew law and therewith the religion of the Hebrews. But this does not seem to me to be sufficient reason to reject the Christian idea of typology or *figura* as providing a model of historical change and transformation. What typology or figure-fulfillment suggests is that a later generation may choose to view itself as an heir of an earlier idea, value, or institution. Like it or not in a specific case, the fact of the matter is that this is the way "history" works.

21. Cf. Frye, *Anatomy*, vii.

Chapter 20 · Storytelling

1. Fernand Braudel, "The Situation of History in 1950," in *On History*, trans. Sarah Matthews (Chicago: University of Chicago Press, 1980), 11.

2. Roland Barthes, "The Discourse of History," in *Comparative Criticism: A Yearbook*, 3, trans. Stephen Bann and ed. E. S. Schaffer (Cambridge: Cambridge University Press, 1981), 16.

3. Roland Barthes, "Introduction to the Structural Analysis of Narratives," in *Image, Music, Text*, trans. Stephen Heath (New York: Noonday, 1977), 123–24.

4. Barthes, "Discourse of History," 6.

5. Georg Lukács, "Narrate or Describe?" in *Writer & Critic and Other Essays*, ed. and trans. Arthur D. Kahn (New York: Grosset & Dunlap, 1970), 143.

6. Ibid., 144.

7. Ibid., 116.

8. Ibid.

9. Ibid., my emphases.

10. Ibid., 121.

11. Ibid., 121–22.

12. David Carr, *Time, Narrative, and History* (Bloomington: Indiana University Press, 1986).

13. C. Vann Woodward, "A Southern Romantic," review of *Judah P. Benjamin: The Jewish Confederate* by Eli N. Evans, *New York Review of Books,* Apr. 14, 1988, 6–9.

14. Ibid., 9.

15. Karl Marx, *The Eighteenth Brumaire of Louis Bonaparte, with Explanatory Notes* (New York: International Publishers, 1969), 8.

16. Louis Hjelmslev, *Prolegomena to a Theory of Language,* trans. Francis J. Whitfield (Madison: University of Wisconsin Press, 1961), 47–60.

Chapter 21 · *The Suppression of Rhetoric in the Nineteenth Century*

1. Quoted in Keith Hoskins, "Making Cobwebs to Catch Flies With" (unpublished essay). Emphasis added.

2. Hoskins, "Making Cobwebs."

3. I. A. Richards, *The Philosophy of Rhetoric* (Oxford: Oxford University Press, 1936), 109.

4. Ibid., 94.

5. Ibid., 116.

6. Paul de Man, "The Epistemology of Metaphor," *Critical Inquiry* 5, no. 1 (1978): 30. [Essay republished in Paul de Man, *Aesthetic Ideology,* ed. Andrzej Warminski (Minneapolis: University of Minnesota Press, 1996), chap. 1.]

Chapter 22 · *Postmodernism and Textual Anxieties*

1. [Stjepan Meštrović, "Will Bosnia Survive Postmodernism?" in *The Postmodern Challenge: Perspectives East and West,* edited by Bo Stråth and Nina Witozek (Amsterdam: Rodopi, 1999).]

2. I use the term *Eastern Europe* in deference to the title of the symposium. I mean to indicate everything between the Urals and the eastern border of Western Europe, including "Central" Europe.

3. This is true even if one takes into account Jean-François Lyotard's definition of postmodernism as the loss of belief in all the "grand narratives" by which the West has imposed "meaning" on history since the time of Hesiod. For, as Lyotard's critics never tire of pointing out, the rejection of all philosophies of history is itself a philosophy of history insofar as it sets a limit on the kinds of meaning that history might be conceived to have.

4. Cf. my essay, "The Modernist Event," in *The Persistence of History: Cinema, Television, and the Modern Event,* ed. Vivian Sobchack (London: Routledge, 1996), 17–38. [This essay has been reprinted in White, *Figural Realism,* chap. 4.]

5. See Janet Staiger, "Cinematic Shots: The Narration of Violence," in Sobchack, *The Persistence of History*, 39–54; and Bill Nichols, "Historical Consciousness and the Viewer: Who Killed Vincent Chin?" in Sobchack, *The Persistence of History*, 55–68.

6. *Collectibles* is a term that names a category of objects for sale in the United States that derive their value, not from either their antiquity, their beauty, or their utility, but only from their possibility of interesting someone who might want to "collect" them. It cannot even be said that the "collectible" is a modern variant on the objects that used to inhabit the "curio cabinet," objects that found their way into the "collection" in virtue of their exotic nature or their provenance from unknown and mysterious places. The collectible is simply an object that might be of interest to someone for any reason whatever. In postmodernist historical sensibilities, the objects inhabiting the past are conceived to possess this aspect of "collectibility."

7. By "virtual" of course I allude to that supreme object of postmodernist interest: virtual reality.

8. And the same is true of any number of historical monuments in Central Europe, monuments so often destroyed and rebuilt that virtually nothing of the original can be said to persist. I think of the Matyas Church in Budapest (Hungary) or the Central Square in Poznan (Poland). These are virtual monuments, producing the effect of "historicity" without the causes thereof—unless, of course, one is thinking in a postmodernist manner and recognizes that "historicity" is nothing but an effect. Has anyone ever tried to define the essence or substance of "historicity"?

9. Gertrude Himmelfarb, "Telling It as You Like It: Postmodernist History and the Flight from Fact," *Times Literary Supplement*, Oct. 16, 1992, 12.

10. Ibid., 12.

11. I say that because law, philosophy, the natural sciences, the social sciences, art, literature, and history all deal in the truth *in one way of another*. The question at issue is what are the differences among these species of truths, how are they produced, what is their scope and utility, and, finally, what is their relative authority? Professor Himmelfarb herself laments the postmodernist's "contempt" for the truth; the truth, she adds, "not as an ultimate philosophical principle but as a practical, guiding rule of historical scholarship" (ibid., 13).

12. Ibid., 15.

13. Ibid.

14. Ibid.

15. She puts down the professional historian's interest in postmodernism to the desire to shock, to appear new, to fashion, careerism, and "bloody mindedness." See ibid., 15.

16. Cf. Roland Barthes, "Texte (Théorie du)," in *Encyclopaedia Universalis* (Paris: Encyclopaedia Universalis France, 1974), vol. 15, 1013–17.

17. Cf. "From Work to Text," in Roland Barthes, *The Rustle of Language* (Berkeley and Los Angeles: University of California Press, 1992); Hayden White, "The Interpretation of Texts," *Berkshire Review* 7 (1984): 7–23. [This essay is included in the present volume as chap. 14.]

18. [Francis Fukuyama, *The End of History or the Last Man* (New York: Free Press, 1992; new ed., 2006).]

19. Cf. "To Write: An Intransitive Verb?" in Barthes, *The Rustle of Language*.

20. As I write these words, the newspapers report a debate amongst the nations belonging to NATO on which and how many of the countries of Central Europe are to be admitted to membership. President Bill Clinton wishes to admit only Poland, Hungary, and the Czech Republic, deferring the admission of other Central European nations until such time as they will have proven themselves worthy of joining a military alliance set up to defend the West against these very nations. Russia demurs, of course, but can do little, since what it ultimately hopes for is admission to this very alliance—at which time it will have reached the "postmodernist" position of having entered into an alliance devoted to defending it against itself.

Chapter 23 · *Guilty of History?*

1. Paul Ricoeur, *Memory, History, Forgetting*, trans. Kathleen Blamey and David Pellauer (Chicago: Chicago University Press, 2004).

2. "[It] is a question here of returning to a lacuna in the problematic of *Time and Narrative* and in *Oneself as Another,* where temporal experience and the narrative operation were directly placed in contact, at the price of an impasse with respect to forgetting the median levels between time and narrative" (xv).

3. The situation may be likened to that in which Joseph K. finds himself at the beginning of Kafka's *The Trial* when, awakening to find himself under arrest by two (minor) agents of the court, he asks what he is accused of and is told that he is accused of being guilty. The crime is "metaphysical," and so is the punishment, since Joseph K. has been voided of all humanity before his ritual murder in the stone quarry.

4. Since *Histoire et vérité* (Paris: Seuil, 1955).

5. Paul Ricoeur, *Time and Narrative,* trans. Kathleen McLaughlin and David Pellauer (Chicago: University of Chicago Press. 1984–88, 3 vols).

6. [See Hayden White's essay "The 'Nineteenth Century' as Chronotope," included in this volume as chap. 16.]

7. Ricoeur, *Memory,* 569.

8. [M. Dufrenne and P. Ricoeur, *Karl Jaspers et la philosophie de l'existence* (Paris: Seuil, 1947).]

9. [Paris: Editions du Temps Present, 1948.]

10. Ricoeur accepts the Socratic idea that all humans seek the good but err through ignorance and lack of foresight, thus bringing doom upon themselves and their communities. This idea is what makes tragedy and the tragic view of life possible. Tragedy is not the struggle of good versus evil (which is melodrama or farce) but the conflict between two or more agents, all of whom seek the good. But he also accepts the Sophoclean idea that this conflict between two notions of the good illuminates the nature of the ultimate good on behalf of which both sides unknowingly militate.

11. Ricoeur, *Memory,* xvii.

12. *Théodicée* (1710) is the title of Leibniz's book purporting to justify the ways of God to humans. It is significant that Ricoeur cites Leibniz's famous "principle of sufficient reason" as a plausible basis for a belief that history, for all its fragmentation and heteroclite

nature, may make sense "as a whole" after all. I cannot forbear remarking that something like this principle has been recently invoked in American culture as the basis for the argument for "intelligent design" and creationism.

13. Ricoeur, *Memory*, xv.

14. Ibid., 497.

15. [Carlo Ginzburg, *The Judge and the Historian*, trans. Anthony Shugaar (London: Verso, 1999)]

16. Ricoeur, *Memory*, 332.

17. [Maxim attributed to Cicero.]

18. Ricoeur, *Memory*, 332.

19. "L'oubli et le pardon désignent, séparément et conjointement, l'horizon de toute notre recherche" (Forgetting and forgiveness designate, together and separately, the horizon of our entire inquiry [ibid., 536]).

20. Ibid., 287.

21. Ricoeur has a longish excursus on the history of the term *modern* and the various "renascences" that have appeared, from the eighth through the twelfth down to the fifteenth and sixteenth centuries, to the Enlightenment that finally succeeds in associating "modern," "the new," "progress," and all the other things that are supposed to indicate "our" difference from and superiority to whatever has preceded us "in history." But while noting the origin of the term in Christian chronosophy, he does not seem to register the significance of the Christian translation of "modernus" as "now" in the sense of "just now" or "right now." This sense of the term suggests that temporal periods are related to one another both by succession and by qualitative change, such that every later period is grasped as a "fulfillment" (which is to say, a cancellation, preservation, elevation, and "sublation") of what had come before. It is this twofold action of cancellation and completion that deprives the "modern" of any negative connotation in its Christian usage. See Waller Freund, *Modernus e altre idee di tempo nel Medioevo*, trans. Gianni Santamaria (Milan: Medusa, 2001).

22. Reinhart Koselleck, *Futures Past: On the Semantics of Historical Time* (Cambridge, MA: MIT Press, 1990).

23. I recently came across the question, in an article on "Change," of whether change itself could change, which I took to mean, could the principles of changefulness themselves change or evolve? Ricoeur, I think, thought that the kinds of changes that historiography registered in the human condition not only were various, but were also themselves evolving.

24. Ricoeur, *Memory*, 300.

25. Ibid.

26. "Material philosophy of history" was the term used to characterize what later commentators called "speculative philosophy of history," by which they meant philosophy of history in the manner of Marx and Hegel. The term suggested that such philosophies of history were based upon the belief that the historical process was a causal force in its own right (a material cause) and not merely a result or epiphenomenon of individual human actions. Reflection on epistemology, theory, and method of historical knowledge was called "formal philosophy of history," corresponding, I surmise, to Aristotle's fourfold theory of

causation: formal, material, teleological, and efficient. Although Ricoeur, like all philosophers, was as Aristotelian as the next guy, he sought to escape the material-formal distinction by claiming for his philosophy of history the designation "critical." Its task: "to reflect upon the limits that a self-knowledge of history, taking itself to be absolute, would attempt to transgress" (ibid., 305).

27. Ibid., 302.

28. Ibid., 333.

29. See Michael Oakeshott, "Present, Future, and Past," in *On History and Other Essays* (Indianapolis, IN: Liberty Fund, 1999), 8, where Oakeshott writes: "We are concerned with our awareness of past and, within it, the character of a distinguishable 'historical' awareness of past."